CIVIC UNIVERSITIES

This is a volume in the Arno Press collection

THE ACADEMIC PROFESSION

See last pages of this volume
for a complete list of titles.

CIVIC UNIVERSITIES

W. H. G. ARMYTAGE

ARNO PRESS

A New York Times Company

New York / 1977

Editorial Supervision: MARIE STARECK

Reprint Edition 1977 by Arno Press Inc.

Reprinted by permission of Ernest Benn Limited

Reprinted from a copy in
The University of Illinois Library

THE ACADEMIC PROFESSION
ISBN for complete set: 0-405-10000-0
See last pages of this volume for titles.

Manufactured in the United States of America

Library of Congress Cataloging in Publication Data

Armytage, W H G
Civic universities.

(The Academic profession)
Reprint of the 1955 ed. published by Benn, London.
Includes index.
1. Municipal universities and colleges--Great Britain. I. Title. II. Series.
[LB2329.A7 1977] 378.41 76-55207
ISBN 0-405-10031-0

CIVIC UNIVERSITIES

RICHARD OF WALLINGFORD

CIRCA 1326

From R. T. Gunther, *Early Science in Oxford*, 1922

See pages 26–7, 42] [*By courtesy of the Clarendon Press*

CIVIC UNIVERSITIES

Aspects of a British Tradition

By

W. H. G. ARMYTAGE

LONDON
ERNEST BENN LIMITED

First published 1955 by Ernest Benn Limited
Bouverie House · Fleet Street · London · EC4
Printed in Great Britain

TO

L. RUSSELL MUIRHEAD

Contents

List of Illustrations

Preface

NEARLY fifty thousand students were registered as attending the eleven civic universities and four civic university colleges of England in the academic session 1950–1. Over six thousand professors, lecturers and demonstrators in those institutions were being supported by large grants of public money: some twenty million pounds annually being granted by the national exchequer alone. What do these civic universities and university colleges represent, and why did they arise? Why are they such a comparative novelty in our educational history?

Clues to the answers of these questions can be found in the standard works of Dean Rashdall and Sir Charles Mallet, and others lie buried in the disorderly folios of Francis Peck and John Ward. Specific answers have been given by the historians of particular universities, but no attempt has been made, as far as I am aware, to provide an answer which will cover the civic universities as a whole. In trying to give this answer, I have been led to consider individuals who could not be claimed by any one university. When Norman Foerster published his book, *The American State University*, in 1937, he acknowledged the debt of that institution to Jefferson, and Jefferson himself acknowledged his own debt to Bacon, Newton and Locke. They in turn but handed on what they received, transmuting knowledge as they transmitted it.

This book, then, attempts to unravel, in the light of modern research, the tradition which the civic universities have inherited. The unravelling of this tradition has been described by Sir Walter Moberly as 'the clue to the reconstruction of the universities'. He has urged that in the re-discovery and re-invigoration of this tradition, it should be 'purged and enriched by relating it to, and expressing it in terms of, a large scale mechanical civilisation'. That is what I have tried to do. It is, admittedly, but a prospector's report, a guide to the wealth of material which awaits the organised industry of more capable scholars. It essays to plot the institutional response to certain social needs, and does not profess to afford continuous histories of all the civic universities and colleges.

Omissions are inevitable and deliberate. For that reason a short bibliographical note has been placed at the end of each chapter to assist the reader to follow any particular subject in more detail. It goes without saying that the dates chosen as landmarks have significance only in their convenience as phasing points for the story.

My thanks are due to the editors of the *Universities Review*, *Notes and Records of the Royal Society*, *The Practitioner*, and the *Vocational Aspect of Secondary and Further Education*, for permission to incorporate material which had been previously published in their journals, and to four tireless friends who grappled with the thankless task of reading and commenting on the manuscript and proofs. To these four, Sir Harold Hartley, L. Russell Muirhead, R. M. Wilson, and Professor Jonathan Tate, a special debt is owed. For though they do not agree with all that I have written, they have unselfishly helped me to say it in as convincing a manner as I could.

'The life of man is founded on technology, science, art, and religion. All four are interconnected and issue from his total mentality.'

A. N. WHITEHEAD: *The Aims of Education*

'Science and the spirit of emulation—these are the forces that have made us what we are.'

E. M. FORSTER: *The Other Side of the Hedge*

CHAPTER ONE

The Monastic Matrix, 596-1154

What happy application, what praiseworthy industry, to preach unto men by means of the hand, to untie the tongues by means of the fingers, to bring quiet and salvation to mortals, and fight the devil's insidious wiles with pen and ink. For every word of the Lord which is copied deals Satan a wound. Thus, though seated in one spot, the scribe traverses diverse lands through the dissemination of what he has written.[1]

SO Cassiodorus encouraged the monks of his foundation at Squillace to undertake the stupendous task of rescuing from the wreck of the Roman Empire such fragments of culture and learning as could be recovered. But for his activity, it is possible that no complete Latin literary work, save that of Virgil, would have reached our time. His foundation coincided with the death of St. Benedict, initiator of a series of efforts to enable man to master his own brutal nature. Benedict's disciples were disciplined like an army. Embracing his rule that work was a form of prayer, their monasteries became oases of quietness in a desert of barbarism and the chief civilising agents of Europe for four centuries.[2]

At that time too, the biographer of St. Benedict was born in Rome. He too was a founder of monasteries—six in Sicily and one in Rome—and he became a monk in one of his own foundations. After a period as papal ambassador in Constantinople he became Pope as Gregory the Great (590-604)—the first monk to be so elevated. Fourth and last doctor of the Latin Church, he was the author of many theological works, but from our point of view the most important act of his pontificate was to send St. Augustine to England in 596.

I

The England to which St. Augustine came was relatively untouched by Christian influence. Christian thought had flourished in the fourth century; indeed Pelagius, an apostle of free will ('If I ought, I can'), was sufficient of a heretic to elicit a missionary visit from St. Germanus of Auxerre who with St. Lupus came over to check the heresies he was spreading. In doing so Germanus also helped to spread the gospel:

he held a disputation at St. Albans in 429, and in the following year he helped the Britons to overcome the Picts by teaching them to cry 'Alleluia'. He came over again in 447 accompanied by Severus of Trèves. His visits certainly brought England into touch with Continental monasteries.

One of the disciples of St. Germanus was his great-nephew Illtyd, the famous Welsh saint, who established at Llantwit Major in Glamorgan a monastery which was described by A. C. Fryer as a 'fifth-century university'. Whether Germanus actually established Llantwit Major or not is immaterial; certainly Illtyd's energy attracted a number of students from Armorica and elsewhere: St. Samson, St. Leonore, St. Paul of Leon and other Armorican missionaries, to say nothing of St. David and St. Gildas—the Celtic Jeremiah, whose influence reached over the centuries to earn from Alcuin the title of 'the wisest of the Bretons'. Llantwit Major continued to attract clerks until the tenth century, and it is not without significance that in the very year when the University of Wales received its charter (1893) A. C. Fryer should have published his study of this remarkable community.

Christian influence was also brought to bear from the west. In curraghs of hide and wickerwork the volatile disciples of St. Columba had penetrated the woods of Scotland, establishing clearings and settlements. Columba himself established Iona in the west of Scotland as a base from which the Christian gospel was carried down to the Humber, and his disciples, especially Barthere after 597, sent preachers and founders of religious communities to Northern Britain. But these influences touched the surface only. They did not uproot the heathenism which frightened St. Augustine and his followers so much that they stopped halfway on their way to England and begged the Pope to release them.

Paulinus (another disciple of Gregory the Great) managed to capitalise the marriage of Edwin of Northumbria to Ethelbert's daughter and secure the destruction of the heathen temple at Goodmanham by the high priest's own hand. But Edwin, whose conversion to Christianity was influenced by his success in the field, died in 633 at the hands of the heathen Mercians, and the Roman Church once more seemed temporarily overwhelmed.

2

In that very year Oswald of Northumbria summoned a bishop from Iona. The bishop came but could meet with little success in view of the obstinacy of Northumbrians and he returned to Iona to report his failure. Among those who listened to the bishop's report was Aidan who asked, 'Were you not too severe to unlearned hearers? Did you not feed them with meat instead of with milk?' The monks agreed and sent Aidan to undertake the task of helping Oswald to establish the Church in Northumbria.

Aidan set out from Iona in 635 to evangelise Northumbria and chose as his centre a convenient place of withdrawal—Lindisfarne, an island at high tide, close to the fortress capital of Northumbria at Bamburgh. He, and others who followed, travelled through the country on foot, preaching the gospel on the hillsides of Durham, Northumberland, and Yorkshire. Aidan himself spoke Irish, his followers, especially those of the second generation like Cedd, Ceadda (Chad), and Cuthbert, spoke their natural tongue, English. Cuthbert, in the year Aidan died, rode up to the Abbey of Melrose and demanded admission at the point of a spear. Thirteen years later he became prior of Lindisfarne, and as such played a great part in the unification of the Roman and Celtic Church effected at Whitby in 663. The apostolate of Aidan, Cuthbert and their followers made Christianity a popular religion not only in Northumbria, but in Mercia, East Anglia and Essex. For in the latter regions, Cedd and Ceadda were especially alive. By making it popular, they removed it from the caprice of court conversion and relapse. Churches were built, land was given to monasteries. A recognisable culture began to take shape which found expression in the famous Lindisfarne Gospels, written and illuminated by Eadfrith, Bishop of Lindisfarne in 698. Its interlaced patterns reveal the surge and tug of the divers influences that had given it birth.[3]

3

Continual contact with Italy animated and energised this vigorous life. Wilfrid (634-709), a novice of Lindisfarne, left England with his friend Benedict Biscop (628?-90), a thane of the King of Northumbria, to visit Italian and Gallic monasteries. Both returned as active agents of the rule of St. Benedict: Wilfrid to refashion Ripon and found Hexham; Benedict Biscop to found Wearmouth (674) and Jarrow (685). Biscop, in addition to classical and ecclesiastical literature, brought back masons and glaziers from France. Lamps and vessels were made for the use of the Church and the craft taught to Northumbrians. Popes helped too: Hadrian was sent over from Rome to assist Theodore at Canterbury in his struggle against the Irish. Glastonbury conformed when King Ine conquered Somerset, and a pupil of Hadrian's, Aldhelm, refashioned Malmesbury. Other monasteries arose in Hampshire and Dorset, while the Bishop of London reanimated Chertsey. Offa of Mercia in turn founded Evesham, Pershore and other monasteries in the Severn Basin, as well as St. Albans.

For a century or more until 787, England developed an active cellular culture. True, many of the foundations which characterise this period were often monasteries only in name, and owed their foundations more to a desire to escape taxation than to any real vocation. But they did succeed in reorganising knowledge, and redeploying its resources after the anarchies of the preceding centuries. In addition to crafts ancillary to Christian worship, music, metre and Roman Law were studied. Theodore's school at Canterbury produced scholars of the calibre of Oftfor (second bishop of Worcester), John of Beverley, and Aldhelm, a West-Saxon princeling.

Aldhelm in fact was a product of all the influences which had so far gone to the making of a Southern English renaissance. Taught by Maildubh, the founder of Malmesbury, Theodore at Canterbury, and at Rome, he built churches at Malmesbury, Bruton, and Wareham, and monasteries at Frome and Bradford. He has been described as 'beyond comparison the most learned and ingenious western scholar of the late seventh century'.[4] Others of his stamp were Boniface, the evangeliser of Frisia; and Tatwine, archbishop of Canterbury from 731-34.

Northern England fructified even more than the South by this cross-pollination with Italy. Benedict Biscop, whom we last met fresh from the Italian and Gallic monasteries, served for two years as abbot of the monastery of Saints Peter and Paul at Canterbury. These names he applied to monasteries of his own creation in the north: St. Peter's, Wearmouth, and St. Paul's, Jarrow. In these two foundations he assembled libraries of books and repositories of relics, accumulated from five separate visits to Italy.

4

From such resources, Bede (673-735) distilled his wide knowledge. His *De Temporum Ratione* not only established in England the custom of reckoning years from the Incarnation, but also contained a remarkable theory of the tides, based on Pliny. His *De Natura Rerum*, also based on Pliny (and on Isidore of Seville) attempted to explain phenomena by natural causes, even though he looked on the earth as a sphere surrounded by a watery heaven. His mathematical speculations *De Loquela per Gestum Digitorum* showed his limitations and those of his age—for it is almost our only source for the study of medieval finger-reckoning. From the scriptoria of Wearmouth and Jarrow copies of these, and other works, issued to the Continent. Well might Professor Knowles hail him as 'the only teacher of the first rank whom the West knew between Gregory the Great and the eleventh century'.[5] For his *Ecclesiastical History* gave men the perspective of their past. It was read wherever Latin was read in England, while it reached over the centuries to influence such men as Alfred, Dunstan, Alcuin, William of St. Carilef, and William of Malmesbury with its theme that monks should co-operate with church and state for the public good: a theme which reanimated successive generations till the twelfth century. Bede saw the monasteries not as retreats from the world but vantage points from which the world could be attacked.

His more immediate influence was felt through the school of York whose founder, Ecgbert, was addressed in his last extant letter. York became a centre of English scholarship under Aethelbert, another library-founder, nourishing Alcuin, who took over the school in 767. Alcuin's thirteen years' administration of the school was highly successful. His *Propositiones ad acuendos iuvenes*, a selection of puzzle problems, exercised a great influence over text-book makers, and showed him as a transmitter of other men's knowledge. In 782 he was invited to assume the headship of the Palace School of Charlemagne, and four years later he retired to make the Monastery of Tours a centre for the diffusion of further texts in the beautiful Carolingian script.[6]

5

Each of these centres of high tension owed something to its predecessor. From Canterbury, from Wearmouth, from Jarrow, from York and possibly even from Lichfield in Mercia, a steady recreative flow of manuscripts and Gospels can be laboriously traced, all combining to present a picture of a culture as pleasant and variegated as any in Europe. Indeed, by the beginning of the eighth century, Anglo-Saxon monasticism was overspilling to the Continent. Willibrord (657?–737?), a Northumbrian who was educated at Ripon and in Ireland, founded the monastery of Echternach in Frisia which was crowded by English and Irish monks in search of medical knowledge.[7] Boniface or Winfrid (680–755) the Devonian, a product of monasteries at Exeter and Nursling, became the apostle of Germany by creating the Thuringian and Hessian church and founding monasteries at Fritzler, Utrecht, Fulda, Amanaburg, and Ordorf. His nephew,

Willibald (700?-86) educated at a monastery at Waltham, continued his work by helping to revive monastic life at the major monastery of the Benedictine order at Monte Cassino.

Just at the end of this overspill period the monasteries themselves were submerged by the Scandinavian invasions. Lindisfarne and Jarrow were sacked for the first time in 793-4; and by the end of the great Danish invasion of 867-70 there was no monastic life left north of the Humber, and little south of the Humber either.

Yet, though the great monasteries had been destroyed, the footing which Christianity had established in the social order enabled the conquerors to be converted.[8]

6

The first deliberate attempt to foster a non-monastic culture was made by King Alfred (849-899). He tried to civilise his ealdormen, reeves and thanes, hoping to fashion not only more enlightened executants of his rule of law, but active preservers of a culture that hitherto had been claustral and monkish. He acknowledged two phases of culture which had preceded his own, the first in the second half of the seventh century, the second immediately antecedent to his own accession. The third, his own, dated from approximately the year 893, when he wrote his preface to the *Liber Regulae Pastoralis.*

This work was intended for every see in the kingdom. It was but one of many translations for which Alfred was responsible: others were Bede's *Ecclesiastical History*, Orosius' *Universal History*, Boëthius *De Consolatione Philosophiae*, and extracts from St. Augustine's works. Alfred was so much in favour of an educated lay élite that he even hoped to found his own court school, where nobles and their sons who were 'rich enough to devote themselves to it' should be 'committed to learning, while they were good for nothing else'.

The Danes, against whom he fought with pertinacity and success, had fortified the burhs of Lincoln, Nottingham, Derby, Stamford and Leicester, and concomitantly this pattern was imposed on Anglo-Saxon England too. Certainly these fortified burhs, or towns with fortified churches and markets, developed into the boroughs of the early Middle Ages, and when the reconquest of the Danelaw was undertaken, and Athelstan recovered York, the revival of learning took root in them.

Alfred was probably in touch with Bald, who wrote the earliest leech book extant in the vernacular, since the *Book of Bald* contains prescriptions sent by Helias, Patriarch of Jerusalem, to Alfred. The herb lore in this, according to J. F. Payne, is more comprehensive than then-existing European knowledge; for the Anglo-Saxon knew and used more than five hundred plants.[9]

Round himself Alfred gathered some of the most active minds of his day. Ohthere came from Norway to his court, bringing with him the knowledge of a journey round the North Cape, having discovered the Barents and White Sea and the mouth of the Dvina. Alfred interpolated these discoveries in his own version of Orosius' *Universal History*. Plegmund was summoned from his hermit-like existence at Plemstall near Chester to help the king in his literary work, and later became Archbishop of Canterbury. Another scholar courtier, Werferth, was consecrated bishop of Worcester and translated Pope Gregory's *Dialogues* into Anglo-Saxon. Grimbold came from the priory of St. Bertin in Flanders to become abbot of the new minster at Winchester, built especially for him by Edward the Elder in 903. Asser (more specifically a product of Alfred's learned household than a recruit, for he studied for six months there each year) was given the monasteries of Amesbury and Banwell and later Exeter and its district. He was Alfred's biographer and the historian of the period, and it is not surprising that the enthusiastic antiquary William Camden (whom we shall meet in another chapter) should regard him as an authority for the myth that King Alfred founded the University of Oxford. In actual fact the passage in Asser's history which Camden chose to select was a pious interpolation by Sir Henry Savile of Bank, and was revealed as such in 1843.

Yet it is significant that early antiquaries should find it congenial to believe that Alfred nourished early centres of learning. More significant too is the fact that Alfred concentrated learned men at his court. Only two monasteries (Athelney and Hyde Abbey) were founded during his reign, and they did not arrest the dispersion and desertion of other monastic scriptoria, which by his death in 901 had almost ceased to exist. The ensuing years under his son Edward saw the reconquest of the Danish area begun, and more burhs established as garrisons to hold in check the reoccupied territory. Alfred's grandson Athelstan set the seal on this policy of unification by annexing York in 927 and defeating the troublesome king of Scotland at Brunanburh in 937. And Athelstan was the second greatest of the West Saxon kings.

7

One of Athelstan's favourites was Dunstan (924-88) who was falsely accused of being a wizard and expelled the court. A practitioner of the arts of metal working, painting and transcription, educated by Irish scholars at Glastonbury, Dunstan was appointed to the abbacy of Glastonbury forty-four years after Alfred's death, and for the ensuing forty-four years he exercised, as adviser to three English kings, a profound effect on English cultural life. With his associates Ethelwold and Oswald, he became the instrument whereby the new monasticism of the Continent was introduced into England.

Dunstan, like Bede, saw in monasticism the effective agency for the moral and intellectual revival of the country. The rules and customs of the new reformed monasticism were adopted at a national council, and the *Regularis Concordia* drafted by Ethelwold was accepted by all monastic houses throughout England. As Professor David Knowles has written: 'Since only in the monasteries could training and shelter be found, and since there also were collected the men and minds of ability and distinction, the newly founded monasteries became at once the homes of learning and art, and the reservoirs whence rulers were drawn for the various episcopal sees.'[10]

From about the year 943, when Dunstan refounded Glastonbury, a new cellular structure of monastic communities began to take shape in England, with foundations that struck deep. Architects of this new network were Dunstan, Ethelwold and Oswald, Dunstan working from Glastonbury, Ethelwold from Abingdon, and Oswald from Westbury (near Bristol). Glastonbury (as we have seen) was founded in 943, Abingdon eleven years later and Westbury in 962.

From these three bastions—Glastonbury, Abingdon and Westbury—the network fanned out. From the first (Glastonbury), Malmesbury, Bath and Westminster were revived; new plantations were made at Milton and Exeter, Muchelney and Athelney, and perhaps Canterbury; and the great western sextet of Cerne, Tavistock, Horton, Cranborne, and Buckfast was completed after Dunstan's death by the addition of Sherborne. From the second (Abingdon), stemmed the Old and New minsters at Winchester, Peterborough, Ely, Thorney, Croyland, St. Neots, Chertsey, St. Albans and, after Ethelwold's death, Eynsham. From the third (Westbury) sprang Ramsey, Winchcombe, Pershore, Worcester, Evesham, and possibly Ripon, and Deerhurst.

These thirty-four monasteries, all the foundations of a most active half century, remained substantially unaltered until the Norman conquest. True some of them suffered during the Danish invasions (Tavistock was burnt in 997, Exeter and Bedford disappeared, and various abbots were taken prisoner), but, as Professor Knowles has shown, there was no kind of general harrying and ravaging of the monasteries. On the contrary Cnut was a patron of the monastic order, and to him must be ascribed the foundations of St. Benet's Holme near Norwich, and Bury St. Edmunds, the first monasteries in East Anglia, hitherto bare of monasteries. Bury St. Edmunds, in fact, at once stepped into the front rank by reason of its superior endowments and immunities. By the Norman Conquest there were forty monasteries in England.

In these, a remarkable revival of learning was cradled. Rich liturgies are said to have evoked the admiration of Cnut, who heard the monks of Ely singing across the water. Wealth enabled them to become generous patrons of the arts. Security enabled scholars like Aelfric (a pupil of Ethelwold), abbot successively of Cerne and Eynsham, to absorb the past, to be a sensitive and broad teacher, to write the first Latin grammar in England and the oldest Latin-English dictionary extant.[11] Aelfric did much to establish the monastic tradition of teaching, although he concentrated on the teaching of Latin. Less narrow in his outlook was Byrhtferth, who knew the great French monastic reformer, Abbo of Fleury, travelled in Europe, and wrote commentaries on Bede. Byrhtferth lived and worked at Ramsey and produced a mathematical and scientific treatise.[12]

Worcester nourished Wulfstan (1012?-95), successively schoolmaster, precentor, sacristan and prior of the monastery. His courageous stand against the slave trade practised by Bristol merchants against their fellow-countrymen helped to secure its abandonment.

At Malmesbury Oliver (alias Eilmer, Elmer or Aethelmar) was an early mechanical experimenter. He is described by the librarian of the abbey as having fitted wings to his hands and feet and attempting to fly off a tower with the help of the wind. He fell and broke his legs, attributing his failure, with commendable scientific detachment, to the lack of a tail. He predicted, amongst other things, the great comet of 24 April 1066.

By that year the English monasteries enjoyed a sixth of the annual revenue of the country. The richest was Glastonbury, with an income of £528; the poorest, Horton with £12. Almost half the houses were in Wessex, eleven of monks and six of nuns; seven houses were in Mercia and seven in East Anglia. The remaining four were St. Alban's,

Westminster and the two Canterbury monasteries. In short they were concentrated west of the Severn, south of the Trent, and east of the Tamar. To the Norman conqueror they presented a unique problem. For unlike lay landowners they could not be dispossessed, though like bishoprics they could be controlled by appointment. They were a conservative force, entrenched and powerful, yet active enough in their conservatism to demand respect.

8

William the Conqueror's Norman duchy had also been revitalised by a remarkable intellectual revival which began a generation before the Battle of Hastings. This revival was embodied in the monastery of Bec (founded 1034), which, from the arrival of Lanfranc in 1041 to the departure of Anselm in 1093, was the supreme educational centre of north-west Europe. It nourished the most progressive minds of the time, and offered an education in letters, dialectic, scripture, and probably also in canon law 'equal to the best given in any contemporary school in northern France. . . . No other monastery had a history or an influence comparable to that of Bec'.[13] Well might Odericus Vitalis say that 'almost every monk of Bec seemed a philosopher, and even the least learned there had something to teach the frothy grammarians'. Its library consisted of a hundred and sixty-four volumes, an indication of the compass of the wisdom of those days.

The intellectual influence of Bec upon English monasteries can be seen after William conquered England. Both Lanfranc and Anselm reanimated Christ Church, Canterbury; Lanfranc's nephew, Paul, became abbot of St. Albans; and Westminster profited by the thirty years' abbacy of Gilbert Crispin. All three houses became educational refractions of Bec.

William the Conqueror himself employed both Lanfranc and Anselm, and recognised his debt to Norman monasticism by founding another monastery at Battle, scene of his greatest victory. Battle was the first stud of a series which was to rivet the kingdom into an intellectual as well as a political whole. Further houses at Chester, Shrewsbury, and Selby showed that the area north of the Trent was to be colonised too; and later foundations at Whitby, York and Durham confirmed this.

Free contact with the Continent established by the Norman administration enabled currents of new thought to pass easily across the Channel and energise English houses. The monastery at Lewes, founded in 1077, was the first of eleven Cluniac monasteries which were to be established in the next fifty years. Monks captured the cathedral chapters too: Rochester, Durham and Norwich being cases in point. The wealth of expertise and ability which poured into England from Norman monasteries was considerable. Tours supplied four monks skilled in medicine: Faricius, who founded a medical school at Malmesbury and became abbot of Abingdon; Grimaldi, a court doctor; John, bishop of Wells; and Baldwin, abbot of Bury. Other professional skills were represented by Gundulph (bishop of Rochester), Ernulf (abbot of Peterborough) and William of Calais; builders all. Historians like Florence of Worcester and William of Malmesbury gave perspective to the new system.

The two leading products of Bec and Caen—Lanfranc and Anselm—set the tone of this new thought. It was Lanfranc, builder of Canterbury Cathedral and archbishop from 1070 to 1089, who established the first hospital in England at Canterbury in 1084. He also provided Paul, abbot of St. Albans from 1077 to 1093, with archetypes for the scriptoria. Anselm, his successor both at Bec and Canterbury, wrote the significantly named *Proslogium sive fides quaerens intellectum* in which he stated that it was necessary to believe in order to understand. Since, he argued, we conceive a perfect being, and that absolute perfection implies existence, so God exists. He maintained that general concepts like this—universals he called them—exist before the individual things modelled upon them (*universalia ante rem*) and so formulated the creed of the so-called Realist School. He was contradicted by Roscelin, a Frenchman, who maintained that universals do not correspond with any objective reality—that they were mere words, and thus the Nominalist School of thought was born.

9

Brought by the Normans back within the European orbit once more, English monks began to stir abroad. Their travels brought them into contact with Muslim science, which had reached a magnificent apotheosis between the eighth and the eleventh centuries. Two monkish travellers are notable in this respect: Adelard of Bath and Robert of Chester. Adelard of Bath, active between the years 1116 and 1142, was early interested in mathematics, and after travelling in France, Southern Italy, Sicily and the Near East, translated into Latin the astronomical tables of the Arabs which contained tables of sines and tangents. He also produced the earliest Latin version of Euclid's fifteen books.

He was aware of the nature of alcohol, and interested in the theory of music. Robert of Chester, after living in Spain (where he would be in immediate contact with Muslim science) returned to London in the middle of the twelfth century. He was the first to use the word 'sine', the first translator of the Koran (with Herman the German), and directly responsible for the beginnings of European algebra. His *Liber de compositione alchemiae*, also a translation from the Arabic, was one of the earliest of such works to appear. In it, he gave directions for chemical experiments, couched in highly allegorical language. Like Adelard, he wrote on the astrolabe.

The beginnings of native experimental endeavour too can be traced in England at this time. Walcher, prior of Malvern for forty years before he died in 1135, had been making observations of the moon and compiled a set of tables. Other monks devoted their time to the study of society, like Florence of Worcester and William of Malmesbury, both of whom wrote histories covering the previous six hundred years.

William was a Benedictine, like Stephen Harding, the English organiser of the white-cowled Cistercians, an order which opened up yet further channels of communication with the Continent. And it is not without significance that Isaac of Stella, author of *Epistola ad quendam familiarem suum de anima*, an early psychological work, was also a Cistercian.

More significant still was the Augustinian canon Alexander Neckham, who became abbot of Cirencester in 1213: for he wrote a popular encyclopaedia of scientific knowledge (*De naturis rerum*) and a technological handbook (*De utensilibus*), both of which contain the earliest European mention of the nautical use of the magnetic needle.[14]

Perhaps the most perfect example of the post-Conquest phase of monastic culture was St. Albans—a Benedictine nursery of abbots which sustained contacts with new thought on the Continent. Simeon (abbot from 1167 to 1183) was a gifted scholar who maintained two or three professional scribes in his apartments, copying the works of Continental teachers. Warin (abbot from 1183 to 1195) brought a group from Salerno, first of the medical schools, and founded a school at St. Albans. John de Celle (abbot from 1195 to 1214) was a Paris graduate skilled in both letters and medicine.[15] St. Albans also produced Matthew Paris, greatest of British chroniclers, who towers above medieval historians until the Renaissance. He took the cowl in 1217, and remained to adorn St. Albans till his death in 1259. Perhaps the most illustrious abbot was Richard of Wallingford, elected abbot on 29

October 1326, a mathematician who played a great part in the introduction of trigonometry into the Christian West. At St. Albans he built a complicated astronomical clock, showing the motions of the sun and the moon, and the ebb and flow of tides. When the king blamed him for spending more money on the clock than on the church, he replied that others could build churches, but not clocks.[16]

10

But such brilliant pacemakers wandered far outside the standard intellectual periphery of the time. The heptarchy of knowledge, allegorically portrayed by Martianus Capella's *Marriage of Philology and Mercury* at the beginning of the fifth century, consisted of grammar, dialectic, rhetoric, geometry, arithmetic, astronomy and music. The seven liberal arts were grouped by Boëthius, last of Romans and first of scholastics, who was the first to use the term *quadrivium* to describe the latter four: geometry, arithmetic, astronomy and music. Boëthius wrote text books on all, but only those on arithmetic and music are extant. Boëthius was a minister of the Ostrogoths in Italy before he was thrown into prison and later executed in 525. He gave the rule for finding any number of combinations of n things taken two at a time, $\frac{1}{2}n(n-1)$, and wrote many translations of Aristotle (from which most medieval scholars derived their knowledge of Aristotle) and commented upon them. In prison he wrote *De Consolatione Philosophiae*, a seminal work translated into English by Alfred the Great.

Cassiodorus, like Boëthius, was a minister of the Ostrogoths. He fixed the number of Liberal Arts at seven on the authority of Scripture, since seven was, to his mind, the perfect number. 'Wisdom hath builded her house; she hath hewn out her seven pillars.' Cassiodorus, to assist his scribes, compiled *De Orthographia*, a synthetic treatise on grammar culled from twelve grammarians from Donatus to Priscian.

The fast-disappearing culture of ancient Rome was caught up by the Bishop of Seville, Isidore, and synthesised in twenty books of Etymologies. These covered not only the liberal arts, but medicine, law and chronology, the Bible, the heavenly and earthly hierarchy, the Church, language, people and official titles, etymology, man, beasts and birds, the world and its parts, physical geography, buildings, stones and metals, agriculture, vocabularies of war, law and games, ships, houses and dress, meat, drinks, tools and furniture. So comprehensive was it that it superseded the study of the actual classical authors.

The Seven Liberal Arts circumscribed learning and culture until men appealed directly to nature. Knowledge until that time remained, in essence, deductive, and the law of nature was regarded as known. Later, when reinforced by the authority of the church, it meant that any dissent from this law implied a charge of heresy and disobedience.

II

In their heyday, the monasteries were conservatories of knowledge. Not only did they preserve it, but by transcription they increased it. In a society too where status was the determinant of life, the monasteries acted as channels of talent, running through class strata to release new forces at the top. For all the apparent tranquillity of individual cells, life did not stand still. The monks' rejection of the earthly and primitive pleasures of those early times enabled them to establish contact with the more creative life of the past, and by so doing, to mould the future. In the metaphor of C. H. Haskins, they were 'stations of high tension, communicating with other centres of high tension'.[17]

This communication fertilised them. In their cloisters were developed all the arts ancillary to Christian worship: illuminated and painted liturgical texts, musical accompaniments and architecture. To men of any mark or race cloistral cells afforded a refuge for talent in an age when petty chieftains had neither the time, inclination, nor resources to act as patrons of the arts. When even royal treasuries were often a mere box under the king's bed, and a scullion could (and did), as late as the time of Edward the Confessor, rob the national exchequer, it was hard indeed for even a king to play the patron.

They not only contributed to the fundamental economic activity of their day—farming—but they organised their own work around their farming. Parchment for the monastic scriptoria was made from membranes and so each collapse of organised society and intercourse made parchment grow scarce and a 'dark' age ensued, unillumined by scriptorial activity. Irish monks, who had experienced such shortages most, adopted a more economic form of writing to save parchment: smaller than the Roman majuscule, it became known as the minuscule. This, more than anything else, illustrates the exclusively monastic character of culture until the tenth century. Styles were not characteristic of countries, but of various scriptoria.

The monastic phase of culture had many drawbacks. Both the means and the instruments of communication were restricted, for monasteries, no less than courts, were islands in an anarchic sea, whose strength lay in resisting the corrosions of localism. A modern Benedictine has stressed that the services of his order in those times to civilisation and culture were 'but by-products'.[18] Its point of focus was the *opus dei*, which slowly extended from four to seven hours a day. Transcription, conversation, discussion, building, farming, and trading were incidental to this main function. Moreover, reading itself tended to be confined to recognised texts, like the Bible and the Fathers of the Church. The Devil was fought by pen and ink, by gloss and by comment and was exorcised by prayer and communion.

The determinative point beyond which the monasteries all but ceased to have any 'directive or formative influence upon the spiritual life of the country' has been fixed at 1154.[19] Overgrowth, with all its dangers, was a real and patent danger, seen at the time, and we at this distance can appreciate it. By 1216, there were no less than seventy Cistercian and over a hundred Benedictine houses in England. They overlay the country, impressing their pattern of life on the newer institutions which were beginning to take shape between these two dates. It is a measure of their strength that they still continued to exist long after these new institutions had developed a life of their own. And their stimulus to college-founders was nowhere more evident than in the seventeenth century, when both Evelyn and Cowley, whom we shall meet in Chapter Six, took as their model a Carthusian monastery.[20]

REFERENCES

1. Crump, C. G., and Jacob, E. F. [ed.]. *The Legacy of the Middle Ages* (Oxford, 1926), 202–3.

2. Chapman, Dom John, *St. Benedict and the Sixth Century* (London, 1929), argues that Cassiodorus, though a pedant and a scholar, was influenced by the Holy Rule.

3. Gougand, L., *Christianity in Celtic Lands* (London, 1932), points out that the Irish monasteries had less reason to fear the pagan associations of the classics, and were thereby able to preserve the classical heritage of the West, and pass it back to Europe.

4. Stenton, F. M., *Anglo-Saxon England* (Oxford, 1943), 183.

5. Knowles, D., *The Monastic Order in England* (Cambridge, 1940), 24; *Bede, His Life, Times and Writings*, ed. A. Hamilton Thompson (Oxford, 1933), calls attention to the symbolism of numbers which fascinated him, and many of his successors. Thus, 3 recalls the Trinity, 4 the Evangelists, 7 universality, 10 the Law, 11 Sin (by transgressing 10), 50 a sign of penitence, and 120 the age of Moses. Larger numbers implied a chain of theological ideas since they were compounded of several symbols. 480 (4 times 120) was the number of years that elapsed before the Temple was built after the Exodus from Egypt.

6. For whom see W. Levison, *England and the Continent in the Eighth Century* (Oxford, 1946), and E. S. Duckett, *Alcuin, Friend of Charlemagne* (New York, 1952).

7. SINGER, C., *From Magic to Science* (London, 1928), 145, indicates the importance of monks' knowing the art of venesection, since bleeding was a regimen for withstanding the lusts of the flesh.

8. FISHER, D. J. V., 'The Church in England between the Death of Bede and the Danish Invasions', *T. R. Hist. S.* (1952), 5th Ser., vol. ii, p. 19.

9. PAYNE, J. F., *Anglo-Saxon Medicine* (London, 1904), 39, points out that the Anglo-Saxons also had the opportunities to assimilate the remnants of Greek and Roman medicine. See also J. W. Adamson, *The Illiterate Anglo-Saxon* (Cambridge, 1948).

10. KNOWLES, D., *The Religious Houses of Medieval England* (London, 1940), 19. See also his *Monastic Order in England* (Cambridge, 1940), 47, where he points out that the monasteries provided the 'soil and the fertilising agency' for talent by 'giving centres of peace, leisure to work, expert tuition and criticism, and a steady demand for objects of beauty and price, focussed and developed the talent of the country in a way that no other institution in the society of those times could have done'.

11. ROBINS, R. H., *Ancient and Medieval Grammatical Theory in Europe* (London, 1951), 72-3.

12. Byrhtferth of Ramsey also drew up a diagram illustrating the close relationship between the external and internal world: the macrocosm and the microcosm. He claimed to see a parallel between the four ages of man and the four seasons; between the humours of the body and the equinoxes; between the four elements and the four cardinal points. One of his diagrams associated the initials of the four cardinal points (Arcton, Dysis, Anatole, Mesembrios) with the name Adam, to whom in the text the term protoplast is attached: a term of liturgical origin, C. Singer, *From Magic to Science*, 142-6.

13. KNOWLES, D., *Monastic Order*, 97.

14. For all these see G. Sarton, *Introduction to the History of Science*, II, i, 125, *et seq.*, 384-6.

15. KNOWLES, D., *Monastic Order*, 309-12.

16. SARTON, *op. cit.*, 662.

17. HASKINS, C. H., *Studies in Medieval Culture* (Oxford, 1929), 94.

18. BUTLER, DOM CUTHBERT, *Benedictine Monachism* (London, 2nd Ed., 1927); *Cambridge Medieval History*, i, 538.

19. KNOWLES, D., *Monastic Order*, 679.

20. JONES, R. F., *Ancients and Moderns, A Study of the Background of the Battle of the Books* (St. Louis, 1936), 333 n. 106.

CHAPTER TWO

Close and College: Premature Regional Universities in England, 1154-1334

THE monastic organisation of cathedral chapters had begun to give way before the Norman Conquest. Canons were exempted from the two vows of poverty and obedience, and allowed to be non-resident on condition that they were employed in scholarship or administration. The secular cathedrals (as they can be called) can be seen emerging in the time of Canute, and owed much to Lotharingian influence. Two Lotharingians, Duduc and Hermann, were appointed by him to the sees of Somerton and Ramsey, while Leofric, who had been educated in Lotharingia, became bishop of Crediton, and transferred his see to Exeter. King Harold, who had travelled extensively and admired the Lotharingian system, appointed Athelard of Liège as head of a college of canons which he established at Waltham, and two other Lotharingians, Walter and Giso, were appointed to the sees of Hereford and Wells respectively.[1]

The Norman Conquest accelerated this secular trend. Sees hitherto sited in small places were transferred to large centres of population: Dorchester to Lincoln, Selsey to Chichester, Elmham to Thetford, Lichfield to Chester, and Wells to Bath. Moreover, three Norman bishops, Osmund of Salisbury (nephew of the Conqueror), Remigius of Lincoln, and Thomas of York allowed prebendal incomes to individual canons who wished to travel abroad and study, and, after joint consultation, introduced a further refinement whereby the duties of cathedral officers like the Dean, Precentor, Chancellor, and Treasurer were specifically outlined.

Further impetus to these developments was supplied by the surges of monastic reform which all flowed to wild and unpopulated places: the Cistercians, for instance, established their new foundations at Waverley (1128), Rievaulx (1131), and Fountains (1132). With secular cathedrals offering every inducement to ambition and talent, it was not surprising that they attracted a diversity of scholastic, legal and administrative talent. Six of these secular cathedrals were especially notable in this respect: Lincoln, Exeter, Hereford, York, London and Salisbury.

The supersession of the cloister by the close was also indirectly assisted by canon law. As early as 826 a synodal decree had stated that bishops should establish schools in order to make the divine commands more manifest. In 1138 the Council of Westminster decreed that masters letting their schools to others for hire should be subject to episcopal censure. This episcopal control took two forms: the giving of instruction in the cathedral school and the issue of licences. The Third Lateran Council of 1179 ordered that every cathedral church should institute a master, endowed with a benefice, to teach clerks and poor scholars, a decree adopted by the Council of London in 1200 and further elaborated by the Fourth Lateran Council of 1215 which required every cathedral to support a master of arts.

I

Contemporary with these decrees, the secular cathedrals had been developing schools. Two of them, Lincoln and Exeter, have been recently described as being 'on the verge of universities, for which they prepared the way'.[2]

Lincoln under its first Norman bishop, Remigius, had, as we have seen, organised the distribution of canonries to scholars: one of his acts was to invite Albinus of Angers to teach in his school. Bishop Robert Bloet (1093-1122/3) was in touch with such leading European figures as Bishop Ivo of Chartres, and Theobald of Étampes. So eminent did the Lincoln school become under him that Henry I sent one of his natural sons there to be trained. By 1160 it had such a reputation that Thorlak, the first saint of the Icelandic church, spent some time there. By 1176 there is evidence of a law school, one of the teachers having formerly been at Bologna, Oxford, and Paris. In 1192 Giraldus Cambrensis studied under the famous William de Monte (Chancellor of Lincoln, 1192-1200)—so called because he had previously lectured on the Mont Ste. Geneviève in Paris.

Exeter, established as one of the first of the secular cathedrals by Leofric, claimed Robert Pullen as a lecturer in theology in 1132, and in the latter years of the twelfth century Alexander of Essebi could refer to the existing teachers of theology in England as 'master Philip of Oxford', a master at Northampton, and 'master John at Exeter'. It also nourished three of the most influential writers of the twelfth century; Bartholomew, whose taste for stinging remarks was most unepiscopal, Baldwin, and John of Salisbury. 'No one can read the earlier letters of John of Salisbury,' wrote Dr. Lane Poole, 'without the persuasion that Exeter about 1160 was a place of studious activity.' Baldwin in fact was born and received his early education in Exeter, and after a period abroad became an archdeacon at Exeter. In 1184 when he became Archbishop of Canterbury, he aroused the anger of the monks there because he wished to build a college for secular canons at Hackington and proposed to endow it with part of the property belonging to the archbishopric, previously alienated in the monks' favour. He also proposed to include on this foundation such men as Hubert Walter, William of Ste. Mère-l'Église, and Henry of Northampton. So great a threat did the monks construe this college of secular canons to be that they tried to secure papal sanction for its suppression.[3]

At Hereford there is not so much evidence of an active school as of an active interest in study of the natural sciences. This was probably due to the influence of the Lotharingian bishop, Robert Losinga, who, as a civil servant, was an active promoter of the use of the abacus in the English Exchequer. As bishop from 1079 he continued to foster the study of calculation, and his successors Gilbert Foliot (1147-63), Robert of Melun (1163-67), and Robert Foliot (1174-86) continued the practice. Robert of Melun had in fact taught at the Mont Ste. Geneviève in Paris as Abelard's successor and opened a school of theology of his own at Melun before his consecration. His *Sentences* contains a plea for a critical outlook to the problems of faith. From Hereford therefore issued some remarkable works on mathematics, astronomy and astrology, together with a tract on metals (*De rebus metallicis*)—all the work of Roger of Hereford. It was here too that Robert Grossteste studied, becoming proficient in, amongst other things, 'the determination of causes and in securing and preserving bodily health.'[4]

At a fourth cathedral, that of St. Paul's, there was 'a university curriculum including faculties in law, grammar, rhetoric, logic and divinity'.[5] Thomas Beckett received his education here, as did two early thirteenth-century chancellors. There too repaired the Cornhills, merchants, politicians and judges: Ralph de Ardern, the son-in-law of Glanville; Henry Fitz Ailwin, the first Lord Mayor; Henry de London and Brian de Insula. When, to foster the law schools of Oxford, Henry III forbade the teaching of law in the City of London, the law students began to obtain their training by acting as clerks to judges and other legal luminaries. In that way William de Insula began his career in the service of Reginal de Cornhill, and Martin de Pateshull to learn from Simon Pateshull. Henry de Bracton, who made the earliest attempt to treat the whole extent of English law in a manner both systematic and practical, also began as a clerk before becoming a justice himself. Such clerks, often enough in the chancery itself, travelled about with the chancellor, and when the chancellor's household separated from that of the King's at the end of the thirteenth century, they took up their residence at the Domus Conversorum, or Rolls House, on the site of the present Public Record Office in Chancery Lane. So, in this way, their 'Inns' or 'Hostels' took shape.

Two other secular cathedrals deserve mention. York attracted Vacarius, the first teacher of civil law in England, and Salisbury, as we shall see, was to cradle the first university college in England.

Of the monastic cathedrals, only Canterbury approached these in activity: Stubbs was so impressed that he compared it to a nineteenth-century university.[6] There gathered round Theobald after he became archbishop in 1138 such men as Thomas Becket, Vacarius (whom he brought over from Mantua) and John of Salisbury (who served him as a secretary). When Thomas Becket became archbishop in 1162, he filled his household with learned men.

Becket did more than provide a haven for scholars. By his courageous stand against the King, and his exaltation of 'benefit of clergy' he endowed the tonsure with a sacrosanctity which materially assisted his brother clerks to win their professional independence of the civil courts. Maitland might call benefit of clergy 'one of the worst evils of the later Middle Ages', but at this very time it played an important part in the enhancement of the university.

2

Becket's quarrel with the King precipitated the recall of the English clerks from Paris: 'the mill where the world's corn was ground and the oven where its bread was baked.' 'Let us suppose,' wrote one, 'that all the sky is parchment, all the sea is ink, and all the stars are Paris masters.'[7]

No star glittered so brightly, and certainly none had such a dramatic eclipse as Peter Abelard. He lectured in the cathedral school of Notre Dame and at the Mont Ste. Geneviève, and attracted a large number of students by his exposition of the dialectical method, i.e. by collecting a number of scriptural and patristic extracts to illustrate the pros and cons of certain disputed theological questions. Universals, he declared, exist only in the minds of men, and previous to that, in the mind of God. Castrated by the uncle of his mistress, and condemned by the Church, he died in 1142 at a Cluniac priory. His influence was transmitted to England by his pupil, John of Salisbury.

Other Englishmen of the twelfth century found in Paris the stimulus which their eleventh-century forebears had found in Lotharingia. Adelard of Bath and Adam du Petit Pont remained to teach in French cathedral schools; Richard of St. Victor and Isaac of Stella to teach in monastic schools; and Alexander Neckham to return to England and diffuse the Paris techniques. Neckham became an Augustinian canon and abbot of Cirencester from 1213-17.[8]

The system established by the cathedral school of Notre Dame of issuing licences to masters stimulated yet another development: that of a gild of masters for mutual protection and regulation. This gild, in the sense that any corporation was a gild, was called a *universitas*, and it emancipated the masters from the fickle patronage of a bishop. As the masters increased in power and number, they overflowed the cloister and migrated to the Mount, where John of Salisbury described how they clustered. In their gild, or *universitas*, it was inevitable that they should demand certain ceremonial requirements of incepting masters, and it was from this incepting ceremonial that the university, as opposed to the cathedral school, was to take strength.[9] Those who were admitted to the degree of Master of Arts were allowed the right to teach—the *jus ubique docendi*.

3

Gilson has indicated the intimate connection between the centralisation of royal power and the canalisation of learning and culture. Henry II, as one of his measures against Thomas Becket, recalled English clerks from Paris in 1167. These scholars made for one of Henry's favourite spots, a centre which was easy of access, the first town on the Thames west of London, an administrative centre with a royal castle and two big monasteries, where a number of scholars had already gathered to hear the lectures of Theobald of Étampes (who described a monastery as 'a place and prison of the damned'), Robert Pullen (whom we have met lecturing at Exeter) and Vacarius (whom we have already met at York). This centre was Oxford, and its Augustinian priory, St. Frideswide's, had at its head Robert of Cricklade from 1141 until 1171. Robert of Cricklade had visited Italy and Sicily, and compiled a collection of extracts from Pliny's *Natural*

History. St. Frideswide's also housed the chest of this nucleus of scholars.[10]

From the middle of the twelfth century onwards, Oxford developed rapidly as a *studium generale* or school of general as opposed to local resort. Giraldus Cambrensis (whom we have found at Lincoln *c.* 1192) read his recently composed *Topographia Hibernica* to the masters and scholars there assembled in 1184–5, and eight years later we are told that the clerks there were so numerous that the city could hardly feed them. This assembly of clerks was not regarded as very significant by the prior of the neighbouring monastery of Osney, who, when puzzled about a point of canon law, consulted his brother prior of Worcester about it. The prior of Worcester was surprised that he should do so, since at Oxford advice could be obtained from clerks 'skilled in mystic eloquence, weighing the words of the law, and bringing forth from their treasures things new and old'.[11]

4

Ubi stabilitas, ibi religio. That the masters were not secure at Oxford might be seen from their migrations in the thirteenth century. These flights, as bright and transitory as shooting stars, illuminate the embryonic universities then taking shape.

The first migration from Oxford took place in 1209. A scholar killed a woman, and the town authorities raided a students' hostel, arresting several members. The King gave permission for the execution of some of the scholars arrested and the rest, together with the masters, dispersed after the fashion of those times. Some went to Reading (where a Cluniac foundation had existed since 1121 as an autonomous abbey) a town on the navigable Thames and at the division of the great western road along which travellers passed to Worcester, Gloucester, Hereford, Bath and Bristol. Its abbey possessed at this time at least 230 books, one of which later contained the earliest of English rounds, *Sumer is icumen in*, which is held to have been composed within its walls round about this time.[12] Other migrants fled to Paris, and others again to Cambridge where a community of regular canons had long existed. Cambridge in fact proved an ideal retreat, for in 1229 further refugees from Paris were offered asylum there, and the Fenland monasteries of Anglesey, Ely, Ramsey and Croyland offered a convenient nucleus of students.

Another migration took place in 1238. The papal legate Otho, lodging in Osney monastery near Oxford, was waited upon by a body of clerks. His brother, who happened to be in the kitchen at the time, threw a cauldron of hot water in the face of a poor Irish chaplain begging at the door, and other servants treated the Oxford clerks rather roughly. Outraged, the clerks set about the legate and his brother: killing the brother and driving the legate to take refuge in the abbey tower. The legate protested to the King, the university was suspended, and the scholars migrated. Some went to Northampton, others to Salisbury.

Northampton was also an ideal refuge. Situated in the middle of the kingdom, it was, with Oxford and Exeter, one of the three theological schools mentioned by Alexander of Essebi, and was sufficiently important for King John to have visited it fifteen times and for him to have held his famous debate with Pandulf there in 1211. It was also recognised as a convenient place of assembly: 46 Benedictine chapters, 20 chapters of Augustinian canons were later held here, and in the very year after the migration (1239) the Dominicans held their first chapter here. Its castle was one of the four most important in the kingdom. Its fair was one of the four or five from which purchases were systematically made for the royal household. There was a Franciscan house (founded in 1224) and a Dominican (founded in 1230). It was also a flourishing industrial town—especially for smiths.[18] Geoffrey de Vinsauf taught there after studying at Paris, and Daniel of Morley planned to study there after assimilating Arabic learning at Toledo. Indeed, it was while Daniel was on his way there that John, Bishop of Norwich, urged him to summarise what he had learned of Arabic science in his *Liber de naturis inferiorum et superiorum*. One recent writer, pointing out that these two taught the *trivium* and *quadrivium* respectively whilst at Northampton, has suggested that a migration thence to Oxford in 1192 might well have enabled the Oxford Studium to establish itself more firmly. With the arrival of the migrant scholars in 1238 (reinforced by others from Cambridge) Northampton seems to have continued to develop as an embryonic university. For twenty-three years this development continued, Henry III encouraging the clerks in February 1261 to persist in their *scholastica disciplina*. But four years later, on 1 February 1265, the baronial council, victorious over the King at Lewes, consulted with the bishops and decided that the 'new university' should be removed, because it might seriously affect the interests of the borough of Oxford, now generally regarded as the home of learning. Their solicitude for that town was touching: and prompted Sir Maurice Powicke to write 'even as late as 1265 a "university of scholars" had no abiding city; the interests of the householders and shop-keepers counted more than academic prestige'.[14] Yet such solicitude for Oxford did not prevent more scholars, from Cambridge this time, migrating to Northampton in 1268.

Salisbury had an even more obvious attraction for seceding scholars than Northampton, for it possessed at this time one of the most famous theological schools of the English secular cathedrals.[15] Richard le Poore, dean and later bishop from 1198 to 1228, was the benignant spiritual influence, Master Henry of Bishopstone, who had previously lectured in canon law at Oxford, the intellectual. So when the secession from Oxford took place in 1238, the students found a school with some tradition, and there is evidence that the tradition lasted for yet another forty-one years, till 1279. In that year, both the chancellor and sub-dean of the cathedral claimed to control the scholars, and the award made shows that Salisbury possessed all the characteristics of a *studium generale*: masters, faculties, and scholars. At least two university colleges existed there: De Vaux College, or the House of the Valley Scholars, founded by Bishop Bridport in 1261 adjoining the southern boundary of the cathedral close; and St. Edmund's College, founded in 1269 by Bishop Wyville for students of theology only. There was a tradition, retailed by Wood, that the scholars of Salisbury could take their degrees at Oxford without further examination. Certainly students lingered at Salisbury even as late as 1540–2, for Leland, visiting Salisbury in those years, wrote, 'part of these scholars (de Vaulx) remaine yn the college at Saresbyri, and have two chapelyns to serve the church there. . . . The residew studie at Oxford'.[16]

The fear of migration certainly had its effect on the ecclesiastical, as well as the town authorities. For we find archbishop Pecham writing to Oliver Sutton, bishop of Lincoln, advising him to walk delicately when dealing with university privileges. 'Do not pull up the tares in such a way as you destroy the wheat,' he wrote in November 1284, 'this your special flock will rather expose itself dispersed to the beasts of the field, than submit to the unaccustomed servitude of this your austerity.'[17]

5

Meanwhile an intellectual tradition in Oxford itself was being built up by the Friars. To galvanise the teaching of the Oxford schools came members of the Mendicant order founded by St. Francis of Assisi in 1209. These mendicants exhaled a new doctrine which rightly earns for them a leading rôle in the rise of modern science.[18] The founder of their order judged knowledge by its results. His manifest apostolate of nature as the open work of God, and his communion with all living creatures tended to work against the verbal subtleties distilled by the scholastic philosophers. In accordance with his mandate, the Franciscans ministered to men's bodies as well as their souls. As the Platonists of their time, they were natural opponents of the Aristotelianism of their contemporary order, the Dominicans, who never wielded in England anything like their influence.

The Franciscans established themselves at Oxford in 1224, three years after the Dominicans.[19] They captured the main channel of English philosophic thought. Alexander of Hales (d. 1245), the first *magister regens* to hold the chair of theology conceded by the University of Paris to the Franciscans, assumed the brown habit in 1222. Adam Marsh (d. 1258), the real founder of the great Franciscan school at Oxford, was the friend and counsellor of Grosseteste and Simon de Montfort. Robert Grosseteste, first chancellor of the University of Oxford, was also the first lecturer to the Oxford Franciscans from 1229 until his appointment as Bishop of Lincoln in 1235. His literary activity and influence were tremendous. The reform of the calendar, the magnifying properties of lenses, the teachings of the Salernitan school of medicine, and the first complete Latin translation of the *Nicomachean Ethics* were only fragments of his mathematical, physical, astronomical and philosophical interests.[20] He was the first man in Western Europe to invite the Greeks to come from the east and he imported Greek books. These ideas were developed even further by his pupil Roger Bacon, the *Doctor Mirabilis*. Of Bacon's span, range, and foresight, much has been written, but nothing apter than Dean Rashdall's remark that in him, 'all the characteristic ideas of the sixteenth century were held in solution'. The Dean added

> it is probable that he was nearer not merely to the physical conception of measurable force but to the wider conception of general laws harmoniously combining to form a general system, than any thinker who lived before the seventeenth century, and this is a greater intellectual achievement than any real or supposed 'anticipations'.[21]

Bartholomew the Englishman, who spent most of his life on the Continent writing an encyclopaedia for plain people (*simplices et rudes*) entitled *De proprietatibus rerum*, was another Franciscan, as were Duns Scotus (d. 1308), whose name now is travestied as a synonym for a dullard or a fool, and William of Ockham.

Perhaps the most astonishing characteristic of the Franciscan order was the rapidity with which it spread throughout England.[22] With their Oxford convent at the head, they established an educational organisation throughout the country. In 1255-6 there were forty-nine convents with 242 friars. By 1334 they had been divided into the custodies of London (nine convents), Oxford (eight convents), Cambridge (nine convents), York (seven convents), Bristol (nine convents), Worcester (nine convents) and Newcastle (nine convents).

In addition to their Oxford teachers, the Franciscans had (*c.* 1237-8) established lecturers at London, Canterbury, Hereford, Leicester, Bristol, and Cambridge, and thus 'the gift of wisdom flowed out over the English province'. The impetus which the friars gave to the theological schools of thirteenth-century England was acknowledged by Roger Bacon, who in 1272 remarked 'teachers of theology are found in every city or borough . . . which has only happened in the last forty years or so'. By 1336 Benedict XII ordered that no friar should become a bachelor unless he had first lectured on the four books of the sentences with writings of the approved doctors in other *studia* which are in the same order called *Generalia*, or in one of the following convents in England: London, York, Newcastle, Exeter or 'Stramforicensis'. So great indeed became the reputation of the English province for learning that when a decree of 1411 forbade a friar from proceeding to the degree of master unless he had attended classes at Paris, the English province was especially exempted.

The Dominican system of schools 'was a kind of distributed university',[23] yet never threw up in England any scholars who even compared with Continental members of the order like Albertus Magnus and Thomas Aquinas, the great reconcilers of Averroistic doctrines with Christianity. Their greatest English representative was Robert Kilwardby, who taught at Paris and Oxford from 1248 to 1261. Kilwardby was English provincial of his order from 1261 to 1272 and archbishop of Canterbury from 1272 to 1278. Though a Dominican, he was anti-Thomist. His *De ortu et divisione philosophiae* has been described by Dr. Sarton as 'perhaps the most important work of its kind in medieval Christendom',[24] for it provides for a complete division of the mechanical arts into seven branches: a *trivium* (agriculture, dietetics, and medicine) and a *quadrivium* (costuming, armour-making, architecture, and commerce).

6

How feebly established the university was at Oxford in 1264 may be seen in the statutes of Walter de Merton for the college which was to bear his name. As Rashdall pointed out, 'the foundation clause contemplates not merely the possibility of a temporary removal of the *studium* from Oxford, but of a state of things in which it might be expedient for his scholars to settle elsewhere'.[25] Five years later, in fact, he acquired a house at Cambridge for his foundation to provide against such contingencies.

Before Merton's foundation, the students lived in hostels. Such hostels were often kept by a tutor. Oliver Sutton for instance, whom we have already met at the end of section 4 as bishop of Lincoln, had rented a lodging house and lecture hall from Osney Abbey on the present site of University College, which he kept until his elevation to the episcopacy. Then again, William of Durham, a former rector of Wearmouth, left in 1249 the sum of 310 marks to support ten or more masters of arts studying theology, which the university used to buy houses. In 1260, four years before Merton's foundation, Sir John de Balliol was publicly scourged by the bishop of Durham, and as a penance promised to provide for poor scholars at the university. But neither of these foundations, nor any of the monastic hostels, developed until after Merton's foundation their distinctive character as colleges.

Merton's regulations provided for virtual autonomy, maintained by an adequate endowment. Freedom from financial control enabled the beneficiaries of his foundation to enjoy relative independence. Merton's idea was to train for *all* the professions: the civil service, the church and medicine.

The college system which sprang from Merton's example owed much to the times. It was, in the completeness of its domestic arrangements, part manor house, part monastery. And, as Sir Charles Mallet truly said, 'Walter de Merton not only founded a community. He gave shape and purpose to a new ideal.'[26] Members of his foundation were to take no vows and enter no cloister. Altar duties were performed for them by chaplains. Under statutes of 1274 the majority of them were to study the liberal arts and philosophy before passing to theology.

From the first Merton College became a pioneer in scientific thought, and its walls housed some of the leading mathematicians of the fourteenth century: Bradwardine, Rede, Simon Bredon, John Mauduith, and others.[27] In spite of prohibition of the study of medicine, it flourished too in the persons of John Gaddesden and John Ashenden. Merton's influence on other founders was great, for sixteen years after his foundation charter, Hugo de Balsham, bishop of Ely, after trying to unite regulars and seculars on the same foundation, founded at Cambridge the college of Peterhouse which later benefactors, notably Simon de Montacute in 1338, remodelled on Mertonian lines.

From the date of its first statutes in 1274, Merton College became the dominant community in the intellectual life of Oxford, and in the following century, of Europe. Within two years of its foundation, Archbishop Kilwardby (whom we have already met as the leading Dominican scholar in England) was regulating its administration, appointing teachers and regulating their payments. Within ten years of its foundation, Archbishop Pecham was stressing the necessity of controlling 'garrulous tongues' and cutting off 'rotten limbs', and indicating abuses like the non-attendance at services, the speaking of the vernacular and neglect of grammar.[28]

But the 'garrulous tongues' were wagging to some purpose. Some fellows of Merton were developing the technique of scientific research, and elaborating instruments more powerful than words to investigate the secrets of nature.[29] William Grizaunte, a physician, wrote four works on astronomy, none of which now exist. John Mauduith drew up astronomical tables and did much to advance trigonometrical studies. Richard of Wallingford, whom we have already met in the preceding chapter, was their contemporary. These three, with Simon Islip (later archbishop of Canterbury) were precursors of many others like Simon Bredon, who migrated from Balliol to enjoy 'the severe discipline' enjoyed at Merton, and took the degree of M.D. in 1330.[30] The greatest mathematicians of them all were John Eastwood, and his partner William Rede. The attraction of such studies[31] can be seen from the 'poure scoler' Nicholas, who appears in Chaucer's *Miller's Tale*.

Nicholas

> 'hadde lerned art, but al his fantasye
> Was turned for to lerne astrologye'

He lived with a carpenter in Oxford where

> 'A chambre hadde he in that hostelrye
> Allone, withouten any compaignye,
> Ful fetisly ydight with herbes swoote;
> And he hymself as sweete as is the roote
> Of lycorys, or any cetewale.
> His Almageste, and bookes grete and smale
> His astrelabie, longynge for his art,
> His augrim stones layen faire aparte,
> On shelves couched at his beddes head.'

Merton's influence was infectious. So satisfied was Simon Islip (a fellow in 1307 and archbishop of Canterbury in 1349-66) with the beneficial effect of the 'secular' education it afforded that he founded a college of mixed monks and seculars, and left 1,000 ewes to improve the breed of the Canterbury monks' sheep. His college at Oxford was, unfortunately, monasticised four years after his death.

7

The northern scholars at Oxford, unofficially organised as a 'nation', were in continual conflict with those of the south—also a 'nation'. One of their great fights in 1274 led to 50 persons being accused of homicide and sent up to London for trial. As a result of this, the chancellor of the university was invested with a control over scholars, whose halls and hostels were freed from civic and fiscal liabilities and placed under his rule. This right, taken in 1275, was a prelude to many others which elevated the university above the normal jurisdiction of the Oxford civic courts and gave it a set of rules and a jurisdiction of its own. In 1288, on a further threat of migration, the university secured more privileges and in 1290 the chancellor's jurisdiction was defined for the first time. These latter privileges, the result of Town being pitted against Gown rather than the antipathies of the two nations, all tended to mitigate the tendency to migrate.

The last of the migrations took place in 1334—this time to Stamford. Whether or not the seceders were northerners, the fact remains that the seventeen masters who began to teach there were all northerners. This university at Stamford undoubtedly disturbed the University of Oxford, which, with consummate tact, seized the occasion of St. Valentine's Day (1334) to petition Queen Philippa. She was a consort of spirit and at that very time was interceding her husband, Edward III, on behalf of the burghers of Calais. After devoutly thanking her 'for the great good and honour that she had so often done to her little university of Oxford', the petitioners went on to explain that

> certain persons, who have received all their honours among us, in destruction, as far as in them lies, of our university, have gone to Stamford, and daily attract others there by their false pretences.

They urged her 'not to allow the town of Oxford be disinherited in this behalf for the honour of another'. They sent another letter to the bishop of Lincoln (in whose diocese both Oxford and Stamford were situated) and a third to the King:

The new assembly of scholars at the town of Stamford for university indwellers, which as it is certain to result in the loss of our school and in being a general seminary of discord for the whole kingdom, we beseech and beg you to extirpate by your royal power, so that what was begun as improvident rashness may be quickly put an end to by the royal wisdom, and be a warning to evil doers.

The seceding masters, for their part, petitioned the King too, pointing out

the great and grievous discords have been for a long time and still are in the University of Oxford, by reason of the great multitude there of different people, and many homicides, crimes, robberies and other evils without number have been done there, and happen from one day to another, which neither the Chancellor nor the force of the town can punish or appease.

as the reason why they seceded to Stamford, and asked

for safety of themselves and other scholars who dare not approach the said town of Oxford, and to staunch the great evils and assaults aforesaid, to stay and study . . . that it may please them of his good grace to grant them his royal assent to take them under his protection, to stop all the evils aforesaid, for the advancement of holy church and of the clergy of his realm.

Queen Philippa evidently had her way, for six months later the King ordered the sheriff of Lincolnshire to go to Stamford and issue a proclamation that no universities were to be allowed except at Oxford and Cambridge: and furthermore instructing him that he should 'without delay certify clearly and openly to us in our Chancery under your seal the names of those whom after such proclamation and inhibition you shall find disobedient'.[32]

But the seventeen masters, all northerners, refused to obey, and three months later, in November, the King once more sent an order to the sheriff to go to Stamford and seize the books and goods of the seceders. By January the following year, Stamford University was still in existence, for the King sent another order, this time to William Trussell, 'escheator this side Trent', to go with the sheriff and execute judgement on the disobedient scholars. The sheriff still did not go. The scholars themselves addressed a further petition to the King saying that they were living under the protection of John Earl Warren. But the King was adamant. On 28 March he wrote again to the escheator to go down to Stamford and take the names of the disobedient. This was done in July 1335, when 17 masters, 5 Stamford clergy, 1 bachelor, and 14 scholars, together with the maniciple of Brazenose were found there. The jury must have sympathised with the seceders, for they professed to find no goods.

The University of Oxford had been thoroughly frightened. For not only did they write to Cambridge asking them not to admit the head of the Stamford institution, William of Barnby, but they also imposed an oath, which remained obligatory on all incepting masters of the university for the next four hundred and ninety-two years, not to lecture *tanquam in universitate* outside the two universities.

So the door was finally closed on any further foundations of a university character outside Oxford and Cambridge. Thus, by the concentration of academic energies, England avoided the dilution which characterised other countries, and as a result Oxford and Cambridge established a tradition for national as opposed to regional scholarship which has only recently been challenged. And it is perhaps ironical to reflect that the right to confer the *jus ubique docendi*, though bestowed by the Pope on the University of Cambridge in 1318, was never similarly bestowed on the University of Oxford.[38]

REFERENCES

1. WELBORN, M. C., 'Lotharingia as a Centre of Arabic and Scientific Influence in the Eleventh Century', *Isis*, XVI (1931), 188–95. A Lotharingian scholar, Ralph, invited his friend Ragimbold, master of the schools of Cologne, to come to the festival of St. Lambert to see his latest scientific instrument. This was the first mention of the astrolabe in the west, R. W. Southern, *The Making of the Middle Ages* (London, 1953), 202.

2. EDWARDS, K., *The English Secular Cathedrals of the Middle Ages* (Manchester, 1949), 188–95. Lincoln came nearest to developing into a University.

3. For much of the detail in this see R. Lane Poole 'Robert Pullen and Nicholas Breakspear' in *Essays presented to T. F. Tout* (Manchester, 1925), 62; E. Rathbone, 'The Intellectual Influence of Bishops and Cathedral Chapters 1066–1216' (Ph.D. thesis London University, 1936), and Dom Adrian Morey, *Bartholomew of Exeter* (Cambridge, 1937), 104–6.

4. SARTON, G., *Introduction to the History of Science* (Baltimore, 1931), ii, pt. 2, 404; J. C. Russell, 'Hereford and Arabic Science in England about 1175–1200' *Isis* (1932), xviii, 14; D. A. Callus, 'The Oxford Career of Robert Grossteste', *Oxoniensa* (1945), x, 19.

5. PAGE, WILLIAM, *London, Its Origin and Early Development* (London, 1923), 169–72; see also C. H. Haskins, *The Renaissance of the Twelfth Century* (Cambridge, Mass., 1907), 8–9; and Charles Mallet, *A History of the University of Oxford* (London, 1924), i, 19, 'A College was planned at Lambeth which might have made London the first of English Universities'.

6. STUBBS, W., *Seventeen Lectures on Medieval and Modern History* (1900), 164.

7. HASKINS, C. H., *Studies in Medieval Culture* (Oxford, 1929), 36.

8. For a good bibliography and discussion of the European setting of these men see M. de Wulf, *History of Medieval Philosophy* (6th ed. trans. E. C. Messenger, 1951), 23–41.

9. DAWSON, CHRISTOPHER, *Religion and the Rise of Western Culture* (London, 1950), 224, saw in the university movement a reaction against the patient scholarship and strict discipline of the cathedral schools: 'it was an intellectual proletariat of needy and ambitious students, contemptuous of the past, impatient of restraint, and following the fashionable teacher and doctrine of the moment.' Rashdall, H., *The Universities of Europe in the Middle Ages* (ed. F. M. Powicke and A. B. Emden) (Oxford, 1936), i, 15, writes: 'They were spontaneous products of that great instinct of association which swept like a great wave over the towns of Europe in the course of the eleventh and twelfth centuries.'

10. See J. C. Dickinson, *The Origins of the Austin Canons and their Introduction into England* (1950), 113-15, 118-19, and Sarton *op. cit.*

11. RASHDALL, *op. cit.*, iii, 1-47.

12. KNOWLES, D., *Monastic Order in England* (Cambridge, 1940), 559.

13. *V. C. H. Northants*, ii (1906), 144-6; iii (1930), 1-28.

14. POWICKE, F. M., *Henry III and the Lord Edward* (Oxford, 1947), ii, 786; *Ways of Medieval Life and Thought* (London, 1949), 200.

15. ROBERTSON, DORA H., *Sarum Close* (1938), 38.

16. LEACH, A. F., *Educational Charters and Documents 598-1909* (Cambridge, 1908).

17. HILL, R. M. T., 'Oliver Sutton and the University of Oxford', *T. R. Hist. Soc.* (1949), 4th Ser., xxxi. 8. For Pecham and the Thomist Movement see Decima Douie, *Archbishop Pecham* (Oxford, 1952).

18. WORKMAN, H. B., *The Evolution of the Monastic Ideal* (London, 1927), 310. 'To Francis Europe owes, to some extent, the rise of science. He really taught men, though he knew it not, to turn from verbal quibblings to the study of nature.'

19. LITTLE, A. G., 'The first hundred years of the Franciscan School at Oxford' in *St. Francis of Assissi: 1226-1926, Essays in Commemoration* (1926). For their impact at Cambridge see F. W. Moorman, *The Grey Friars at Cambridge* (Cambridge, 1952).

20. POWICKE, SIR MAURICE, *Ways of Medieval Life and Thought* (1949), 223, calls him 'the greatest Oxford man in this age, probably the greatest in any age' but points out that 'his work was done and his reputation made as much after as while he was at Oxford'. For a full study see A. C. Combie, *Robert Grosseteste and the Origins of Experimental Science* (Oxford, 1953).

21. RASHDALL, *op. cit.*, iii, 246; for a view that he was a scholastic genius inspired by a vision of unusual knowledge, not a forerunner of modern scientific method see Stewart C. Easton, *Roger Bacon and his search for a Universal Science* (Oxford, 1952).

22. LITTLE, A. G., *Franciscan Papers, Lists and Documents* (Manchester, 1943), 62, shows that nearly 30 teachers were distributed throughout the English provinces of the order. See also his 'Theological Schools in Medieval England' *E.H.R.* (1940), lv, 624–30.

23. POWICKE, F. M., 'Some Problems in the History of the Medieval University' in *Christian Life in the Middle Ages* (1935), 97.

24. SARTON, G., *Introduction to the History of Science* (Baltimore, 1931), ii, 950. For Kilwardby's fusion of Latin and Islamic Scientific thought see Marshall Clagett 'Some General Aspects of Physics in the Middle Ages', *Isis* (1948),

xxxix, 35. The intellectual authority of Kilwardby was such that when the Master-General of the order wanted philosophic advice, he went to Kilwardby and Thomas Aquinas, *Mélanges Mandonnet*, Paris, 1930, i, 126. For the view that Kilwardby insisted that human knowledge depended upon divine illumination see E. M. F. Sommer-Seckendorff, *Studies in the Life of Robert Kilwardby* (Rome, 1937), 152.

25. RASHDALL, *op. cit.*, iii, 194, adding 'it is worth mentioning that the founder in 1269-70 acquired a house at Cambridge for his college, no doubt in view of the possibility of a migration to that University'.

26. MALLET, C., *op. cit.*, i, 115.

27. GUNTHER, R. T., *Early Science in Oxford* (Oxford, 1923), ii, 22-68.

28. MALLET, C., *op. cit.*, i, 118.

29. William Merle, one fellow of Merton, was also the most important meteorologist of the first half of the fourteenth century, his weather predictions being least affected by superstitious and occult method. E. L. Thorndike, *A History of Magic and Experimental Science* (Columbia, 1934), iii, 141-5.

30. It is now suggested that Chaucer may have written the *Equatoris of the Planetis* hitherto ascribed to Bredon. See *Times Literary Supplement* (29 February, 26 March 1952).

31. Richard Kilmington, Thomas Bradwardine, William of Heytesbury (Tisberus) and Roger of Swineshead (Suisset) were active agents in preparing men's minds for the advent of modern science, Powicke, *Ways of Med. Life*, 224-5.

32. *V. C. H. Lincs.* (1906), ii, 468-74, Leach, *Educational Charters*, 283-9.

33. HASKINS, G. L., 'The University of Oxford and the jus ubique docendi' *E.H.R.* (1941) lvi, 281–292.

CHAPTER THREE

Laicisation of the Professions and the Concentration of Collegiate Effort, 1334-1546

I

THE *jus ubique docendi*, which endowed a teacher with freedom of movement, was deliberately withdrawn by the University of Oxford. In the alarm provoked by the Stamford secessionists, the university imposed an oath upon all incepting masters: 'tu jurabis quod nec leges nec audies Stamfordiae tanquam in universitate studio aut collegiō generali'. This effectively paralysed any further attempts by Oxford masters to establish themselves elsewhere.

Yet one university remained to draw further strength from its region. For, within eighteen years of the Stamford secession, Cambridge added four further foundations, three stemming from East Anglian endeavour. Gonville Hall (1349) was founded by the vicar-general of the diocese of Ely, Trinity Hall (1350) by the bishop, and Corpus Christi (1352) by the gild of that name in the town of Cambridge. Apart from East Anglia, however, the rest of the kingdom had to look to Oxford, where, channelled for a century, the founts of charity flowed, nourishing a number of colleges which became veritable universities within the university. The hiving off and migration, which was creating numerous universities in Europe at this time, stopped in England earlier than elsewhere.

Servants of the crown showed the way to future patrons. Queen Philippa's own chaplain set the example six years after the Stamford secession. Intending to strengthen the church in Cumberland and Westmorland, he endowed a college, not in the district, but in Oxford. Giving it a regal title (Queen's College), he laid down certain rules designed to commemorate the Last Supper. These rules were the first categorically to define the status of a fellow (*socius*) and ran in the medieval tradition by obliging such a fellow to take orders.[1]

Other royal servants followed suit. John Huyton, of Huyton, near Liverpool, after rising to hold the Privy Seal, wished to found a college for Lancashire men. He made regulations for its establishment at Oxford after his death in 1363. But, owing to the greediness of his heirs in taking the case to law, the endowment was swallowed up.[2] Sixteen years later, another royal servant, William of Wykeham, who had risen from a surveyorship of royal works to a bishopric, personally supervised the erection of a building which was, as its name implied, to be a New College. Its novelty lay in the fact that it was to provide instruction for its members in the arts, canon and civil law, medicine and astronomy, hitherto the province of university lecturers. New College was virtually a *universitas in universitate*. Its secular priests enjoyed all the privileges of withdrawal from the world, and even from the University of Oxford. Though affording preference to scholars from his own diocese of Winchester, it was intended to train the nucleus of an anti-heretical army of the church.[3]

2

Such training for the secular clergy was imperative at the time. For not only had the church lost a considerable proportion of clergy in the Black Death, but signs were evident that it was unable to keep abreast of the times. The urban gilds were taking responsibility for education in the towns and ecclesiastical preferments tended to become more exclusively the perquisites of civil servants—spoils of office. The Black Death, with its attendant social and psychological reactions, accentuated the need for trained secular clergy. The years 1334–81 witnessed a general erosion of the foundations of church and state symbolised by a general anti-clerical feeling. Whether, as Cardinal Gasquet declared, this was due to the hasty ordination of illiterate clerks, or whether, as Dr. Coulton maintained, the priests as a body had fallen far below the height of their sacred office in not attending to their duties, is a matter of opinion.[4] Certainly it resulted in the efflorescence of superstition, heresy, and criticism of the established order.

These forces animated the career of Yorkshire-born John Wyclif, an Oxford master of arts, who attacked William of Wykeham in his tract *Why Poor Priests have no Benefices* as a source and example of the troubles. Wyclif went on to label the Pope as anti-Christ, and to initiate the production of two vernacular translations of the Vulgate which provoked much opposition. Even more significantly, he declared that high office, whether secular or ecclesiastical, was held only by virtue of the grace of its holder. This theory of dominion was a challenge which the crown itself could not ignore.

Coincident with Wyclif's assault on intellectual and religious authority was the revolt of the peasants in 1381. In the following year, at a synod convoked by the archbishop of Canterbury, Wyclif's main doctrines were condemned as heresies. Transubstantiation was reaffirmed, apostolic poverty denied, oral confession declared necessary *in articulo mortis*, and the autocephalous character of the English church refuted.

The masters and students of Oxford loyally supported Wyclif, whose disciples had become a veritable university extension movement. So the archbishop commanded the university to suppress Wyclifism in all its forms, under pain of excommunication, and dispatched Dr. Peter Stokes, a Carmelite, to publish his mandate. But the chancellor would give him no assistance, and Stokes was forced to write back to the archbishop: 'venerable father, I dare go no further for fear of death.' Town and gown had united against him.

But the church had other resources at command. The chancellor of Oxford University was summoned to Lambeth and forced to beg pardon on his knees. Wyclif was suspended, and his supporters forced to retract or be expelled. Wyclif himself withdrew from the University to Lutterworth where he sadly declared 'an unlearned man with God's grace does more for the Church than many graduates'. There he died.

Though his translation of the Bible, indeed any translation issued without episcopal authority, was forbidden; though university teachers were forbidden to teach heretical doctrines; and though a monthly inquisition to discover heretics was instituted in all colleges and halls; the fires he lit took time to damp down. Only in 1411, after a series of riotous and tumultuous encounters, was the right of the archbishop to visit the university for inquisitorial purposes acknowledged. Three years later, in 1414, the bishop of London announced his intention of carrying out such a visitation and met with no protest.

Oxford seemed to petrify after this: As Rashdall remarked, 'all life had been taken out of it: all real, fresh, intellectual activity was beginning to divert itself into other channels'. Though Rashdall's latest editor has remarked that he was 'disposed to make too much of the effects of Archbishop Arundel's visitation', since the archbishop gave a present of books, yet the fact remains that further foundations took good care to insulate their scholars from anything which might infect them with heretical ideas.[5] Richard Fleming, whose timely renunciation of the doctrines of Wyclif was rewarded with the see of Lincoln, founded a college which bore the name of his see expressly for the defence of the church against the heresies he had so successfully abandoned. His fellow Yorkshireman and successor to the see of Lincoln, Thomas Rotheram, added to the foundation, strengthening the obligation on its graduates to take priests' orders.[6]

3

In 1333 Richard of Bury became bishop of Durham. He had studied at Oxford, before entering the Benedictine monastery of Durham, whence he had emerged to become the tutor of Edward III. He recognised that the regular clergy in monasteries no longer cherished their functions as preservers of culture and dedicated his own energies to the preservation of their books: 'Ears full of corn, to be rubbed only by apostolic hands; golden pots of manna; Noah's ark and Jacob's ladder', he apostrophised in his *Philobiblon.* Since moths and mice consumed what the monks neglected, he issued special injunctions, for the collection of a large library, with which Durham College, Oxford, was to be enriched. This library was to be free to all scholars to borrow any book of which there was a duplicate. Though it did not come to Durham College, the intention was important in that it helped to stimulate the establishment of the university library.[7]

Richard of Bury's story of the abbot of St. Albans who sold him thirty-two books for £50 in order to refurbish the abbey kitchen, was typical of monastic carelessness for learning. This was symptomatic of a more general decay. It is therefore not surprising that Richard's pupil Edward III confiscated the revenues of alien priories in 1337, and did not restore them again till 1360. Succeeding kings were more thorough. Henry IV's privy council took evidence in the early years of the fifteenth century, and in 1414 Archbishop Chichele was able to confiscate the revenues of a hundred and twenty-two houses whose foreign affiliations were not obscured by charters of 'denization'.

These confiscations removed a number of monastic roots in England. Okeburne, the wealthiest cell in England, which reverted to the crown, was a dependency of the once famous abbey of Bec; Tyldeshyde in Cornwall and Felsted in Essex were dependencies of the abbey of Caen. Many acres of Warwickshire, Worcestershire and Norfolk were also mulcted from the abbey of St. Peter of Conches.

That further collegiate foundations at Oxford and Cambridge were considered necessary to discharge duties hitherto regarded as monastic may be seen from the fact that Archbishop Chichele utilised some of the proceeds of the confiscation to found All Souls in 1438. This college, intended on the one hand to serve as a memorial to the great French wars, had a further utilitarian and secular character in that sixteen of its forty fellows were to study law. Chichele's royal master, Henry VI, also utilised his share of impropriated priories to found King's College at Cambridge; where fellows were obliged to take an oath not to maintain the 'damnable errors' of Wyclif or the contemporary heresiarch Pecock. These fellows were also exempted from both episcopal and archepiscopal jurisdiction. And further to illustrate the fact that these new colleges were virtually universities in themselves, a statute exempted King's College from the authority of even the Chancellor of Cambridge University.

Cambridge now began to rise above its region, and rival Oxford. In 1432, by means of a forged charter of Pope Honorius I, it successfully asserted its independence against the bishop of Ely at the great Barnwell Trial. The university asserted that this pope had been moved by gratitude to grant such exemption in the year 624—six centuries before the university was actually founded. So complacently did it emulate Oxford in fabricating its antiquity, that one of its most distinguished sons, F. W. Maitland, tolerantly acknowledged 'the earliest of all university contests was a lying-match'.[8]

4

Yet, though Cambridge might allege forged charters to gain national status, some of its members were not blind to the trends of the times. The anti-sacerdotal character of the grammar schools, and the consequent distress of the clerical schools excited the attention of William Byngham, who tried to remedy the serious shortage of clerical teachers. He had noticed, on a journey between Hampton Court and Ripon, no less than seventy grammar schools 'voide or mo' because of the lack of teachers to fill them. He petitioned the King in 1438 for permission to establish a training college, where scholars would be bound on graduation to accept an appointment at any grammar school in the country. Byngham's activity was informed by fifteen years experience of a parish in London, where he had been friendly with the founder of the City of London School, the master of the Mercers' Company, and several prominent lay civil servants.

Byngham's proposal was an attempt to check the anti-sacerdotal character of many of the London grammar schools then taking shape. One such had been founded in 1432 by William Sevenoaks: its secularity excited comment.[9] Byngham, as a priest, had often acted as an executor of merchants' wills, and could appreciate the anti-sacerdotal intensity of their minds. His Cambridge foundation, Godshouse, licensed on 13 July 1439, admitted to masterships postulants whose qualifications lay, partly in terms kept, but also years spent in actual teaching. Unfortunately for Byngham, Godshouse was pulled down to make room for the King's College, and refounded as a more conventional Cambridge foundation and christened Christ's College.[10]

Royal munificence towards the universities was not confined to King's College. In addition to a princely foundation at Eton (intended to bear the same relationship to King's as Winchester did to New College), another Cambridge college, known as St. Bernard's (later Queens') College was chartered, together with two new universities in the English dominions in France. The first of these universities, Caen, was established by Henry in 1432 for students of civil and canon law, in the hope of keeping his French subjects away from Paris. The second, Bordeaux, was founded nine years later for the same purpose.

Just as Cambridge had originally benefited from Oxford practice, now Oxford benefited from new developments at Cambridge. William Patten of Waynflete, a provost of Henry VI's college at Eton, emulated his royal master by establishing, out of the revenues of monasteries which he received leave to suppress, another college at Oxford in 1448. This foundation, Magdalen College, was also influenced by Byngham in that both grammar and arts were to be studied within its walls. Though theology was to be the norm of the course, law or medicine could be studied by special permission. And to keep a steady flow of recruits, Waynflete established a class of demies—admitted from the age of twelve—on the model of Winchester and Eton.

Waynflete's foundation certainly rekindled the study of Latin grammar, thanks to the first two masters of the school, Stanbridge and Whittington. Indeed, it was to nourish the revival of classical studies which formed such a prominent feature of the so-called Renaissance, as well as giving to Wolsey his first preferment. Well might the church, now that the colleges were completely under their control, reinstate exemption from visitation in 1479. For there was little remaining that was worth visiting. With the chancellor an absentee, the colleges all-powerful, the corporate spirit of the university, as such, scarcely existed.

5

The papal schism of 1378 affected English university development still further. Up to that time, Scots students had, for nearly a century, gravitated to Balliol College, Oxford, which was, in a sense, the first of the great 'Scots Colleges' which were founded all over Europe in following centuries. After the War of Independence, Scots students had seemed to prefer Paris, where in 1326 the Bishop of Moray had created an endowment for such of them as came from his diocese.

With the advent of the Great Schism, fifty-two years later, the flow of Scots to French universities was increased, since France and Scotland recognised the Avignon Pope and England did not. But when in 1408 France followed the lead of the University of Paris and defected from the Avignon Pope, Scots students at Paris were left with nowhere to study, since Scotland still remained loyal to him. Faced by a further feud between the Burgundians and Armagnacs, they returned home.

Congregating at St. Andrews, seat of the greatest bishopric and the largest monastery in Scotland, it was but natural that the prior of the monastery, James Bisset, an Augustinian, and the archdeacon of the cathedral, Thomas Stewart, should lecture to them. The lectures were so successful that the bishop, Henry Wardlaw, formally incorporated them as a university on 25 January 1412.

By so doing, he provided them with the necessary privileges as a corporation of teachers. The other, more important right, that of conferring degrees, lay with Benedict XIII, the Avignon Pope, now exiled in Aragon. Benedict responded to the appeal made to him. On 28 August 1413 he issued a bull confirming Wardlaw's charter: two further bulls allowing beneficed persons to study at the university so created; a fourth appointing 'Conservators'; and a fifth allowing students of Paris and other 'schismatic' universities to study at St. Andrews.[11]

Papal recognition of similar efforts at Glasgow in 1451 gave Scotland a second university, thanks to Bishop Turnbull, who obtained the bull. Buildings were given in 1460 when James, the first Lord Hamilton, endowed a college in the old High Street, which was used for the ensuing four hundred years. A third, a University at Aberdeen, was also founded through the effort of a bishop and the pope in 1494. Eleven years after its foundation it established the first chair of medicine in these islands.[12]

6

Singularly enough, it is also in about the year 1340 that we can trace the increasing displacement of the clergy as civil servants of the crown. In that year Edward III returned from the Continent after a long period of preoccupation with war and diplomacy, and inaugurated one of the greatest series of reforms in the history of English medieval administration. He appointed a layman to the chancellorship: the first in our history. In 1371 laymen also captured the treasurership and keepership of the Privy Seal. Though the minor staff of these offices still tended to be in orders, it was, as Professor Tout has so carefully shown, usually because they needed the income of benefices in order to live. Some lay civil servants were men of calibre like Geoffrey Chaucer and John Gower.[13]

To produce lay law officers of the crown, professional law schools began to emerge in London. Groups or gilds of students began to congregate around the King's courts in London in much the same way as their forebears had congregated around the Mount in eleventh-century Paris. Ambitious for posts in the Chancery, their hostels were, naturally enough, called Inns of Chancery. These Inns had been gradually peopled outside the city walls of London, in what was then the village of Holborn.

Holborn was connected with the river Thames by a lane flanked by a palace of the bishop of Chichester, and called, since one of the bishops had been Chancellor of England, Chancellor's Lane; later corrupted to Chancery Lane. In the village of Holborn itself were scattered other houses. One belonged to the barons Grey de Wilton; another was the property of the Knights Templar; and a third was the property of the earls of Lincoln.

These schools were in London because policy had confined schools of law to the metropolis and the students were laymen because the pope had prohibited the clergy from teaching common law. As their number rose with the increasing demands of the Royal Courts, the need for accommodation became more pressing. Bishop, earl and baron leased their properties as hostels or inns for the students. The Temple, leased to the Hospitallers by the needy King Edward III before he embarked for France in 1340, was in turn farmed by them seven years later to professors and students of the law who had migrated from Thavie's Inn, Holborn.[14]

The congeries of hostels crystallised out into formal collegiate bodies. Four Inns of Court (Inner Temple, Middle Temple, Lincoln's Inn, and Gray's Inn) were fed by ten tributary Inns of Chancery (which included Clifford's, Clement's, Barnard's, Furnival's, Staple, Thavie's, and Lyon's Inn). The Inns of Court were 'Hospitia Majora, such as receive not gudgeons and smelts, but the polypuses and Leviathans, the behemoths and giants of the law'. By the time Sir John Fortescue became a 'gubernator' of Lincoln's Inn in 1425, they had developed a collegiate character with over two hundred students apiece, larger in fact than any of the Oxford or Cambridge colleges.

'In these greater Inns,' Fortescue wrote, 'a student cannot well be maintained under £28 a year (£800 now). For this reason the students are sons of persons of quality, those of inferior rank not being able to bear the expense. There is in both the Inns of Court and the Inns of Chancery a sort of Academy or Gymnasium, where they learn singing and all kinds of music, and such other accomplishments and diversions (which are called revels) as are suitable to their quality and usually practised at Court. Out of Court the greater part apply themselves to the study of the law. All vice is discouraged and banished. The greatest nobility of the kingdom often place their children in those Inns of Court, not so much to make the law their study, but to form their manners and to preserve them from the contagion of vice.'[15]

These were the first institutions of higher education where men could study for a profession without becoming clerks, and their lawyer students were the first of the learned laymen. The Inns were, as Maitland observed, part club, part college, and part trade union: *universitates* in fact if not in name. They provided the rising squirarchal class with the one professional skill they needed—knowledge of the law to preserve their property in an age more than ordinarily litigious. John Paston the first (1421-66), who inherited most of the estates of Sir John Fastolf (a would-be founder of a college at Caistor) on a doubtful will in 1459, spent the rest of his life fighting to retain them. He had attended the neighbouring university of Cambridge before going on to the Inner Temple. 'Resorte ageyn to your college, the Inner Temple', a correspondent wrote, and his mother had shown wise prescience when she advised him to study law. When his son Walter in turn went to the university, John Paston's wife was suspicious of the clerical influence there: 'I would love him better,' she wrote, 'to be a good secular man than a lewit priest.'[16]

7

Another lay vocation was emerging under the pressures of war and plague: that of surgery.[17] Cannon-shot was first used at Crécy in 1346, and it was the French wars which produced John Arderne, the first great English surgeon. He had served under the two dukes of Lancaster at Antwerp in 1338, at Algeciras in 1343 (where gunpowder is said to have been used for the first time) and at Bergerac in 1347. From 1349 until 1370 he practised at Newark-on-Trent, and for the rest of his life at London. Arderne's bold surgery, scrupulous cleanliness, and imaginative dressings, were distilled for the benefit of others. His *Practica de fistula in ano* (1376), and *De arte phisicali et de cirurgia*, attained a wide circulation. A manuscript of the latter was found in Sweden in the eighteenth century, and nearly eighteen MSS of Arderne's survive in the British Museum today. They were copied till the seventeenth century, and three of his pharmaceutical preparations appear in the second edition of the first *Pharmacopœia* of 1618.

St. Bartholomew's Hospital, founded at Smithfield in 1123 for the collective reception of the sick, the aged, and fallen women, was in point of time the nineteenth hospital in England. From the twelfth to the fourteenth centuries, the number of hospitals in England increased by over 700. The first notable writer connected with them seems to have been John of Mirfield, whose observations at St. Bartholomew's were systematised in his *Breviarium Bartholomei* (written between 1380 and 1395) and the *Florarium Bartholomei* (*c.* 1404).

In addition to becoming more articulate, surgeons were also developing a corporate sense in the same way as scholars had done in the twelfth century. But their corporate sense did not lead them to appropriate the title of a *universitas.* The master-surgeons formed a gild of their own in 1368, and recognised women physicians in 1389. In about 1421 they formed a joint faculty with the physicians and in 1422 under Gilbert Kymer, Rector of Medicine in the City of London, jointly petitioned the King for authorisation of their professional status. They sought to provide a hall where reading and disputations in philosophy and medicine could be regularly carried on. The London barbers, who formed the preponderant lay element in the profession, obtained a separate charter from the crown on 24 February 1462 which was, a year later, enrolled by the Court of Common Council. The surgeons obtained a separate charter in 1492.

Both surgeons and barbers united in 1540 to form the Barber Surgeons Company. Their first president was Thomas Vicary, who with his fellows, was painted by Holbein in the act of receiving a charter from the King. As Sir Arthur MacNalty acknowledged, 'The Company of Barber Surgeons undoubtedly raised the study and practice of surgery to a high level, organised professional teaching and standards, raised the social status and general education of the surgeon, and opened a new era in observation and treatment of surgical maladies.'[18]

8

Medical skill was increasingly fostered as larger numbers of English students began to study at the University of Padua. Padua, after coming under the republic of Venice in 1405, became a civic studium whose pre-eminence in the arts and law, as well as medicine and physics, was generally acknowledged. Venice proved a generous patron, erecting a public amphitheatre for dissections in the following century, where Harvey is said to have derived his idea of the circulation of the blood. Not without reason did it become the university where Galileo taught. Perhaps the most distinguished Englishman who studied there during the fifteenth century, however, was not a doctor but an administrator: John Tiptoft. Tiptoft, a ruthlessly efficient servant of the crown, a patron of Caxton and the Oxford University Library, was executed in 1470. It was reliably reported that the people crowded round his scaffold crying out that he must die 'for he had introduced the law of Padua where he used to study'.[19]

We know of twenty Englishmen who took degrees at Padua in the fifteenth century, and four of them became ambassadors: John Tiptoft, Peter Courtenay, Thomas Langton, and John Doggett. As Miss R. J. Mitchell has truly written, 'a degree from Bologna, Padua, or Ferrara gave a lustre which it seems that Oxford and Cambridge were in the fifteenth century considered powerless to provide'.[20] It was certainly so in Venice, for no one was eligible for office in the senate unless he had spent a term in study in Padua.

Perhaps the most interesting of these graduates was Thomas Linacre, who, after a period at Oxford, took his M.D. at Padua and returned to England in about 1492, where, in the next decade, he became the king's physician. Linacre was one of those who applied the new classical techniques to the study of medicine, translating Galen, and writing Latin grammars. His medical works owed much to Galen, and included treatises on hygiene (1517), therapeutics (1519), temperaments (1521), natural faculties (1523), the pulse (1523), and semiology (1524). His influence with King Henry VIII undoubtedly led to the incorporation of the Royal College of Physicians in 1518. This body owed much to the Italian schools, and was intended as a means of ensuring that incompetent practitioners would be repressed. Like the Oxford colleges, it was endowed with the power of holding lands, and of making ordinances for the governance of a particular profession. Other Paduan graduates were amongst its earliest members. Perhaps the most notable fellow in the generation after its incorporation was John Caius, who, as a student at Padua, had lodged at the same house as Vesalius. Caius, significantly enough, had been professor of Greek at Padua as he learned his medicine, another indication of the way in which the classics were being reinterpreted and rediscovered. He was admitted as fellow of the Royal College of Physicians in 1547.

9

In other universities of Italy, the lively spirits of the time found exciting nourishment. To listen to the Greek teachers from the East, and to obtain the new manuscripts of classical learning, scholars travelled across the Alps. Robert Fleming, nephew of the founder of Lincoln College, went there to gather manuscripts for his uncle's foundation. William Gray of Balliol brought back even more for his college library, while his fellow collegian, John Free, taught medicine at Ferrara, Florence and Parma with such success that the pope nominated him for a bishopric. From Cambridge, John Gunthorpe accompanied Free, returning, not only with manuscripts, but with valuable experience which enabled him to become one of the earliest of the great Tudor diplomats. Professional scribes were set to work copying Greek manuscripts for the great men of England.

These early travellers were followed by William Grocyn (1446?–1519) who went to Italy in 1488–90, where he studied Greek with Politian and Chalcondyles, met Aldus the printer, and returned to lecture in Greek at Oxford. His circle included three men who represented a new order in the academic world: Erasmus, Thomas More, and Richard Foxe.

The subtle interpenetration of the conventional Christian framework by a pervasive secularism, refined and formalised by the humane but earthly ideals of classical literature, is evident in the writings of Erasmus. His unique receptiveness to the secular bias of Roman literature and thought is all the more important in that he was the pre-eminent scholar of his day and age.

A few examples only must suffice. When in the Spring of 1496 he fell ill, it was with an ironical lament to the stars that he recollected his misfortunes in tranquillity. He never accepted scholasticism: 'I don't approve of philosophising too much,' he wrote in his *Colloquies*, 'for it is a very jejeune, barren and melancholy thing. When I fall into any calamity or sickness, then I betake myself to Philosophy, as to a Physician; but when I am well again, I bid it farewell.' For him the theologians were like Epimenides, who meditated in a cave 'biting his nails . . . and making many discoveries about *instances* and *quiddities* and *formalities*' and fell asleep. Awaking after forty-seven years, Epimenides found the world changed beyond all recognition. 'I am ready to swear,' Erasmus wrote, 'that Epimenides came to life again in Scotus.'[21]

While accepting the framework of medieval catholicism—monasticism, prayers to saints, the allegorical interpretation of the classics for the benefit of the Christian faith—there was yet an obverse side to Erasmus' mind. He was no fanatic. By allowing that the sources of moral learning could be derived from Greek and Roman authors as well as Writ and Revelation, he was guilty of a subtle ambiguity which his pupils were to misinterpret profoundly. For the rediscovered classics of Greek and Roman thought contained powerful solvents of the established order. Lucretius, for instance, became widely known during the Renaissance, as did Plato, Plotinus, Epictetus, Plutarch and Lucian, to say nothing of Archimedes and Hero. The recovery of proficiency in the Greek and Roman tongues enabled mathematical works to be translated for the first time. Erasmus first came to England in 1499 unknown. Sir Thomas More became his friend as did Grocyn, Linacre, Charnock, and Colet. He returned again in 1506 almost famous, and a third time in 1511 as the leading northern scholar, to teach Greek at Cambridge. He wrote his *Praise of Folly* in More's house and his *Novum Instrumentum* called for serious reform of the academic system.

Erasmus in turn influenced his friend Sir Thomas More, who had been a pupil of both Linacre and Grocyn before entering Lincoln's Inn. More decisively rejected the inclination to become a priest, and became in 1529 the lay successor to Cardinal Wolsey as Chancellor. Though he was beheaded in 1535 for his refusal to recognise the king as head of the church in England, More wrote the most convincing plea for academic freedom yet written in England. His *Utopia* not only sketched a system of national education open to men and women alike, but categorically recognised that man could not be made to believe anything. The rules of *Utopia*, wrote More, 'do not drive any man to dissemble his thoughts'.

The third of these influential men was Richard Foxe—both a Tudor statesman and an adherent of the new learning. With his fellow bishop, Hugh Oldham, he founded Corpus Christi College, Oxford: the first college to make permanent provision for the teaching of Greek. For this purpose, a fellow or scholar was allowed to reside in Italy for three years to qualify as a teacher. A number of foreign scholars were admitted to the college, notably Juan Luis Vives and Nicholas Kratzer.

Another more eminent Tudor statesman, Cardinal Wolsey, founded within the precincts of St. Frideswide's his aptly-named Cardinal College which mirrored the extravagant secularity of the age by its very sumptuousness. The priory of St. Frideswide's was transferred to Osney, and the wits said that the Cardinal had founded a college and finished an eating house. Wolsey also gave more extensive privileges to the university than it had ever enjoyed before: appropriating monastic resources to such an extent that even the King had to intervene and send him a 'rude yet loving' letter of rebuke.

The impropriation of monastic foundations which took place before the great dissolution of the monasteries also benefited Cambridge where the nunnery of St. Mary and St. Radegund was dissolved by the bishop of Norwich and converted to academic uses as Jesus College. Another bishop, John Fisher, was successful in diverting the charity of Margaret Beaufort, Henry VII's mother, to pious uses in the university of which he was chancellor. Christ's College (1505) and St. John's College (1511) bore marks of his advice. St. John's, founded in place of the suppressed hospital whose name it bore, became the centre of the New Learning in Cambridge, Ascham, Cheke, and Watson being outstanding members.

The old conservative ideas persevered at Oxford in the foundation of Bishop Smyth and Sir Richard Sutton, who acquired Brasenose Hall, one of the most famous of the many halls which still studded the university town, to found in 1512 a new college for study of sophistry, logic and philosophy as preparatory to theology.

10

By the sixteenth century it was from the Inns of Court that the lawyers and administrators were increasingly recruited for the Tudor civil service and parliaments. Gray's Inn had monopolised from 1426 to 1525 the chief justiceship of the King's Bench. Lincoln's Inn produced, in the person of Sir Thomas More, the first lay chancellor of England. Edmund Dudley, the formidable instrument of Henry VII, was a Gray's Inn man who, reflecting in prison on the working of his own society, wrote in his *Tree of the Commonwealth* (1509)

> Looke well upon your twoe universities, how famous they have ben, and in what condicion they be nowe. Where be your famous men that were wonte to reade Divinitie in every Cathedrall Church, and in other great Monasteries? Where be the good and substanciall scollers of grammar that have ben kepte in this realme before this tyme, not onlie in every good toune and citie, and in other places, but also in Abbies and Priories, in prelates houses, and oftentymes in the houses of men of honour of the temporalitie? Wherefore the greate prelates with the help of other of the clergie, pare of theis paringe of the increase of vertue and connynge, and throwe them into your universities in plenteous mauner, soe that every one of you in your diocese do this, as well in your Cathedrall church as in Abbies and Priories, and in all other places convenient.

Just how significant the Inns of Court were in the education of the Tudor élite can be seen from the views and career of Sir Thomas Elyot. Son of a judge of the common pleas, he studied, not only law, but medicine,[22] and graduated through being a J.P. for Oxfordshire to becoming clerk of the Privy Council from 1523–30. A friend of Erasmus on one hand, he was also an agent of the crown on the other: representing Henry VIII twice at the court of the Emperor Charles V, and becoming M.P. for Cambridge in 1542. Elyot's period at the privy council secretariat led him to write *The Boke called the Governour* (1531) which has been called 'the first full exposition of the humanistic point of view, not only in England, but in English'. His university had been at Sir Thomas More's house at Chelsea, and his book was aimed primarily at the sons of the new Tudor gentry. His proposal was that, after an early education based on the utilisation of play and infant participation in language speaking, on reaching the age of fourteen the boy should begin to study, not only classical authors, but contemporaries, geometry, and astronomy and the use of maps. At seventeen he should begin the study of philosophy, and at twenty-one he should study the laws of his country, not with the purpose of becoming a professional lawyer, but because they were part of a liberal education to one whose life was to be spent in the public service. He also recommended such outdoor pursuits as wrestling, swimming, hunting, hawking, and archery. Elyot's book reveals the class nature of his ideal system. It was intended only for young 'governors' and those were the very people with whom the courts of Oxford and Cambridge became increasingly thronged as the century progressed.

II

It was Thomas Cromwell, a friend of Elyot's, a member of Gray's Inn, who became the agent of Henry VIII. A harsh enemy of the monasteries, his zealous prosecution of the king's interests brought about a divorce with medieval practice. Cromwell appointed two visitors, Richard Layton and John London, to visit Oxford University, neither of whom showed much respect for monks and schoolmen. As one of them wrote:

> We have set Dunce in Bocardo, and have utterly banished him from Oxford for ever, with all his blind glosses . . . and the second time we came to New College, after we had declared your injunctions, we found all the great quadrant court full of the leaves of Dunce, the wind blowing them into every corner. And there we found one Mr. Greenfield, a gentleman of Buckinghamshire

> gathering up part of the same book leaves, as he said, to make him sewells or blawnshers, to keep the deer within his wood, thereby to have the better cry with his hounds.[23]

Yet iconoclast as these commissioners were, they did make provision for the teaching of the subjects we have met emerging in the foregoing pages. Greek and Latin, Medicine and Civil Law were established, monastic property which had sustained certain foundations was confiscated, Oxford colleges which depended upon Gloucester, Durham and Canterbury disappeared with the spoliation of those great foundations. All monastic colleges and friaries were seized, whether of the Franciscans, Dominicans, Carmelites, or Augustinians. Anything which savoured of the old order was destroyed. At Cambridge the monastic Buckingham College was dissolved and reconstituted in 1542 by Lord Audley of Walden as Magdalene College.

The great despoiler Henry VIII was liberal enough to the secular aspects of the universities. 'I tell you Sirs', he said, 'I judge no land in England better bestowed than that which is given to our universities. For by their maintenance our realme shall be well governed when we be dead and rotten.' But the Reformation he had precipitated affected the universities in one particularly adverse respect. Hitherto, they had been full of poor scholars, maintained by scholarships from the free schools. But the dissolution of these schools in the general appropriation of monastic resources, coupled with the subsequent rapid rise in the cost of living, led them to become dependent on the sons of the new Tudor bureaucracy. Well might Latimer complain to Henry's son, Edward VI, in 1549: 'There be none now but great men's sons in colleges, and their fathers look not to have them preachers.'[24]

12

Scotus and the schoolmen provided a good run for more than Mr. Greenfield's hounds. Indeed, from the time a fourteen-year-old university student entered his name on the *matricula* or master's roll till he incepted as a bachelor, he would spend anything up to seven years in the Faculty of Arts listening to commentaries, attending disputations, and exercising himself in logical arguments—all in Latin. By so doing he could move far more easily than his modern counterpart from a university in one country to that of another: Scotus himself, for instance, was, as his name implies, a Scot, who studied at Paris, lectured at Oxford, and possibly at Cologne and Bologna. To become a master or doctor (itself a professional degree), a further period of study was necessary.

An arts course was the essential preliminary to such professional training, and it comprised, as we have seen, not only the logical components of the *trivium*—grammar, rhetoric and dialectic—but the corpus of natural science in the *quadrivium*—arithmetic, music, geometry and astronomy—the latter four all stemming, as we have seen, from the earlier phases of our story. But more noteworthy is the technique of teaching represented by the term scholasticism, a technique embodied in the very organisation of the *Summa* of Thomas Aquinas, and comprising the ritualised disputation. These disputations, the *ordinaria* and the *quodlibet*, comprised those based on topics raised by the master and those by the student, the latter being not so frequently held.

Well might John Stuart Mill praise the schoolmen for their unrivalled capacity to invent technical terms, and Sir Maurice Powicke point out that modern science began in such circumstances. For though the schoolmen derived their knowledge from the encyclopaedias compiled from the debris of the ancient world and not from direct observation and experiment, their studies sharpened the very terms which later generations were to use. It is to the memory, exactness and gifts of expression cultivated by scholasticism that we owe such terms as 'property', 'substance', 'accident' and 'equivocal'. Or, as a medieval schoolman would have said, they became 'common-places'.[25]

REFERENCES

1. Magrath, J. R., *The Queens College*, i, 40-60ff.

2. Tout, T. F., *The English Civil Servant in the Fourteenth Century* (Manchester, 1916), 27.

3. Rashdall, H., and Rait, R. S., *New College* (Oxford, 1901).

4. Gasquet, F. A., *The Black Death of 1348-9* (London, 1908), and A. M. Campbell, *The Black Death and Men of Learning* (New York, 1931).

5. Rashdall, *op. cit.*, iii, 271.

6. Clark, A., *Lincoln College* (1898). H. E. Salter (*Snappe's Formulary*) does not agree that Fleming was once a Wycliffite.

7. *Richard d'Aungerville of Bury. Fragments of his Register and other documents Surtees Society Publications*, cxix (Durham, 1910). M. R. James, *Wanderings and Homes of Manuscripts* (London, 1919), 78, was inclined to think he was a humbug.

8. Quoted by G. G. Coulton, *The Medieval Scene* (Cambridge, 1930), 123.

9. Leach, A. F., *The Schools of Medieval England* (London, 1915), 244 citing Sevenoaks School, founded in 1432.

10. LLOYD, A. H., *The Early History of Christ's College* (Cambridge, 1934).

11. CANT, R. G., *The University of St. Andrews* (Edinburgh, 1946), 1-5. The rebel Owen Glendower also offered to recognise the Avignon Pope in 1406 if universities for North and South Wales could be established to help him break free from English domination. D. Emrys Evans, *The University of Wales* (Cardiff, 1953), 1.

12. See Rashdall, *op. cit.*, ii, 301-20.

13. TOUT, *op. cit.*

14. MAITLAND, F. W., *Collected Papers*, ii, 482; W. S. Holdsworth, *History of English Law* (1923), ii, 314-15, 494 ff.

15. HOLDSWORTH *op. cit.* shows how the lectures, tests and enforcing an *inceptio* was after the fashion of the great Medieval Universities. It becomes at any rate possible to understand how Fortescue, Coke, and Selden speak of the Inns of Court as Universities for the study of the law on the same footing as Oxford and Cambridge.

16. Quoted G. M. Trevelyan, *English Social History* (London, 1946), 77.

17. SARTON, *op. cit.*, v, 1700-4.

18. GARRISON, F. H., *An Introduction to the History of Medicine* (London, 1921), 234-5. Vicary is also credited with the first English work on Anatomy; S. Young, *The Annals of the Barber Surgeons of London* (London, 1890), 83 ff; J. W. Bridge, 'Thomas Vicary: A Famous Maidstone Surgeon' *Archaeologia Cantiana*, lxii (Ashford, 1950), 91–3; Sir A. MacNalty 'The Renaissance and its influence on English Medicine', *Annals of Royal College of Surgeons*, 1. (London, 1947), 8–30.

19. MITCHELL, R. J., *John Tiptoft* (London, 1938), 89, 149: 'Then did the axe at one blow cut off more learning than was left in the heads of all the surviving nobility.'

20. MITCHELL, R. J., 'English Students at Padua, 1460-1475', *Trans. R. Hist. Soc.*, J. H. Randall 'The Development of Scientific Method in the School of Padua', *J.H.I.* (1940), i, 197.

21. RICE, EUGENE F., 'Erasmus and the Religious Tradition 1495-1499', *J.H.I.* (1950), 385-411; Fritz Casperi, 'Erasmus on the Social Functions of Christian Humanism', *J.H.I.* (1947), 78-96.

22. It is interesting to note that in his book *The Governour*, Elyot refers to Galen frequently, especially to his *De Sanitate Tuenda* which was translated by Linacre, cf. p. 73 (Everyman Edition).

23. MALLET, C., *History of the University of Oxford* (London, 1924), ii, 62.

24. SMYTH, C. H., *Cranmer and the Reformation under Edward VI* (Cambridge, 1926), 142–3.

25. COPLESTON, F., *A History of Philosophy* (London, 1950), ii, 212–15.

CHAPTER FOUR

The Emergence of a Scientific Spirit: 1546-1600

It cannot be trueli denied, but that in this oure time god hath steared up excellent vertuous witts whiche so straitli call to examination all the doctrine and documents lefft from the auncients, waeing, & so advuisedlie trieing, the sincere from the contrarie, that if thei procead as thei haue begun, it is like within feu yeares, that science will be so renued, refreshid, and purged, that thei whiche hitherto haue boren al the bruit & haue obtainid all autorite, will leese a greate portion of there creadit.[1]

THOSE were Thomas Raynalde's reflections on the revolution of his time, published in 1561 just as its nature was being revealed. It was a positivistic revolution, one in which the relations of man with himself, with others and with his inanimate environment were being deepened and extended.[2] In England, these years witnessed the laying down of a new educational mould in which the formal pattern of the age of genius was to be cast. The metallic metaphor would have been appreciated at the time, for it was an age when the technologies were advancing rapidly. Yet the historian of ideas prefers another, less rigid: for him the slow osmosis of practice and theory from the handicrafts to the academies suddenly quickened in this period: indeed, handicrafts themselves were radically modified by theory and we enter a new age.[3] And in so far as landmarks are convenient to indicate stages in the process, we begin in the year 1546, just when the silver from the mines of Potosì was beginning to flow into Europe.

I

That year saw the publication in English of Polydore Virgil's *De Inventoribus Rerum*, a book which summed up for Englishmen the main constructions and activities of mankind to that date, and drew attention to the new devices which were being daily produced. This sixteenth-century essay in scientific synthesis was proudly regarded by its owner, and avidly read by a European public,[4] which had already been given, three years before, two books which were to alter their ideas of man and the universe. The first, Vesalius' *De Fabrica Humani*

Corporis, was eloquently silent on man's relation to the cosmos, but shatteringly matter-of-fact in its account of man's physiological structure and its analogies with animal nature. The second, Copernicus' *De Revolutionibus Orbium Coelestium,*[5] dethroned the Aristotelian theory of a fixed and immovable universe, supplanting it by the stimulating and exciting heliocentric theory, particularly congenial to the new technologist who was winning from flame and fire the materials for ships, cannon, and the new inventions.

It was also the first year in which England was without the comfortable insulation of the clerical schools, for Henry VIII had confiscated the endowments of many of the monastic colleges, chantries, and hospitals.[6] On this *tabula rasa* a more secular network was established, and education was considerably laicised. The risk of infection (or inspiration) from the new ideas was correspondingly greater.

From the point of view of the Weber–Tawney thesis of the rise of capitalism[7] the year is perhaps more significant still, since Humphrey Baker first issued his *Well Spring of Sciences,* which professed to teach 'the perfect work and practice of arithmetic'. Though he was not quite the first in this field (Hugh Oldcastle, a schoolmaster in the parish of St. Olave's, London, had published his *Brief Instruction and Maner how to keep Books of Accounts* three years earlier) he was the most significant, for he went on to keep a school on the north side of the Royal Exchange in London, where he was firmly established when the second edition of his book was issued in 1562.[8]

But the year is only selected as a convenient vestibule. Leading up to it is a path from the previous decade, when Juan Luis Vives had in his *De Corruptis Artibus* lamented the traditional disdain for seeking wisdom in workshops, and in his *De Tradendis Disciplinis* outlined his positive contributions to education. In it he advocated observation and experiment in the natural sciences, and employment of the inductive method.[9] His collected works were first published posthumously in 1555, but before that he had lectured at Corpus Christi College, Oxford. To Vives' high and noble arguments, Rabelais had made his own inimitable contribution. Describing the method by which Ponocrates used to teach Gargantua, he stressed the essentially technological nature of that education: how they learned to 'consider the industry and invention of the trades' by going to see

> the drawing of metals, or the casting of great ordnance; how the lapidaries did work, as also the goldsmiths and cutters of precious stones . . . the alchemists, money coiners, upholsterers, weavers, velvet workers, watchmakers, looking glass framers, printers, organists and other such kind of artificers.[10]

In rainy weather they would recreate themselves by 'bottling up hay, in cleaving and sawing of wood, and in threshing sheaves of corn at the barn. Then they studied the art of painting and carving.' With the increased study of history that marked that very time the curious could see further precedents for such realist instruction from the time of Aristotle himself.[11]

In this year of portent, no date looms so significantly as December 19, when, by letters patent, a royal college was established within the University of Cambridge for the study of literature, the sciences, good arts, and sacred theology, consisting of a master and sixty fellows and scholars. Its name, Trinity College, had a twofold significance: not only because it was dedicated to God, one in three persons, but also because it embodied three old houses. Its endowment and conception were truly regal. As one Cambridge historian has finely said:

> No Cambridge foundation and probably no academic institution in Europe furnishes so striking an example as does Trinity College of the change from the medieval conception of learning and education. It rose on the ruin of the monasteries. For many a long year after, the Franciscans' precincts exhibited only a wide expanse of orchard ground, whereon a few outbuildings were all that remained of the stately structure which had once moved the admiration of the passer-by. If it were asked to what use the former fabric had been converted, men pointed to where, scarcely a hundred paces distant, a new and noble college met the view.[12]

Even in its endowments the college was modern, for, like the gentry who were to rise to great places in the State out of the confiscation of monastic lands, Trinity derived its chief revenues from the impropriation of livings.

The scholars who were incorporated into this new foundation were themselves the most enlightened members of the university at that time, and set the precedents for the foundation to become for many years the most distinguished nursery of natural philosophers in the English-speaking world. For among the first members of the society was John Dee, whose clever stage effects at a performance of the *Peace* of Aristophanes made him a reputation. The effects included that of enabling Scarabeus to mount upwards with his human burden and the basket of victuals at his back, to the very presence of Jove: a fine allegory of the subsequent career of Dee himself. Astronomer, mathematician, alchemist, and astrologer, his bright and erratic genius touched most of the activities of the succeeding sixty years. He suggested a national library of manuscripts, explained the appearance of new stars, doctored Queen Elizabeth, mapped and charted the new geographical discoveries at her express command, was responsible for the introduction of the Gregorian calendar into England, and headed a small and select fraternity which looked for the secret of the transmutation of matter: a man of great span and vision who tumbled into spiritualism and died in poverty and obscurity in the first decade of the following century. His influence would itself repay investigation by the historian of ideas.

The decade also marked the recognition of medicine at Oxford and Cambridge by Henry VIII's establishment of Regius Professorships. Paracelsus, the violent intemperate emancipator of chemistry, had initiated a chain-reaction of ideas which reverberated throughout the fields of natural science; and even those Englishmen who were confessedly anti-Paracelsian[13] nevertheless followed the new fashion of watching the purification of copper, iron, and marcasite in the new forges of London, Cornwall, Cumberland, and Ireland. The 'metallic medicines' of which Paracelsus was such an acknowledged master (mercury for syphilis proved a great success) involved preparations of antimony, copper, iron, lead, and milk of sulphur.[14] Paracelsian iatrochemistry, iatro-physics, and vitalism drew the quick wits: and Thomas Hill, the Elizabethan Huxley, though he 'neuer tasted of the learned Laake' was nevertheless 'taughte among the smythes of Vulcanes forge', and embellished his books with woodcuts of furnaces.[15] His manuscripts were bequeathed to a distiller of St. Paul's Wharf, John Hester, through whose busy activity both as a salesman and a publicist the new knowledge became common.[16]

2

The bold and forward spirits of the age continued to find their intellectual vent in medicine.[17] From 1518, when the College of Physicians had met at Linacre's house, till 1560 that vent was little used: but in the latter year when the College moved to premises at Amen Corner, it began to attract men of calibre. Contemporary with it, the informal fellowship of Barber Surgeons was formally incorporated in 1540 and opened a common hall in Monkwell Street, where in 1572 attendance at quadrennial demonstrations of anatomy was made compulsory on all fellows. With the study of anatomy thus generalised, the College of Physicians soon followed suit, and, thanks to John, Baron Lumley's endowment of a lectureship, they were able to offer a stipend of £40 a year to attract men of ability from Oxford or Cambridge.[18] The extent of their success in so doing may be gauged from the fact that it was as Lumleian lecturer that Harvey first publicly stated his theory of the circulation of the blood though he had graduated M.D. from Cambridge and Padua fourteen years earlier.[19]

John Caius, who became a Fellow of the College of Physicians in 1547, lectured on anatomy in London. Caius, though an avowed Galenist, nevertheless was of an experimental nature: his observations of the sweating sickness at Shrewsbury and Norwich were an interesting essay in social medicine. Anxious to promote the study of medicine at Cambridge, he refounded Gonville Hall, obtaining from the crown the permission to dissect one subject annually at the new foundation. In spite of the fact that he personally endowed three fellowships and twenty scholarships, his more conservative colleagues could not appreciate him and he was ousted.[20]

Caius having taken his doctorate at Padua was also a Vesalian, yet for the definite hall mark of Vesalian influence in England we look to the publication of Thomas Raynalde's *Byrthe of Mankynde*, a book which ran through seven editions by 1600, and a further six afterwards. This has been called 'the most interesting work on mid-wifery in the English language' and accorded 'a place of honour at the head and source of English obstetric literature'.[21] Here was human anatomy laid bare: from these studies a positivistic outlook stemmed as naturally as the metallic fancies of Paracelsus had emerged from the mines of the Tirol.

The foreign wars of Elizabeth's time accelerated the study of anatomy: John Banister at the age of twenty-three served as surgeon to the Earl of Warwick's forces at Havre and with Leicester's expedition to the Low Countries twenty-three years later, and was able to write, edit, and compile a number of medical works;[22] John Woodall, who was a military surgeon in Lord Willoughby's regiment in 1591, went on to add lustre to the Barber Surgeons by becoming not only their master, but also the first surgeon to the East India Company.[23] The knowledge spread, and with it further institutions for medical education: Peter Lowe settling in Glasgow in 1598 and founding the Glasgow Faculty of Physicians and Surgeons.

Such case histories can be multiplied. As medieval chivalry was dying on the field of Zutphen, so English medicine was being born. William Clowes the elder could not see enough active service: after acting as an army surgeon in France in 1563, he served with the navy till 1569, returning to St. Bartholomew's Hospital during the years 1581-5 before resuming service with the army in the Low Countries from 1585 to 1587, and with the navy again in the following year. His surgical treatises synthesised much of this first-hand experience. Of an earlier generation, Thomas Gale did not restrict his service to English forces: he was with the Spanish Army at St. Quentin in 1557, came back as Master of the Barber Surgeons' Company in 1561, and two years later published his volume on surgery containing the prescription for his styptic powder.[24] As the times grew quieter, subsequent surgeons obtained their experience in great houses: George Baker, Master of the Barber Surgeons in 1597, attached himself to the household of the Earl of Oxford, whose violent temper and extensive travels afforded much of interest to a physician.[25]

By 1576 English doctors had acquired such a reputation that Ivan the Terrible of Russia wrote to [Queen] Elizabeth asking her to send him a doctor, an apothecary, and men 'cunning to seek out gold and silver'. He promised to take them into his service and reward them. Dr. Reynolds, Thomas Carver, and three or four others went, but they tired of the barbarous conditions prevailing there and returned. German-born Eliseus Bomelius, an M.D. of Cambridge who had been arrested in 1567 for practising without a licence from the College of Physicians, was then sent, but he soon found it was more profitable to play on the Czar's credulity by astrological practices, and was subsequently arrested in Russia and died in prison. Ivan's successor tried to get the notable Dr. Dee, and failing there, he secured Timothy Willis, who travelled overland in 1597 and returned in 1601. The whole negotiations were conducted on the assumption that the doctor should be an envoy, and none of those sent was of outstanding calibre.[26]

There is also strong evidence of a scientific interest in the working of men's minds. Dr. Thomas Phaer, in addition to writing legal handbooks and translating the *Aeneid* into English verse, composed a popular treatise on *The Regiment of Life* dealing with child health. Ten years later in 1563, William Fulwood translated Gratorolus' *Castle of Memory*. The subject of memory attracted William Perkins, just about to begin a great teaching career at Cambridge, where he was to win for himself a reputation little inferior to that of Hooker: in the year 1584 he published his *Libellus de Memoria*. Indeed, medicine attracted the teachers so much that Christopher Johnson, the headmaster of Winchester School from 1560 to 1570, left to proceed to Oxford for his M.D. in 1571 and became a practising physician, being admitted a Fellow of the Royal College of Physicians in 1580. The subject attracted country gentlemen of leisure too, and in far Cornwall

Richard Carew from his estate at Antony translated Juan Huarte's *Examen de Ingeniis* under the apt title *The Examination of Men's Wits*. Nor was such an interest confined to specialists, for as L. C. Knights has pointed out 'psychology was becoming popular . . . and the melancholy man presented a case for analysis'.[27]

This was not the only discipline which was branching out from the research of the medical men. There were doctors who made notable advances in fields which today are far removed from their parent disciplines. Botany owes much to William Turner, whose *De Re Herbaria* marks the beginning of the scientific study of the subject in England. Turner had met Gesner, the Swiss naturalist, whose new and friendly attitude to nature has been already noted by Wolf, and whose employment of belladonna to relieve pain in 1540 was a real discovery.[28] Turner's scientific spirit is reflected in his strong stand against such superstitions as the mandrake. He was so rationalist that in 1564 he was suspended from his deanery of Wells for nonconformity, and his religious works were forbidden to be read in England in English. Such an innovatory mind was also responsible for the introduction of lucerne into England.[29] Epitomised in him is the rational, positivist spirit, hostile to all authoritative statements unless they could be demonstrated by reason, or reinforced by observation, and he deserves a competent biographer. The trail Turner blazed was followed at a discreet distance by John Gerard, a member of the court of assistants of Barber-Surgeons, who superintended the gardens of Lord Burghley as well as his own in Holborn, and by his diligent collection of simples and plants was able to publish his *Herball* in 1597—the first of its kind of practical value to horticulturists, though the pundits might oppose it by William Bullein's *Book of Simples* published thirty-six years earlier. The quarrel, if one there were, does not detract from the theme that it was in medicine that these new disciplines were being conceived, for Bullein himself was a physician, and wrote *A Dialogue against the Fever Pestilence*, published two years before his death in 1676. To these three pioneers should be added Edward Wotton, the first reader in Greek at Oxford University, an M.D. of Padua, and an F.R.C.P., whose *De Differentiis Animalium* gave him a European reputation when it was published in 1552. This was a pioneer work in zoology, and it antedated by many years the treatises of Aldrovandi whose first work on birds was not published till 1599. Though Wotton largely followed the Aristotelian classification of animals, his objective account of the animal organism and its affiliations in the rest of the natural world makes it a seminal work. Lastly, there were the medical virtuosi: Andrew Boorde, secret agent and traveller, and Thomas Newton, the physician of Butley, who wrote medical, historical, and theological works with a fluency which showed how the currents of thought were flowing between the different subjects, energising them with the same new potential.[30] Such a process, needless to say, finds its climax in Francis Bacon.

The opening up of the animal organism revealed to many minds, through the grimly realistic woodcuts that adorned the pages of the medical works, physical secrets which were capable of being applied to the inanimate world of nature. The lever, the crank, the ball-joint lay bare for the genius to apply them, and soon the value was to be revealed. The chemistry of blood itself was appreciated, and, as the new influx of sugar from the Indies began to flow inwards, it was found that bullock's blood afforded a suitable refining agent for it, and was so used. This inspirational value of a medical education can be even more fully illustrated in the work of Gilberd of Colchester, whose position as physician to Queen Elizabeth enabled him to find both the time and opportunity for research. To him we will later return.

3

Mathematics had been an element in culture long before the period under review, but now it became a cultural force. Thanks to Leonardo da Vinci, the mathematical method was now in the ascendant in Europe, and the old hierarchy of sciences was revised in these terms. Leonardo had said: 'he who scorns the very great certainty of mathematics is feeding his mind on confusion, and will never be able to silence the sophistical teachings that lead only to an eternal battle of words.'[31]

Here again the realism of a medical education shows itself in Robert Recorde, who graduated M.D. at Cambridge in 1545. Recorde taught mathematics and other subjects both at Oxford and Cambridge, and his techniques were in marked contrast to the verbal quibbling of the theologians. It has been aptly said by his recent biographer that 'his aim was the intensely practical one of arousing interest in the many useful applications of mathematical knowledge, and so training his pupils that they would, at the earliest possible moment, be able to employ their new leisure in solving specific problems'.[32] Visual aids, a highly dramatic style, and a series of practical applications mark his work: 'many thynges in the makynge, and in the use also of instrumentes, are better perceaved by a lyttle sighte, then by many wordes.'[33]

His books literally introduced the language of technology into England for he was the first writer in English on arithmetic,[34] and geometry,[35] and an astronomer[36] besides being responsible for the introduction of algebra into England.[37] Indeed, he was the first to see the independence of an algebraic operation and its numerical interpretation. His first book, *The Grounde of Artes*, ran through twenty-seven editions, and was being republished as late as 1699, a century and a half after its first publication.[38]

Recorde's initiation of the English school of mathematical science, with all its consequences, was perceived by a later English mathematician, who in his own day and generation fought the battle for freedom of thought.[39] He was followed by a crop of lesser publicists: Humphrey Baker, author of *The Well-spring of Sciences* (1562); William Bourne, the self-taught ship's carpenter and gunner of Gravesend, who published works on those subjects, and left others unpublished; and Thomas Blundeville, a country gentleman of Newton Flotman, whose ready pen was already employed in popularising other subjects as well. Their very versatility is a testimony to the stimulus of the new technological language, and their literary fertility is a testimony of their scientific evangelism.

By 1570, Euclid had been translated into English by Henry Billingsley, who, after an education at both Cambridge and Oxford, had gone into trade, and, seeing the practical value of the new subject, published his translation with a preface by John Dee. This preface not only surveyed the existing state of mathematical knowledge, but alleged that the chief reason for publishing it was to 'assist the common artificers' who with 'their owne Skill and experience already had, will be hable (by these good helpes and informations) to finde out, and devise, new workes, straunge Engines, and Instrumentes: for sundry purposes in the Common Wealth'. The common artificers were grateful: Robert Norman, a maker of mathematical instruments, said as much in his *Newe Attractive*, published eleven years later; as also did Edward Worsop in his *Discouerie of Sundrie Errours committed by Landemeaters ignorant of Arithmetike and Geometrie*, published in 1582.[40]

Educators seized the new discipline and urged its adoption. Richard Mulcaster, who in 1561 had become the first headmaster of the Merchant Taylors' School in London, had seen the introduction of mathematics at Cambridge under Buckley, and, in his *Positions, Wherein Three Primitive Circumstances be Examined, Which are necessarie for the Training up of Children, either for Skill in their Booke, or Healthe in their Bodie* (1581), he advised the beginning of mathematical subjects in the school, directly after the elementary subjects were acquired. He also advocated the establishment of a separate mathematical college, and contemplated writing a book on the teaching of the subject.[41] Mulcaster's idea was brought to fruition by Thomas Smith, who, like Billingsley, was a haberdasher, and in 1588 took the lead in raising funds to endow a mathematical lectureship in London, the first lecture being given in his own house, and subsequent ones in the chapel of the Staplers' Company.[42]

The new cosmic pattern evolved through the mathematical teachers reached out of the classroom and up to the stars. Leonard Digges, whom the latest historian of Oxford University has seen fit to ignore, published his *Tectonicon* in 1556, and his *Geometrical Practise, named Pantometria* was published fifteen years later. Contemporary military forays to the Continent, which provided so much stimulus to the physicians, certainly called forth his *Arithmeticall Militare Treatise, named Stratioticos* in 1579. But his attention was not confined to the mechanics of this world, and if his son Thomas Digges is to be believed, he can be also regarded as the inventor of the telescope.[43] This was to prove the basic instrument of the new cosmology.[44] His son Thomas was even more significant, for he actually was the muster-master-general for the English forces in the Netherlands in 1586, and a projector of an expedition to China and the Antarctic. It is to him that we owe the first exposition of the heliocentric theory in English.

The exploitation of this new knowledge by its dissemination among those likely to make the most effective use of it led to a quickening of old traditions, and to a very vocal and practical movement for the establishment of new institutions which would sustain the teaching and research of the new subjects. Along with this was an industrial advance, to which economic historians, with due caution, have not scrupled to apply the name of 'revolution'.[45] J. M. Keynes asserted that 'the boom period in England definitely began with the return of Drake's first important expedition . . . in 1573'.[46]

4

'On the whole,' a recent historian of the period has written, 'easterners went to Cambridge and westerners to Oxford.'[47] Oxford attracted the politically minded owing to the fame of Laurence Humphrey, President of Magdalen College from 1561 to 1589, a notable Calvinist. Elizabeth is said to have remarked to him: 'Mr. Doctor, that loose gown becomes you mighty well; I wonder your notions should be so narrow.' He gave an edge to many earnest Puritan minds and his influence was felt long after his death.

From this very time 'education' begins to have a secular connotation.[48] The incorporation of the two universities of Oxford and Cambridge in 1571 shows that the government of the day realised just how important those two institutions were becoming in the national economy. Certainly the Elizabethan economic expert, Sir Thomas Smith, realised how important it was that the new economic order should benefit the universities, so that the universities should be able to rest secure in devotion to non-factitious enterprises.[49] Successive legislation by the governments, enhancing the importance of the universities, reached a climax in 1603 when they received the right to send representatives to Parliament—a right that has only recently been extinguished.

To feed them new schools arose to meet the new demand for a lay, administrative class.[50] Shrewsbury (1552), Westminster (1560), Merchant Taylors' (1561), Rugby (1567), and Harrow (1571-1608) added five to what were to become the 'big nine' of the so-called public schools.[51] The very concept of the 'public school' as an institution where the scions of the ruling class might be suitably indoctrinated dates from these years, since it was formerly customary to place such sprigs in the households of great men.[52] Indeed, educational theorists went to great pains to indicate the advantages of such schools over the old method, which savoured of apprenticeship, and was often not attended with all the useful knowledge that it might have been. In these new schools, the masters were men of attainment and culture, such as Richard Mulcaster, the first headmaster of the Merchant Taylors' school, whom we have mentioned.[53] Hitherto, educational historians have tended to concentrate on the mere number of schools founded, and have instanced this as evidence of the paucity of educational provision at this time.[54] Not for nothing were Philip Sidney and Fulke Greville sent to the newly founded Shrewsbury School; and Merchant Taylors' produced such men as Lancelot Andrewes, Thomas Lodge, Sir Edwyn Sandys, Sir James Whitlocke, Matthew Gwinne, and Edmund Spenser.

5

The new Tudor aristocracy looked to the Inns of Court rather than to the universities for their professional education. And this was indeed the golden age of the Inns. Lincoln's Inn acquired Furnival's Inn (1547) and Thavie's Inn (1550), and the estate of the bishop of Chichester

(1580) to complete the architectural design inaugurated by the construction of its gatehouse in 1521. The Hall of the Middle Temple was finished in 1570, thanks to Edmund Plowden. But of the four, Gray's Inn was most outstanding. There gathered a cluster of ability such as seldom congregated in any one seat of learning in England.

The exceptional prestige of Gray's Inn was due to three men, who lost no opportunity of advancing it: Sir William Cecil, Sir Nicholas Bacon, and Sir Gilbert Gerrard. Cecil and Bacon were brothers-in-law, and they favoured the idea of applying the revenues of monasteries to establish a university in London.[55] Their plan fell through, but they seem to have persisted in carrying it out on a smaller scale in Gray's Inn. Cecil was in a particularly favourable position to do this, for he was, in addition to his other high offices of state, the Master of the Court of Wards. He introduced his two sons, Thomas and Robert, and his son-in-law, Edward de Vere. Bacon introduced his five sons, of whom Francis was the youngest. Others who added their brilliance to this constellation of ability were Sir Francis Walsingham, Sir Henry Sidney, Charles Howard of Effingham, John Whitgift, Sir John Wolley, Sir Charles Parry, and Sir Philip Sidney.

Indeed, one of the reasons for the liveliness of the Elizabethan House of Commons was the quality of the education which its members received. Of the 420 members in the 1563 Parliament, no less than 108 went to the Inns of Court, and only 36 of these had prefaced that education by sojourn at either Oxford or Cambridge. By 1584 the proportion was: 164 had an Inns of Court education and 90 of these had already been to a university. By 1593, 197 members had been to the Inns of Court of whom 106 had attended the universities. The figures of those who had received a university education alone were 67 in 1563, 145 in 1584, and 161 in 1593. The general increase in the higher education of members is therefore striking.

The close inter-relationships of these men form a fascinating pattern of Elizabethan life. Sir Philip Sidney, introduced by Cecil to Gray's Inn, married the daughter of Sir Francis Walsingham, another member. Henry Wriothesley, third Earl of Southampton, also introduced by Cecil, was the patron of Florio the translator, and a close friend of Shakespeare, who dedicated *Venus and Adonis* to him. And it was Gray's Inn which, after Trinity College, Cambridge, nourished the philosophic genius of the age to come: Francis Bacon. Admitted in 1576, he became a bencher ten years later. Between the years 1597 and 1600 he laid out their garden, and it was to their society that he retired after his fall from power.

6

The explorers and pioneers themselves valued the new techniques highly, and were anxious that succeeding generations should continue to blaze the trails which they had started. Sir Humphrey Gilbert, Raleigh's step-brother, founder of the first British colony in North America, was so anxious that he drafted for Lord Burghley a scheme to establish a special academy. These proposals, laid before the Queen in 1570 by Burghley, reveal what the most forward spirit of the day thought of education and its basic requirements. Moral Philosophy, Mathematics, Geography, Physic, and Surgery constitute the basic elements of the course which was to be offered, although Greek, Latin, Hebrew, Logic and Rhetoric, make a conventional appearance. But what is really interesting is his further provision that the Natural Philosopher and the Physician should 'continually practize together . . . to try owt the secreates of nature, as many waies as they possibly may. And shalbe sworne once euery yeare to deliuer into the *Tresorer* his office, faire and plaine written in Parchment, withoute *Equiuocacion* or *Enigmaticall phrases*, vnder their handes, all those their proofes and trialles made within the forepassed yeare.' It almost reads like the preamble to a bill establishing a state atomic project. Gilbert continued that at his proposed academy he wished the researchers to enjoy immunity from the Statute of 1404 which forbade alchemical experiments having as their aim the multiplication of gold. Among the thirty professors and instructors who were to teach he suggested specialists in 'Spanish, Italian, French, and High Dutch', a Librarian of a Copyright library, and a teacher of law who should 'sett downe and teache exquisitely the office of a justice of the peace and sheriff'. Among the regulations were: that language teachers should publish translations of works which would advance the studies of the academy; and that the readers in arts and common laws should 'set forth some new bookes in printe, according to their several professions'. This might well be a new college president determined to raise the status of his faculty. Gilbert closes with the downright certainty of an empiric: 'by erecting this Achademie there shalbe hereafter, in effecte, no gentleman within this Realme but good for some what, Whereas now the most parte of them are good for nothing.'[56]

The ideas of a leading overseas voyager never got beyond writing, but similar ones, drafted at the same time by the dominating figure of Elizabethan finance did. The wealthiest merchant of his day, Sir Thomas Gresham, whose achievements included raising the exchange value of the pound sterling from sixteen shillings to twenty-two shillings, had certainly earned the right to be heard. But what is even more important, as an international financier he was one of the most powerful destroyers of the traditions and attitudes of his ancestors.[57] Four years after Sir Humphrey Gilbert's abortive scheme, he announced his intention to found a college in London for the free instruction of all who wished to attend. Naturally enough, the scheme excited the apprehension of the University of Cambridge, whose public orator exerted all the resources of his latinity to set forth the prior claims of the university on its former alumnus. His technique was obsolete; had he broken with tradition and couched it in the vernacular it might have had more effect. Few, least of all Lady Burghley (wife of the great Elizabethan minister), could really believe that *detrimentum, pene etiam ruina* faced those venerable collegiate foundations if Gresham's scheme were carried into effect. For so it was, by his will of July 1575, destined to be. Salaries of £50 a year for professors of Law, Physic, and Rhetoric showed that he was infected with the new ideas: while similar provision for Mathematics and Astronomy, no less than for Geometry and Music, showed that he intended no narrow vocational course, although his scheme was avowedly designed to assist those already actively engaged in some professional activity. The close connection between the city and the college was emphasised by the use of the same bell to call merchants to the Exchange, and to summon students to a lecture. When Lady Gresham died in 1596, the Mercers' Company (to whom Gresham had bequeathed the right of nominating the professors of Law, Physic, and Rhetoric) and the Corporation of the City of London (to whom he bequeathed the right of nominating the remaining four professors) got cold feet. Fearing their own judgments might be clouded, they requested the two universities of Oxford and Cambridge to nominate for them. Nevertheless, the choices made were good ones, and set notable precedents.[58] John Bull, the first professor of Music, gave his lectures in English, and Henry Briggs, the first professor of Mathematics, not only calculated complete tables of logarithms, but also introduced the present notation of decimal fractions, one of the most important advances in the history of arithmetic; and published works on navigation.[59] As an institution, the importance of its foundation can be seen in the fact that its professors were intimately bound up with the formation of the Royal Society, so much so that after 1660 the term *Greshamite* covered both.[60]

Not so obviously linked to the driving needs of the times was another foundation, the first Society of Antiquaries, formed in London in 1572, ostensibly for the study of antiquity and history.[61] Its real purpose, as Dr. Wittlin has recently pointed out, was to 'separate falsehood from truth and tradition from evidence', sifting records of the past by the same technique as we have seen both the doctors and the mathematicians applying: penetrating into origins without fear of the conclusions which might arise therefrom.[62] In their application to the Queen for a charter of incorporation, the society stressed the example of Germany, Italy, and France, where public lectures, libraries, and academies ensured that the treasures of the past were not forgotten. At the same time, they pointed out the value of such studies 'to qualify persons for public characters and offices'. Among the thirty-eight members[63] were many like Sir Robert Cotton[64] and William Hakewill,[65] who found in antiquity the necessary legal precedents which were to serve the constitutionalists of the following century with arguments against monarchical tyranny, and it is not surprising that James I saw fit-to dissolve it as a 'treasonable cabal'.

7

'It is for each age under the spur of necessity to point out what is best for its own circumstances, and the State must exercise its wisdom and policy in bringing this about.' So Richard Mulcaster, a great Elizabethan educationist, saw the problem of university reform, and his suggestions bear detailed examination.

'I would have it understood', he wrote, 'that I have no great fault to find with the present constitution of the universities, but granting that things are well done there already, there is no discourtesy in wishing that they might be managed a good deal better.' And to 'manage them a good deal better' Mulcaster put forward four points.

1. That the Colleges should be divided into faculties 'according to the professions for which they prepare'.
2. That students of similar age studying for the same profession should be 'all bestowed in one house'.
3. That College livings should be made more valuable 'by combination', and that the Colleges themselves should be strengthened by being 'lessened in number'.
4. That there should be life fellowships for learned scholars.

Mulcaster looked to the State as the agent of these reforms. 'Hath not the State authority to carry them out?' he asked, 'seeing that it hath already given its sanction to the making of foundations, with a reservation of the right to alter them if sufficient cause should be

PLATE I

HENRY VIII PRESENTING THE COMPANY OF BARBER SURGEONS WITH THEIR CHARTER

From a painting by Holbein in possession of the Royal College of Surgeons

See page 57]

PLATE 2

GRESHAM COLLEGE

From John Ward, *Lives of the Professors at Gresham College*, 1740

See page 79]

shown?' He envisaged a separate College for Languages, where some 'wishing only a general culture, will be content to rest in this literary faculty, taking delight in the writings of the poets and historians, and not passing on to any professional study'. Another College was proposed for Mathematics, 'the sure means of direction for all skilled workmen, who without such knowledge can only go by rote, but with it might reach genuine skill'. A third College for Philosophy, Natural, Political, and Moral, was suggested, with the responsibility of training future doctors, lawyers, and theologians: each of these three professions was to be endowed with its particular College. Another College was to be for teachers. Thus the Mulcasterian scheme comprised three Colleges of General Study (Languages, Mathematics, and Philosophy) through which all postulants for the professions should pass, and four specifically professional Colleges (Medicine, Law, Divinity, and Education).[66]

Mulcaster was animated by a desire to train the élite: 'it were better for the country to have a few well trained and sufficiently provided for, than an unlearned multitude.' But during this period, there was a steady groundswell of opinion on behalf of what we today would call the 'extra-mural' population of the universities. 'That meane sort of men' described by John Dolman, whose quickness of wit could 'conceive all such points of art, as nature could give'.[67] A host of writers put out books for the adult common reader, and among this host schoolmasters were prominent. It was a period of rapid assimilation of knowledge, and the popularisers and translators were incorporating into the general fabric of culture the discoveries of their times. Richard Sherry, formerly headmaster of Magdalen College School, published a spirited defence of his native tongue in 1550. His aim was revealed by his title: *A Treatise of Schemes and Tropes very profytable for the better understanding of good authors*, in which he categorically asserts: 'Thoughe vnto greate wittes occupyed wyth weightye matters, they do not greatelye pertayne, yet to such as perchance shal not haue perfect instructoures, they may be commodious to helpe them selues for ye better vnderstandynge of such good authors as they reade.'[68] For the next half-century the movement gathered impetus till it culminated in Philemon Holland, the master of the free school at Coventry, whose translations of Livy (1600), Pliny (1601), and Plutarch (1603) were used as late as Southey's time.

Nor was this activity confined to schoolmasters. Other writers were soon popularising the *expertise* of their particular professions. Thomas Wilson, Secretary of State, member of parliament, secret agent, and man of affairs, published the first English translation of Demosthenes in 1570, insisting that it should be read by 'yong and olde, learned and vnlearned' since 'none euer was more fitte to make an English man tell his tale praiseworthily in any open hearing, wither in Parliament or in Pulpit, or otherwise, than this onely Orator was'.[69] Only a year before this Edward Fenton, captain, navigator, and voyager to China, translated *Certaine Secrete Wonders of Nature* which he hoped would supplant the unprofitable Arthurian stories which 'besides that they passe all likelihood of truth, are vtterly without either graue precept or good example. Whereby I am in better hope that this booke containing such varietie of matter bothe pleasant to read and necessary to know, being sprinkled throughout with great wisdome and moralitie, shall be the rather embraced and allowed of all.'[70] The first tract or treatise on English political economy, written by John Hales (who had converted his grant of St. John's Hospital in 1548 into a free school where Philemon Holland was later to teach) was published in 1581. This, as Max Beer has pointed out, is medieval in sentiment, but modern in practice: combining ethical views with mercantilist aims: stressing that the duty of every citizen was to increase the wealth of the country by industry and frugality, by working up raw materials into valuable goods, and by eschewing foreign trifles and luxuries. He admonished his countrymen not to export native raw materials, but to work them up into goods, the value of which consisted mainly in craftsmanship, since such goods brought in new riches in gold and silver.[71]

This exhortation to the technologists was not wasted. Coal mining and iron founding were extended, copper and zinc were exploited, ships were built, glass and paper were manufactured, beer, spirits, and sugar were brewed, distilled, and refined, and foreign technicians were eagerly welcomed,[72] and, in these last three decades, the English middle class started on its manufacturing and maritime career equipped with a positive teleology that admitted no barriers. Medieval usury laws fell unlamented in 1571, and, as well as committing his cargoes to the protection of God, the Elizabethan merchant who was bent on expanding the export trade took good care to insure them, relying on the practical treatise of William West which showed him how to do it.[73]

Protected by royal patents of monopoly,[74] all adventurers and manufacturers took great pains to secure proper vocational training for their employees. There was no danger under a monopolistic system, that the trained workman would reveal trade secrets to a native competitor, as was the case in England as late as 1884.[75] At the very bottom of the scale, the Statute of Apprentices of 1563 regulated some thirty crafts and mysteries, and imposed upon the whole country the seven-year period of learning the trade. It stressed that apprentices should be of English blood and should belong to a certain class, and aimed at the production of English goods of a high order. There was no stigma attaching to the custom: indeed, the craftsman had become, by the end of Elizabeth's reign, the hero of drama and fiction. In Thomas Delony's *Gentle Craft*, Peachy and his shoe-makers beat two sea-captains; and the theme was still further exploited by Dekker in 1599 in his *Shoemaker's Holiday*. Apprenticeship cut right across the class stratification of society, and the popular motif of the time was that of the apprentice who, like Dick Whittington, rose to be Mayor of London and a great man; just as today the movies portray the poor boy who works his way through college to become a successful business executive.[76] Learning in those days was best done on the job itself, and the numerous cases involving non-observance of the Statute of Apprentices only serve to illustrate that the vitality of the growing crafts was not stultified by regulations.[77]

We are already in the age of the manager and the secretary, however, for three handbooks published at this time show that the secretary needed instruction. Angel Day, son of a parish clerk, and himself a stationer, wrote *The English Secretarie . . . in which is layd forth a Pathe-waye, so apte plainer and easier, to any learners capacity, as like whereof hath not at any time heretofore been delivered*. This, the Elizabethan counterpart of the secretarial course, ran through five editions from its first publication in 1586, and has been described as 'the most thorough-going book on letter writing in English, perhaps in any language, of the time'.[78] Nor was it the first: Abraham Fleming, prolific author of some fifty-nine works, had ten years earlier published *A Panoplie of Epistles* for the same purpose. Already the new educational network was producing its clerks, and the term itself was being significantly laicised.[79]

Case histories of individual training can be further adumbrated. The Muscovy Company, the best organised, most ambitious, and most fruitful of all overseas enterprises up to that date, maintained 'one learned man in the science of Cosmographie' paying £200 a year—four times more than Gresham allowed for his professors—to instruct their mariners, and carry out plans for navigation.[80] Similarly, Walter Raleigh was much indebted to his own mathematical tutor, and sent him to survey Virginia in 1585; when Raleigh's star waned, he entered the service of the ninth Earl of Northumberland, who earned the title of 'the Wizard Earl' by his scientific experiments. There were even those who sought to educate the most conservative of all classes—

the farmers—and Thomas Tusser, who introduced the culture of barley, threw into verse form a *Hundred Points of Good Husbandry*, which was first published in 1557 and further amplified in 1570 and 1573. This quickly became a farmers' bible, and it showed that even in agriculture some measure of rationalisation was possible. From 1574 dates also the first practical treatise on hop-culture in England, written by Reginald Scott, *The Perfect Platform of a Hop-Garden*.[81]

Over all this busy ferment of new knowledge and education brooded the Elizabethan statesman, anxious to ensure the continuance of some sort of social discipline, but at the same time anxious to avoid too much. Licences for schoolmasters were reinstituted, and diocesan visitations were once more revived to inspect possible disseminators of sedition. The pulpit was also supplied with State homilies from 1571 onwards. Similarly, text books, like Christopher Ocland's *Anglorum Praelia*, were recommended for use in schools by virtue of their moral quality.[82] Perhaps the increasing measure of control is but another testimony to the efficacy of the new educational agencies. And surely the comprehensive measures taken to control the Press in 1586 showed that the printed word was certainly having its effect on the mass of the populace![83]

8

This aspect of education began to loom ever more prominent as the century drew to its close. Questions were being posed that literally fulfilled Thomas Raynalde's reflections of a generation before: science had 'renued, refreshid and purgid' men's minds so much that the authorities began to lower an iron curtain. The simple, consequential application of scientific techniques to the study of society followed as naturally as the transference of training from medicine to technology and back again. The specialisms were only just emerging, and, even in the following century the 'curiosi', 'otiosi' and 'virtuosi' were still encyclopaedic by nature.

So it is not surprising that by 1600 two currents of thought should be clearly apparent: dialectically working on each other to produce the century of genius. We have been concerned here with the building up of the thesis that the new view of Nature as an oyster to be opened without inhibitions was gaining ground steadily in the educational world. This view was influenced partly by the new scientific cosmology, partly by the new technologies, but chiefly by the formulation and popularisation of new techniques in all branches of human experience. The antithesis is sufficiently inherent in the general pattern of society not to be stated with such emphasis. That general pattern, or great chain of being, has been sketched by E. M. W. Tillyard in his *Elizabethan World Picture* (1943). In this, Dr. Tillyard has gone to great pains to insist on the 'purest medieval tradition' of the Elizabethan cosmology. 'The Puritans and the courtiers,' Dr. Tillyard goes on, 'were more united by a common theological bond than they were divided by ethical disagreements.' This common theological bond Dr. Tillyard finds in the Great Chain of Being: a chain stretching from the foot of God's throne to the meanest of inanimate objects. Between God and man were the angels as guardians, Nature was the 'direct and involuntary tool of God himself', and every Elizabethan felt the pervasive operation of an external fate in the world. All Dr. Tillyard writes, is of course, counter to the general opinion of the writers in *Shakespeare's England*. But we are not concerned with the validity or otherwise of Dr. Tillyard's argument. We merely wish to state it as a classical exposition of the antithesis which is embedded in the general pattern of society. The thesis here propounded gains rather than loses from the elaboration of this antithesis. That the thesis had taken possession of men's minds can be seen from Marlowe's *Dr. Faustus* (published just after the turn of the century), but even more from Shakespeare's *King Lear*. Shakespeare was in direct contact with this new cosmology: he drew on the works of the translators for his histories, and on the writings of Reginald Scot's exposé of witchcraft for details in *Macbeth*. He certainly knew Digges the mathematician, both as a neighbour and a writer.[84] And when he wrote *King Lear* he was so obsessed by the word Nature and its conflicting interpretations, that he rung the changes on it more than forty times, covering all its known imputations. That is why the soliloquy of Edmund, the Bastard and outsider, rings so curiously modern, and hypostatises the new philosophy.[85]

9

By 1600 certain fresh developments can be discerned. The framework created for the generation after the dissolution of the monasteries has lost their elasticity and is hardening. A new secular authoritarianism is beginning to make itself felt. But the products of those moulds are abroad and themselves changing the shape of things to come. For in this very year Gilberd, the President of the College of Physicians, declared the earth to be a magnet: his *De Magnete Magneticisque Corporibus* looks out, not over the palæotechnic age which was to follow, but right into the neotechnic age that was to find its prime mover in Electricity. This was the supreme event of the year: the publication of the first scientific textbook in the English language.[86] The first rails had been laid at Nottingham,[87] and the stocking frame had been adopted.[88] Illustrating that medieval concepts had no validity, the rising of Essex in the following year proved an abortive failure: for from now onwards the great households were to serve as shelters not for armed retainers but for scientists and men of letters.

The morphology of Elizabethan society explains so much that occurred later, for it was the last time that England was a community within its borders. On 31 December 1600, a date as ominous as any in history, the East India Company was given its charter, and the greatest trading and empire-building corporation in English history began its activities, fortified by all the techniques and advances of the preceding two generations. Some inkling of what was afoot in those times stirred Samuel Daniel, the tutor to the colonially minded third Earl of Pembroke, when he wrote his *Musophilus, or a Defence of All Learning* with its prophetic passage:

> Who can tell for what great work in hand
> The greatness of our style is now ordain'd?
> What powers it shall bring in, what spirits command,
> What thoughts let out, what humours keep restrained,
> What mischief it may powerfully withstand,
> And what fair ends may thereby be attain'd?[89]

The fission in Elizabethan society was complete, and Lear in his madness could cry, at the same time as Francis Bacon was publishing his *Advancement of Learning*:

> You sulphurous and thought-executing fires,
> Vaunt-couriers of oak-cleaving thunderbolts,
> Singe my white head. And thou all-shaking thunder
> Strike flat the thick rotundity o' th' world,
> Crack Nature's moulds, all germens spill at once
> That makes ungrateful man.[90]

REFERENCES

For a standard picture of the age see *Shakespeare's England* (O.U.P., 1916); for some of the contemporary contrivances of mechanical science see HODGES, C. W., *The Globe Restored* (Benn, 1953).

1. *Compendious Declaration of the Excellent Vertues of a certain lateli invented oile*, quoted Paul H. Kocher, *J.H.I.*, XI (1950), 14.

2. For which see R. P. Adams, 'The Social Responsibilities of Science in Utopia, New Atlantis, and After', *J.H.I.*, X (1949), 374-98.

3. The Zilzel-Koyré controversy as to whether the craftsman or the theorists were responsible for the eotechnic revolution is very pertinent here. Zilzel's

thesis that the symbiosis between workshop practice and higher culture led to the fresh, empiric, positive approach of man to nature is accepted as outlined in previous articles in the *J.H.I.*, and in *Am. Jour. of Sociology*, XLVII (1942); Koyré, 'Galileo and Plato', *J.H.I.*, IV (1943), 401-29, insists that Galileo taught the artisans and craftsmen of the shipyards of Venice more than they taught him. I hold that both these groups contributed to mould a fresh educational matrix for England in two generations. For a general discussion see R. P. Stearns, 'The Scientific Spirit in England in Early Modern Times', *Isis*, XXXIV (1943), 293-312.

4. Between its first publication in 1499 and Polydore Virgil's death in 1555, it ran through twenty-four editions. The first English edition published in 1546 by Thomas Langley was dedicated to Sir Anthony Denny, a favourite of the King, who had obtained much monastic wealth after the Dissolution. By 1551 it had passed through four editions. See John Ferguson (whose magnificent library of early scientific works is now in the University of Glasgow), 'Bibliographical Notes on the English Translation of Polydore Virgil's work, 'De Inventoribus Rerum', *Archaelogia*, LI, pt. 1 (1888), 107-41. For the most up-to-date account of Polydor Virgil's life, see Denys Hay in *Journal of the Warburg and Courtauld Institutes*, XII (1949), 133-51.

5. ARMITAGE, A., *Copernicus, The Founder of Modern Astronomy* (1938), points out that the theory was not 'an original product of his genius', but a synthesis and development of ideas already existing (p. 90).

6. LEACH, A. F., *English Schools at the Reformation, 1546-8* (1896), sustains the thesis that the endowments of schools were swept away wholesale for distribution among courtiers, and that the schools called after King Edward VI are misnamed.

7. e.g. TAWNEY, R. H., *Religion and the Rise of Capitalism* (1927), for the close affiliation between the new mercantile class and the reformers, and his 'Rise of the Gentry, 1558-1640' in *Econ. Hist. Rev.*, XI (1941).

8. WATSON, Foster, *The Beginnings of the Teaching of Modern Subjects in England* (1909), 321-2.

9. *Journal of English and Germanic Philology* (1915).

10. Quoted by L. F. Anderson, *History of Manual and Industrial School Education* (London, 1926), 8.

11. Aristotle, *Politics*, 1, 7; Columella, *Re Re Rustica*, 1 Praef., 5, 6; Lampridius, *Alexander Severus*, 44; *Patrologia Latina*, CLXXII, 1245, and CLXXVI, 752; J. Johnson, *Laws and Canons* 1, 4422 (Canon of A.D. 960).

12. MULLINGER, J. B., *The University of Cambridge from the Royal Injunctions of 1535 to the Accession of Charles the First* (1884), 81.

13. As was John Jones, who had studied at both Oxford and Cambridge, and practised at Bath and Buxton, from the last-named place deriving his material for his book on baths in 1572. In 1574 he translated *Galens Bookes of Elementes*. See Paul H. Kocher, 'Paracelsian Medicine in England, 1570-1600', *Jour. Hist of Medicine*, II (1947), 451-80.

14. WOLF, A., *A History of Science, Technology, and Philosophy in the 16th and 17th Centuries* (1950), 439.

15. For whose life see the *Dictionary of National Biography* and the *Huntington Library Quarterly*, VII (1944), 329-51.

16. The titles of his pamphlets in the British Museum show his range:

A Joyfull Jewell . . . contayning . . . orders, preservatives . . . for the Plague (1579); *A Short Discours . . . upon Chirgurgie . . . translated out of the Italian* (1580 and 1626); *A Compendium of the Rationall Secretes of L. Phioravante* (1582)—a translation of Fioravanti; *The Sclopoturie of J. Quercetanus* (1590)—which made known the use of calomel as advocated by *Joseph de Chesne*; *An Excellent Treatise teaching howe to cure the French Pockes* (1590)—a translation of P. Hermanni; *A Breefe Aunswere . . . to the Exposition of J. Aubertus . . . concerning the Origin of Metalles . . . whereunto is added divers rare secretes* (1591); *The First part of the Key of Philosophie* (1596); *The Secrets of Physic and Philosophy* (1633); *The Pearle of Practise . . . for Physike and Chirurgie* (N.D.) and *These Oiles, Waters, Extractions, or Essence . . . ready made to be sold*, which seems to have been his sales catalogue.

17. NEWMAN, Sir G., *The Rise of Preventive Medicine* (1932), 138, calls attention to the fact that Sir Thomas More was a friend and pupil of Linacre, and that when the College of Physicians was founded, it not only regulated the practice of physic in the whole country, but 'exerted a powerful stimulus on the science and art of medicine'. Vesalius' mother was an Englishwoman called Isabella Crabbe.

18. Equal to that of the Regius Professors at Oxford and Cambridge.

19. The influence of Padua in this connection should not be forgotten, since from the time of Pietro d'Abano at the beginning of the 14th century till that of Cremonini at the beginning of the 17th century it was a school of scientific method, see J. H. Randall, Jr., 'The Development of Scientific Method in the School of Padua', *J.H.I.*, I (1940), 177-206. Paduan-trained Forest and Bontius also set up an anatomical theatre and physic garden at Leyden, where in 1578 the first medical student matriculated. This was John James, an Englishman who had already graduated at Cambridge, and in 1581 he was the second to receive the M.D. degree. 'He was the first swallow to invade the University of Leyden, an invasion that was to culminate in the Boerhaavian summer of the early 18th century'; R. W. Innes Smith, *English Speaking Students of Medicine at the University of Leyden* (1932).

20. ALLEN, Phyllis, 'Medical Education in Seventeenth Century England', *Jour. Hist. of Medicine* (1940), 115-43.

21. BALLANTYNE, J. W. (ed. 1907), *The Byrthe of Mankynde*, gives a full bibliographical treatment. The first edition (not Raynalde's) was published in 1540, and was followed by Raynalde's in 1545, 1552, 1560, 1565, 1584, 1593, 1598, 1604, 1613, 1626, 1634, 1654, 1676.

22-25. See *Dictionary of National Biography* (1926), and H. J. Webb, 'English Surgery during the reign of Elizabeth' in *Bulletin of the History of Medicine* (Baltimore, 1944), 15.

26. CHENEY, E. P., *History of England* (1926), I, 314-15.

27. KNIGHTS, L. C., *Drama and Society in the Age of Jonson* (1937), 316, who continues, 'Even during the first half of Elizabeth's reign Ascham had devoted several pages of *The Schoolmaster* to a discussion of the different characteristics of "quick wits" and "hard wits", and Lyly had made Euphues declaim on the theme that "Education can have no show where the excellency of Nature doth bear sway". These discussions find parallels in modern textbooks of Psychology.'

28. WOLF, A., see 14 above, 440. Gesner's illustrations in his *Historia Animalium* (1551-87) provided much new and original zoological material.

29. For further agricultural improvements see 81 below, and *The Setting of*

Corne by Sir Hugh Plat, 'the most ingenious husbandman of his age', and also 89 below.

30. For all these see the *Dictionary of National Biography*, the *British Museum Catalogue*, and 14 above.

31. For a general discussion of this point see Hans Baron, 'Evaluation of the Fifteenth Century Renaissance', *J.H.I.*, IV (1943), 45-51, to which I am indebted for much of this argument.

32. JOHNSON, F. R., 'Robert Recorde's Mathematical Teaching and the Anti-Aristotlian Movement', *Huntington Library Bulletin* (1935), vii, 60; L. D. Patterson 'Recorde's Cosmography', *Isis*, XLII (1951), 208-18.

33. *Op cit.*, 71.

34. *The Grounde of Artes* (1540).

35. *The Pathway to Knowledge* (1551).

36. *The Castle of Knowledge* (1551).

37. *The Whetstone of Witte* (1557). He discovered the method of extracting the square root of multinomial algebraic expressions, and was the first to use the sign =. A. Wolf, *History of Science*, etc., 192, says that this book was the first English book to contain the + and — signs.

38. 1540, 1542, 1543, 1549, 1551, 1552, 1558, 1561, 1570, 1571, 1573, then with additions by John Dee and John Mellis (the latter of whom said 'I had no other instruction at my first beginning, but only this good author's booke') 1582, 1583, 1590, 1600, 1607, 1610, R. Norton re-edited it 1618, and R. Hartwell 1623, 1636, 1646, 1648, 1652, 1654, and Thomas Willsford 1558, 1662, and Edw. Hatton 1699.

39. Augustus De Morgan, who resigned his professorship of mathematics at University College, London, when the council refused to elect James Martineau to the chair of mental philosophy and logic because of his rationalism. See *Arithmetical Books* (1847), and *Companion to the British Almanac* (1837).

40. This characteristic artisan flavour clung to Mathematics till after the first quarter of the following century, when John Wallis (whose *Arithmetica Infinitorium* of 1655, contained the first hints of the differential calculus) declared, 'Mathematicks (at that time, with us) was scarce looked upon as Academical Studies, but rather Mechanical, as the business of Traders, Merchants, Seamen, Carpenters, Surveyors of Lands, and the like; and perhaps some Almanac Makers in London. . . . For the study of Mathematicks was at that time more cultivated in London than in the Universities.' T. Hearne, *P. Langtoft's Chronicle* (1725) cxlvii, and C. E. Mallet, *History of the University of Oxford* (1924), ii, 147.

41. Mulcaster also proposed Colleges for teacher training, languages, philosophy, and for specific professions.

QUICK, R. H., *Educational Reformers* (1917), 90-102; Foster Watson, *The Beginnings of the Teaching of Modern Subjects in England* (1909), 259, gives Mulcaster's three reasons: (1) 'The Mathematicalls . . . do some good thing, sensible even to simple people by number, figure, sound or motion.' (2) They induce a habit 'inexpungable by bare probabilities and not to be brought to believe upon light conjectures in any other knowledge, being still drawn upon infallible demonstrations'. (3) They supply an antidotal training to false rhetorical similes. When Mulcaster was at Cambridge in the reign of Edward VI, William Buckley had been appointed to read arithmetic and geometry to the students, and had presented them with a number of Euclids at his own cost. For Buckley, see *D.N.B.*, vii, 215.

42. For his inaugural address see F. R. Johnson's works and the article in the *J.H.I.*, III (1942), 94-106. For the most up-to-date review of Billingsley's Euclid and its source see *American Mathematical Monthly*, LVII (1950), 443-52.

43. Though the invention is usually ascribed to Hans Lipperskey, a Dutch spectacle maker, in 1608, see A. Wolf, *op. cit.*, 76.

44. Johnson, F. R., and Larkey, S. V., 'Thomas Digges, The Copernican System, and the Idea of the Infinity of the Universe', in *Huntington Library Bulletin* (1934), V. D. P. Pattison, 'Leonard and Thomas Digges', *Isis*, XLII (1951), 120-1.

45. For an account of which see J. U. Nef, *Industry and Government in France and England, 1540-1640* (1940).

46. Keynes, J. M., *A Treatise on Money*, II, 156-7, who continues that 'the booty brought back by Drake in the *Golden Hind* may fairly be considered the fountain and origin of British Foreign Investment'. L. C. Knights, *Drama and Society in the Age of Jonson*, 41-2, who quotes this, deals very fully with the economic developments of the period in an attempt to discover whether there was in fact any sociological relationship between the 'two worlds' and literature. For the general cultural picture there is also L. B. Wright, *Middle Class Culture in Elizabethan England* (1934), which is comprehensive and important.

47. Neale, J. E., *The Elizabethan House of Commons* (London, 1949), 303.

48. De Montmorency, J. E. G., *State Intervention in English Education* (1902), 82-3.

49. His Act stipulating that one-third of the college rents should be paid in corn insulated them from the price revolution going on at the time, J. B. Mullinger, *op. cit.*, 377. In 1583 (six years after his death) appeared his important work *De Republica Anglorum*.

50. The first school which was set up as a purely lay corporation was Sherborne in May 1550. The Lady Chapel was converted into a house for the headmaster, and the new governors were 'the first body whose, last, and only duties were educational'. *The Sherborne Register 1550-1937* (1937), xxvii.

51. Mack, E., *British Public Schools and Public Opinion* (1941).

52. As late as 1577 Hugh Rhodes' *Book of Nurture* was being published, and William Kempe, author of *The Arte of Arithmeticke* (1592), published in 1588 his *Education of Children in Learning*, which was a counter apologetic. Rhodes was a Roman Catholic and Kempe a Protestant. Kempe was also, curiously enough, headmaster of Plymouth Grammar School from 1581 to 1605 and must have educated many boys who later sailed from that port. For a general discussion of this change, see M. St. C. Byrne, *Elizabethan Life* (1925), who points out that Thomas More was placed in the household of Cardinal Morton when he was a young boy.

53. See 41 above.

54. Watson, Foster, *E.H.R.* (1900), XV, 58-9 argues that there were only 185 schools founded from 1501 to 1601 and 186 from 1601 to 1660. There is need for someone to work through such works as E. P. Hart, *The Merchant Taylor's School Register*, which shows 4,000 boys passing through the school between its foundation in 1561 and 1607. The Grammar School was exhaustively studied by Foster Watson, *English Grammar Schools to 1660* (1908), but

he based his study on certain seventeenth-century generalisations. He omits the remarkable revival which took place in the last quarter of the century, a revival which led Sir Wasey Sterry, *The Eton College Register 1441–1698* (1943), to remark 'for the first twenty or thirty years of the sixteenth century, the school was never full, but from 1560 onwards till the civil war the school was flourishing'.

55. BENHAM, C., and others, *The Inns of Court* (London, n.d.), 178.

56. For the provisions of which see *Early English Text Society, Extra Series*, VIII (1869), 1–12. It should also be noted that Richard Hakluyt, a chief adventurer in the South Virginia Company, was interested in an enterprise for the endowment of a public lecturer, in navigation, towards which Sir Francis Drake promised to contribute £20 p.a., see E. G. R. Taylor, *The Writings and Correspondence of the two Richard Hakluyts* (1935), I, 23–5, 175–81, 208–10.

57. 'The foreign exchanges confronted the traditional doctrines with an *experimentum crucis*. Plain men were frankly bewildered by the whole business, and could only murmur helplessly: "there is some mystery in the matter, pray God it may be discovered to the weal of our realm".' R. H. Tawney, Preface to Thomas Wilson, *A Discourse upon Usury*, 85.

58. Isaac Barrow, Robert Hooker, Sir William Petty, and Sir Christopher Wren were all professors, and Isaac Newton was a frequent visitor. See J. W. Burgon, *Life of Sir Thomas Gresham* (1839) and John Ward, *Lives of the Professors of Gresham College* (1740).

59. SCHUSTER, A., and SHIPLEY, A. E., *Britain's Heritage of Science* (1917), declared that it ought to have developed into a University of London.

60. For which see F. R. Johnson, 'Gresham College: Precursor of the Royal Society', *J.H.I.*, I (1940), who suggests that it was the weekly lectures at Gresham College which led to the meetings in 1645 and so to the foundation of the Royal Society. Miss R. H. Syfret, *Notes and Records of the Royal Society*, V (2), 75–137, has criticised this view as Professor Johnson has presented it, but agrees (p. 85) that the 'connection was a close one'.

61. HUNTER, Joseph, in *Archaeologia* (1847), XXXII, points out that it was also designed to take the place of the dissolved religious houses as a repository of records.

62. WITTLIN, Alma S., *The Museum* (London, 1949), 60, 68.

It was an English version of the contemporary European movement for establishing academies as in Florence (1470), Naples (1560) and the Kunst and Naturalienkammer of the Elector Augustus of Saxony (inspired by the writings of the mineralogist Agricola). The significance of these bodies was pointed out by A. Harnack, *Geschichte der Kgl. Preussischen Akademie der Wissenchaften* (1910), I, 5, 'The Universities of Europe were born at the high tide of the Middle Age, and their institutions corresponded to the medieval view of transmitting the body of knowledge in fixed terms. The European Academies are an expression of the new spirit which was henceforth to obtain its power in the domain of life and thought.' Private cabinets in the following century, like those of the Tradescants and Sir Hans Sloane, stemmed from the same radical purpose, as also did the Royal Society, which last institution actually discharged the functions of the Society of Antiquaries till it was revived once more in 1717.

63. Arthur Agarde, Lancelot Andrewes, Robert Beale, Henry Bowchier,

William Bowyer, Richard Broughton, William Camden, Richard Carew, Cliffe, Lord William Compton, Walter Cope, Robert Cotton, John Davies, Sir William Dethicke, John Doddridge, Thomas d'Oyley, Sampson Erdeswicke, William Fleetwood, Abraham Hartwell, Michael Heneage, Joseph Holland, William Jakewill, Thomas Lake, William Lambart, Francis Leigh, James Ley, Michael Oldesworth, William Patten, Savel, Spilman (Sir Henry Spelman?), John Stowe, Strangeman, Thomas Talbot, Francis Tate, Francis Thynne, Robert Weston, Joseph Whitlocke, Wiseman.

64. Sir Robert Cotton was himself a collector of books and coins, and allowed Bacon, Raleigh, Camden, Speed, Ussher, and Selden to use his library. His firm stand against Charles I as M.P. for Castle Rising led to his being excluded from his library by Royal Command from 1629 until 1631. His *History of Henry III* (1627) and *Dangers wherein the Kingdom now standeth* (1628), were powerful tracts on behalf of the Parliament.

65. 'Out of his grave and long conversation with Antiquity, he extracted several curious observations concerning the liberty of the subject and the manner of holding Parliament.' Wood, *Ath Ox.*, II, 112.

66. *The Educational Writing of Richard Mulcaster* (1532–1567), ed. J. Oliphant (Glasgow, 1903), 90–99.

67. For a comprehensive treatment of this see L. B. Wright, 'Translations for the Elizabethan Middle Class', *The Library*, 4th Ser., XIII, 311–31.

68. *Op. cit.*, 316, n. 1.

69. Conley, C. H., *The First English Translators of the Classics* (1927), 52, adds the further reason that it was 'to incite England to resist Spain', an unlikely argument, as L. B. Wright has shown.

70. Dedicated to Lord Lumley, founder of the lectureship at the College of Physicians *et supra*.

71. *A Briefe Conceipte of Inglish Policie* (1581), republished 1751, 1808, 1813 and 1876, and in 1893 edited by Miss Lamond as *A Discourse of the Commonwea[l] of this Realm of England*. It was a dialogue between a doctor, a knight, a merchant, a husbandman, and a craftsman 'rehersing the common and universall greifes that men complaine on now a dayes' and seeking for 'the causes and occasions of the same'. For further discussion see Max Beer, *Early British Economics* (1938), 86–94.

72. For which see Sir J. H. Clapham, *Concise Economic History of Britain* (1949), 230ff.

73. *Simboleography* (1598). For the emergence of British Insurance at this time see H. E. Raynes, *History of British Insurance* (1948), which points out that from 1575 all such registrations were made compulsory. For Francis Bacon's part in the promotion of further bills, see p. 56. Bacon's description of insurance as 'the loadstone that draws the merchant on the adventure, and stretch even the very punctilio of his credit' shows just how far men were prepared to prognosticate disasters.

74. A classic instance is the saltpetre monopoly, important in this period for the manufacture of gunpowder. Elizabeth first put the industry into the hands of two Dutchmen, and paid one of them £500 to teach two of her subjects how to make saltpetre. A few years later the first patent for the industry was granted to George Evelyn (1530–1603) grandfather of the famous virtuoso and his son John. This fortune provided for a family of 16 sons and 8 daughters

ınd made possible the leisured activities of the virtuoso, who was thus enabled o travel in the 1640's. See Nef. *op. cit.*, p. 89.

75. See the trouble that faced the civil servant, John Donnelly, at that time n his evidence to the *Royal Commission on Technical Education* (1884) in *The Vocational Aspect of Secondary and Further Education*, No. 4 (1950), 6–21.

76. The whole theme is expanded by C. W. Camp, *The Artisan in Elizabethan Literature* (1924).

77. In the textile industry, which employed one-third of the industrial workpeople in the country, evasion of the Statute of Apprentices was widespread n East Anglia, Lancashire, and Yorkshire, and the South West of England. Building, the next largest industry, also evaded the regulations. Nef. *op. cit.*, 44.

78. WATSON, Foster, *Curriculum and Text-Books of English Schools* (1903). *The Beginnings of the Teaching of Modern Subjects in England* (1909), (1948).

79. MATHEW, D., *The Social Structure in Caroline England* (1948), 75–6, points out 'the new type of secretary' that was emerging, and gives a brief study of he Countess of Northumberland's gentleman of confidence, George Gerrard.

80. CHENEY, E. P., *History of England* (1926), 1, 314.

81. He also wrote the *Discouerie of Witchcraft* (1584), which was an attempt o prevent the persecution of aged persons who were popularly believed to be vitches.

82. Written, significantly enough, in Latin, published in 1580, and the year fter ordered to be used in grammar schools. Foster Watson, *The Beginnings f the Teaching of Modern Subjects*, 79–88.

83. For which see *A Dictionary of Printers and Booksellers in England 1557–640* (1910), ed. R. B. McKerrow, xiv–xv.

84. According to Leslie Hotson, *I, William Shakespeare, Esq.* (1937), 115.

85. BALD, R. C., 'Thou Nature art my Goddess', in *Joseph Quincy Adams Memorial Studies*, 337–49. J. F. Danby, *Shakespeare's Doctrine of Nature* (1949), 2, 'the sentiments of Edmund's speech must have been fairly widespread in hakespeare's society'.

86. ZILZEL, E., 'The Origins of William Gilbert's Scientific Method', *.H.I.*, II, 1–32, shows that his physical instruments were actually common at he time for sailors. Sir James Jeans, *The Growth of Physical Science* (1947), 76, also agrees that the phenomena of magnetism were 'fairly widely known'.

87. JENKINS, Rhys, *Collected Papers* (1936), 36–7.

88. Invented by William Lee, B.A., St. John's College, Cambridge, 1583, vho found that workers were so opposed to it that he went to France.

89. cf. PLAT, Hugh (1595), *A Discoverie of Certaine English Wants*. 'Now herefore, I see it is high time to let the world and all posterity to understand, hat if our English artists (whereof sundrie in my knowledge are of such are and singular conceipt as they were able, yea, and would also be found villing, if the stipend of honour and merit were now propounded, fully to iscover a world of new inventions, whereof no Polidore hath as yet taken ny note or notise) were sufficiently emploied in the fulness and height of their pirits, that they would bring foorth so many, so rich, and so inestimable lossoms of skill, as neither any civill pollicy . . . nor any religious charity . . . ould yet produce or shew any comparable effects unto them.' (Reprinted in *Harleian Miscellany* (1812), IX, 107).

90. DANBY, J. F., *op. cit.*, 181.

CHAPTER FIVE

The Baconian Blueprint, 1600-60

I

'MAN is the helper and interpreter of Nature. He can only act and understand in so far as he has observed Nature's order practically or theoretically. Outside this he has no knowledge or power.'[1] So Francis Bacon in his *Novum Organum* proclaimed his breach with the old philosophical tradition of the schools. The title itself was significant, an answer to Aristotle's *Organon*. A revolution was required not only in knowledge, but in the conditions of life. 'The difference between civilised men and savages,' he proclaimed, 'is almost that between gods and men. And this difference comes not from soil, not from climate, not from race, but from the arts.'

It was to advance these 'arts' that Bacon confined his main energies to authorship. In the preface to a proposed work *On the Interpretation of Nature*, composed in 1603, he wrote:

> Now among all the benefits that could be conferred upon mankind, I found none so great as the discovery of new arts, endowments, and commodities for the bettering of man's life. . . . But above all, if a man could succeed, not in striking out some particular invention, however useful but in kindling a light in nature—a light which should in its very rising touch and illuminate all the border-regions that confine upon the circles of our present knowledge; and so spreading further and further should presently disclose and bring into sight all that is most hidden and secret in the world—that man (I thought) would be the benefactor indeed of the human race—the propagator of man's empire over the universe, the champion of liberty, the conqueror and subduer of necessities.

In 1605 he published a description of the means whereby this great aim could be accomplished in *The Advancement of Learning*. An essential pre-requisite was an examination of the universities. 'Among so many colleges in Europe,' he recalled, 'I find it strange that they are all dedicated to professions, and none left free to arts and sciences at large.' He lamented: 'It is esteemed a kind of dishonour unto learning to descend to inquiry or meditation upon matters mechanical, except they be such as may be thought secrets, rarities, and special subtilities.' Again and again he directed his attacks against professors who accepted the finality of existing knowledge, and thought only of interpreting commenting, compounding, or abridging. 'Everything is found averse to the progress of science,' he continued in his *Great Instauration* (1620), describing the existing colleges and universities, 'for the studies of men in these places are confined, and, as it were, imprisoned in the writings of certain authors, from whom if any man dissent, he is straightway arraigned as a turbulent person or innovator.'

Bacon was the most turbulent of all. The real purpose of his *Great Instauration* was to restore the *commerce* of the mind with things, and overthrow the old philosophies. He hoped that King James, to whom he dedicated the work, would sponsor and finance a grand encyclopaedia of nature and the arts, without which his design had no hope of a successful issue:

> I have a request to make—a request no way unworthy of your Majesty, and which especially concerns the work in hand; namely, that you who resemble Solomon is so many things . . . would further follow his example in providing for the collection of a Natural and Experimental History, true and severe, unencumbered with literature and book-learning, such as philosophy may be built upon, such, in fact, as I shall in its proper place describe: that so at length, after the lapse of so many ages, philosophy and the sciences may no longer float in air, but rest on the solid foundation of experience of every kind, and the same well examined and weighed. I have provided the machine, but the stuff must be gathered from the facts of nature.

The 'machine' was Salomon's House. In his *New Atlantis* (published by his devoted secretary Dr. Rawley in 1627 as an appendix to *Sylva Sylvarum*—a collection for the projected encyclopaedia) he sketched the organisation of Bensalem. This, usually regarded as a utopian learned society, was a series of laboratories devoted to every conceivable subject of experimental research. 'The End of our Foundation is the knowledge of Causes, and secret motions of things; and the enlarging of the bounds of Human Empire, to the effecting of all things possible.' For this end, Salomon's House—as his foundation was to be called—embraced observatories on high towers, experimental stations and lakes, underground laboratories, 'engines for multiplying and enforcing of winds', experimental gardens, dissection rooms, breeding stations and dispensaries, 'furnaces of great diversities', 'perspective-houses', 'sound houses', 'perfume houses', and all the equipment conceivably necessary for the interrogation of Nature.

To operate this elaborate research institution, Bacon described the Father or principal as 'a man of middle stature and age, comely of person, and had an aspect as if he pitied men'. His coadjutors were specified as 12 Merchants of Light who brought back books, abstracts of experience and patterns of experiment from other countries; 3

Depradators to 'collect the experiments in all books'; 3 Mystery-men to 'collect the experiments of all mechanical and liberal arts'; 3 Pioneers of Miners to try new experiments. The results of the labours of these four groups were to be organised 'into titles and tables, to give the better light for the drawing and observations out of them' by Compilers. Above these were three Dowry-Men or Benefactors to 'cast about how to draw out of the experiments of their fellows things of use and practise for man's life and knowledge as well for works as for plain demonstration of causes, means of natural divinations, and the easy and clear discovery of the virtues and parts of bodies'. After 'divers meetings and consults' of all these, three more, called Lamps, were to 'direct new experiments, of a higher light, more penetrating into nature than the former'. These new experiments were to be executed by three Inoculators. At the summit of this researching hierarchy were to be placed three Interpreters of Nature, to 'raise the former discoveries by experiments into greater observations, axioms, and aphorisms'. It is interesting to notice that Bacon, discussing the degree of secrecy to be observed, suggested that some of their conclusions might not be revealed to the State.

It is ironical to notice that Bacon did not recognise scientific investigators when he lived amongst them—he never tired of vilifying Harvey and the circulation of the blood nor did he select any of his other contemporaries in the field of science as examples to be emulated.

2

Now James I, before he became King of England in 1603, had been King of Scotland. There, he had granted a charter in 1582 to a university founded by the town council and clergy of Edinburgh. This, the fourth and youngest of the Scottish Universities, had been initially opposed not only by his mother, Mary Queen of Scots, but by the other universities of St. Andrews, Aberdeen, and Glasgow as well. Its nucleus, obtained after some difficulty from Mary, was the ancient collegiate church of St. Mary-in-the-Field, commonly known as the Kirk o' Field, and the university authorities extended this by buying out other occupants of the Kirk grounds. This civic university remained for many years the chief nursery for Scottish Presbyterian clergy, and began with only one regent and an assistant. It expanded four years later to a principal and four regents, each of whom taught all the subjects of the curriculum. By 1621, an Act of the Scottish Parliament conferred upon the new foundation all the rights, immunities, and

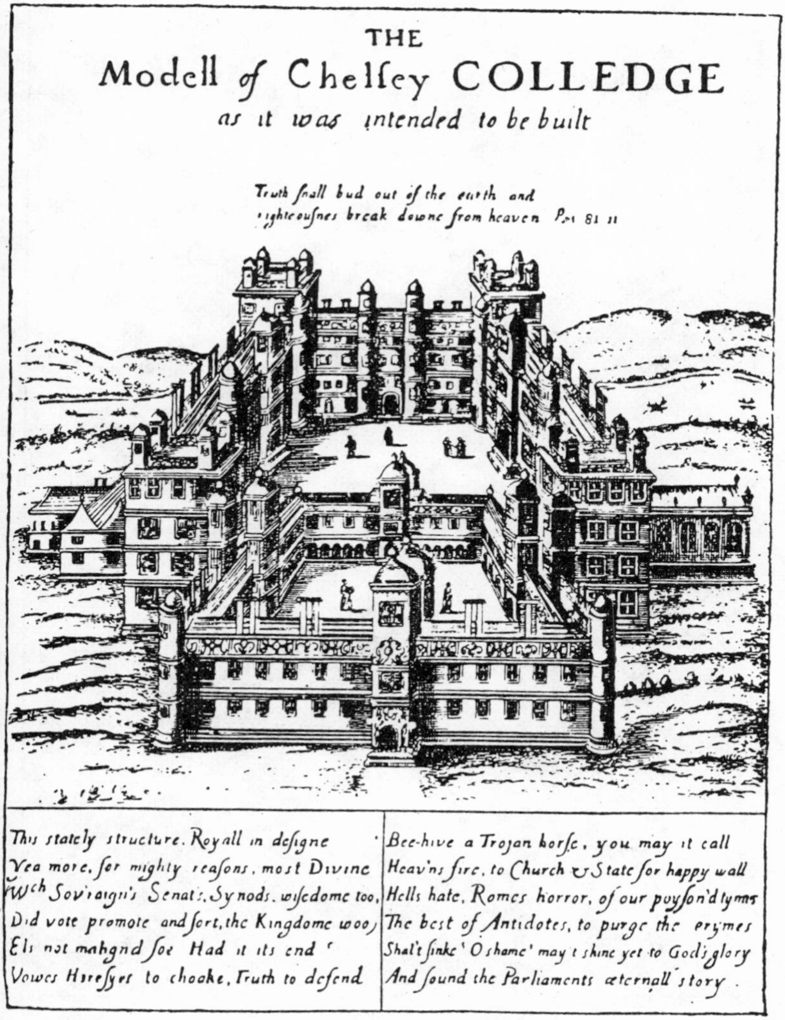

THE
Modell of Chelsey COLLEDGE
as it was intended to be built
Truth shall bud out of the earth and
righteousnes break downe from heaven Psa 81 11
This stately structure. Royall in designe
Yea more. for mighty reasons. most Divine
Wch Soveraign's Senats. Synods. wisedome too.
Did vote promote and sort, the Kingdome woo
Els not malign'd soe Had it its end
Vowes Heresyes to chooke, Truth to defend
Bee-hive a Trojan horse, you may it call
Heav'ns fire, to Church & State for happy wall
Hells hate, Romes horror, of our poyson'd tymes
The best of Antidotes, to purge the erymes
Shal't sinke O shame may t shine yet to God's glory
And sound the Parliaments æternall story.

CHELSEA COLLEGE

From John Darley, *The Glory of Chelsey Colledge Revived*, 1662

See page 97]

PLATE 4

(a)

(b)

WARRINGTON ACADEMY

THE TWO SUCCESSIVE BUILDINGS

From H. Maclachlan, *Warrington Academy*, 1943

(a) The first building, 1757 (b) The second building, 1762

See page 154]

privileges enjoyed by other universities in Scotland, and it remained under the control and patronage of the Town Council until 1858.[2]

Once King of England, however, James was primarily an Erastian, and his collegiate benefactions were directed towards strengthening the links between the church and the throne. In 1609 he laid the foundation stone of a polemical college at Chelsea, allowing it to bear his name in a charter of incorporation given the following year. He also supported it by grants and benefactions, gave timber from Windsor Forest for its building, and ordained that seventeen of its nineteen fellows were to be in holy orders.

Chelsea College was, as Thomas Fuller declared, 'intended for a spiritual garrison, with a magazine of all books for that purpose; where learned divines should study and write in maintenance of all controversies against the Papists'.[3] It never fulfilled its aim. True John Howson, a fellow whose abilities brought him to the sees of Oxford and Durham in turn and earned him interment in St. Paul's, declared that he would loosen the Pope from his chair 'though he were fastened thereto by a ten-penny nail', but his colleagues were not as aggressive. The scholarship which Bacon disparaged was well represented amongst the other fellows: John Boys was the most eclectic quoter of his time; John Overall a subtle theologian who wrote on predestination and passed through three bishoprics; Robert Abbot (whose brother George was consecrated archbishop of Canterbury, and subsequently achieved the enviable distinction of shooting a keeper while out hunting) became a Regius Professor of Divinity at Oxford; while Miles Smith paid so much attention to his oriental books that he allowed his cathedral church of Gloucester to fall into decay.

Perhaps the two appointments which redeemed the foundation were those of William Camden and Thomas Heywood. Camden, after being excluded from an All Souls fellowship in 1571, spent his vacations in compiling his *Britannia*. Both discharged their duty to 'faithfully record and publish to posterity all memorable passages in church or commonwealth'.

King James's College was a failure. Only one side of the first quadrangle was ever built, and that cost £3,000. In spite of a royal hint to Archbishop Abbot, a national collection in all the dioceses of the kingdom barely covered the fees of the collectors who made it.

More promising indeed was the project of Edmund Boulton, a Roman Catholic, whose faith prevented his scholastic preferment. A friend of Camden, he was also a zealous antiquary and historian. In 1617 he proposed that Windsor should become the site of a Royal

College, where a synthesis of all secular learning should be undertaken.[3] He secured an enthusiastic supporter in Lord Admiral Buckingham, who, on 5 March 1620 proposed in the House of Lords that persons of 'Honour and Quality' should contribute freely and voluntarily 'to erect and maintain an Academy' for 'the breeding and bringing up of the Nobility and Gentry of the Realm'. The House of Lords warmed to the subject, discussed the 'Arts, Sciences and Exercises' to be taught, and appointed a committee to consider ways and means of establishing it. Boulton's scheme for tutelaries (or patrons), auxiliaries (a selected group of the nobility 'both at home and in the plantations'), and essentials (who were to prosecute the necessary research) caught the Royal imagination, and things looked promising. But Buckingham was assassinated, and Boulton, deprived of a patron, was soon forgotten.[4]

Scarcely a proposal, but none the less indicative of the contemporary mood, are the remarks of Robert Burton in his *Anatomy of Melancholy* (1621). Looking back upon the destruction of nearly a century before, he wryly commented:

> Methinks, therefore, our too zealous innovators were not so well advised in that general subversion of Abbeys and Religious Houses . . . Some Monasteries and Collegiate Cells might have been well spared, and their revenues otherwise employed, here and there one, in good Towns and Cities at least, for men and women of all sorts and conditions to live in, to sequester themselves from the cares and tumults of the world . . . to the perfection of arts and sciences.

He called attention to the work of the bishop of Lincoln in establishing a library at Lincoln as 'a noble precedent for all Corporate Towns and Cities to imitate'.

But the idea of an academy for noblemen persisted, and in 1635 Sir Francis Kynaston set up a *Musæum Minervae* in London, for which he obtained a licence, a grant of arms and a common seal from King Charles I. The King contributed £100 from the Treasury, but Kynaston provided the premises in Bedford Street, Covent Garden, and furnished them with books, manuscripts, musical and mathematical instruments, paintings and statues. Kynaston planned a full seven-year course, and those who completed it were to be septennals, as opposed to those triennals, who took only half the course.

Under Kynaston as Regent, there were six professors: Edward May (Medicine), Thomas Hunt (Music), Nicholas Phiske (Astronomy) John Spidell (Geometry), Walter Salter (Languages), and Michael Mason (Fencing). Some of the nobility made payments to support it, Sir George Peckham bequeathed £10 to it in 1636, but his example does not seem to have been followed by many others. Indeed, one contemporary records that Kynaston was actually collecting money for his professors' salaries 'with a bason'.

Kynaston, a scholarly man who had been a cup-bearer to King James but had to resign because he trembled so much, had an interest in mechanics as well as music, and was well aware of the hostility which his Musæum might provoke in the existing universities. In the preface to his *Constitutions* describing the academy, he went to great pains to repudiate suggestions already made by 'personages . . . of note' that it would divert young men from Oxford, Cambridge, and the Inns of Court, and re-affirmed his determination not to detract from their worth. He maintained that the *Musæum Minervae* would concentrate upon arts not practised in these institutions. But the disclaimer was not taken seriously, and, according to Samuel Hartlib, the opposition of the universities led to the failure of Kynaston's plan. And when the plague raged in 1636, Kynaston asked the King if he might move his museum to Chelsea College. The King was willing but the provost of the college, Dr. Featley, was not, and counter-petitioned Archbishop Laud. As a result Kynaston had to move elsewhere. At this time Laud referred to Chelsea as 'Controversy College'.[5]

3

Further advances in scientific training and research at this time stemmed from the professional needs of the apothecaries and surgeons. Apothecaries relied upon the flora of Nature for their drugs, and in 1617 were incorporated as a society.[6] Severed by their charter from an embarrassing professional connection with the grocers, they began to take their botany very seriously, arranging 'simpling excursions' for members, with fines for those who did not participate. Not without cause did they produce the two leading English botanists of the age in John Parkinson and Thomas Johnson.[7] Even more significant, however, from the point of view of our story was their assumption of the power of examining apprentices: as early as 1619 we find apprentices being 'dismissed until they can give better proof of their sufficiency'. Gowned and hooded like a Livery Company, the Society of Apothecaries soon commanded the respect of the Lord Mayor of London, who would send them objects to be investigated. By 1633 the Society of Apothecaries was buying its own hall in Blackfriars. They soon developed other characteristics of a learned body: a library was established in 1633 with Gerard's *Herball* as the first book, and in 1641 one member offered £500 of his own money to build a laboratory.

The corporate strength of the society was developed to safeguard them from the attacks of physicians, grocers, and distillers, to each of whom the apothecaries appeared as a professional challenge.

The Company of Barber Surgeons also developed the professional education of its members and made advances in this direction after the bequest of Thomas Arris, a master of the company, which brought £510 to endow lectures on anatomy.

Less dramatic, but equally significant, was the progress of the College of Physicians. Since Harvey's election to the Lumleian lectureship in 1615, and the announcement of his famous discovery the following year (the notes of which are in the British Museum) it had grown in buildings and equipment. Much of this was due to Harvey himself, indeed he endowed it with his estate in the year before he died. They acknowledged his gift of a library to them by the institution of the Harveian oration.

Harvey's outlook was admirably summarised in his *De Generatione Animalium* (1651) in which he wrote:

> Sensible things are of themselves and antecedent; things of the intellect, however, are consequential and arise from the former . . . and hence it is that without the due admonition of the senses, without frequent observation and reiterated experiment, our mind goes astray after phantoms and appearances. Diligent observation is, therefore, requisite in every science, and the senses are to be frequently appealed to. We are, I say, to strive after personal experience, not to rely on the experience of others; without which indeed no one can properly become a student of natural science.

But, taking the broad view, one is forced to admit that the real centres of medical research and education lay on the Continent. There, the University of Leyden was capturing much of the prestige and loyalty formerly accruing to the University of Padua. As a matter of fact, Peter Forest and Gerard de Bontius, the earliest teachers of medicine at Leyden, were both graduates of Padua. And Leyden, from its first foundation in 1574, opened its doors to students of all persuasion, from Jews to Roman Catholics. John James, who received the second doctorate of medicine to be awarded at Leyden, was the first Englishman to graduate there, and he was followed by a stream which steadily increased as the civil state of England grew more troubled. This increasing stream poured into other universities as well: Franeker (founded 1585), Groningen (founded 1614), and Utrecht (1640) offered the additional attractions of courses in law, but Leyden rose above them all to the brilliant heydey of its Boerhaavian maturity in the following century.[8]

4

These tendencies seemed to be caught up and manifested in the career of Samuel Hartlib. Son of a German merchant, he had, since his permanent adoption of England in 1628, endeavoured to further Bacon's plan of linking education with things rather than words. To his friend and associate John Dury he was 'a cursitor and agent for universal objects', 'a conduit pipe for things innumerable'. 'He setteth more men aworke, both within and without Great Britain,' wrote Dury, 'than perhaps ever any man did of his rank and position.' Immersing himself in the intellectual life of London, Hartlib soon became an active helper of exiled foreign scholars, disbursing some three to four hundred pounds a year to forward the projects of his versatile imagination. In 1637, at his own expense, he circulated two hundred and ninety-four copies of the *Conatuum Comeniarum Praeludia*, following it two years later with an expanded edition entitled *Pansophiae Prodromus*. This appealed for financial support for the pansophic ideas of the great Czech educator, John Amos Comenius, and outlined the essentials of Pansophism: universal books, a universal language, universal schools, and an academy of science drawing its members from the whole world.

'These tymes of distraction (like troubled waters) will hardly recive the image of it now so well as they otherwise might', one correspondent advised him in 1639, but Hartlib was not to be dissuaded. The Dutch were interested in Comenius, and some of them were actively attempting to invite him to settle in Holland, so Hartlib moved every stone to find supporters to counteract this design and attract him to England. Comenius himself declared to Hartlib that now was the time for the Baconian plans to be executed, and asked Hartlib to read the preface to Book 2 of the *De Augmentis Scientarum* to see whether the supplications addressed there to King James πολύτεχνον could not with more right be transferred to King Charles πολυτεχνότερον. If Bacon desired a Universal College of learned men, could not such a project be essayed in England?[9]

Comenius, urged by his friends and 'pricked by his conscience' arrived in England on 21 September 1641. A month later, Parliament showed interest by discussing a possible building for the Pansophic College. The Savoy, Winchester (Saint Cross), and Chelsea College were specifically named. Dury, Hartlib, and Comenius compacted each to pursue his respective task by a formal agreement dated March of the following year.

The realisation of the Baconian dream did not seem so impracticable. Comenius admitted that 'even now men will say that we are drunken and dreaming', but he added, 'the answer is to make all men drunk'. Hartlib, striking while the iron was hot, circulated a fictional version of the plan under the title *A description of the famous Kingdom of Macaria*, in which he urged the application of scientific techniques to the study of agriculture, health, industry, and other human activities, with public rewards for discoveries that contributed to human welfare. But the times were against it. Civil war broke out in Ireland in November 1641, and King Charles left London in January of the following year. Comenius responded to pressing invitations from Sweden, and left England on 21 June 1642. John Pym, who was one of the leaders of the Parliamentary party (his arrest had been attempted by King Charles in January 1642) wrote to Hartlib just as Comenius was leaving, asking him 'to consult with Mr. Comenius, if he be not gon as I hope he is not'.[10]

5

The outbreak of Civil War nipped another interesting venture in the bud: a scheme for a university of the north at Manchester.

Dissatisfaction with the condition of Oxford and Cambridge was fairly widespread. Never before, and never again, were those two universities to enjoy the monopoly they possessed in the early seventeenth century. As Dr. Venn nostalgically wrote in 1897: 'Absolutely—not relatively merely—the number of graduates in the years about 1625-30 was greater than was ever attained again till within living memory. When allowance is made for the growth of the population, it must be frankly admitted that, as far as concerns the number of trained men sent out into the country, the Old Universities have not yet regained the position they occupied two centuries and a half ago.'[11]

This position, dominant as it was, was by no means unchallenged. In 1604, following attempts in 1590 and 1596, the Corporation of Ripon had petitioned the queen for the application of the confiscated revenues of their minster to a college 'after the manner of a university'. These revenues had been in crown hands for over a century, and the Corporation called attention to the 'manifold benefit' which both the borders of England and Scotland would enjoy by the granting of their petition: lectures on market days would be given by the tutors, and students would teach the surrounding villages. The King actually made provision for some such college, but the outcome was a collegiate church, now the cathedral.[12]

The desire for a Northern University was not however extinguished by the failure of the attempt at Ripon, and on 4 August 1617, the citizens of Carlisle petitioned King James I when he visited the town. They asked that 'a nobleman might lye in Carlyle Castle' and that King James 'for the honour of his name and posterity' would 'create one university in this poor sity of Carlisle'. Needless to say, the attractions of the city of London, and the general unwillingness of the King to disturb the Erastian nurseries of Oxford and Cambridge prevented any such petition being granted.[13]

As the Erastian policy of the crown developed, the universities became vestibules for places in the King's service. In the twenties, John Webster could raise a laugh by inserting the lines in his play, the *Devil's Law-Case*:

> 'Letters of commendation—
> Why, 'tis reported they are grown stale
> When places fall i' th' university'

So obvious did the policy of linking gown and crown become that the House of Commons discussed a special bill to prevent such corruptions. The bill, read a second time and referred to a committee on 23 February 1629, would have become law had not Parliament been dissolved in the following March.

Archbishop Laud anchored the high tables of the colleges even more closely to the court. 'Never before, and not again,' wrote Archbishop Mathew, 'were the ancient universities to be brought so close within the orbit of the Government.'[14] Oxford seemed closest, partly because it produced both Laud and Juxon, archbishop of Canterbury and bishop of London respectively, and partly because it was more national. Cambridge on the other hand was more provincial, more securely set in the general framework of Puritanism and East Anglian life. Yet even Cambridge, home as it had been to Francis Bacon, afforded no secure haven for the scientists. John Dee had deserted the Trinity high table, first for Manchester, then for Mortlake; William Gilberd lived in London; William Harvey published his great *Exercitatio Anatomica de Motu Cordis et Sanguinis in Animalibus* at Frankfurt; and William Oughtred, anticipator of mechanical calculation, was allowed to retire to Aldbury.

Such innovations as there were flourished in spite of the prevailing temper. At Oxford in 1619, Sir Henry Savile, who had assisted Bodley to found his library, founded the professorships of Geometry and Astronomy which bore his name: no small feat in an age which reckoned 'the most Useful branches of Mathematics were spels, and her Professors limbs of the Devil'.

As the universities became the vestibules to great place in Church and State, the provinces became concerned. The nobility, gentry, clergy, freeholders, and other inhabitants of the northern parts of England met together in Manchester and passed certain propositions concerning a university for the northern parts. These resolutions were embodied in a petition, which Henry Fairfax, a fellow of Trinity College, Cambridge, forwarded to his brother Ferdinando, Lord Fairfax, who, as M.P. for Yorkshire, could present them to Parliament. The petitioners complained that:

> divers gentlemen are induced to send their sons to foreign universities, or else allow them only country breeding. The great charges of the other universities, necessarily occasioned by the multitude of scholars; the dearth of provisions, the want of fuel and scarcity of lodgings, forcing many men of indifferent and competent estates, able enough to maintain their children in another convenient place of the kingdom, either to debar them of university breeding, to make them servitors, or, at best, to allow them only two or three years' maintenance, and then to provide them of a country cure, or, which is worse, without any degrees, without university learning, to procure them holy orders, and so obtrude them upon the Church, which (we speak from sad experience) hath occasioned many ignorant and unlearned ministers amongst us.

They pointed with confidence to the patrons who would be forthcoming, to the antiquity, fame, and 'happy traffic' of Manchester which could afford a proper setting for such endowments, and above all to the necessity of avoiding an illiterate ministry.

The letter was dated 20 March 1640, and Ferdinando replied on the 22 March that the proposed bill would cost a hundred marks. He added, 'those well affected to the now universities (which include, indeed, every member of our House), will be in danger to oppose this. I should be most glad to have such a bill pass, as beneficial not only to that, but all the northern counties'. He promised to consult with the knights and burgesses of the county 'and go the way they shall think fittest', but he concluded, 'I much fear a happy issue of it, especially now that the House has made an order to entertain no new matter till some of those great and many businesses we have grasped be ended'.

Those 'great and many businesses' began with the trial of Strafford, but Henry was not to be put off and suggested to his brother that a deputation be sent to the council. Ferdinando replied on 20 April in a really discouraging vein: 'I have advised with several gentlemen who serve for the counties of Lancashire and Chester, concerning a University at Manchester, but find them hopeless of having it.' In the meantime, York, not to be outdone, put forward a similar claim, and tried to enforce it in two petitions. But, as with Manchester's claims, they were laid aside in the press of events.[15] Yet pressure from the Yorkshire petitioners continued, and seven years later they were asking that 'Liberty may be granted and Means allowed for laying the Foundations of a University within York for educating scholars in all learning which may fit them for the discharging of their ministerial functions in the church'. The argument of the petitioners was that the older universities were not able to provide for the country's needs.[16]

6

The outbreak of the great Civil War intensified the issues. On 29 October 1642 Oxford became the headquarters of the Royalist cause, and London that of Parliament. It was therefore to be expected that within a year certain members of that university should petition Parliament to consider 'the contrival of a college somewhere about London' where provision could be made for the 'godly and scholastic instruction of students', who might in time 'go on for their degrees'. Parliament welcomed the petition, elaborating it for presentation to the Lords by further suggesting 'a sage religious governor' assisted by twelve graduates. As it was being read, Anthony Burgess, a fellow of that Puritan stronghold, Emmanuel College, Cambridge, was foremost in commending it, suggesting with some warmth that 'some collops might be cut out of deaneries and chapters for the cherishing of young scholars'.[17]

To Hartlib, undaunted by the failure of his Comenian project, John Milton addressed his pamphlet *Of Education* in 1644. In it, he proposed a new Academy of learning which would satisfy all interests, and not, like Oxford and Cambridge, be restricted to those of the clergy. He wrote:

First to finde out a spatious house and ground about it fit for an *Academy*, and big enough to lodge a hundred and fifty persons, whereof twenty or thereabouts may be attendants, all under the government of one, who shall be thought of desert sufficient, and ability either to doe all, or wisely to direct, and oversee it done. This place should be at once both School and University, not needing a remove to any other of Schollership, except it be some peculiar Colledge of Law, or Physick, where they mean to be practitioners; but as for those generall studies which take up all our time from Lilly to the commencing, as they term it, Master of Art, it should be absolute. After this pattern, as many edifices may be converted to this use, as shall be needfull in every City throughout this land, which would tend much to the encrease of learning and civility everywhere.

This scheme, visionary as it was, clearly envisaged civic colleges wherever they could be sustained. Hartlib was impressed, and referred to Milton as 'a great traveller, and full of projects and inventions', and Milton in his turn referred to Hartlib as 'a person sent hither by some good providence from a far country to be the occasion and incitement of great good to this island'.

Hartlib's incitement was particularly concerned with the establishment of a university in London. Two pamphlets, dated 1647, have recently been found amongst his papers with this end in view, one of them entitled *Motives grounded upon the Word of God and upon Honour, Profit, and Pleasure for the Present founding an University in the Metropolis London*. He also proposed that the existing professorships at Gresham College in Divinity, Civil Law, and Rhetoric should be replaced by others in the scientific principles of trades, like glass and metal working.

In this connection, he tried to have twenty-six-year-old William Petty set apart to advance experimental science and mechanical knowledge at Gresham College in 1649. For Petty had 'flying thoughts, concerning the advancement of real learning' and embodied them in *The Advice of W.P. to Mr. Samuel Hartlib of Some Particular Parts of Learning* (1648). This argued that time spent in apprenticeship should be shortened, vocational guidance practised, and a *Gymnasium Mechanicum*, or College of Tradesmen, together with a *Nosocomium Academicum*, or Academic Hospital, should be established.

There were others who bombarded Hartlib with similar ideas. In 1649 George Snell came to Hartlib's house in Duke's Place with a scheme to have rural colleges established in every county town or city, in which all arts, sciences, and faculties should be represented. In that year too Dr. Bathurst proposed the establishment of a teachers' training college, supported by a state subvention of £4,000 a year, to 'bee an Inspector and Seminarie of all Schoolmasters . . . throughout the Kingdom'. A third suggestion came from Cressy Dymock for the establishment of a college of husbandry at Fulham to which pupils should be admitted at the age of fifteen. Adolphus Speed had ideas about an academy for gentlewomen as well as young men.[18]

At the same time as these suggestions were being made, Sir Balthasar Gerbier enlisted Hartlib's support for his projected Academy at Bethnal Green. This was to teach languages, history, and 'in particular, the secret motions of sceances and the like'. Hartlib told him of the hostility which he suspected the universities had entertained towards a previous venture of this kind initiated by Sir Francis Kynaston. Gerbier was an optimist; his academy was to be the Minerva of

Albion; but at the same time he took care to ask Hartlib to destroy copies of his prospectus *To All Fathers*, since it contained proposals for the teaching of Latin 'which perhaps would prove a stumbling block and move the Universities against my Academy'. This opposition from Oxford and Cambridge was a very real thing: Hugh l'Amy and Peter le Pruvost evidently thought better of their scheme for an academy in London, and in their proposal to Hartlib, they amended it by noting in the margin that perhaps it would be better to establish a special college at Oxford or Cambridge.

The most interesting of the many schemes mooted in this *annus mirabilis* is contained in a letter from Hartlib to twenty-two-year-old Robert Boyle. On 18 May 1649 he wrote: 'Fauxhall is to be sett apart for publick uses, by which is meant making it a place of resort for artists, mechanicks, etc. and a dépôt for models and philosophicall apparatus'; there, added Hartlib, 'experiments and trials of profitable inventions should be carried on' which 'will be of great use to the Commonwealth'. Five years later, in another letter, he wrote, 'The Earl of Worcester is buying Fauxhall from Mr. Trenchard, to bestow the use of that house upon Gasper Calehof and his son, as long as they shall live, for he intends to make it a college of artisans. . . . Yesterday I was invited by the famous Thomas Bushel to Lambeth March, to see part of that foundation.'[19] Thomas Bushell and the Earl of Worcester were both Royalists who had recently been allowed to return to England. Bushell, a noted mining engineer, had learned mineralogy from Francis Bacon, whose page he had been, and the Earl of Worcester was then writing his *Century of Inventions* in which he suggested a calculating machine (No. 84) and an ingenious adumbration of a steam engine (No. 68). The attempt to found a Salomon's House in Lambeth Marsh was a gallant failure.

7

Even the Puritans of the extreme left wing, like Gerrard Winstanley, were affected by the new philosophy, and wove it into their schemes for social regeneration. Thus Winstanley had a scheme for annually elected ministers, who should 'set forth the benefits of freedom' were to make speeches

of all Arts and Sciences, some one day, some another; As in Physick, Chyrurgery, Astrology, Astronomy, Navigation, Husbandry and such like. And in these speeches may be unfolded the nature of all herbs and plants from the Hysop to the Cedar, as *Solomon* writ of.

Likewise men may come to see into the nature of the fixed and wandering stars, those great powers of God in the heavens above; and hereby men will come to know the secrets of Nature and Creation, within which all true knowledge is wrapped up, and the light in man must arise to search it out.

Speeches may be made, sometimes of the Nature of Mankind, of his darkness and of his light, of his weakness and of his strength, of his love and of his envy, of his sorrow and of his joy, of his inward and outward bondages, and of his inward and outward freedoms.

But the ministers were not to monopolise the dissemination of knowledge. On the contrary 'everyone who hath any experience, and is able to speak of any Art or Language, or of the Nature of the Heavens above, or of the Earth below, shall have full liberty to speak' provided that they speak 'nothing by imagination, but what he hath found out by his own industry and observation in tryal'.

In Chapter V of his *Law of Freedom* (1652), which contains these ideas, he treats of the education of mankind. Winstanley has no place for 'Schollars trained up only to book learning', but wanted everyone to be educated 'in every Trade, Art, and Science, whereby they may finde out the Secrets of the Creation, and that they might know how to govern the Earth in right order'. These Arts and Sciences flow from what he calls 'the Five Fountains': husbandry, mineral employment, 'the right ordering of Cattel', 'the right ordering of Woods and Timber trees', and 'the exercise of reason upon the secrets of Nature to observe the Sun, Moon, Tides and Seas'.

Infusing the whole argument was his contempt for 'Traditional Knowledg', which 'leads to an idle life'. He welcomed technological change, and urged

let no young wit be crushed in his invention, for if any man desire to make a new tryall of his skil in any Trade or Science, the Overseers shall not hinder him, but incourage him therein; so that the Spirit of knowledge may have his full growth in man, to find out the secret in every Art.

He concluded

when men are sure of food and raiment, their reason will be ripe, and ready to dive into the secrets of the Creation, that they may learn to see and know God (the Spirit of the Whole Creation) in all his works.

So the argument of the advanced Puritan ran, and, like an underground river, it unobtrusively sustained many suggestions for social reform in the arid century ahead.

8

Contemporary with all these 'flying thoughts', movements for provincial universities were under way. John Dury complained in

A Seasonable Discourse (1649) that Oxford and Cambridge 'monopolise all means of Learning, as if without the formalities and constitutions of old settled in them, there could be no truth of Learning'.

A more effective agitation was set on foot by the people of Durham, where on 30 April 1649, consequent on the passage of the Act dissolving all cathedrals and cathedral chapters, the castle and college were left vacant. So, on 20 August, they petitioned for a new college. Parliament referred the matter to a committee which was then dealing with the sequestered lands, and it got no further. After two years of waiting, the local authorities moved again. This time a deputation rode over to Edinburgh, where Oliver Cromwell was visiting. He approved of their scheme, and wrote a letter to Speaker Lenthall, praising the scheme as a pious and laudable work. Still nothing was done. So, in 1652, a third petition was sent, pointing out that Parliament was indebted to the counties of Durham and Northumberland for some £25,000 incurred in buying off the Scots. But this evoked no response.

Yet Cromwell was interested. 'Truly,' he told Lenthall, 'it seems to me a matter of great concernment and importance, as that which, by the blessing of God, may much conduce to the promoting of learning and piety in those poor, rude, and ignorant parts.'[20]

Zealots of the Parliament were threatening Oxford and Cambridge with disendowment and abolition, and their views were forcibly expressed by John Hall, a clever young friend of Hartlib, in *An Humble Motion to the Parliament of England concerning the Advancement of Learning and Reformation in the Universities.* John Hall was a Durham man, and accompanied Cromwell to Edinburgh when the second Durham petition had been received. His pamphlet was published just before this visit. Its indictment had a Baconian flavour, and made articulate convictions which were lurking in the minds of many who had neither the wit nor courage to express them:

we have hardly professours for the three principall faculties, and these but lazily read—and carelessly followed. Where have we anything to do with Chimistry, which hath snatcht the Keyes of Nature from the other sects of philosophy by her multiplied experiences? Where have we constant reading upon either quick or dead *anatomies*, or occular demonstrations of herbes? Where any manuall demonstrations of Mathematical theorems or instruments? Where a promotion of their experiences, which if right carried on, would multiply even to astonishment? Where an examination of all the old tenets? Review of the old experiments and traditions which gull so many *junior* beliefs, and serve for nothing else but for idle priests, to make their sermons more gaudy? Where is there solemn disquisition into history? A nice and severe calculation and amendment of the epochs of time? Where a survey of antiquities and learned descants upon them? Where a ready and generous teaching of the tongues? Free from pedantisme, and the impertinencies that that kind of learning hath been pestered with? And all this done, not by some stripling youngster, who perhaps understands that which he professes as little as anything else; and mounts up into the chaire twice or thrice a yeare, to mutter over some few stolne impertinencies, but by some stayed man, of tried and known abilities in his profession, allured by a competent encouragement to stay in the university.[21]

To secure 'the effectual advancement . . . not the permissive propagation of learning' Hall suggested that their funds should be controlled by 'a select committee of able and knowing men (wherein some representatives of the University should be mingled)': a striking anticipation of a twentieth-century expedient. He also referred to the possibility of 'some better way of disposing of those few colledges which are thinly scattered up and down the land, and make them either collaterall or subservient to this designe'.

William Dell, the Master of Caius, followed this up by *The Right Reformation of Learning, Schools and Universities*, itself a polemic against the award of degrees in Divinity. Arguing that the civil power was entitled to erect schools, he asked why more universities could not be established:

why universities and colleges should only be at Oxford and Cambridge, I know no reason. . . . It would be more advantageous to the good of all the people, to have universities or colleges, one at least at every great town in the nation, as in London, York, Essex, Bristol, Exeter, Norwich and the like; and for the State to allow to these Colleges competent maintenance for some godly and learned men to teach.[22]

But Cromwell defended Oxford and Cambridge; Parliament was dissolved, the reaction set in, and order reigned there once more.

By 1656 Cromwell went forward, and the Privy Council authorised the founding of a college at Durham. On 15 May 1657, letters patent were issued to the following effect: it was to be on the old prebendal site, to consist of a provost, fourteen fellows, twenty-four scholars and twelve exhibitioners, and was to be known as a body corporate under their names. The first provost was Philip Hunton, an Oxford Master of Arts. The two senior fellows came from Oxford and Cambridge, and one of the junior fellows was later destined to become the master of Trinity College, Cambridge. Rent charges totalling £900 a year were granted to it, with permission to purchase lands to the amount of £6,000 a year. It was allowed to set up a printing press, and all its members were exempted from watching, warding, mustering, and other social obligations of a normal citizen of those times.

But the college, though it petitioned for university powers, never succeeded in obtaining them: Oxford and Cambridge opposed it strongly, as also did the Quakers, since it aimed at preparing candidates for the ministry. So when the Restoration came, and the Church was restored to its old privileges and endowments, the Cromwellian college was swept away, along with other 'intruded' persons throughout the kingdom.

The second venture was equally unsuccessful. The West of England Presbyterian divines were anxious to establish a university at Shrewsbury, to serve Wales and tap the rich springs of Puritan opinion there and in neighbouring counties. Richard Baxter, the divine, was active in the year 1646, and approached Colonel Mackworth, the governor of Shrewsbury, but with no result. Ten years later, he approached James Berry, a one-time clerk in a Shropshire ironworks and then Cromwell's Major-General of Hereford, Shropshire and Wales. Berry, wrote Baxter, 'promised me his best assistance, but the want is money'.

Continuing in a letter to his friend John Lewis, he wrote:

> Till we see a probability for that it is in vaine to gett authority. I heard of a Shrewsbury man liveinge in London worth £40,000 that had no child to leave it to, and wrote to him—though a mere stranger—my strongest arguments to move him to bestow on such a foundation; but could not prevail. If you could but get £1,000 stock to build so much of a College as would containe an hundred students and but £200 or £300 per annum at first laid to it, I say if you could first procure assurance of this much either from one yt shall be ye founder, or by contribution, I make no doubt to procure authority from ye Protector and Parliament, and some hundred pounds per annum additional from my friends, perhaps many, for many will give to such a work when they see it in a hopefull way, yet will not begin it as not knowinge who will helpe it on.

Baxter considered that the site of this new university college should be at Shrewsbury: 'ye only fitt place in many respects', adducing six reasons for his choice.

> 1st It's a capable place where may be sufficient accomodations and a place of some name: 2nd A Little within ye verge on England is best that your sons may learne English; 3rd It's a place of strengthe, if warre should arise ye students may be secured: 4th It's a strength where they may live without military entanglements. Ludlow Castle will not be trusted to scollars unless they turned soldiers and ye town would not secure them, nay ye castle will draw ruine on them; 5th It is a healthfull seat; 6th There is a gallant free schoole

allready to perceive for ye academy, and I know no reason but £100 or £200 per annum might be allowed out of ye now superfluous maintenance of ye schoole.[23]

In spite of Richard Baxter's efforts, the project for a Western University at Shrewsbury came to nothing.

9

The significance of Durham College from the Baconian standpoint was considerable. Ezerell Tonge, one of the four 'Fellows and Tutors', was well known to Samuel Hartlib, who thus described him: 'He desired the foundation of a Mechanical Schoole and acquainted mee with the whole designe of founding a Coll[ege] of Sciences with several Schooles and a Library, a worke-house in Durham. . . . Also well acquainted with Dr. [John] Wallis.'; adding that Tonge wanted apprentices to be employed at learning and mechanics, when otherwise they would be standing idle in their shops. Tonge was communicating these aspirations to Hartlib as early as 1656, before the letters patent for the college were issued, and was evidently agitating for work to begin. Another of the fellows was William Sprigg, whom Tonge described as 'excellent for drawing and painting and very optical also'; while a third, John Peachell, was 'a universall schollar'. The fourth of these fellows, Thomas Vaughan, was described by Hartlib as 'a very learned man and minister, who is haunted with a Platonical genius, who talkes to him at nights. Hee is very didactical, and hath many several Tables to teach m[ore] readily the grammar of the Latin Tongue and hath given specimina in teaching of languages'. Vaughan, also according to Hartlib, had 'invented a mechanical way for common-places with removable notes' and had a secret recipe to cure the stone.[24]

Tonge, though he took up residence at Durham and described himself as engaged on 'perpetuall imployments', met little encouragement. 'I am here left alone with many youthes, more enimies, great hindrances, noe helpes nor helpers but God', he lamented.

Some of the 'Fellows and Professors' of the college were also significantly interested in the various sciences. Robert Wood wrote a pamphlet entitled *Ten to One*, proposing a decimal coinage, and was also engaged in making 'a Catalogue of matter for all trades artificers etc.'. He also knew Lady Ranelagh, the sister of Robert Boyle, having met her through Hartlib. Another 'Fellow and Professor' was John Kiffler (Johannes Küffeler), the son-in-law of Cornelius Drebbel, a

Dutch inventor who bequeathed him all his secrets before dying in 1634. One of these was 'an engine' which would sink any ship at a blow. This so intrigued the Commonwealth Council of State that they invited him to England, where Cromwell promised him £10,000 for the secret. After a successful demonstration on 4 August 1658, Drebbel's son-in-law waited in vain for the money.

That such men were appointed was an indication of the instruction to be given, and, if further evidence were needed of the desire to persevere with it, the presence of Major Tolhurst on the committee of visitors would provide it. For Tolhurst, according to Hartlib, had 'found out devices for facilitating the workes in the mines at Newcastle'. Unfortunately, other visitors did not think that Durham College should enjoy university status, and one of them, Benjamin Whichcote, was also a member of the delegation from Cambridge University which with Oxford, petitioned Richard Cromwell to that effect on 18 April 1659.[25]

10

One of the recipients of the *Conatuum Comeniarum Praeludia* from Samuel Hartlib was another refugee, Theodore Haak. He suggested that a group of those interested in the '*New Philosophy* or *Experimental Philosophy*' should meet weekly in London on a certain day 'to treat and discourse of such affairs'. Such meetings were no new thing: Queen Elizabeth's physician, William Gilberd, used to hold them in his house on St. Peter's Hill.

But Haak's suggestion fell among men of great talent. In 1645 there were in London, for one reason or another connected with the Civil War, a number of these men. George Ent, Christopher Merrett, and Francis Glisson, three physicians, were interested, and a fourth, Jonathan Goddard, offered hospitality at his house in Wood Street, where he kept 'an operator for grinding glasses for telescopes and microscopes'. Naturally enough, the professor of astronomy at Gresham College, Samuel Foster, came along, and with him another astronomer, Dr. John Wilkins, 'a very ingeniose man, and had a very mechanical head. He was much for trying experiments and his head ran much upon the perpetuall motion'.

Sometimes the group would meet at Foster's house in Cheapside, and sometimes at Gresham College. John Wallis, a mathematician who was employed by Parliament to decipher important dispatches, used to attend these meetings, and later left an account of them:

Our business was (precluding matters of theology and state affairs) to discourse and consider Philosophical Enquiries and such as related thereunto; as Physick, Anatomy, Geometry, Astronomy, Navigation, Staticks, Magneticks, Chymicks, Mechanicks, and natural Experiments; with the state of these studies, as then cultivated at home and abroad . . . with other things appertaining to what hath been called the *New Philosophy*, which from the times of Galileo at Florence, and Sir Francis Bacon in England, hath been much cultivated in Italy, France, Germany, and other parts abroad, as well as with us in England.[26]

For three years these meetings continued, till in 1648 Wilkins moved to Oxford as Warden of Wadham. And though the London group continued to meet, a far stronger new group assembled at Oxford, among them being William Petty (whom Samuel Hartlib had wished to be 'set aside' to advance scientific studies at Gresham College), Willis, Ward, and Bathurst. Petty, since he lodged with an apothecary who had plenty of drugs, seemed to have acted as host at first, but left Oxford for Ireland on government business. Wilkins as Warden of Wadham seems to have housed the group until 1659 when he was appointed Master of Trinity College, Cambridge. The host then became Robert Boyle. The group called themselves the Philosophical Society, and their weekly meetings were described by Sprat, their historian, as proceeding

'rather by action than by discourse, chiefly attending some particular trials in Chymistry or Mechanicks; they had no rules nor method fixed. Their intention was more to communicate to each other their discoveries which they could make in so narrow a compass, than united, constant and regular disquisitions.'

So inspired, indeed, did the members become that a number of them established private laboratories to 'perform those things which the memory of man could not reach'. Boyle himself equipped a laboratory in an ancient hall called Ram Inn, where Peter Stahl lectured to several classes, including John Wallis, Nathaniel Crew, Ralph Bathurst, Richard Lower, and Christopher Wren. Boyle even considered a scheme, and suggested it to the Council of State in which 'a matter of twelve thousand pounds, sterling was to purchase confiscated lands and houses . . . in Ireland'. The profits of this purchase were to be committed 'into the hands of certain trustees, for to employ it in the entertainment of an agent, secretary, translators, for keeping intelligence, distributing rewards, *etc.*, in order to realise the Baconian dream. But the magic circle at Oxford broke: a severe winter disturbed men's minds, and Cromwell died. Wren went to London as Professor of Astronomy at Gresham College and Wilkins went as Master to Trinity College, Cambridge.[27]

Indeed after 1658, the majority of the Oxford group returned to London where they could hear Lawrence Rooke, Professor of Geometry since 1657, lecture at Gresham College. His previous Gresham Chair of Astronomy, which he had held since 1652, was now taken over by Christopher Wren. It was at a discussion after Wren's lecture on 28 November 1660 that 'something was offered about a design of founding a college for the promoting of *Physico-mathematical Experimental Learning*'. High enthusiasm for the new philosophy inspired one to write 'In praise of the choice company of Philosophers and Witts who meet Wednesdays weekly at Gresham College':

> 'At Gresham College a learned nott
> Unparalleled designs have layed
> To make themselves a corporation
> And know all things by demonstration.
>
> These are not men of common mould,
> They covet fame but condemn gold.
> The Gresham College shall hereafter be
> The whole world's University.
>
> Oxford and Cambridge are our laughter;
> Their learning is but pedantry.
> These new Collegiates do assure us
> Aristotle's an ass to Epicurus.'[28]

REFERENCES

1. FARRINGTON, B., *Francis Bacon, Philosopher of Industrial Science* (1951), 99.

2. GRANT, Sir Alexander, *The Story of the University of Edinburgh* (London, 1884).

3. CROSSLEY, J., *The Diary and Correspondence of Dr. John Worthington* (1841), i, 69–75.

FULLER, T., *Church History* (ed. J. S. Brewer, Oxford, 1845), v, 387.

4. PORTAL, Edith M., 'The Academ Roial of King James I', in *Proceedings of the British Academy* (1916), vii, 189–208.

5. TURNBULL, G. H., 'Samuel Hartlib's Connection with Sir Francis Kynaston's Musaeum Minervae'. *Notes and Queries* (1952), 197, 33–37.

FAULKNER, T., *An Historical and Descriptive Account of the Royal Hospital at Chelsea* (London, 1805), 36.

6. BARRETT, C. R. B., *The History of the Society of Apothecaries* (1905), 5–48.

7. RAVEN, C. E., *English Naturalists from Neckham to Ray* (Cambridge, 1947), 248–97.

8. INNES-SMITH, R. W., *English Speaking Students of Medicine at the University of Leyden* (1932).

9. Turnbull, G. H., *Hartlib, Dury and Comenius* (Liverpool, 1947), 350.
10. *ibid.*, 365.
11. Quoted, J. Bass Mullinger, *The University of Cambridge* (1911), iii, x.
12. Peck, F., *Desiderata Curiosa* (London, 1779), vii, no. xx, 283-91; F. Bussby, 'An Ecclesiastical Seminarie and College General of Learning at Ripon,' *Journal of Ecclesiastical History* (1953), iv, 154-61. Peck (1692-1743) also published an account of the early university at Stamford.
13. Creighton, M., *Carlisle* (London, 1889), 152.
14. Mathew, David, *The Age of Charles I* (1951), 22.
15. Thompson, J., *The University of Manchester* (1886), 512-16.
16. Rushworth, J., *Historical Collections* (1680), II, iv, 854.
17. Bass Mullinger, J., *op. cit.*, iii, 264.
18. For these schemes see G. H. Turnbull, *Hartlib, Dury and Comenius*, 57-65.
19. Weld, C. R., *History of the Royal Society* (1848), i, 53.
20. Firth, C., *Oliver Cromwell* (London, 1947), 355, *Letters and Speeches*, ed. E. S. C. Lomas (1904), ii, 186.

James, M., *Social Policy during the Puritan Revolution* (1930), 324-6.

Cromwell also had a scheme for establishing a new college at Oxford, St. Mary's Hall, and endowing it by voluntary subscription, for the purpose of supporting 'poor Protestant ministers and scholars', and effecting a 'generall Synopsis of the true reformed Protestant Christian Religion professed in this Commonwealth'. James, *op. cit.*, 318.

21. Watson, Foster, 'A Clever Young Man: John Hall of Gray's Inn', in the *Gentleman's Magazine* (1894); *The Advancement of Learning*, ed. A. K. Croston (Liverpool, 1953), 27.

Turnbull, G. H., 'John Hall's Letters to Samuel Hartlib', *Review of English Studies*, iv. (Oxford, 1953), 230, for a plan for another academy.

22. For William Dell see *Cyclopaedia of Education* (ed. Paul Munroe), New York, 1911, ii, 290–1, and H. R. Trevor-Roper *E.H.R.* (1947), lvii, 377-9.

Evans, Emrys, *The Universities of Wales* (1953).

Dr. John Ellis, the rector of Dolgallan, suggested Ludlow as the site of a Welsh University, but feared that the Universities of Oxford and Cambridge would oppose the project.

23. Auden, T., *Memorials of Old Shropshire* (1906), 233-4.
24. Turnbull, G. H., 'Oliver Cromwell's College at Durham', in *Research Review* (London, 1952), No. 3, 1-7.
25. *ibid.*
26. Ornstein, Martha, *The Role of Scientific Societies in the Seventeenth Century* (Chicago, 1938), 93-102.
27. More, L. T., *The Life and Works of the Hon. Robert Boyle* (Oxford, 1944), 101-2.
28. Ornstein, *loc. cit.*, and R. H. Syfret, 'The Origins of the Royal Society', *Notes and Records of the Royal Society*, v, No. 2, 75-137.

CHAPTER SIX

The Royal Society and its Influence, 1660-1731

I

JUST before the Restoration, John Evelyn the diarist wrote to Robert Boyle:

> since we are not to hope for a mathematical college, much less a Salomon's House . . . why might not some gentlemen, whose geniuses are greatly suitable, and who desire nothing more than to give a good example, preserve science, and cultivate themselves, join together in a society and resolve upon some orders and economy, to be mutually observed, such as shall best become the end of their union.

and proceeded to suggest the purchase of an estate near London where a library, laboratory, aviary, museum, herb and vegetable garden, conservatory, and lodgings might be provided. To show his good faith he offered to sustain both the building and maintenance of such a college. Two years later Abraham Cowley, in his *Proposition for the Advancement of Experimental Philosophy*, designed a college which should 'give the best education in the world gratis'. Expressly disclaiming any imitation of Salomon's House (which he described as 'a project for experiments that can never be experimented'), he proposed an establishment of twenty professors, sixteen fellows, and two hundred scholars, researching and teaching in a manner truly Baconian. In his preface, he stressed the inadequacy of existing university education, which, medicine and mathematics apart, ignored the application of knowledge to practical living, and held 'that idle and pernicious opinion . . . that all things to be searched in nature had been already found and discovered by the ancients'. He continued: 'no man can hope to make himself as rich by stealing out of others' trunks as he might by opening and digging of new mines.' Four of his college professors were to travel beyond the seas, like Bacon's merchants of light, and were to report on all things pertaining to natural and experimental philosophy. In their reports, they were to be strictly enjoined 'never to write anything . . . but what, after very diligent examination, they shall fully believe to be true, and to confess and recant it as soon as they find themselves in error'. The weekly faculty meetings, the academic conditions of tenure, the relationship between instructing staff and trustees, the frequent written reports of research: all show that Cowley realised the manifold implications of modern university life.

The idea of a college was very much in the minds of the group which we have noticed, at the end of the last chapter, meeting at Gresham College. Indeed, they sporadically discussed it for many years after 28 November 1660 when 'something was offered about the design of founding a Colledge for the promoting of Physico-Mathematicall Experimentall Learning'. But instead they resolved to 'improve' their meetings 'to a more regular way of debating things . . . according to the manner in other countries where there were voluntary associations of men in acadamies for the advancement of various parts of learning'.

On 5 December 1660, some forty-one of them agreed to debate and consult, and two years later were formally incorporated as the Royal Society. In promoting the Baconian ideal they ignored class and sect. Fellows like Chief Justice Hale and Lord Keeper Guilford wrote scientific works as well as discharging their duties. Bishops like Ward of Salisbury, Wilkins of Chester, and Sprat of Rochester were also attracted to the early meetings of the Royal Society, together with Irish landowners like Lord Brouncker (the first president) and Robert Boyle (one of its leading members), and virtuosi like John Evelyn. They were joined by expatriates like Theodore Haak and Henry Oldenburg. The Royal Society was a real institute of advanced studies, with its own publications, meeting house, and (although a meagre one) endowment.[1]

But as the garrulous Anthony Wood recorded in his diary:

> The Royal Societie instituted this yeare—the Universitie looke upon it as obnoxious; they desire to confer degrees; the Universitie stick against this. Stubbe writes against them; Dr. Fell favours him.[2]

Fell, subject of the well-known nursery-rhyme, became Vice-Chancellor of Oxford in 1666. Cambridge was little better: in 1669, Dr. Gunning refused to grant Peter du Moulin a licence to print his poems unless he omitted one in praise of the Royal Society. Du Moulin wrote to Boyle that it grieved him 'to see a feud between that noble society and the Universities . . . your great credit, prudence and moderation may stop that growing if anything in the world may'.[3] The dispute was not so much between two institutions as between two philosophies. It had been going on, as we have seen, between the adherents of Aristotle and the Anti-Aristotelians and was to reach a climax in the last decade of the century with the famous *Battle of the Books*.

2

For at the Restoration, the universities were obliged to filter their intake by religious tests, designed to secure them as nurseries of partisan thought. 'Masters and other heads, fellows, chaplains, and tutors of, or in, any colledge, hall, house of learning or hospital, and every publique professor and reader' were constrained both to take such oaths, and also to administer them. The penalty for not so doing was loss of office—'as if any person so failing were naturally dead'. These oaths, imposed by the Uniformity, Conventicle, Five Mile and Test Acts, left no interstices through which Dissenters could creep. Conformity was essential, and non-conformists were driven out.

Thirteen heads of colleges from Oxford and six from Cambridge went into the wilderness, followed by some seventy-five fellows.[4] Those who remained were few. John Wallis, it is true, continued to adorn the Savilian Chair of Mathematics for another thirty-three years, Robert Plot became the first curator of the Ashmolean, Robert Morison was appointed to the Chair of Botany, Thomas Willis to the Chair of Natural Philosophy, and the great Christopher Wren accepted the Chair of Astronomy. But they can be numbered on the fingers of one hand, and constituted Oxford's leading lights. At Cambridge the position was similar. Isaac Barrow and his successor Isaac Newton established a mathematical tradition, but even Newton, whose brilliance far outshone all his contemporaries, was very unhappy about the false position in which the universities now found themselves. 'I do not know a greater abuse of religion than that sort of oaths,' he wrote in a manuscript which Rouse Ball found amongst his papers, 'they being harder to be kept than the Jewish law.'[5] Even Newton's brilliance was a handicap in one sense, for as Lange pointed out seventy-five years ago, his contemporaries were content to leave further progress to the Continentals.[6] Deprived of the stimulus of a free and open society at Cambridge, he turned to London, where he found a sympathetic and receptive audience in the Royal Society.

The purging of the two universities was not accompanied by any startling improvements in undergraduate behaviour. Freed from Puritan discipline, students broke out into orgies of bad manners and excesses, so much so that birchings were still being recorded as necessary. After 1670, Balliol had only twenty-five undergraduates on its rolls and was casting about for more. Antony Wood, who commented on the scarcity of students in 1682, was himself expelled from Oxford in 1693 for libelling the author of this penal legislation, Lord Clarendon, who had been Chancellor of the University for the first seven years following the Restoration.[7] There was also a prejudice against education itself. Edward Chamberlayne, private tutor to the Duke of Grafton and to Prince George of Denmark, in his *Angliae Notitiae or the Present State of England* (1669), a book which ran to twenty editions in thirty-three years, attributed the recent 'Sedition and Rebellion' to the tendency of country grammar schools to draw pupils from the lower classes. Christopher Wase began his *Considerations touching Free-Schools* (1678) with the observation:

> 'There is an opinion commonly receiv'd, that the Scholars of England are overproportion'd to the preferments for letter'd persons', and that those 'whom Nature or Fortune had determin'd to the Plough, the Oar, or other Handicrafts' were being diverted 'to the study of Liberal Arts'.

The increase of foundations, concluded Wase, was seen to be 'dangerous to the Government'.[8]

But men, not walls, make universities, and men are susceptible to the contagion of ideas. The Royal Society's outlook did affect them, and some of the results of that influence can be seen if one considers the relative progress of the universities in the period.

Oxford undoubtedly suffered by the withdrawal of Wren, Hooke, and Boyle to London, following Ward, Wilkins, Goddard, and Rooke. Yet among those who remained there were some, like Dr. Edward Bernard, who hoped that 'in a short while the Royal Society will approve itself so great a friend and near ally of the Universities that by the munificence of some members of the noble fellowship, there may be occasion given of frequent experiments in both Universities and consequently of a lasting commerce'.[9]

That munificence was forthcoming. In 1669 a chair in Botany was established and Robert Morison occupied it to study the 'nature and distinction of herbs and others plants' in the Physic Garden. Fourteen years later, a chair of Chemistry was established by Elias Ashmole in connection with his Museum, and Robert Plot, its first occupant, began to lecture on the ground floor of the Ashmolean three times a week on 'Naturall Bodies relating to, and made use of in Chemical Preparations'.[10]

We know, from the letters of an undergraduate at the end of the century, that the 'new philosophy' was affecting the tutors. His own recommended him to buy Bacon's *Novum Organum*, Robert Boyle's *Philosophical Essays, Sceptical Chymist* and tracts on the Saltness of the

Sea. He even bought a quadrant and a pair of compasses to help him n his mathematical work.[11] By 1690, experimental scientific demonstrations had begun, thanks to David Gregory and his pupil James Keill.

At Cambridge, the new philosophy went even more forward, hanks to a previous reception of Descartes and the revival of interest n Plato. Though one student declared that 'new philosophy was a ort of heresy', the fact remained that Newton was a Fellow of Trinity College, and became in 1669 second occupant of the Lucasian Chair of Mathematics—six years after its creation, succeeding, incidentally, saac Barrow, who had previously been Professor of Geometry at Gresham College. Newton significantly chose optics as the topic of is first lectures. In the last two decades of the century, it proved ossible to study chemistry with Francis Vignani, though not, unappily, under the auspices of the university.[12]

3

In 1667, the heyday of the religious persecutions under the Clarendon Code, Sprat's *History of the Royal Society* (1667), came out with the emarkable announcement:

> As for what belongs to the Members themselves, that are to constitute the ociety, it is to be noted that they have freely admitted men of different Religions, Countries, and Professions of Life. This they were obliged to do, or lse they would come far short of the largeness of their own declarations. For they openly profess not to lay the Foundation of an English, Scotch, Irish, Popish or Protestant Philosophy, but a Philosophy of Mankind.

By 1669, it embodied such a cluster of talent that the public orator f Oxford enviously derided the Fellows as admirers of nothing except fleas, lice, and themselves', in a speech made at the opening of Oxford's great auditorium, designed by Christopher Wren and nanced by Archbishop Sheldon, the University's Chancellor. Dr. Vallis, the Savilian Professor of Geometry, and Keeper of the Public Archives, was perturbed, and told Boyle they had been 'damned . . . *d inferos, ad gehennam*'. So was John Evelyn, who described the malicious and indecent reflections on the Royal Society by the Public Orator' as 'underminers of the University' as being 'foolish and ntrue'.[13]

The challenge of the Royal Society was discerned by other proessional bodies too. The College of Physicians, then passing the hundred and fiftieth year of its establishment, numbered amongst its fellows and benefactors Dr. Baldwin Hamey. Hamey was not as forthright as Dr. South, the Oxford Public Orator, preferring to commission 'the most noted Latinist and Grecian of his age', Henry Stubbe, to carry on a vigorous propaganda against the Royal Society. This was a shrewd move, for Stubbe had a wide ranging mind, was not afraid to criticise (he had previously been expelled from Oxford for writing against the clergy and the universities), and was a great friend of Thomas Hobbes. Stubbe claimed to stand for common-sense: 'neither the ancients nor modern academicks were so foolish as they painted them out to be, nor the Royal Society so inquisitive as they would seem', he wrote, pointing to the virtuosi as either 'very great imposters, or men of little reading' who were desirous 'to overthrow the universities and all others as idiots and ignoramuses'.[14]

But Fellows of the Royal Society were anxious to disclaim any challenge, and expressed a positive desire to co-operate. 'The Royal Society doth in no way disturb or meddle with *University Learning and Education*', wrote Joseph Glanvill in reply to Stubbe. We have already noted the remarks of Dr. Edward Bernard, private tutor and university don, who praised the balance of books and experience so happily struck by the Society.

Lasting commerce, however, took some time to develop and in the meantime experimental philosophy, involving as it did the patient collection of specimens of every kind, brought down showers of ridicule on the Royal Society. Even their royal patron Charles II laughed when they tried to weigh the air. To stem this ridicule Sprat wrote a *History of the Royal Society* when it was barely five years old for he 'dreaded the power' of the wits of the age, who 'by making it ridiculous . . . may do it more injury than all the Arguments of our severe and frowning and dogmatical Adversaries'. This the wits, like Thomas Shadwell and Aphra Behn, attempted to do. Thomas Shadwell ransacked the *Philosophical Transactions* and Sprat's *History* for material for his play *The Virtuoso* (1673) in which he charged the Fellows of the Society with 'the artificial folly of those who are not coxcombs by nature, but with great art and industry make themselves so'. In this play Sir Nicholas Gimcrack was such a success that Addison revived him again early in the following century.[15] Shadwell's success was followed fourteen years later by Mrs. Aphra Behn, who used the foibles of an F.R.S. for her *Emperor in the Moon*, where two amorous youths deceive the jealous guardian of two young girls by preying on his scientific credulity.[16]

The Royal Society had other handicaps too. Charles II gave them a mace, but little else. For though in 1669 he endowed them with the lands of Chelsea College, the property was so dilapidated and encumbered that the Fellows could do little with it. Attempts to sell it failed, partly owing to objectionable fumes from a glassworks that Prince Rupert, one of the Fellows, had established nearby. In May 1678, though £30 had previously been spent on repairs, the roof collapsed, and on Wren's advice the Council of the Society then ordered that 'the tiles and timber of Chelsea College be taken down and stored in some place near the same' and that their Vice-President should 'direct some person to go about the pulling it down forthwith'.[17] Fourteen years later, Charles II took the lands back again, promising them £1,300, which they never got. Nor were they any luckier with gifts from their own members. Bishop Wilkins's legacy had to be demanded from his executors, and when that was invested after much trouble, the revenues soon froze. Moreover their own officers, besides being handicapped by lack of funds, were often crippled by other calls. Oldenburg, the secretary in the first fourteen years, was imprisoned for suspected fifth-column work; Boyle, one of their brightest luminaries, refused the presidency because of scruples about the oaths, while the three men who might have carried much of the burden on their shoulders, were deeply committed elsewhere—Pepys at the Admiralty, Evelyn with the sick and wounded from the Dutch war, and Wren with the rebuilding of London.[18] Such powerful noblemen as they did secure to help them were mostly failures: Lord Carbery, President for three years, was described by Pepys himself as 'one of the lewdest fellows of the age'; and the Earl of Pembroke, Carbery's successor, never attended a single meeting during his year of office. Nor were the ordinary Fellows prepared to back the efforts of their scientific brothers, for by 1675 unpaid dues amounted to over £2,000—no small sum when we remember that each single Fellow was obliged to pay one shilling a week.

In spite of everything, the Royal Society survived. Perhaps the greatest tribute to it was that Newton published his *Principia* under its name in 1687. Certainly its greatest asset was when Newton became President and moved it to Crane Court where its library (initiated by the generosity of Henry Howard at Arundel House after the Great Fire, from his collection of 500 manuscripts and 3,000 printed books), and the collections (amassed from all over the globe by assiduous correspondence) were housed. As Addison wrote in the *Spectator* (No. 262 of 1711) of the advantages of the Society:

it draws men's minds off from the bitterness of party and furnishes them with subjects of discourse that may be treated without warmth or passions. This is said to have been the first design of those gentlemen who set on foot the Royal Society; and had then a very good effect as it turned many of the greatest geniuses of that age to the disquisitions of natural knowledge, who, if they had engaged in politics with the same parts and applications, might have set their country in a flame.

It is not too fanciful to see in various committees of the Royal Society the first real acknowledgement that specialism by a group of experts is essential if any real extension of the frontiers of knowledge is to be won. These committees concentrated on most aspects of life which would repay investigation: agriculture, music, medicine, botany, history, and the various branches of natural science; throwing up work of lasting distinction. In such an atmosphere of mutual encouragement and help, publications by individual members reached a very high standard. Often the Society's assistance extended to the actual cost of publication, and under their aegis such works as Evelyn's on *Trees* (1664), Hooke's *Micrographia* (1665), Wilkins's *Essay toward . . . a Philosophical Language* (1668), Malpighi's *Anatome Plantarum* (1675), Willughby and Ray's *Ornithologiae* (1676), and Flamsteed's *Tide Table for 1687* were given to the public. Crowning this cluster was, of course, Newton's *Principia* (1687), which was paid for by Halley, whose own exertions in the cause of science led him to St. Helena, Danzig, the top of Snowdon, across the Atlantic, round the Adriatic, and up and down the English Channel.

All these activities were presented through the *Philosophical Transactions*, the oldest scientific journal in the English-speaking world This, in the Hartlib tradition, was intelligencing on a systematic scale It assuaged the fever which so many researchers had (and have) t burst into print. 'That jealousy about the first authors of experiments' as Henry Oldenburg called it, was undoubtedly a factor in its establishment. And Oldenburg's assiduity and courage in face of financia hardship launched this disseminator of ideas, which, apart from three-year lapse in the sixteen-eighties, has continued down to our ow day, fathering a numerous progeny.

4

The College of Physicians also numbered amongst its members som who found the inspiration of the Royal Society a very real thing, lik Francis Glisson, a physiologist of note, and Thomas Lower, wh performed before the Royal Society an experiment on blood transfusion which attracted much attention. The Society of Apothecaries too, seized the opportunity offered after the disastrous fire of London to build themselves a new hall, and to establish therein a laboratory which was so busy that tenants of the Society near their Hall in Blackfriars complained that the stench was 'ready to suffocate them, and makes them soe sicke they are not able to endure it'. Its third 'operator', Nicholas Staphorst, taught chemistry to Sir Hans Sloane, and contributed, like John Coniers, James Petiver and Samuel Doody —other apothecaries of talent—to the *Philosophical Transactions*.[19] The Barber Surgeons, too, sustained the Leyden-trained Dissenter, Richard Mead, as their reader on anatomy, and he did much to enhance the reputation of St. Thomas's Hospital, as William Wagstaffe, another reader on anatomy to the Barber Surgeons, did for St. Bartholomew's.[20]

John Bellers, a Quaker cloth merchant, in his tract *Towards the Improvement of Physic* (1714), proposed that the Royal Society should receive State aid 'the better to Enable them to carry on that Useful and Great Design, of improving Men in the Knowledge of NATURE (and the MECHANICS) of which MEDICINE is a principal branch'.

In this essay he proposed that each of the two universities should possess a hospital, that all hospitals should be allowed to dissect the bodies of those who died in them, that public laboratories and physical observatories be provided to 'make general search among the *Vegitables* and *Minerals*', and that gratuities or prizes should be awarded to those 'who shall discover any thing New in *Nature*, or in *Mechanicks*'. He also urged the Colleges of Physicians and Surgeons to 'draw up a Summary of Advice, in both their Faculties, in the plainest manner, of what common Errors should be avoided in Practice, as well as what is fit to be done . . . and that there may be a Committee appointed to attend at the College of *Physicians* every Post Day to correspond with the Country *Physicians* in Case any of them should meet with a Difficulty'.[21]

Bellers' last proposal was timely, for the College of Physicians was now limited to graduates of Oxford and Cambridge. Since its formation in 1518 it had welcomed graduates of Padua, Leyden, and other Continental schools. Now, with Sir Charles Scarburgh as its Lumleian lecturer (a post which Harvey had held), it did not offer that free vent to medical ability which it had previously done. Scarburgh was also the reader in anatomy to the Barber Surgeons' Company. So it is not surprising to find that the original research of this time was done by Thomas Sydenham, who learnt much of his medicine at Montpellier. Sydenham's work on fevers and the current diseases of the time was of such importance that the great Boerhaave was accustomed to raise his hat with respect whenever Sydenham's name was mentioned. A friend of Boyle, Locke, and Sir Hans Sloane, Sydenham also received pupils. Mrs. Mary Beale, the mother of one of them, painted his portrait which was presented to the College of Physicians in 1691.[22]

The wide interests of the medical men at this time are well known. Locke's contribution to psychology and philosophy, Petty's to demography and economics, Lister's and Woodward's to geology, were continued by the generation that succeeded them, though in a more literary way. Radcliffe, Mead, Garth, Arbuthnot, and Blackmore were bright lights in the cultural history of Queen Anne's times. Others conserved their energies for the teaching of their craft. William Cheselden began to lecture in 1711 on anatomy, and a year later became a fellow of the Royal Society. He, like Edward Nourse, owed his medical education to facilities afforded in the metropolis itself. These facilities began to increase at this time with the population when, to the hospitals of St. Bartholomew and St. Thomas, were added the Westminster in 1720, and Guy's in 1724.

5

Amateur virtuosi began to be supplemented by professional science teachers at this time. At the beginning of the period we see Sir Kenelm Digby, whose wife drank viper wine for her complexion (and died), employing Hans Hunneades, and 'in the last faire house westward in the North portico of Covent Garden' maintaining a regular academy, attended by wits, experimentalists, occultists, philosophers, and men of letters. Yet we also recognise such 'professionals' as Nicholas Le Fevre, whose chemistry lectures had been attended in Paris by John Evelyn in 1647, and who was entrusted with the management of the Royal Laboratory in St. James's Palace. His *Traité de la Chymie*, a popular book which passed through many editions, was translated into English by a gentleman of the Privy Chamber. George Wilson kept his furnaces burning furiously till the mob broke them up in 1688. John Dwight at Fulham pioneered a miniature centre of glass technology, manufacturing salt-glazed stoneware that greatly interested the London Company of Glass Sellers. But perhaps the two most notable laboratories in London were those kept by Robert Boyle after he finally left Oxford in 1668. The first was at the back of Lady Ranelagh's house in Pall Mall, where he experimented with the calcination of metals. The second was in Southampton Street, fitted up *c.* 1680, where his assistant A. G. Hanckwitz prepared phosphorus from urine, and for long remained the only manufacturer of phosphorus in Europe.

It was Boyle who, in the year before the Restoration, had introduced the first regular teacher of practical chemistry into Oxford, Peter Sthael. Sthael was originally assistant to Boyle, on the recommendation of Samuel Hartlib. He stayed at Oxford for about five years, his classes being attended by John Wallis, and Christopher Wren, amongst others. But in 1664, for want of pupils, he too went to London, where he became 'operator' to the Royal Society. It was a London courtier, Elias Ashmole, who decided to endow a scientific institute in Oxford on the model of Gresham College and the Royal Society. His foundation, amply supplemented by the University, was finished by 1683, but never attained the scientific eminence of its models, retaining in great measure the archaeological atmosphere by which its projector had been surrounded. However, it supported Robert Plot and John Freind, and with Hart Hall (where John Keill and J. T. Desaguliers lectured) formed the nucleus of scientific teaching in the university.[23]

Yet, as the Oxford historian of science R. T. Gunther has pointed out, most of the experiments for which Desaguliers was famous were carried out after his removal from Oxford to London. This move, which took place in 1713, marks the first course of lectures in the new experimental philosophy to be given in the metropolis. Desaguliers lectured in Channel Row, Westminster, on a syllabus printed both in English and French entitled *Course of Mechanical and Experimental Philosophy*, for a fee of three guineas. In addition to inventing a machine for taking sea-soundings, he was the first to classify materials as electrics and non-electrics, according to whether or not they would conduct electricity.[24] Squat, thickset, and short-sighted, he nevertheless was such a successful lecturer that, when he went to Holland, Huyghens and Boerhaave came to listen to him. When his house in Channel Row was pulled down owing to the rebuilding of Westminster Bridge, he removed to a lodging over the great piazza of Covent Garden where he continued with unabated success till 1744. He lived by his lectures, and died in poverty.

Nor was Desaguliers the only lecturer to popularise experimental philosophy. William Whiston, who had succeeded Newton in the

Lucasian Professorship at Cambridge, was banished from the university and deprived of the chair in 1710 for publishing an essay on the *Apostolic Constitutions.* He thereupon began lecturing, not only in London, but as far afield as Bristol, Bath, and Tunbridge Wells, on meteors, eclipses, and earthquakes. Francis Hauksbee also began lectures on natural philosophy at this time. George Wilson, who gave lectures in his own house, was the most notable writer on chemistry since Boyle's time. His book of 1691, which embodies these, was the clearest exposition then known of the major processes required by the pharmacist and maker of chemical remedies.[25]

6

By serving as an office for enquiries and a central clearing house for scientific knowledge, the Royal Society revealed that a number of provincial physicians, apothecaries, and surgeons were pursuing interesting and profitable investigations. To take two examples from the West Riding of Yorkshire alone: Henry Power (1623-68), impressed by the 'incomparable artifice' of the microscope, published in 1663 his *Experimental Philosophy* in three books, becoming in the same year an F.R.S. He was a good country physician, who attended most of the noble families of the county.[26] In Sheffield at the same time the Fisher brothers, one a physician and the other a surgeon, and both dissenters, used to communicate their observations to the local squire, Francis Jessop, who in turn relayed them to the Royal Society. And Jessop was the type of person who was counted amongst the intimate friends and helpers of John Ray and Francis Willughby.[27] Similar cases could be adduced from other counties in England.

7

The Fishers' brother-in-law, Timothy Jollie, directed from 1688 to 1714 the fortunes of a nonconformist academy at Attercliffe, near Sheffield. These nonconformist academies were established by tutors ejected from Oxford and Cambridge, who found themselves unable to subscribe to the tests and so went into the metropolis and the provinces to found academies of their own.[28] Two of these, Nettlebed and Tubney, are said to have actually awarded degrees. The realistic education demanded by the age was afforded by over a score of these private academies.

One of these Nonconformists, Charles Morton, had been a student at Wadham College, Oxford, when that college had been the nucleus of the body that later became the Royal Society. Morton loved science throughout his life, and for long after his death his textbook, *Compendium Physicae*, remained a standard work. He was 'the very soul of philosophy, the repository of all arts and sciences, and of the graces too'. His academy was opened at Stoke Newington in London in 1675, and of the five nonconformist academies established in the metropolis by the first generation of dissenters, his most deserves notice. 'A poor Hackney may put a Race Horse upon his brisker Career. This may stir up . . . a greater Diligence and Industry in the Universities', he quipped. Samuel Wesley, who was educated under Morton, acknowledged that his academy was 'the most considerable of any in England . . . for the number of its pupils and its polite learning'. Morton offered a course of five years for all those seeking an advanced education, whether intending ministers or not. Believing with the savants of the Royal Society that God was magnified the more one laboured to understand his revelation in the wonders of nature, Morton provided a garden, a bowling green, and a fishpond in the precincts of the academy, and built up a collection of 'all sorts of mathematical instruments' to illustrate his lectures, among them an air pump and thermometers.

It is little wonder therefore that many sons of the nobility and gentry were sent there to avoid the 'debaucheries of the universities'. Morton avowed that his purpose was 'to have knowledge increased, and not only confined to the clergy, or learned professions, but extended or diffused as much as might be to the people in general'. To that end, he ran the academy on self-governing lines: students formed a council, teaching was conducted in the vernacular, and modern studies like history, geography, and contemporary languages were part of the curriculum. Morton was well aware of the purpose of his work. Although he did not formally confer degrees, he protested strongly against the system which confined universities to conformists only. 'This securing of the Key of Knowledge and tying it fast to some men's girdles, or making it too hot or heavy for others to touch on any terms,' he wrote, 'might well enough comport with popish designs to keep people in the dark, that they may lead them the more quietly by the nose.'[29]

His attitude, as well as his success, brought down upon him the inevitable punishment. He was accused of breaking his oath as an M.A. not to lecture *Stamfordiae tanquam in universitate* and harassed by processes from the episcopal court. Unable to continue, he emigrated to New England in 1685, where he became a Fellow of Harvard, and later its first Vice-President. But his twenty years at Newington Green had not been wasted. His academy had nursed, not only such divines as Timothy Cruso, Joseph Hussey, Richard Lardner, and Thomas Reynolds, but also Samuel Wesley and Daniel Defoe. The last-named testified that he had read widely: five languages, mathematics, natural philosophy, geography, history, and logic showed that Morton's range was a wide one. No wonder Defoe lamented that the academy had but one deficiency—'want of conversation'. A new tradition had been established.

This tradition was being established in the provinces too. At Bromsgrove, Coventry, Dartmouth, Lincoln, Nottingham, Rathmell, Sheriffhales, Shrewsbury, Sulby, Taunton, Whitchurch, and Wickhambrook, the piety and learning of individual nonconformists stirred provincial minds, kindling the imagination of those to whom the doors of the university were irrevocably shut. These tutors, Henry Hickman, John Bryan, John Flavell, Edward Reyner, John Whitlock, Richard Frankland, John Woodhouse, Francis Tallents, John Shuttlewood, Matthew Warren, J. Maulden, and Samuel Cradock, were the pioneers. Others who came after reaped what they had sown. Two of them, Richard Frankland and Francis Tallents, especially illustrate the continuity of university teaching in their academies: Frankland as a former tutor designate of the projected Cromwellian University of Durham, and Tallents as a former Vice-President of Magdalene College, Cambridge.

The success of the academies was so great that attempts were made to institutionalise them. Migratory and furtive as they were, outside help was essential if they were to maintain any standards. Moreover, specialist teaching, especially for the second generation of nonconformists, was becoming increasingly necessary. So in 1689 the Independents and Presbyterians established a common fund to support academies for training their ministers, and six years later the Congregationalists followed suit. In the first decade of the following century they were further enriched by a substantial legacy from Sarah, Lady Hewley, and in 1730 the Calvinists founded yet a fourth sustaining fund administered by the King's Head Society. These funds were not specifically interested in the training of potential ministers, and stressed the importance of 'humane learning' as well as 'knowledge of divinity'. By sustaining students at the academies, they made it possible for many of the tutors to lay down more intensive courses of study, and to undertake research themselves.

The larger academies of the second generation showed that much untapped ability lay in the provinces. Attercliffe, Alcester, Bedworth, Bridgnorth, Bridgwater, Bolton, Bristol, Exeter, Findern, Gloucester, Saffron Walden, Stratford-on-Avon, Hungerford, Ipswich, Lyme Regis, Manchester, Newport Pagnell, Northampton, Tiverton, Tewkesbury, Warrington, and Whitehaven all maintained a lusty life, throwing up many students of real ability.

Of the northern academies, Attercliffe was first in importance. Originally established by Richard Frankland, whose activity at Rathmell has been already mentioned, it was continued by Timothy Jollie from 1689 until 1714. In Attercliffe Hall, near Sheffield, he built up Christ's College, which numbered amongst its pupils a professor of mathematics at Cambridge (Nicholas Saunderson, 1682–1739), a lord chancellor of Ireland (John Bowes, 1690–1767), an archbishop of Canterbury (Thomas Secker, 1693–1768), and the most popular non-conformist divine in London (Thomas Bradbury, 1677–1759), as well as numerous distinguished divines. Secker, after conforming, followed the example of Samuel Wesley in disparaging the place, referring to it in slighting terms: 'only the old philosophy of the schools was taught there; and that neither ably nor diligently. The morals also of many of the young men were bad. On the whole, I spent my time there idly and ill.'[30] But he was not the only bishop of the established church who was produced by a dissenting academy, for Joseph Butler, later Bishop of Durham, was educated at Tewkesbury, and while he was there carried on his famous correspondence with Dr. Samuel Clarke, which was later published. Butler is particularly relevant in this context, for he commented adversely on his own later education at Oxford in terms similar to those which Secker used of Attercliffe: 'we are obliged to misspend so much time here in attending frivolous lectures and unintelligible disputations that I am quite tired with such a disagreeable way of trifling.'

That the Establishment realised just how big a challenge these academies were offering to the universities of Oxford and Cambridge may be seen from the concerted attacks which were kept up throughout the early decades of the eighteenth century. Samuel Wesley's attack in 1702 was followed three years later by an official denunciation by the Irish Church. And when the second part of Clarendon's *History* was published in 1704, the writer of the dedication to the queen asked with a vehement rhetorical flourish that betrayed his uneasiness:

what can be the meaning of the several seminaries, and as it were universities, set up in divers parts of the kingdom, by more than ordinary industry, contrary to law, supported by large contributions, where the youth is bred up in principles directly contrary to monarchical and episcopal government?[31]

The answer is implicit in the foregoing pages, and can be further illustrated ten years later. For when in 1714 the Schism Act was passed to crush these academies (Lecky called it 'one of the most tyrannical measures enacted in the eighteenth century, especially shameful from the fact that those who took the most prominent part in carrying it were acting without the excuse of religious bigotry'), a notable exception was made of those which taught 'any part of mathematics relating to navigation, or any mechanical art'.[32] The practical aspect of their curricula was thus recognised to be a national necessity. Yet as late as 1732 a diocesan chancellor was prepared to institute legal proceedings against Philip Doddridge for opening an academy at Northampton.

8

Social needs stimulated a number of schemes for other sorts of academies. John Aubrey, also an F.R.S., drafted a scheme in 1684 and gave it to Elias Ashmole for safe-keeping. This was as lively as his *Lives*. His scheme was that six or seven establishments which should be 'both school and university' should be established in various parts of England to train the élite. A celibate Provost and celibate Informators were to superintend instruction in classics, mathematics, English, accounts, military science, drawing, and gentlemanly accomplishments. Boys were to remain till they were eighteen years old, and were then to go to Leyden rather than an English university. Such establishments were to be set up in Kensington, Lancashire, Wiltshire, Dorset, North Wales, Glamorgan, and Oxford, where 'it would be envied by the Colleges'. His latest biographer, Mr. Antony Powell, tells us that at the end of the manuscript Aubrey wrote: 'But now (methinkes) I see a black squadron marching from Oxford, led up by a crossier staffe to discomfort this pretty little Flock: and so this my pleasing Dream is all at an end', and then the name 'Dr. Fell'.[33]

Not all the black squadrons were blind to the serious condition of the existing universities. Bishop Burnet was so appalled by the deficient education of his ordinands that he determined to establish an episcopal school at Salisbury for them. As he wrote:

that on which my heart was most set was that which raised up such hatred against me especially at Oxford, and answered my expectations so little that after I had kept it up 5 years at the rate of 300*l*. a year I saw it was expedient to let it fall. I thought the greatest prejudice the Church was under was from the ill education of the Clergy. In the Universities they for the most part lost the learning they brought with them from schools, and learned so very little in them that too commonly they came from them less knowing than when they went to them.

His diocesan venture apparently lasted from 1689 until 1694. 'Those at Oxford,' he wrote, 'looked on this as a publike affront to them and to their way of education, so that they railed at me not only in the street but in their Acts unmercifully for it.'[34]

In his first book, published at Bristol in 1697, Daniel Defoe wrote, 'this is the projecting age . . . past ages have never come up to the degree of projecting or inventing . . . which we see this age arrived to'. Naturally enough, Defoe himself had his own particular project for an academy which should be erected by the public and sustained by revenues from the Crown. It was to consist of four colleges, and was to be four times as big as Chelsea College. Its list of studies was formidable: geometry, astronomy, navigation, arithmetic, trigonometry, dialling, gauging, mining, fireworking, bombarding, gunnery, fortification, encamping, intrenching, approaching, attacking, delineation, architecture, surveying, bodily exercises, and history. Its experiments, he continued, 'would be as well worth publishing as the acts of the Royal Society'. Were it established, he forecast that it would prove the greatest, gallantest, and most useful foundation in the world. He supplemented this by a further suggestion that every county should have an academy for women.[35]

Lewis Maidwell's scheme, embodied in a petition to the House of Commons in 1699, was for a public academy. For this, he offered a large house 'with spatious ground and outhouses, well-walled about' in which he proposed to erect an auditorium, and on which he proposed to settle a suitable endowment. He supported his petition by three pamphlets appealing for public support: the third of these outlined the subjects to be studied as 'navigation, surveying, mathematics, architecture, and modern languages'.

The universities were quickly aroused. When Maidwell's project was referred to a committee of the House of Commons, Dr. John Hough (President of Magdalen College, Oxford) wrote to Dr. Charlett (Master of University College): 'I do not beliefe tis possible to effect such a thing under any regulations whatsoever without prejudice to the Universitys.' Dr. Leopold Finch (Warden of All Souls), also wrote to Charlett: 'Of my own Accord I apply'd myself to my Ld. Weymouth to use his interest in the house of Commons to spoile Mr. Maidwel's Project, which by the best reasons I could urge I endeavoured to prove to be injurious to the two Universities.' Cambridge, in the person of Dr. Thomas Greene (Master of Corpus and Vice-Chancellor), was of like mind. 'I have this day wrote to Mr. Boyle, at the desire of all the heads,' he wrote to Charlett, 'to desire him and his Partner to use their utmost endeavours to put a stop to its further proceeding in the house.' Their efforts were rewarded. Maidwell was not only frustrated in this attempt, but two further attempts made in 1704–5 were similarly discouraged. For the universities feared the insidious precedent of his bill which 'might be stretcht to authorise him and future governours to set up teachers of University Learning . . . yea and of unsound Divinity too, though he praetends particularly onely to teaching mathematics, Navigation, fortification, etc. . . .'[36]

At the same time as Maidwell was finally discomfited, Jonathan Swift published a powerful satire on theological shams and pedantries in his *Tale of a Tub*.[37] 'Your Grace sees I am a projector too,' he wrote eight years later to Archbishop King, outlining his scheme for an academy to 'correct, improve, and ascertain the English tongue'. King encouraged him, adding that his scheme would fare better in peacetime, adding, 'I wish some other name were given it, for I find the generality so prejudiced against all French precedents that as parties are more formed I apprehend the name will be of great disadvantage'. It was. When peace did come, larger problems exercised the minds of statesmen, and yet another proposal was shelved.[38]

9

The 'mechanic trades' and 'manual arts' like agriculture, navigation, dyeing, clothing, building, furniture making, and printing, together with inventions to improve these were especially in the mind of Sprat when he wrote his *History of the Royal Society*. He pointed out that it was possible for such arts to reach higher stages of development, and argued that the artificers might learn something from an F.R.S. Thus:

> The Tradesmen themselves, having had their Hands directed from their Youth in the same Methods of Working, cannot when they please so easily alter their Custom, and turn themselves into new Roads of Practice. Besides this, they chiefly labour for present livelihood, and therefore cannot defer their Experiments so long, as is commonly requisite for the ripening of any new Contrivance. But especially having long handled their Instruments in the same Fashion, and regarded their Materials with the same Thoughts, they are not apt to be surpriz'd much with them, nor to have any extraordinary Fancies or Raptures about them. . . . Whereas the Men of Freer Lives have all the contrary advantages.[39]

The ideal was, of course, as Sprat acknowledged, 'when either the Mechanic Labourers shall have Philosophical Heads, or the Philosophers shall have mechanical Hands'. But until that time, other members of the Royal Society attempted to give a more vocational aspect to education generally. Two of these call for especial comment: Joseph Moxon and John Locke.

Joseph Moxon was a self-educated hydrographer and mathematician, who after settling in London became a prolific populariser of the new knowledge in astronomy, geography, architecture, and typography. But from our point of view, his most significant act was to publish a series of pamphlets on mechanical processes beginning on 1 January 1677. These were brought together as a volume entitled *Mechanick Exercises or the Doctrine of Handiworks* in 1683, which embodied the fourteen parts of his serial. His subjects show just how far the concept of vocational education had developed. 'Smithing; Hinges, Locks, Screws, Keys and Nuts; the Making of Jacks and Bullet Moulds, the Twisting of Iron, the Case Hardening of it: Also of several sorts of Steel, the manner of softening, hardening and tempering them; The Art of Joynery (in which the theory and application of tools is discussed); The Art of House-Carpentry; The Art of Turning'—these encompass a wealth of information on the technology of the day. Moxon said that he thought his was the first work of this character in the English language, and we might well believe him, since his outlook was wide and deep. As he said in the preface:

> The Lord Bacon in his Natural History reckons that Phylosophy would be improv'd by having the Secrets of all Trades lye open; not only because much Experimental Philosophy is Coucht among them: but also that the Trades themselves might by a Philosopher be improved. Besides, I find that one Trade may borrow many Eminent Helps in Work of another Trade.

Locke was a Fellow of the Royal Society (elected in 1668) and had taken a degree in medicine (in 1674). The development of natural sciences had a profound effect upon his thinking. In particular, it affected three of his writings: his *Essay on Human Understanding* (1690), *Some Thoughts Concerning Education* (1693), and his scheme for 'working schools' elaborated in 1697 when he was a Commissioner of Trade and Plantations. Locke openly admitted that 'of a great part of the learning now in fashion in the schools of Europe . . . a gentleman may in good measure be unfurnished with, without any great disparagement to himself or prejudice to his affairs'. Locke blessed the system of private education that now came into vogue, and by his bold and forceful empirical psychology reinforced the argument that individual exercise in habits of practical usefulness contributed more towards the development of a judicial and reflective capacity than education in the established curriculum of the universities. His opinions were shared by others who preferred foreign academies or private tutors for their sons. Admiral Penn sent his son William to Saumur, while Lord Wharton sent his sons to Caen under the chaperonage of Theophilus Gale. Indeed, for the next century, the great Whig houses were to serve as shelters and laboratories for men of science and learning, so that the position of tutor often meant that the intellectual could thereby establish himself near the centres of political and economic power.[40]

10

However they made a livelihood, whether gentleman virtuoso, or private tutor, or clergyman, many of those whom we have already met in the foregoing pages belonged to clubs. We know that coffee houses became, in the seventeenth century, centres of discussion. In 1660, James Harrington, author of *Oceana*, founded the 'Rota Club' in New Palace Yard, Westminster, as a 'free and open society of ingenious gentlemen'. Some idea of the procedure adopted in this and other coffee-house clubs like the one in Threadneedle Street kept by the Greek Constantine where F.R.S. used to meet, can be gathered from a pamphlet published in 1670 entitled *Character of a Coffee House*.

> A numerous company is present and each group is occupied with its subject. One is quoting classics, another admires Euclid, a third for a lecture, a fourth a conjecture, a fifth for a penny in the pound. Theology is introduced, Masques, Balls and plays are condemned. One cries up philosophy, and whether Harrington's Rota or Boyle's Virtuosa be the nobler design they determine. The company is mixed and prentice boys call for their coffee in Latin.

Some of them were forced to adopt almost the character of a secret society, so latitudinarian were their aims. Thus the Robin Hood Society, originally founded in 1613 by Sir Hugh Myddleton the great water engineer, threw open its doors to the public in 1667 in order to 'diffuse useful knowledge'. These doors were those of the Essex Head Tavern. The Society lasted right up to 1773, and has recently been described as 'undoubtedly . . . one of the great forums of the eighteenth century, and played an important rôle in educating the adult population of London'.[41]

Then there was the Kit-Cat Club, probably founded by the publisher Jacob Tonson at the Fountain Tavern in the Strand, where the club met for twenty years. Locke's friend John Somers, Sir Isaac

Newton and Sir Samuel Garth were members. Perhaps its outlook was best expressed by other members like Sir Richard Steele and J. Addison, whose weeklies like the *Tatler*, *Spectator*, and *Guardian* served as sounding boards for club opinion. As Addison himself said: 'I shall be ambitious to have it said of me that I have brought philosophy out of closets and libraries, schools and colleges, to dwell in clubs and assemblies, at tea-tables and in coffee-houses.' A third club, in which Swift and Pope were prominent, was the Brothers Society founded in 1709. This in turn gave birth to the Society for the Encouragement of Learning (1710–14).

These clubs were not confined to the metropolis either. At Salisbury, Peter Chubb, a member of the London Robin Hood Society, was president of a similar group, while John Henley lectured at Newport Market on a variety of subjects, urging that education should have a vocational bias. At Manchester a 'Mathematical Society' was founded in 1718, which instituted public lectures on mathematics, employing John Jackson to deliver them.[42]

Permeating these clubs, particularly those of the metropolis, was the Rosicrucian influence of the seventeenth century, slowly being transformed into the speculative Freemasonry of the eighteenth. And as evidence of the close link between the spread of scientific ideas through lectures and masonic ideas we have only to consider the fact that J. T. Desaguliers, the intimate of Isaac Newton and the pioneer of metropolitan courses in mechanical and experimental philosophy, was instrumental in regenerating the order in 1717, and became its third Grand Master in 1719. Other masons of note were also members of the clubs we have mentioned. The masonic lodges, as their historians have acknowledged, often employed lecturers 'who were learned men and gave exhibitions of skill in arts and sciences'.[43]

The scientism of such groups drew caustic comments from at least one member of them, Dean Swift, who ridiculed their activities. In the third part of his *Gulliver's Travels* (1726), Gulliver visits Laputa, where the mathematical preoccupations of king and people are so great that flappers have to strike them gently on the mouth and ears to remind them to speak and listen. Everything is in mathematical shapes: the meat and bread they eat, their houses, and clothes. Gulliver is measured for a suit by a tailor who, though he used a quadrant, a rule and compasses, returned with an atrocious fit. Even a pretty woman, he noted, was compared to a rhomb, a circle, or an ellipse. His most penetrating satire, however, was reserved for the capital city of Lagado. Throughout the whole kingdom, he wrote, 'there is not a town of any consequence without an Academy of Projectors'. As a result desolation prevailed:

In these colleges, the professors contrive new rules and methods of agriculture and building, and new instruments and tools for all trades and manufactures, whereby, as they undertake, one man shall do the work of ten; a palace may be built in a week, of materials so durable as to last for ever without repairing. All the fruits of the earth shall come to maturity at whatever season we think fit to choose, and increase an hundred-fold more than they do at present, with innumerable other happy proposals. The only inconvenience is, that none of these projects are yet brought to perfection, and in the mean time the whole country lies miserably waste, the houses in ruins, and the people without food or clothes. By all which, instead of being discouraged, they are fifty times more violently bent on prosecuting their schemes, driven on equally by hope and despair.

The Lagado Academy had, as its most venerable student, one who had been trying to reduce human excrement to original food. Others calcine ice into gunpowder, spin silk from spiders, and use bellows for intestinal operations. Their speculations revolve around the condensation of air, the softening of marble, the petrifying of horses' hooves, and the sowing of chaff, and the rearing of a woolless sheep. One ambitious savant had even invented a mechanical epitome of knowledge.[44]

II

Swift's friend, and his Vanessa's legatee, was George Berkeley. In the very year in which *Gulliver's Travels* was published, the House of Commons debated Berkeley's own project for establishing a great Anglo-American University at Bermuda. With only two dissentients, they agreed that Berkeley should receive certain lands in the island of St. Christopher as an endowment. Private charity subscribed a further £3,400, and in 1728 Berkeley set sail.

Berkeley's original idea was to found a centre of Christian civilisation at Bermuda, where learning and enthusiasm were to be used for the enlightenment of the colonies. From this fountain or reservoir (the metaphor was Berkeley's) rivulets of learning and religion were to stream through all parts of America, 'purging away the ill manners and irreligion of our colonies, as well as the blindness and barbarity of the nations around them; especially if the reservoir be in a clean and private place'. Berkeley as President was to be assisted by nine Fellows, who were to have the power of making statutes, conferring degrees in all faculties, and be enabled to receive benefactions as a corporation.

The unhappy issue of his project has been recently told by Professor

Luce. Short-sighted politicians like Lord Townshend, enmeshed in European politics, thought that the dependencies would cease to be dependent if Berkeley's scheme was carried out: with Lord Wilmington, he held that Britain's interests lay in Europe not overseas. The Duke of Dorset, then Lord Lieutenant of Ireland, where Berkeley held the deanery of Derry, was persuaded that Berkeley was a madman for deserting his deanery, where there were Papists to convert, for Bermuda where there were none. Who, added another, would go to Bermuda, but a Don Quixote, since nothing was there to nourish men beyond onions and cabbages.

Berkeley himself soon realised how thin were the prospects of success. Within a fortnight of arriving in Rhode Island, he wrote to a friend saying that he 'would not demur one moment' about establishing his college in America itself. Friends who should have promoted his interests became too engrossed in promoting their own. Finally the Bishop of London bluntly asked the Prime Minister when the promised grant would materialise, and Walpole characteristically replied that Berkeley had better return home.

So, in the October of 1731, Berkeley came back to England, his project unrealised. But, as Professor Rand has shown, his visit was an educational event of the first magnitude. The enduring value of his inspiration and influence was recognised by the celebration, on 23 January 1929, of the bicentenary of his arrival. Directly, his stimulus was great: Jan Smibert, who had helped him dispose of Vanessa's pictures and accompanied him to America, stayed on to become the pioneer of American art; and Peter Harrison, another disciple, of American architecture. Indirectly, the interaction of Berkeley's ideas with those of the American Samuel Johnson, influenced both men: 'to his influence,' writes Professor Rand, 'are most largely due the enduring characteristic idealistic tendencies in America.'[45] Indeed, in the composition of *Alciphron, or the Minute Philosopher*—the product of Berkeley's enforced abstention from college-founding—Johnson's opinions might well be those of Crito and Berkeley's those of Euphranor, a supposition which is confirmed by Johnson's dedication of his own *Elementa Philosophica* to Berkeley some twenty years later.

On American universities, Berkeley exercised a great influence. Columbia University (when King's College) owed much to his advice during its inception, especially through Samuel Johnson. The present University of Pennsylvania owed a similar debt. The moneys subscribed for his own Bermudian college were returned to the donors with Berkeley's advice that they be given to Yale, as the college which 'came nearest' to his own plans. To Yale too went his library, described by the rector in 1766 as 'the finest collection . . . that ever came together at one time into America'.[46] Today, symbolising this very influence, the seat of the University of California is a town bearing his name.

12

The attraction of the Americas to academic reformers was no new thing. Dr. J. Beale of Somerset wrote to Robert Boyle on 31 October 1666:

> SIR—I have moved Mr. Oldenburg to find a way to use Sir Robert Atkins the recorder of Bristol, and what means else he could to frequent the correspondence with our American Plantations, and more particularly with New England, amongst whom there is some fear of God, but too notional in the bulk of wavering creeds. They may grow as we shrink. They are the granary, and husbandmen for all other colonies. They begin for a university, and by the paucity of seducing libraries, and the necessity of useful and accommodable supplies, may be at leisure, to be imbued with our suggestions. And it is fit to put new wine into new vessels.[47]

For over half a century talent had been flowing across the Atlantic, fertilising Harvard, and founding newer colleges. Charles Morton, hounded from the Islington nonconformist academy, became, in S. E. Morison's words, 'the principal agent for spreading in New England the scientific discoveries of the age of genius'.[48] Leonard Hoar, too, found in Harvard a haven where he could essay the educational practices of the Royal Society: building 'a large well-sheltered garden and orchard for students addicted to planting; an ergasterium for mechanic fancies; and a laboratory chimical for those philosophers, that by their senses would culture their understandings . . . for readings and notions only are but husky provender',[49] as he told Robert Boyle.

Theophilus Gale left his library to Harvard, and Penn projected his great scheme for religious toleration in the state which now bears his name. Such activity persuaded those wealthy but obscure nonconformist merchants that their money was better left to such foundations than to the closed, restricted corporations in old England. And significantly enough, in the very year in which Berkeley returned to England, a wealthy South Yorkshire merchant left a large sum of money to found chairs of mathematics, natural philosophy, and divinity, as well as ten scholarships, to Harvard. But for the unhappy history of the previous sixty years, it might well have been diverted to a university in his own home county. The bequest of Thomas Hollis afforded a text for the times.[50]

REFERENCES

1. See *The Record of the Royal Society* (4th ed. London, 1940); C. R. Weld, *A History of the Royal Society* (London, 1848), Dorothy Stimson, *Scientists and Amateurs* (London, 1949), and various articles in *Notes and Records of the Royal Society*.

2. *Life and Times*, ed. A. Clarke (Oxford, 1891).

3. SYFRET, Rosemary, 'Some Early Reactions to the Royal Society', in *Notes and Records of the Royal Society*, VII (1950), 220.

4. MATTHEWS, A. G., *Calamy Revised* (Oxford, 1934), xiii-xvi.

5. ROUSE BALL, W. W., *Cambridge Notes* (1921), 258.

6. LANGE, F. A., *History of Materialism* (trans. E. C. Thomas), London, 1877, i, 315. See 'The Newtonian Epoch', in W. C. D. Dampier-Whetham, *A History of Science and its Relation with Philosophy and Religion* (Cambridge, 1929), 160–216, *op. cit.*

7. See 'The Oxford of Antony à Wood', in C. E. Mallet, *History of University of Oxford*, ii, 405–63.

8. WALLIS, P. J., 'The Wase School Collection', in *Bodleian Library Record* (August, 1952), 78–104.

9. *Correspondence of Scientific Men of the Seventeenth Century*, ed. Stephen J. Rigaud (Oxford, 1841), 1, 158–9.

10. *Collecteana*, 1, VI, 298–9.

11. See Phyllis Allen, 'Scientific Studies in the English Universities of the Seventeenth Century', *Journal of the History of Ideas* (1949), X, 243.

12. COOPER, C. H., *Annals of Cambridge* (Cambridge, 1852), IV, 53.

13. STIMSON, *op. cit.*, 77.

14. *ibid.*, 87, Syfret, *op. cit.*, 227ff.

15. BORGMAN, A. S., *Thomas Shadwell* (New York, 1928), 161–73.

16. WOODCOCK, G., *The Incomparable Aphra* (London, 1948), 185–92.

17. DEAN, G. C. T., *The Royal Hospital, Chelsea* (London, 1950), 31–2.

18. CLARK, G. N., *Science and Social Welfare in the Age of Newton* (Oxford, 1948), 14.

19. For Staphorst see *Notes and Queries*, CXCVII (1952), 390–1, and CXCVIII (1953), and for the others see R. H. Semple, *Memoirs of the Botanic Garden at Chelsea* (1878).

20. MUNK, W., *The Roll of the College of Physicians* (London, 1878), ii, 40 and 60.

21. FRY, A. Ruth, *John Bellers 1654–1725* (London, 1935), 109–38.

22. PAYNE, J. F., *Thomas Sydenham* (London, 1890), 193.

23. GUNTHER, R. T., *Early Science at Oxford*, 21–42, 43, 51–61.

24. WHITTAKER, Sir E., *A History of the Theories of Aether and Electricity* (London, 1951), 41–3.

25. GIBB, F. W., 'Peter Shaw and the Revival of Chemistry', *Annals of Science* (London, 1951), VII, 213 n.13.

26. WALKER, J. W., 'Medicine in Seventeenth Century Yorkshire', in *Yorkshire Archaeological Society Transactions* (1947), xxvi, 288–96.

27. ARMYTAGE, W. H. G., 'Francis Jessop 1636–1691: A Seventeenth Century Scientist', in *Notes and Queries*, CXCVII (1952), 343–6.

28. PARKER, I., *Dissenting Academies in England* (Cambridge, 1917).
29. MCLACHLAN, H., *English Education under the Test Acts* (Manchester, 1931), 77.
30. ARMYTAGE, W. H. G., 'Attercliffe Academy', in *Sheffield University Gazette* (1949), v, 2-3.
31. *Cambridge History of English Literature* (1912), ix, 394.
32. LECKY, W. E. H., *History of England in the Eighteenth Century* (London, 1888), i, 95. It is worth noting that John Eames, F. R. S., a tutor in the Fund Academy, Moorfields, was not only a friend of Isaac Newton, but also, with John Martyn, F. R. S.—an apothecary—responsible for the 1719-32 abridgement of the *Philosophical Transactions.*
33. POWELL, Antony, *John Aubrey and his Friends* (London, 1948), 283-7.
34. CLARKE, John, *Bishop Gilbert Burnet as Educationist* (Aberdeen, 1914), 138-9.
35. DEFOE, D., *Essay on Projects* (1697). For other suggested women's colleges see John Duncon, *Lady Lettice, Vi-Countess Falkland* (ed. M. F. Howard. London, 1908) and Mary Astell, *A Serious Proposal to the Ladies* (London 1697); the latter opposed by Bishop Burnet and ridiculed by the *Tatler* (Nos. 32, 59 & 63).
36. *Collectanea, First Series* ed. C. R. L. Fletcher (Oxford Historical Society, 1885), 291-4.
37. STARKMAN, M. K., *Swift's Satire on Learning in A Tale of a Tub* (Princeton, 1950).
38. BALL, F. Elrington, *The Correspondence of Jonathan Swift* (London, 1910), 325, 331, 347-8.
39. *Philosophical Transactions*, No. 255, August, 1698.
40. LOCKE, John, *Some Thoughts Concerning Education* (1693), 94. Even the university libraries were in poor shape and scholars had to rely on those of the aristocracy, see David Douglas, *English Scholars 1660–1730* (London, 1951), 264–5.
41. HANS, N., *New Trends in Education in the Eighteenth Century* (1951), 168-71.
42. *ibid.*
43. KNOOP, D., and JONES, G. P., *The Genesis of Freemasonry* (Manchester, 1947).
44. EDDY, W. A., *A Critical Study of Gulliver's Travels* (Princeton, 1923), 157-70.
45. RAND, B., *Berkeley's American Sojourn* (Cambridge, Mass., 1932), 70.
46. LUCE, A. A., *Life of George Berkeley* (London, 1949), 148, who adds 'it helped to turn an academy into a university'.
47. MASSON, J. I. O., *Three Centuries of Chemistry* (London, 1927), 48-52.
48. MORISON, S. E., *Harvard College in the Seventeenth Century* (Cambridge, Mass., 1936), i, 249.
49. MASSON, I., *op. cit.*, 53, who comments, 'This design, if it was carried out, would give probably the earliest specially built chemical laboratory in the world.'
50. GUEST, J., *Historic Notes of Rotherham* (Worksop, 1879).

CHAPTER SEVEN

The Rise of Corporate Patronage, 1731-1810

ROUND about the year 1731, Malachy Postlethwayte set about the compilation of *The Universal Dictionary of Trade and Commerce*; a task that engaged him for the next twenty years. In this, as in his other works, he showed the preoccupation of his generation with the 'arts', which not only kept 'the mass of people in useful action', but also kept 'their minds engaged upon inventions'. It was his firm belief that such 'arts' were mechanical, and furthermore, he contended that they would improve the mind more than any form of ideal speculation.[1]

Such emphasis was not new. Sir William Petty and the founders of the Royal Society had pointed out that such arts were on a par with land, labour, and capital as the fourth pillar of a country's greatness. 'Arts, and mills, and engines,' said Petty, 'save the labour of many human beings.' Defoe, embroidering the theme, contended that in Russia labour was not assisted by art, and was therefore, technologically speaking, backward. For the Russians 'had no other way to cut a large plank, but by felling a great tree, and then with a multitude of hands and axes hew away all sides of the timber, till they reduc'd the middle to one large plank'. The 'artful' method would have been to 'cut three or four, or more planks of like size from one tree by the help of saws and sawmills'.

Postlethwayte carried this idea to its logical conclusion when he said that such arts should be encouraged by the State, which would thus be fostering invention and discovery. He suggested that a Mercantile College should be established which among other things should preserve 'accounts of many distinguished and eminent merchants deceased'. By so doing, civilisation would improve, for, as David Hume went on to elaborate 'the same age which produces great philosophers and politicians, renowned generals and poets, also abounds with skilful weavers and ships' carpenters.'[2]

I

There was a feeling that London should afford such instruction in the arts. Three years before he died in 1731, Daniel Defoe opened a pamphlet on the means by which London might become the most flourishing city in the universe by suggesting the establishment of a university.[3] The idea persisted, and on 31 March 1742 it was announced that:

> At the East End of Exeter Change in the Strand, this evening at 6 o'clock will be opened the London University, where all liberal Arts and Sciences will be most usefully, critically and demonstratively taught in the mother tongue in proper courses of lectures, composed by men of the greatest learning and delivered with good address, so as to be entertaining to all. . . . The opening lecture will be a rational view of the nature, reality, origin extent, past and present state of all liberal Arts and Sciences with the means of improving them.[4]

Nothing came of this, nor of a similar scheme conceived by Dennis Chevalier de Coetlogon, who opened an Academy of Sciences three years later, following it with a *Universal Dictionary of Arts and Sciences.*

As the centre where the nobility of the kingdom tended to congregate, London nourished a number of societies for the encouragement of the arts and sciences. Peter Shaw, an associate of Hauksbee, edited the works of both Bacon and Boyle, published in 1731, *Proposals for a course of chemical experiments with a view to practical philosophy, arts, trade and business,* and in that and the following year conducted a course for over twenty students at a fee of five guineas each. His 'noble audience' requested the publication of his lectures, and Lord Lonsdale, amongst others, read them. These seem to have been the first public lectures on chemistry to have been delivered in the metropolis.

Other public lecturers on natural and experimental philosophy followed. Dr. Triboudet Demainbray, F.R.S., who discovered the influence of electricity in stimulating the growth of plants, delivered a course in 1754-5. So too did Benjamin Martin, James Ferguson, and Dr. Bryan Higgins. The last named founded a school of practical chemistry in Greek Street, Soho, in 1774, and a Society for Philosophical Experiments and Communications whose members made contributions of papers.[5]

Bishop Sprat had urged the gentlemen of England to become experimental philosophers, and in 1731 was born one who followed that precept throughout his life: Henry Cavendish. Grandson of the second duke of Devonshire, Cavendish was a millionaire who used his fortune, not only to experiment in the natural sciences, but also to disseminate a knowledge of them. For not only did he discover the constitution of water and air, experiment in electricity, and gauge the density of the earth, but he also maintained three houses. One, at the corner of Montague Street and Gower Street, was furnished with books and apparatus; at another, in Clapham, he maintained a laboratory, forge, and observation platform; while a third in Dean Street, Soho, he furnished with 'a large and carefully chosen library of works on science', open to all engaged in research. To this he would go for his own books, signing a formal receipt for such as he took away with him.[6]

Fellow noblemen, if they could not emulate his achievements, followed similar paths. Some extended their patronage to scientists, and others became generous patrons of the arts in a more aesthetic sense, and in 1734 associated as the Dilettanti Society, meeting once a week with elaborate ritual to toast 'Viva la Virtù'. History, poetry, philosophy, and theology were discussed in gay convivial sessions ostensibly devoted to painting. To young men of promise in the arts—liberally interpreted to include sculpture and architecture—they afforded the present day equivalent of travelling scholarships. One of their members, Lord Charlemont, suggested and led an expedition to Smyrna, taking with him Richard Chandler the antiquarian and Nicholas Revett the architect. From this was written *Ionian Antiquities* (1769) and *Inscriptiones Antiquae* (1774) which played their part in fostering the classicism of the period. Their efforts inspired Sir Osbert Sitwell to observe: 'these untoiling butterflies accomplished more for English art than all the labouring stage elephants of the next century.'[7]

2

Association was not limited to noble patrons: it grew among those whom they had patronised. By association, professional feeling and standards were fostered. Attorneys and solicitors began the custom. Soon after the passing of the Act of 1729 which initiated a system of practical training for those appearing before the courts, they formed a 'Society of Gentlemen Practisers in the Courts of Law and Equity'. Soon after its foundation in 1734 this began to be known as the Law Society. It mooted a 'Royal College of Attorneys-at-Law and Solicitors', which never came to fruition because the sponsors could not agree whether they wished to be incorporated by Royal Charter or by Act of Parliament. In that same year 1734, the artists established their own dining-club at the Foundling Hospital, and conceived the idea of holding exhibitions of their work in order to raise money. This grew, after many vicissitudes, into the Royal Academy, formally founded in 1768 'for the purpose of cultivating and improving the arts of painting, sculpture, and architecture'. They undertook to train students and raise funds by exhibition, and for nearly a century they remained as the sole institution affording training in such subjects.[8]

Other professional groups clubbed together, usually in taverns, to discuss matters concerning their craft. Dr. Johnson's met at Horseman's chop-house in Ivy Lane, and he acknowledged that 'the tavern chair' was to him 'the throne of human felicity'. Similarly, the great Leeds engineer Smeaton, whose ingenuity helped to carve canals across the face of England and stud it with bridges, initiated the club which bore his name. It later developed into the Society of Civil Engineers. In 1771 it was proposed to him 'that it would be well, if some sort of an occasional meeting, in a friendly way, was to be held . . . that thus the sharp edges of their minds might be rubbed off, as it were, by a close communication of ideas, no ways naturally hostile; might promote the true end of public business upon which they should happen to meet in the course of their employment'. Similarly the architects associated twenty years later.

A sign of the private patron's displacement was the State purchase of Montague House in 1753. This, one of the few private palaces in London, was purchased by the Treasury to house the once private collections of Sir Hans Sloane and Lord Oxford. These, together with the Cottonian collection (already purchased in 1730, twenty-three years before) served as the basis for the British Museum collection, the finest and widest collection of human accomplishments yet established. In 1757 King George II gave yet another 10,000 volumes and 1,800 manuscripts to the many thousands comprising the other three collections, with the further privilege that the British Museum should obtain a free copy of every book entered at Stationers' Hall. This vast quarry for students of the arts and sciences, unlike the private collections of the virtuosi of the preceding century, was open to everybody. As a repository of knowledge and learning, the English-speaking world had not yet seen its equivalent, and rivulets from its vast and ever-increasing store trickled down to irrigate and animate less comprehensive efforts elsewhere. One of the correspondents of Bishop Berkeley's widow was 'delighted to see Science in this Town so Magnificently and Elegantly lodged', but confessed her uneasiness that it might prove 'a storehouse of Arms open to every Rebel Hand'. There was little of the rebel about one of the earliest readers—Thomas Gray—who often 'passed through the jaws of the great Leviathan into the belly of Dr. Templeman, Super-Intendant of the Reading Room'.[9]

3

'Encouragement is much the same to Arts and Sciences as culture is to vegetables: they always advance and flourish in proportion to the awards they acquire and the honours they obtain.' Such were the sentiments of a Northampton drawing master, William Shipley, whose brother was a great friend of Benjamin Franklin. He wished to raise a fund by subscription in order to distribute premiums for improvements in the Liberal Arts and Sciences and Manufactures.

He failed to secure support in the locality, and went to London. There a Turkey merchant and his brother-in-law (Viscount Folkestone and Lord Romney) proved sympathetic and enthusiastic, and largely by their efforts a 'Society for the Encouragement of Arts, Manufactures and Commerce in Great Britain' was founded on 22 March 1754. Other promoters included Defoe's son-in-law, Henry Baker; a director of the Bank of England, Gustavus Brander; a botanist with a laboratory at Teddington, Stephen Hales; a surgeon, Husband Messiter; a watchmaker, Nicholas Crisp; and an optician, James Short. Within eight years, more than 2,500 other members had joined, and the annual income of the society was £4,614. In 1765 they were formally associated.

Shipley's successor as secretary was Dr. Peter Templeman, who had previously been keeper of the Reading Room at the newly established British Museum. He was a physician who had graduated at Leyden in 1737, and an assiduous correspondent with learned foreigners. That the society grew so extensively under him was due primarily to the fact that it supplied a great want. Public Health, Agriculture, Forestry, Colonial Affairs, Trade and Technology all came within the purview of the Society's operations, and premiums were freely offered for ideas and practicable suggestions in these fields. Six specialist committees were set up to deal with suggestions, and a repository was established. The provinces showed interest: the Corporation of Liverpool sent a subscription of £100 to help along the work.[10]

Other supporters included eleven dukes, two marquesses, fifty-one earls, and twenty-five barons. Many professional groups also adhered; the architects were represented by the Adam brothers (who built the premises for the Society in the Adelphi, occupied since 1774), Chambers, Dance, and Paine; scientists by Henry Cavendish, Franklin, and Morton; bankers by Baring, Coutts, and Drummond; medical men by Addington, Fothergill, Hunter, and Pitcairne; painters by Hogarth and Reynolds; and musicians by Arne. In this stimulating society, the men of letters like Johnson, Boswell, Goldsmith, Richardson, and

Sterne found much to interest them. Johnson in fact found that the meetings which he attended were so distinguished that when he tried to speak 'all his flowers of oratory forsook him'.

The impact of the Society's work can be traced in many spheres of national life, chiefly in agriculture, then the country's staple industry. Arthur Young, who was chairman of the Committee on Agriculture in 1774 (the year after he was elected to fellowship of the Royal Society) wrote in 1784, 'it is probable that the Kingdom has been benefited a thousand pounds for every guinea these men have expended'. To secure adequate supplies of winter meat in the days when most people lived off salt meat, the society offered prizes for winter food for cattle. These resulted in the cultivation of the swede and the mangel-wurzel by English farmers. Their premiums were distributed for improvements in the quality and yield of wheat, barley, oats, and rye; for new grasses and roots; for better techniques of cultivating; for new types of agricultural machinery; for manures; and for soil analysis. Not the least of its efforts was to promote afforestation: source of the country's fuel and ship-building material. Over fifty million trees were planted as a result. The Duke of Beaufort received a gold medal for raising oaks in Gloucestershire, and Colonel Thomas Jones received six gold medals for planting four million trees in Cardiganshire.

Benjamin Franklin was chairman of the Committee on Colonies in 1761. It did much to extend its activities on the mainland of North America. The famous Captain Bligh qualified for a gold medal for transplanting bread-fruit and other plants to the West Indies, and later medallists included John McArthur, the founder of the Australian wool trade.

Not the least of the Society's activities was the active encouragement of drawing, as the basis of technical instruction. In the first century of their existence, over three thousand awards were made, among the recipients being such notables as Sir Thomas Lawrence, Sir Charles Eastlake, and Sir John Millais. To further this interest in art, the Society held exhibitions, and in 1760 the first public exhibition of contemporary art was staged. This was so successful that a year later another exhibition, one of agricultural machinery, was held.

4

The Society for the Encouragement of Arts, Manufactures and Commerce in Great Britain, usually known as the Society of Arts, was supported most strongly by the medical profession, as rigid a hierarchy as existed anywhere at the time. Entry to this profession was in 1731 through two main channels: the university or apprenticeship. University training by-passed Oxford and Cambridge, and generally ran through Edinburgh or Leyden, and in some cases both. Apprenticeship, usually to an apothecary, was the custom. The Bevan brothers in London, or such typical provincial apothecaries as Benjamin Bartlett of Bradford not only maintained 'a seminary of ingenious physicians', but also contributed much to the intellectual life of their districts. For the Apothecaries had grown steadily in status since 1703, when the House of Lords gave their famous decision in the case of *The Royal College of Physicians* v. *Rose*, that apothecaries were not only to dispense medicine, but also entitled to prescribe. Nineteen years later they were empowered by Act of Parliament to inspect the stocks of their members and in 1748 were yet further empowered to examine all persons dispensing drugs within a seven-mile radius of London.[11]

Moreover, from 1732 onwards, their Physic Garden at Chelsea was extensively reorganised 'for the improvement of useful knowledge' and became a nursery of a number of distinguished botanists. The great Linnaeus, pioneer of the sexual system of classification of plants, visited it four years later, and was much impressed with the achievements of Isaac Rand, the demonstrator, and Philip Miller, the gardener. Both these men became Fellows of the Royal Society, and Miller, in the course of nearly half a century's work at Chelsea, was responsible for a gardeners' dictionary which ran to eight editions in his own lifetime, and long after his death was reissued with additions by Thomas Martyn, the Regius Professor of Botany at Cambridge. Miller's son, in fact, became the first curator of the Botanic Garden established at that university, and it was under Miller that Sir Joseph Banks learnt the first rudiments of botany.

Of the many distinguished apothecary-trained scientists, space will only permit mention of three who adorned other fields than medicine. The first, William Hudson, was the first botanist in England to adopt the Linnaean system of classification in his *Flora Anglica* (1762), published a year after he was elected F.R.S. The second, William Cookworthy, an apprentice of the Bevans', discovered the Cornish deposits of china clay and can be considered the founder of the English porcelain industry based on their use. The third, William Watson, sent an electric current along the Thames in 1747, gave the Leyden jar its present form, and, by observing that electric sparks could be transmitted for some distance through an exhausted glass tube, anticipated the discovery of cathode and X-rays.

Other apothecary-trained doctors, who reinforced their qualifications by further study, played their part in the advancement of medical education in the metropolis. John Fothergill, a Quaker, assembled in 1752 a number of hospital physicians to discuss various diseases and their cures. From these meetings emerged *Medical Observations and Inquiries*, a publication lasting from 1757 to 1784. He also inspired the Licentiates of the Royal College of Physicians to break through the cordon which limited fellowship of that body to graduates of Oxford and Cambridge. When that attempt failed, he founded the Society of Licentiate Physicians, which met once a fortnight to read papers to each other on the newest medical and surgical discoveries. His own range of scientific correspondence was wide: Dr. William Cuming of Dorchester, Dr. Falconer of Bath, and Dr. Percival of Manchester were some of his many English correspondents, while his numerous American friends included the Bartrams, Franklin, and Benjamin Rush. His own collections of shells and drawings were inherited by William Hunter.[12] His fellow-Quaker, John Lettsom, worked in much the same way, proposing in 1773 the formation of the Medical Society of London. This was the first professional group to embrace surgeons, physicians, and apothecaries, three members of each being represented on its governing council. For fifteen years it met in Crane Court, and at the end of that time he endowed it with buildings in Bolt Court, near by. The names of both these pioneers are commemorated in the Lettsomian and Fothergillian Lecture foundations.[13]

But these societies, important as they were, depended for their success upon the hospitals: these cradled the new ideas. The heavy load of London's sick, borne since the Reformation by St. Bartholomew's and St. Thomas's, had been as we have seen, redistributed among a number of new foundations. The Westminster was founded in 1719 by the banker Henry Hoare and Samuel Wesley; Guy's in 1725 by the bookseller Thomas Guy; and St. George's in 1733 with the help of the Court.

St. Thomas's had students in 1695 and in 1740 when the London Hospital was founded permission was given for a 'pupil in surgery' to be entered on the books, who was to receive a certificate at the end of his course. By 1782 the London Hospital was fully organised as a teaching hospital. The opportunities of first-hand clinical practice afforded by these and subsequent foundations encouraged the formation of medical schools, whose teachers became famous in the history of medicine. John Freke, Edward Nourse, Percivall Pott, the Pitcairns, and John Abernethy at St. Bartholomew's; Cheselden at St. Thomas's;

and William Hunter at St. George's were some of those whose work so effectively lowered the death rate of the country, that the population began to increase by leaps and bounds.[14] Such medical instruction was at first opposed, partly because it was described as less efficient, partly because it was suspected of changing the 'prentice apothecary into a city surgeon in a matter of months. Indeed, as late as 1783 John Hunter was at first opposed when he tried to set up a medical school at St. George's on the lines of that existing at Guy's.

This tradition of medical teaching resulted in the establishment of private medical schools. William Hunter established such a school in Great Windmill Street, where he collected a museum of useful specimens, now preserved in Glasgow University, and his brother John, who first arrived in London in 1748, had a distinguished roll of pupils, many of whom also opened medical schools. These pupils, Abernethy, Astley Cooper, Cline, Clift, Parkinson, Blizard, Home, Alanson, Wright Post, and Physick carried his experimental skills across two continents. Perhaps the best known was Edward Jenner, pioneer of vaccination, whose statue was erected in Boulogne, Brünn, and Kensington Gardens, as well as his native Gloucester. Even a mystic like William Blake could draw inspiration from 'Jack Tearguts' (as Hunter appears in *An Island on the Moon*), confessing

> . . . every Generated Body in its inward form
> Is a garden of delight & a building of magnificence.

Few poets reviled natural science so much as Blake, yet few owed it more.

These medical lecturers often spanned the whole range of natural philosophy as it was then known. Thus George Fordyce, who began a thirty-year teaching career in 1759 when he was only twenty-three, devoted his attention to agriculture and chemistry as well as publishing the standard medical text-book of the period *The Elements of the Practice of Physic* in 1770. His chemical researches, published in the *Philosophical Transactions* of the Royal Society (of which body he became a Fellow in 1776) show that he was working towards the same solution of the problem of phlogiston as Priestley and Lavoisier, though by a different way. In 1787 he was elected F.R.C.P. although such an honour was reserved almost exclusively for Oxford and Cambridge graduates. Undoubtedly his work at St. Thomas's Hospital (where he was physician from 1770–1802) affords a classic example of the intellectual span possessed by many of these medical teachers in the eighteenth century.

Indeed, medical specialisms extended in all directions. As an index of this, the Surgeons, inspired by the brilliant teacher William Cheselden, decided to sever their corporate connection with the barbers, to whom they had been linked for over two hundred years. So in 1745 the City Company of Barber Surgeons was split into two separate companies. The Barbers were left to their wigmaking, with the hall, library and plate of the old company. The Surgeons, appropriating the Arris (1643) and Gale (1698) foundations for public lectures, were reconstituted as the 'Masters, Governors, and Commonalty of the Art and Science of Surgeons of London'. This new body was empowered to examine and license all practitioners of surgery within London and a seven miles radius of it. Though they lost vigour and interest at the close of the century, by 1800 they were re-chartered as the Royal College of Surgeons of London, and forty-three years later became the Royal College of Surgeons of England. And not a little credit for securing the charter goes to William Blizard, whose enthusiasm for medical education had led him to find most of the cost of the London Hospital Medical School in 1785.[15]

In the provinces, too, hospital founding proceeded. Liverpool (1749), Newcastle (1751), Manchester (1752), Leeds (1767), Leicester (1771), Birmingham (1779), Nottingham (1782), Hull (1784), Durham (1793), and Sheffield (1797) were ten of seventy-nine which had been founded by the first quarter of the nineteenth century. At the same time, it was calculated that of the six thousand practising surgeons and physicians then recorded, not more than a hundred possessed a university qualification. As to which provincial centre was the first in the field of medical education, opinions differ. Vincent and Hinton, in their recent history of the University of Birmingham, published in 1947, claim that John Tomlinson, surgeon to the Town Infirmary, 'was the first surgeon outside London ever to offer any regular anatomical lectures'. This was 'in about the year 1768'. Yet it is on record that Page and Ford were giving similar lectures in the old Barber Surgeons' theatre at Bristol from 1746.[16] But whatever town claims pride of primacy, the fact remains that during this period such lectures were becoming increasingly common, and were to lead directly to the establishment of medical schools early in the following century. Even Oxford, 'moved', as her historian writes, 'by jealousy if not by science', hastily summoned an anatomy lecturer from London.[17] Moreover, some of these provincial practitioners were themselves cultural beacons in their districts. James Currie of Liverpool was the editor and biographer of Robert Burns; Samuel Kay of Manchester acted as a peripatetic lecturer on natural philosophy in 1743, popularising the work of Newton, Boyle, and others; and John Heysham at Carlisle made observations on births, deaths, and marriages which formed the basis of the Carlisle Mortality Table drawn up by Joshua Milne. This table formed for many years the basis on which insurance companies used to calculate their premiums. Perhaps the most eminent of these provincial medical men was John Roebuck who abandoned his profession to concentrate on the refining of metals and the mass-production of sulphuric acid. By so doing, he became one of the leading figures in the so-called Industrial Revolution.

5

John Roebuck was a dissenter, educated, before graduating at Edinburgh and Leyden, at the Northampton Academy. This, one of the most distinguished of its kind, began in 1729 and flourished till 1751, for the last twelve years of which it was housed in the former home of the Earl of Halifax. Nor was Roebuck the only industrial pioneer to be so educated, for John Wilkinson, who established the first blast furnace in this country and bored the accurate cylinders which made possible the efficient use of the steam engine, was educated at Kendal Academy. Kendal lasted from 1733 until 1753, and possessed 'a considerable apparatus in mechanics and hydrostatics'.[18] Not only as vestibules for the Scottish and foreign universities, but as institutions of advanced education in themselves, these academies attracted pupils from the nobility as well as the mercantile classes. It is to these that Dissent probably owed its close connection with the industrial innovations of the time, and the latest historian of the Industrial Revolution, Professor T. S. Ashton, has acknowledged that 'broadly speaking, the Nonconformists constituted the better educated section of the middle classes'.[19] It was this superior education, rather than their exclusion from Oxford and Cambridge (though the two are of course interconnected) which animated them to become the architects of the industrial state. Indeed, the catalogue of their achievements is an impressive one. The Huntsmans of Sheffield pioneered in the casting of steel, the Darbys of Wolverhampton in the smelting of iron ore by coke, and as Dr. Raistrick has recently shown, other members of the Society of Friends were responsible for similar innovations in clockmaking, banking, pharmacy, brewing, and corn-milling.[20] James Watt was a Presbyterian. So attached were these dissenting industrialists to the Dissenting Academies, that Joshua Walker, a member of the great iron-founding family second only to Wilkinson in the magnitude of their enterprises, built a magnificent collegia building to house such an institution in Rotherham.[21] Dr. Warwick, Unitarian minister in that town, made notable discoveries in the art c fast dyeing. He started a business with his brother-in-law in 1801, an at the same time began a series of Sunday afternoon lectures o physiology. On leaving the town he undertook similar lectures else where, and went on to invent a new type of microscope.

Some idea of this superior education can be obtained from the histor of Warrington Academy, which justified its reputation as the 'Ather of the North', by educating, during its existence from 1757 to 178 over a hundred business men, twenty-four lawyers, and twenty-on doctors. Its driving force was Joseph Priestley, whose chemic researches isolated such gases as nitrous oxide, hydrogen chlorid ammonia, sulphur dioxide, nitrogen peroxide, carbon monoxid and oxygen.[22] He caught up and made current the electrical discoveri of Benjamin Franklin. Yet Priestley was in addition a teacher of ra depth and breadth of vision; his introduction of the study of histor and politics at Warrington was so successful that when his lectur were published, the professor of modern history at Cambridge sa fit to recommend them. Nor was Priestley the only bright star in th cluster that adorned Warrington; for John Reinhold Forster left t travel with Captain Cook on his second voyage, and was later appointe to a chair at the University of Halle, then at the zenith of its reputatio To Warrington came students from as far afield as the West Indie then not only the sugar bowl of Europe, but the source of seven-tent of British cotton imports. 'They say he has rum and sugar enoug belonging to him, to make all the water in the Thames turn int punch,' mused a servant in a London play called *The West India* and it is suspected that such elements contributed to the disruption c the academy by attempting a similar feat in the Mersey. For th indifferent discipline was one of the causes of the academy's dissolu tion in 1786. Yet not all the students were anti-social: Edward Rigb went on to publish a book on uterine haemorrhage in 1776 which wa translated into French and German; T. R. Malthus to win a fellowshi at Jesus College, Cambridge, and publish his famous *Essay on Populatio* in 1798; and John Goodericke to win the Copley medal of the Roya Society for astronomical discoveries. Priestley's teaching of politics bor fruit too: Henry Beaufoy became an M.P. for Minehead in 1780, an for Great Yarmouth in 1784 and 1790, in which capacity he laboure long but ineffectively for the repeal of the Test and Corporation Acts.

Indeed, it was the adverse political climate which killed the Dissenting Academies. The legatee of Warrington's scientific apparatus was a new foundation: Hackney College. With a large capital fund, and a long list of supporters, it was able to purchase Homerton Hall, and in the eighteen acres of ground to build accommodation for seventy students. The liberal nature of its curriculum (intended for 'youth in general, whether they are intended for civil or commercial life, or for any one of the learned professions') is attested by the fact that a Roman Catholic and several members of the Established Church were numbered amongst the students. If anything, it was too liberal, evoking from Burke the opprobrium of being 'the new arsenal in which subversive doctrines and arguments are forged'. Burke had in mind, not only the teachings of Priestley (who came to London after the sacking of his house by the Birmingham mob) but the even more forthright views of Richard Price, whose warm approval of the French Revolution was the reason why he wrote his *Reflections on the French Revolution*. Price was known as the leading statistician of his time. Condorcet regarded him as one of the formative minds of the century and Pitt is said to have been influenced by him to re-establish the sinking fund for the national debt. With the aid of Baron Mazeres, Price also propounded an elaborate scheme of contributory old age pensions. But Burke's fulminations struck the consciences of many Dissenters, who, now that the more odious restrictions on their educational activity had been removed in 1779, viewed with considerable alarm the doctrinal lapses of Price and his fellow lecturer Thomas Belsham. Belsham had already been forced to resign from a tutorship at Daventry Academy because of his progress along the Arian path, and at Hackney his toleration of a republican supper (with Tom Paine as the guest of honour) was followed by the arrest of an ex-student for treason. When one of the governing body of the college was actually imprisoned for attempted rebellion, it was realised that such a state of affairs could no longer continue. So in Midsummer 1796 the college was dissolved, the buildings sold, and the students dispersed. But its ten years of life had not been in vain. In a biography of William Hazlitt, who was a student at the college in 1793, Augustine Birrell wrote: 'As things went in England in 1793, Hackney College was a better Studium Generale than either Oxford or Cambridge at the same date.'[23]

So, having produced some of the seminal minds of the following half-century like William Godwin, Hazlitt, and William Johnson Fox the Dissenting Academies became subject to the same restrictions as had paralysed Oxford and Cambridge after the Restoration. Tests were imposed and admission was restricted to those students who intended to become Dissenting ministers. But by this time the Dissenting Academies had ceased to reflect the energies and ingenuity of the provinces.

6

The rising towns of the provinces provided a rich field for the scientific lecturer. Manchester as we have seen, sustained a 'mathematical Society' as early as 1718, which engaged John Jackson to deliver public lectures in 1719. Newcastle-on-Tyne provided audiences for the lectures of Isaac Thompson and Robert Harrison, whose *Short account of a course on natural and experimental philosophy*, was published in 1757. Charles Hutton, map-maker, mathematician, and Copley medallist of the Royal Society, taught there too.

Usually, however, the lecturers were peripatetic. John Ferguson obtained £100 in the Spring of 1763 by a tour of Bath and Bristol, and published his lectures in 1760, acknowledging his indebtedness to earlier exponents of his art like Keill, Cotes, Desaguliers, Whiston, and Hauksbee. Benjamin Donn, who obtained a prize of £100 from the Society of Arts for his map of Devonshire, was an energiser of the West-Country, as was Adam Walker of the North. Walker's lectures were published in 1770, 1771, 1772, and 1799.[24]

Of the various societies which took shape in the provinces during the period, one of the best known was the Lunar Society of Birmingham. It derived its name from the fact that its members met on the night nearest the full moon—an important consideration when roads were unlit. Like the clubs of the metropolis, its ostensible purpose was convivial: dinner would be served at two in the afternoon before each member presented his paper or communicated his observations. 'Lord!' wrote Erasmus Darwin, the Doctor whose imagination conceived the society, 'what inventions, what wit, what rhetoric, metaphysical, mechanical and pyrotechnical will be on the wing, bandied like a shuttlecock from one to another of your troupe of philosophers!' in a letter to Matthew Boulton, apologising for not attending a particular meeting. Other apostrophes from Dr. Darwin revealed the interests of his associates:

> 'Soon shall thy arm, UNCONQUERED STEAM, afar
> Drag the slow barge, or drive the rapid car;
> Or on wide waving wings expanded bear
> The flying chariot through the fields of air.

Fair crews triumphant, leaning from above,
Shall wave their fluttering kerchiefs as they move;
Or warrior bands alarm the gaping crowd,
And armies shrink beneath the shadowy cloud.'

He used to define a fool as 'a man who had never made an experiment in his life', and his own interest in mechanics is shown by his design of a flint mill for Wedgwood and by the fact that he shared Watt's secret before the steam engine was patented. Others in the Lunar Society experimented too. James Watt's experiments had improved the steam engine; Josiah Wedgwood's had devised that cream-coloured and Jasper ware with which his name is always associated; and John Baskerville's had resulted in that fine fount of type which led Cambridge University to appoint him as their printer. Not all the experiments of the members were so successful, however: Thomas Day experimented with the education of two orphan girls in an attempt to find a perfect wife. Needless to say, neither married him. Others outside the immediate circle at Birmingham and Lichfield were enrolled: Joseph Banks of the Royal Society and William Herschel the Hanoverian hautboy player who in 1800 discovered infra-red solar rays, together with Joseph Priestley, all helped to make the meetings a success.[25]

More public, and less like a private club, was the Manchester Literary and Philosophical Society, which was formed in 1781 at the house of Dr. Thomas Percival, formerly the first enrolled student of Warrington Academy. Percival became the president of the 'Lit. and Phil.' from its commencement till 1804; corresponding with distinguished men all over Europe and America. When Warrington Academy was dissolved, he assisted in transferring some of its effects to Manchester to establish an academy there. Percival's two associates were Thomas Henry, a surgeon-apothecary, and Dr. Thomas Barnes, a unitarian divine. Henry became secretary of the Literary and Philosophical Society, and Barnes proposed that a College of Arts and Sciences should be established in the town. Barnes's suggestion was followed: the governors were appointed under Thomas Percival as president, and Henry undertook to lecture on chemistry, bleaching, dyeing, and calico-printing. But the College of Arts and Sciences never seems to have enjoyed much success, probably owing to the fact that the Manchester Dissenting Academy in Dawson Street (now Mosley Street) was proving so successful. From 1793 until 1800, the academy enjoyed the services of John Dalton, the Quaker, who in 1808 published his tabulation of the atomic weights of elements. Robert Owen, the father of British Socialism, was a member of the Manchester Philosophical Society.

The American Revolution encouraged a number of such societies in other towns.[26] At Newcastle, Thomas Spence was expelled from one in 1775 for political heterodoxy. As the political scene grew grey, such groups tended to accentuate their political outlook, and at Sheffield in 1794 the local Constitutional Society had to dissolve when its leading member fled the country to avoid the charge of high treason. Bristol was the scene of a singular experiment by Thomas Beddoes—a 'Pneumatic Institution'—to investigate the properties of 'airs and gases' upon the sick. Beddoes had been a successful teacher of chemistry at Oxford, but had to resign because of his opinions. As the superintendent of his laboratory he selected young Humphry Davy, who, in 1799, his second and last year at the Pneumatic Institution, published discoveries concerning nitrous oxide.

It was Southey who once said: 'From Beddoes I hoped for more good to the human race than any other individual.' Such optimism, especially as to the beneficial effects of a realistic education, was particularly rife in England at this period. From 1741, when Isaac Watts (himself a former student at Newington Green Dissenting Academy) published his *Improvement of the Mind*, till Richard Lovell Edgeworth (Beddoes' father-in-law) published his *Practical Education*, there was a steady pressure of such opinion. In this tradition, the important work of Priestley and Godwin played its part.

From all this, Oxford and Cambridge seemed insulated. Bishop Butler, who would never have been able to enter Oriel had he retained his Nonconformist conscience, confessed that the lectures he heard there were 'lifeless and unintelligent'. Dr. Johnson agreed—his own tutor's lecture on logic not being worth (in his opinion) half the twopenny fine imposed for missing it. Gibbon's indictment of the dull and deep potating dons who presided over 'the most idle and unprofitable period' of his life were echoed by another Oxonian, Jeremy Bentham who observed that the only effects of education there were 'mendacity and insincerity'. When Richard Watson was elected to the chair of chemistry at Cambridge in 1764, it was no false modesty that led him to confess that 'he had never read a syllable on the subject, nor seen a single experiment'. Forsaking his chair for a see, he then most unepiscopally confined his researches to the production of a cheaper gunpowder. It was his experience in these fields of scientific endeavour which led him to suggest in his *Chemical Essays* that an Academy of Chemistry should be founded at the public expense:

'The improvement of metallurgy and the other metallic arts dependent on hemistry, might best be made by the public establishment of an Academy, ie labours of which should be destined to that particular purpose. The utility f such establishments has been experienced in Saxony and other places . . . id . . . one may hope that a Chemical Academy may, in time of peace and anquillity, become an object not unworthy the attention of the King or the egislature of the British Nation.'

'orson, who was perhaps the most remarkable scholar at Cambridge in ie latter part of the century, lost his chance of a fellowship at Trinity ecause he refused to take orders, and even when elected to the chair of ;reek remained in London to tipple and talk. He was under no lusions concerning the attainments of his colleagues, and suggested ie epitaph:

'Here lies a Doctor of Divinity,
Who was a Fellow, too, of Trinity.
He knew as much about Divinity,
As other Fellows do of Trinity.'

Villiam Wordsworth, who had hoped for better things, decided:

'Such life might not inaptly be compared
To a floating island, and amphibious spot
Unsound, of spongy texture, yet withal
Not wanting a fair face of water weeds
And pleasant flowers.'

ind with experience of Oxford in mind, Adam Smith was bluntly ragmatic. 'In the universities', he wrote in the *Wealth of Nations*, he youth are neither taught, nor always can find proper means of eing taught, the sciences which it is the business of those incorporated odies to teach.'[27] Such a statement, however, did not apply to Germany, Scotland, or America at that time.

7

Eighteenth-century England was burdened by Hanover. 'The devil ike the whole island, provided I can get out of it and go to Hanover,' emarked George II to his Queen, and he showed where his real iterests lay by establishing an ultra-modern university at Göttingen i 1734. There, under the inspiring teaching of J. M. Gesner and his uccessor, C. G. Heyne, the humanism inherent in the classics was evived and the range of studies expanded, with the result that Göttingen became the nursery of such men as Wilhelm von Humboldt.)ther German states were equally active: the first technological istitution was founded at Brunswick in 1745, followed by similar istitutions at Freiburg in 1756 and Clausthal in 1775; medical colleges like that at Dresden in 1748 and Frankfurt-on-Main in 1768, together added to the reputation which German education had been gaining since the foundation of the University of Halle in 1694. These German colleges sent men like John Reinhold Forster to succeed Priestley at Warrington, and Joseph Planta to assist in the building up of the British Museum. They were also centres for the advanced education of Dissenters, and some of the educational trusts, like that of the Presbyterians, encouraged students to study in Germany.

But with the period of peace that followed the 1745 rebellion, the Scottish universities attracted the majority of English students. There pre-eminent professors lectured in the vernacular, class-distinctions (which enabled a nobleman at Oxford and Cambridge to proceed to his M.A. as he matriculated) did not exist, and expenses were small. No university regulations cramped the individual students. Glasgow in the middle of the century offered such lecturers as Hutcheson, Leechman, Simpson, Muirhead, Moore, and Adam Smith, to say nothing of Joseph Black, whose experiments on heat gave the initial impetus to Watt (then an instrument maker near the university) to improve the steam engine. Glasgow especially maintained close links with the Dissenting Academies. The first head of Warrington was a personal friend of Leechman, who proposed him for the degree of D.D. in 1756. Edinburgh was, of course, the mecca of the medical students, and thither Joseph Black migrated in 1765 to spend the next thirty-one years as Professor of Chemistry and Medicine. In the Royal Society of the town, the science of geology, which was to play such a part in the developments of the extractive industries for the next century, was being carefully exploited by James Hutton, John Playfair, and Sir James Hall. Both Glasgow and Edinburgh were intimately connected with the life of their respective districts, being in many respects what we should now call civic universities.

8

More imponderable, yet ever more powerful throughout the period, was the pervasive influence of America. The Philadelphian Prometheus, Benjamin Franklin, was the central figure. His establishment in 1727 of the Junto (a weekly philosophical club working for personal improvement) and later, in 1743, the American Philosophical Society (an intercolonial Junto) showed that he was an active practitioner of the ideas which he put forward in *A Proposal for Promoting Useful Knowledge among the British Plantations* (1743). This tract, as the historian of the Royal Society of Arts has pointed out, antedated William Shipley's proposals in England, and in this connection it is not without interest that one of Franklin's English friends was William Shipley's brother Jonathan, later Bishop of St. Asaph and a protagonist of the repeal of the Test and Corporation Acts.

Another of Franklin's English friends was Peter Collinson, who acted as the English agent of the Junto. Collinson, a Quaker merchant engaged in the North American trade, secured their books and sent Franklin apparatus with which to make his famous electrical experiments. Collinson also secured their publication in England as *Experiments and Observations on Electricity*, which appeared in 1751 with a preface by Dr. John Fothergill, whom we have already encountered as a pioneer of medical education. These discoveries were fundamental, Franklin being the first to print the English electrical terms, armature, battery, brush, charged, charging, condense, conductor, discharge, electrical shock, electrician, electrify, minus, and plus. They were given a wider English currency by Joseph Priestley's *History of Electricity*—written, let it be noted, at Warrington Academy, in the intervals of Priestley's five-hours-a-day lecture schedule.[28]

It was Franklin's stimulus which led in 1755 to the founding of the University of Pennsylvania, originally a purely secular foundation. Other colleges, too, were added by the religious bodies: Columbia (1754) was an Anglican foundation; Princeton (1746) was Presbyterian; Brown (1765) Baptist; Rutgers (1766) Dutch Reformed; and Dartmouth (1770) Congregational. So, by the time the American Colonies broke away from the British Empire, these six foundations, together with Harvard (1636), William and Mary (1693), and Yale (1701) constituted 'the venerable nine': all for a population of two and a half million whites and blacks, less than a third of the population of the mother country. And in this great war of independence, it should not be forgotten that most of those we have already met in these pages —Fothergill, Priestley, and others—were actively sympathetic to the colonists.

American influence became more pervasive still after 1783. The writings of Bartram, Hearne, and Carver exercised a profound influence on Wordsworth, and can be seen in his sketch of an ideal university in the third book of *The Prelude*. With Coleridge and Southey he had much talk, in the hope that such a project might materialise on the banks of the Susquehanna. In the following century, with the movement westwards, America was to become the great escape hatch for English social reformers.

The very last year of the eighteenth century witnessed the architectural embodiment of American ideas on higher education in a foundation established by Benjamin Thompson of Massachusetts, a sometime student of Harvard. This was the Royal Institution in London. Thompson came to England during the War of Independence, communicated a number of papers to the Royal Society, and after a brief period of service under the Crown, migrated to serve the Elector of Bavaria. For these services he was created Count von Rumford.

He returned to England, and in 1797 he was elected a life member of the newly formed Society for Bettering the Condition of the Poor. In this society, the moving spirit was another American, Thomas Bernard, and at one of the meetings Thompson (or Rumford as he can now be called) suggested a further establishment which would 'diffuse the knowledge and facilitate the general introduction of useful mechanical inventions and improvements . . .' and teach 'by courses of philosophical lectures and experiments, the application of science to the common purposes of life'.

This frank utilitarianism struck chords in the minds of those who had remembered Priestley's phrase 'the greatest happiness of the greatest number'. Rumford's further proposal to 'diffuse the knowledge of all new and useful improvements, in whatever quarter of the world they may originate' and to 'teach the application of scientific discoveries to the improvement of arts and manufactures in the country . . . to the increase of domestic comfort and convenience', chimed with the spirit of the age. So the Royal Institution was born: aptly enough in the house of Sir Joseph Banks in Soho Square, on 9 March 1799. By June it was housed in Albemarle Street, and in the same year it had received a Royal Charter.

Rumford intended that the foundation should exhibit in a 'repository' such useful inventions as his own stove (the Rumford Roaster), looms, farming implements, and distilling apparatus. Such exhibits were to be ticketed with the price and the maker's name so that quick sales could be effected. But he also planned to establish a lecture room, laboratory, and other necessary facilities for conducting experiments and delivering lectures upon scientific and technical subjects.

But he did not remain to sustain the foundation with his guidance and help. On his departure for Bavaria, the managers (elected from the subscribers) decided to discontinue the repository and technical school, and concentrate on developing the laboratory and reference library. This, in the light of subsequent events, was a very wise decision.

9

The Royal Institution chair of natural philosophy and chemistry was awarded to Thomas Garnett, a physician, who after taking his degree at Edinburgh, had practised at Bradford, Knaresborough, and Harrogate. In the last-named place he examined the waters, and published the first analysis of them. Going to Anderson's Institution at Glasgow, he initiated a series of lectures on natural philosophy at the Trades Hall. These lectures were continued by his successor at Glasgow, Dr. George Birkbeck, who in the year 1800, established the cheap courses of lectures on science with which his name is always associated, and from which the Mechanics' Institute was to rise.

An even more powerful influence was exerted from the Royal Institution when twenty-three-year-old Humphry Davy was appointed in 1801 as director of the chemical laboratory. Davy was such an intrepid experimenter that in the year before his appointment he had nearly died after breathing water gas made by passing steam over charcoal. F.R.S. in 1803 at the age of twenty-five, Copley medallist in 1805, he was at once a synthesiser of knowledge already gained and a blazer of new trails. His *Discourse Introductory to a Course of Lectures on Chemistry*, delivered at the Royal Institution in 1802, shows how much had been achieved. Davy contrasted human beings 'in what is called a state of nature . . . unable to discover causes, and quietly and passively submissive to the mercy of nature and the elements' with the position now reached, when man was civilised:

> informed by science and the arts, and in control of powers which may be almost called creative; which have enabled him to modify and change the beings surrounding him, and by his experiments to interrogate nature with power, not simply as a scholar, passive and seeking only to understand her operations, but rather as a master, active with his own instruments.

The second professor of natural philosophy was Thomas Young—'Phenomenon Young' as he was nicknamed at Cambridge from the depth and width of his interests. Trained in medicine at Edinburgh and Göttingen after a period of study at St. Bartholomew's Hospital, he was elected to the Royal Society at the age of twenty-one, and only went up to Cambridge as a fellow-commoner of Emmanuel at twenty-four. As a physicist, he made important contributions to optics, and as an egyptologist he deciphered the Rosetta Stone. Perhaps he is best known for his experiments on light: experiments in which he originated the wave theory, so little appreciated at the time, and so widely recognised today. The two years in which he held office at the Royal

Institution were not marked by any startling developments, but soon afterwards, when Rumford severed his connection with it, the school for mechanics and the kitchens and model workshops were abolished, and a determined attempt was made to popularise it amongst the middle and upper classes.

As a middle and upper class body, the Royal Institution was a great success. The Rev. Sidney Smith lectured on moral philosophy, S. T. Coleridge on poetry, and Landseer on art. To Sir Joseph Banks, such developments were 'profane' and he resolved 'not to attend in future'.

But of all the lecturers, none had so great an influence as Davy. His own metamorphosis from a country boy to an English gentleman symbolises the change in the Institution. His imaginative experiments and lectures made these two activities characteristic of the Institution. And both his experiments and his lectures had a most practical bearing. Tanning and the chemistry of agriculture were two of his early lecture courses, while his experiments literally created the science of electro-chemistry. By utilising the recent invention of the voltaic battery in which plates of copper and zinc were immersed in cells of dilute acid, he discovered that he could decompose a number of substances in aqueous solution, by immersing the positive and negative wires of the battery in separate vessels connected by a moistened thread. With a large battery he succeeded in decomposing potash and soda and isolating the metals potassium and sodium. In addition he isolated the new metals, barium, strontium, calcium and magnesium, and in 1810 demonstrated the elementary nature of chlorine. And in that same year, an Act of Parliament converted the Institution from a semi-private to a public body, with powers to promote 'chemical science by experiments and lectures, improving arts and manufactures, discovering the uses of the mineral and natural productions of this country, and the diffusion and extension of useful knowledge in general'.[29]

This was the prelude to the achievements of his successors at the Royal Institution, some of whom were to be honoured, as he never was, by the award of degrees at Oxford and Cambridge. Their names represent the masterful interrogation of nature which was to follow in the century and a half to come: Young, Faraday, Tyndall, Frankland, Dewar, Rayleigh, J. J. Thomson, Rutherford, and Bragg.

10

Such associations as these, whose members were sustained and animated by corporate spirit, were in a very real sense the institutional ancestors of the civic universities. For not only did they help to pioneer the technological changes of the times, but they also bequeathed an enthusiasm for science and the arts to a far wider circle than was ever affected by the two existing universities. Nor, in this connection, should the work of the private scientific lecturers be forgotten. Many of them explained and demonstrated the laws of motion, hydrostatics, pneumatics, and optics to appreciative circles. One of them, a Mr. Tatum, who lectured at 52 Dorset Street, Fleet Street, numbered Michael Faraday among his pupils. Other popularisers of science were the instrument makers. Men like Benjamin Martin, George Adams, and Jesse Ramsden by improving microscopes, theodolites, and other tools for the investigation of nature gave the scientific workers greater facilities. Adams, in addition, was a clear exponent of the new techniques.[30]

The rise of the cities, the growth of professional classes, the increasing specialisation of knowledge all influenced, and were influenced by, the economic progress of the time. Knowledge of the laws governing the world of nature had become essential, not only for further progress, but also for the ordinary business of government and administration. And it was to advance and diffuse this knowledge that the nineteenth-century counterparts of the people we have met in the foregoing pages were to promote and establish professional societies.

REFERENCES

1. POSTLETHWAYTE, Malachy, *Universal Dictionary of Trade and Commerce* (London, 1751), which owed much to J. Savary de Brulone.

2. JOHNSON, E. A. J., 'The Mercantilist Concept of "Art" and "Ingenious Labour",' *Economic History* (1931), ii to 234–53.

3. *In Augusta Triumphans* (1728).

4. HANS, N., *New Trends in Education in the Eighteenth Century* (London, 1951), 136ff.

5. *ibid*, 149–50.

6. WHITTAKER, *op. cit.*, 54–5.
RAMSEY, Sir Wm., *Essays Biographical and Chemical* (London, 1908), 19.

7. *The Age of Johnson* (ed. A. S. Tuberville) (Oxford, 1933), ii, 21–2.

8. CARR-SAUNDERS, A. M., and WILSON, P. A., *The Professions* (Oxford, 1933), 45–6.

9. ESDAILE, Arundel, *The British Museum* (London, 1948), and *British Museum Quarterly*, xviii (1953), 28.

10. WOOD, H. T., *History of the Royal Society of Arts* (London, 1913).

11. HAMILTON, Bernice, 'The Medical Professions in the Eighteenth Century', in *Economic History Review* (1951), IV, 141–69; Lloyd G. Stevenson, 'The Siege of Warwick Lane', together with a 'Brief History of the Society

of Collegiate Physicians 1767-1798', *Journal of the History of Medicine and Allied Sciences* (Connecticut, 1952), vii, 105-21.

12. Fox, Hingston, *Dr. John Fothergill and his friends* (1919), 157-82.

13. For other Quaker apothecaries see A. Raistrick, *Quakers in Science and History* (London, 1950), 288-315, and works previously cited Chapter V, note 6, and Chapter VI, note 19.

14. Moore, Sir Norman, *The History of St. Bartholemew's Hospital* (1918).
Parsons, F. G., *The History of St. Thomas's Hospital* (1932-6).
Morris, Sir Ernest, *A History of the London Hospital* (1926).
Wilks and Bettany, *A History of Guy's Hospital* (London, 1892).
Ives, A. G. L., *British Hospitals* (1948).
Campbell Thomson, H., *The Story of the Middlesex Hospital 1835-1935*.
Peachey, G. C., *Memoir of William and John Hunter* (1924), points out that Hunter tried to stop the practice of students, fees being pooled when some surgeons did no teaching.

15. Cope, Z., 'William Cheselden and the Separation of the Barbers from the Surgeons' *Annals of Royal College of Surgeons* (London, 1953), xii, 1; E. Morris, *op. cit.*, 131.

16. Vincent, E. W., and Hinton, Percival, *The University of Birmingham* (Birmingham, 1947), 38.
Garrison, F. H., *Introduction to the History of Medicine* (London, 1921), 416.

17. Mallet, Charles, *History of the University of Oxford* (1923), iii, 125.

18. McLachlan, H., *English Education under the Test Acts* (Manchester, 1931).

19. Ashton, T. S., *The Industrial Revolution* (London, 1948), 19.

20. Raistrick, A., *Quakers in Science and Industry* (London, 1950).

21. Guest, J., *Historic Notes of Rotherham* (Worksop, 1879), 500.

22. Fulton, J. F., 'The Warrington Academy (1757-1786) and its influence upon Medicine and Science', *Bull. of the History of Medicine* (Baltimore, 1933), i, 54-9, H. MacLachlan, *Warrington Academy* (Manchester, 1943).

23. Birrell, Augustine, *William Hazlitt* (1902), 29.

24. Hans, *op. cit.*, 144ff.
For the Spalding Society see J. Nichols, *Antiquities of Leicestershire* (London, 1790), iii, 1-35.

25. For descriptions of the Lunar Society, see E. Krause, *Erasmus Darwin* (London, 1879), and Hesketh Pearson, *Doctor Darwin* (Penguin, 1943), J. G. Crowther, *The Social Relations of Science* (London, 1941), 417-23, and Andrew Cook (ed.) *An Eighteenth Century Lectureship in Chemistry* (Glasgow, 1950), 47.

26. Gillespie, C. C., *Genesis and Geology* (Harvard, 1951), 20-40, gives a good description and bibliography of these, which should be supplemented with studies of various individual groups like Spence Watson, R., *The History of the Literary and Philosophic Society of Newcastle-upon-Tyne* (London, 1897), 1-32.

27. *Wealth of Nations* (Everyman Edition), ii, 250.

28. Van Doren, C. C., *Benjamin Franklin* (London, 1939), 171.

29. Martin, T., *The Royal Institution* (1948).
Bence Jones, H., *The Royal Institution* (London, 1871).
Foote, G. A., 'Sir Humphrey Davy and his audience at the Royal Institution', *Isis*, XLIII (1952), 6-12.

30. *London and the Advancement of Science* (London, 1931), 301-11.

CHAPTER EIGHT

The Metropolitan Apotheosis and the New Clerisy, 1810-51

THE great electric battery of the Royal Institution enabled Davy to hold an exciting inquisition of nature. This opened up new industrial vistas, especially round about the year 1810 when he demonstrated the elementary existence of chlorine. Two years later he appointed twenty-one-year-old Michael Faraday as his assistant. His close friend Coleridge, who had lectured at the Royal Institution two years before, evolved a new social concept: that of the 'operatives in science, literature, and the learned professions', later described as 'The Clerisy'. This group, exempted from the play of economic pressures by a secure income, were to devote their time to increasing the spiritual possessions of the race. They were the Nationality, embracing not only the National Church, but an establishment essential to the orchestral efficiency of society. In an analogy which might have almost been drawn from his experience at the Royal Institution he said:

> All harmony is founded on relation to rest—on relative rest. Take a metallic plate, and strew sand on it; sound an harmonic chord over the sand, and the grains will whirl about in circles, and other geometrical figures, all, as it were depending on some point of sand relatively at rest. Sound a discord, and every grain will whisk about without any order at all, in no figures, and with no points of rest.
>
> The clerisy of a nation, that is, its learned men, whether poets, or philosophers or scholars, are these points of relative rest. There could be no order, no harmony of the whole, without them.

I

New universities for the clerisy of the new industrial society were strongly advocated by Charles Kelsall and James Yates. Kelsall proposed, in his *Phantasm of a University* (published in 1814 and again in 1821, and dedicated to Francis Bacon) that, at both Oxford and Cambridge, colleges should be re-grouped according to certain specialities thus:

Colleges of Civil Polity and Languages: Christ Church (Oxford) and Trinity (Cambridge)

Colleges of Moral Philosophy:	Magdalen, Queen's, and University (Oxford) St. John's, Magdalene, and Sidney (Cambridge)
Colleges of the Fine Arts:	New College and Trinity (Oxford) Downing, Christ's, and Emmanuel (Cambridge)
Colleges of Natural Philosophy:	Brasenose, Balliol, and Oriel (Oxford) Clare and Queens' (Cambridge)
Colleges of Agriculture and Manufactures:	The remaining five halls at Oxford and Pembroke and Peterhouse at Cambridge.

The remainder of the foundations, Kelsall suggested, should become Colleges of Mathematics.

Since such a re-grouping would be difficult to accomplish, Kelsall detailed architectural designs for a new university with special colleges for the specialities indicated above. With remarkable foresight he wrote:

For the situation of the new University, let a healthy and cheerful spot be chosen in the county of Stafford; and let the silver Trent meander at the end of the University Grove.

Not as unashamedly innovatory as Kelsall's plans, but influenced by it, were the proposals of a northern unitarian pastor, whose *Thoughts on the Advancement of Academical Education in England* ran to two editions in the years 1826–7. Yates, who had been born in Liverpool, and had experience in both Sheffield and Birmingham, asked his readers:

Why should not Yorkshire and Lancashire . . . and the adjoining counties, have the benefit of at least one university, planted in the midst of them, and accessible upon as easy conditions as possible to all their inhabitants?

And after the north of England, he asked, should not the west claim attention?

But both Kelsall and Yates lacked the support of a powerful and interested group, so their voices descanted rather than demanded. Real pressure could only be exercised from the metropolis and it was from there that the significant institutional developments of the period were stimulated.[1]

2

Davy was succeeded as professor of chemistry at the Royal Institution in 1813 by apothecary-trained W. T. Brande who held the chair for 41 years.[2] He had also studied at the Windmill Street Medical School and at St. George's Hospital, and at the time of his election was professor of chemistry and superintending chemical operator to the Society of Apothecaries. That he should have accepted this latter office after lecturing at the new medico-chemical school in Windmill Street was both a testimony to, and an accelerant of, the progress made by that Society towards achieving professional status.

This professional status, enriched by more expert knowledge of the fundamental scientific basis of medicine and enhanced by labour among the growing populations of the new industrial towns (labours which were partly responsible for the falling death rate), though John Mason Good had written and worked to promote it, was as yet unrecognised by the State. And to secure its recognition, a forty-year-old London doctor, G. M. Burrows, began to press for parliamentary action against the charlatans who still flourished. After five years' oscillation between the claims and counter-claims of the Colleges of Physicians and Surgeons, the Society of Apothecaries finally secured the passage of the statute 55 Geo. III.

This statute was one of the most significant of the century. It endowed the Society of Apothecaries with the power of awarding its licentiate on the results of a written examination conducted by a court of twelve examiners (of which Brande's brother, Everard Augustus, was one), to candidates who had served a five-year apprenticeship and attained their majority. These examinations, together with those instituted fifteen years before by the Royal College of Surgeons of London, constituted standard qualifications for the general practitioner, and, indeed, created the status. The licence of the Royal College of Physicians was useless until 1861 because of the disabilities it entailed in matters of dispensing.

The professional qualification now afforded by the licence of the Society of Apothecaries stimulated a number of medical schools in London and the provinces. In London, perhaps the most notable was that of Charing Cross Hospital, founded in 1818. For this was the first foundation to begin as an integrated medical school and hospital, and its 'Objects and Intentions' dated 31 March 1821 underlined this by proclaiming that it was intended 'to promote . . . not only the welfare of the Poor but the improvement of the Healing Art and the good of the Community at large'.[3] Bellers had come into his own at last.

3

In six of the eight provincial towns where medical schools were forming to prepare students for these examinations, there were proposals to establish local universities. And though these proposals had, in some cases, to wait for half a century before being accepted, it does not invalidate their significance, nor minimise their importance. In Leeds John Marshall read a paper to the local Philosophical Society in January 1826 with that end in view.[4]

In Newcastle, T. M. Greenhow read two papers before the Newcastle Literary and Philosophical Society on the 5 April and the 7 June 1831 stressing the 'expediency' of establishing 'an academical institution of the nature of a college or university for the promotion of literature and science'. The papers were printed and published, together with plans for the proposed buildings. The Home Secretary was memorialised, and a joint-stock company with a capital of £15,000 was mooted. The project fell through, however, and the Corporation of Newcastle diverted their munificence to helping the pioneers to start a school of medicine which opened its doors on 1 October 1834.[5]

Then again at Birmingham, the founder of the local medical school, Dr. Sands Cox, scoured the Continent for ideas to improve the teaching of medicine in the Midlands, and on his return in 1831 determined to make Birmingham 'the seat of a grand scientific and commercial college'. Within ten years he had secured sufficient help to build, not only a substantial clinical hospital, but also to establish Queen's College, which by 1843 was offering Architecture, Civil Engineering, Law, Theology, General Literature, and Arts to such students as might wish to study there. This ambitious scheme was consistently financed to the tune of some £25,000 by one of Cox's former patients, to whom Cox wrote exultingly: 'May we not, with the powers we now enjoy, lay the foundation of a great central university, based upon sound Church of England principles?' That they did not do so was in great measure due to the representative of the Church, J. T. Law. As Chancellor of the Diocese of Lichfield, he not only tried to emancipate the theological department from the exuberance of Sands Cox, but actually proposed after fifteen years of such bickering, that Queen's College should be sold, and two separate colleges for medicine and divinity refounded with the proceeds.[6]

In 1836, after the reformed corporation of Liverpool was elected,

Dr. Carson suggested that a university was needed to complete the civic structure.[7] In 1836 the Pine Street School of Medicine at Manchester sponsored a similar proposal,[8] while in 1840 the leaders of the medical profession in Bristol formally discussed the possibility that the city might become 'the seat of a medical university'.[9]

Incubating the growth of these schools both in London and the provinces was the steady and increasing protection of professional status afforded by the State. The Anatomy Act of 1832, by affording to the schools a sufficient supply of bodies for dissection, freed them from the unpleasant necessity of negotiating with resurrection men, and gave them status in the public eye. Just how good the schools were becoming might be judged from the agonised cries of the Scottish graduates practising in England, who were not exempt from the penal clauses of the Apothecaries Act. Until it became law, they had captured most of the medical students debarred from Oxford and Cambridge. Now, they expressed

> . . . strong reasons for doubting the competency of any Society of London Apothecaries to examine an Edinburgh graduate or licentiate, as to his proficiency; as these men are utterly unknown in the history of medicine, and bear the same rank in medical science as does the Fishmongers' Company in Natural History, or the Stationers' Company in general literature, being little more than dealers in raw materials.[10]

This umbrage, expressed in a memorial addressed to the Prime Minister in 1833, was further aggravated by the restless activities of Thomas Wakley, founder and editor of the *Lancet*, who later entered politics to further his schemes for medical reform. It stimulated the government to appoint a select committee to examine the whole question of medical education. The report of this committee endorsed the efficacy of the Apothecaries' examination (to which the presidents of both the Colleges of Physicians and Surgeons bore witness) and the excellence of the provincial medical schools preparing for them. It also helped to precipitate, amongst other things, the grant of a charter to a University of London.[11]

4

This university represented, in its origins, the aspirations of utilitarians and secularists, who, with the Dissenters, were excluded from Oxford and Cambridge. Founded as a result of the enthusiasm kindled by Thomas Campbell's visit to Germany, built on an old rubbish dump in Gower Street, financed on the joint-stock principle, and governed by a council in which Brougham was a leading spirit, it was a political challenge to the ascendancy of the Tory party, which was based on Oxford and Cambridge. Robert Peel saw it as such, and, as M.P. for Oxford and Home Secretary, communicated with the Dean of Christ Church commenting on the exclusion of religious education from the scheme and adding:

> This must be opposed and rejected, but I have hardly time to give to such an important project all the attention which it deserves. Can you tell me where I can look for that which it would be useful for me to know. Was there any public discussion on a London University? on the impolicy of forming a university, a place of education for adults, in the Metropolis.[12]

This was on 26 May 1825, the day on which Brougham moved in the House of Commons for leave to bring in a bill of incorporation. Though unsuccessful, Brougham's vigour persisted, and three months later he wrote to the wealthy radical Sir Francis Burdett (who had been twice imprisoned for his activities on behalf of popular suffrage) soliciting subscriptions to the new university, declaring:

> It is an event of infinite moment in my view which will do more to crush bigotry and intolerance than all the Bills either of us will ever see carried, at least until a Reform happens. Accordingly the monasteries (Oxford and Cambridge) are loud in their Howlings, but it all won't do.[13]

Praed, who knew Francis Gilmer, the 'talent scout' for Jefferson's non-sectarian University of Virginia, and introduced him to likely men, saw the significance of this London counterpart to the American scheme. Though himself a Cambridge graduate, he wrote the well-known verses which appeared in the *Morning Chronicle* between the writing of Peel's and writing of Brougham's letters quoted above:

> 'Ye Dons and ye Doctors, ye Provosts and Proctors,
> Who are paid to monopolise knowledge,
> Come, make opposition, by vote and petition
> To the radical infidel College:
> Come, put forth your powers, in aid of the towers,
> Which boast of their Bishops and Martyrs,
> And arm all the terrors of privileged errors,
> Which live by the wax of their Charters.
> Let MACKINTOSH battle with CANNING and VATTELL
> Let BROUGHAM be a friend to the Niggers,
> BURDETT cure the Nation's misrepresentations,
> And HUME make a figure in figures;
> But let them not babble of Greek to the rabble,
> Nor teach the Mechanics their letters;
> The labouring classes were born to be asses,
> And not to be aping their betters.'

Praed did not mention that Brougham had enlisted a formidable medical group, who hoped to improve medical education and research. Most notable was Charles Bell, who had bought the Great Windmill Street Medical School in 1812, and sold it to Herbert Mayo to become a professor at Brougham's foundation. 'His assistance was of the first importance to the establishment of the medical school, and his influence upon the appointments to the medical chairs seems to have been great.'[14] Other attempts to enlist professional groups can be seen in the establishment of chairs of Law, Economics, Geography, Modern Languages, Chemistry, Natural Philosophy, and abortive attempts to create chairs of Mineralogy, Engineering, Design, and Education. Unchartered, jeered at, and ostensibly despised, it had enrolled over five hundred students within five years of its foundation.

The Established Church first opposed the grant of a charter but soon saw it was more practicable to establish a rival institution, affording the same professional facilities under Anglican control. George D'Oyly, rector of Lambeth, expressed this point of view in an open *Letter to the Right Honourable Sir Robert Peel on the Subject of the London University*. More universities were certainly needed, according to D'Oyly, to satisfy the needs of an increasing population and the 'spread of a strong spirit of intellectual improvement': another in London and one in the North, together with an expansion of Oxford and Cambridge. At a meeting held on 21 June 1828, with the Duke of Wellington in the chair, flanked by the two archbishops, City financiers, surgeons, and a not inconsiderable number of provincial men of substance promised to support a college which should imbue the minds of youth with a knowledge of the doctrines and duties of Christianity as inculcated by the United Church of Great Britain and Ireland'.

Orthodox as this new foundation—King's College—might be, it agreed with the 'godless' institution in Gower Street in three important particulars. The first was the construction put upon the term 'university', as a place where universal or general knowledge was to be taught. For the catalogue of studies which was to afford the 'liberal and enlarged' course of education offered at King's College included religious and moral instruction, classical learning, history, modern languages, mathematics, natural philosophy, medicine and surgery, chemistry, jurisprudence, etc.'—the last opening endless vistas. The second was a recognition of the needs of the time, that to sustain the foundation 'specific preparation for the particular professions' had to be undertaken. That 'specific preparation' applied especially, as at London University, to medical students. In 1834 these numbered 347 of the

469 students at Gower Street, and 241 of the 446 students at King's. And in this connection it is worth noting that Herbert Mayo, who had bought the Great Windmill Street Medical School from Charles Bell on his departure for London University, now himself sold it to take a similar appointment at King's. The third was its frank recognition of the importance of physical science. J. F. Daniell, inventor of the hygrometer which bears his name, was elected to the chair of chemistry in 1831, and went on to construct the first electric battery which was able to give a constant current; while Charles Wheatstone, elected to the chair of physics in 1834, was a pioneer of spectrum analysis, of submarine telegraphy, of electrical recording instruments, and of the stereoscope.[15]

With such common ground between them, combination was almost inevitable. A charter granted in 1836 enabled them to associate as the University of London: a title relinquished by the college in Gower Street for that of 'University College'. Oxford, Cambridge, and the College of Surgeons which had sustained a strong opposition to the whole project, were overborne by the support which the City of London gave to its own university. The Liberals rejoiced in it as the first non-sectarian university to be established in England with powers to grant degrees in Arts, Laws, and Medicine.

It seemed as if the University of London would go too far, even for Liberals like Thomas Arnold, one of the original senate. In 1839 he resigned because he could not induce them to impose a compulsory examination in Scripture on undergraduates. He wrote to the Bishop of Norwich:

> I cannot disguise from myself that the University of London, in its public capacity, cannot be considered as a Christian institution, although it may happen that all its branches individually may be Christians; and therefore I must withdraw from it. . . . To see my hopes for this new University thus frustrated, is one of the greatest disappointments I have ever met with.[16]

Its soulless, impersonal character disappointed others too—Charles Bell amongst them. For, from being a teaching university, it developed into a vast examining machine, to which the energies of many flourishing provincial institutions were orientated. By 1851, 29 general and nearly 60 medical colleges were affiliated. Of the general colleges London, Somerset, Lancashire, and Yorkshire each possessed four: Staffordshire (and Ireland) three; Hertfordshire two; and Bedford Devon, Durham, Gloucester, and Carmarthen one each. Almost all the medical schools of the United Kingdom were included, as well as those of Malta, McGill, Bengal, and Ceylon. And, to emphasise the real source of strength, one third of the graduates were medicals. And it was at one of the newest of these medical schools, that of Charing Cross Hospital, that T. H. Huxley learnt, between the years 1842 to 1846, to love science, and obtained the first insights into physiology which were to make him Darwin's watchdog.

By holding a non-sectarian umbrella over these, and numerous other 'affiliated institutions' London helped many provincial pioneers to weather strong and damping antipathies.

5

If liberal churchmen like Thomas Arnold were chilled by the attitude of Gower Street, the chapter of Durham was almost frozen with horror. Prebendary Durrell addressed his Bishop on 20 July 1831:

> It appears to be morally certain that as soon as the Reform Bill is disposed of, an attack will be made on dean and chapters, and as certain that Durham will be the first object. It has occurred to us that it will be prudent if possible to ward off the blow, and that no plan is so likely to take as making the public partakers of our income by annexing an establishment of enlarged education to our college.[17]

Van Mildert, last of the great palatine bishops, was more than favourable, but he advised his correspondent to keep the matter quiet 'until more mature', so to anticipate not only any 'mongrel affair at Newcastle', but 'any fierce attack upon Church dignitaries in the House of Commons'. Furthermore, the bishop suggested that it would be unwise to seek powers through a House of Commons Bill, as the Radicals 'would be for cutting up root and branch, not for lopping off portions'.

The chapter of Durham was a wealthy oligarchy. Stalls, then on an average worth £3,000 a year, were held by a dozen clerics, among whom were the four bishops of St. David's, Bristol, Chester, and Exeter. Phillpotts, the Bishop of Exeter, might therefore be excused for holding the view that to establish a university from the chapter incomes was unwise, for, he argued, it would only increase discontent in the country, and add to the excess of educated people for whom there were already too few positions. Gaisford, the prebendary (best known perhaps for the celebrated observation that 'the advantages of a classical education are twofold—it enables us to look down with contempt on those who have not shared its advantages, and also fits us for places of emolument not only in this world, but the next') deprecated the establishment of a university and proposed 'a superior school' for poor ordinands to be housed in Sherburn Hospital. Of the curriculum he wrote:

Divinity, ancient languages, Mathematics and Natural Philosophy I con-sider essentials: the numerous tribe of medical sciences with names terminat-ing in -ogy I consider non-essentials and excrescences; they are amusing an to a certain degree instructive, but are not wholesome discipline for the min —are more suitable to the *dilettante* than the sober student.

But Van Mildert's persistence won through. By giving £1,00 outright and a further £1,000 a year, he was able to set the universit on its feet. The chapter co-operated by enfranchising the South Shields estate for £80,000, which enabled them to give the universit a further £3,000 a year. The bishop introduced a Bill through th House of Lords to enable this to be done, and his successor, Dr. Maltby handed over the castle for the university's use. A warden was appointed and in 1837 they obtained a charter to award degrees.

The university was, like King's College, soon forced by the pres-sures of the time to make provisions for professional training. Natur-ally, they trained Anglican clergy, but they also commenced engineer-ing classes in the very year they received their charter—to the bishop' great pride. Unlike King's College, London, Durham maintained th residential character of the old universities by opening Hatfield Hall i 1846 and Cosin's Hall in 1851. J. F. W. Johnston, who taught chem-istry and mineralogy there for twenty-two years, was a contributo to the *Edinburgh Review*. His *Catechism of Agricultural Chemistry an Geology* ran to thirty-three editions, and was translated into mos European languages.

6

The fears of the Durham chapter that the Radicals 'would be fo cutting up root and branch, not for lopping off portions' had som real foundation, for James Mill was credited with the suggestion tha the Church of England should be converted into a National Mechanics Institute.[18]

These Mechanics' Institutes stemmed from the efforts of the variou scientific societies and lecturers, and were brought into flower throug the efforts of Henry Brougham, Dr. Birkbeck (a Glaswegian pro-fessor who originated the idea), and the London working-class leaders who rallied to support the London Mechanics' Institute when i opened in Southampton Buildings in 1824: so successfully, in fact, tha the *St. James Chronicle* described it in the following year as 'scatterin the seeds of evil the extent of which the wisest amongst them canno anticipate'. The roll numbered a thousand industrious students i its early years, and inspired a number of similar ventures in the pro-vinces. One of the early lecturers, C. F. Partington, showed his ow

ntellectual affinities by editing the journal of the seventeenth century
Earl of Worcester, whose scheme for establishing a college of artisans we
nave already met in chapter Five.

Brougham wrote a pamphlet, *Practical Observations upon the Educa-
ion of the People addressed to the Working Class and their Employers*
which ran to twenty editions, following it up by helping to found the
Society for the Diffusion of Useful Knowledge. This was ridiculed four
years later by Thomas Love Peacock in *Crotchet Castle* (1831) as 'the
Steam Intellect Society'. But unfortunately, as Brougham himself
dmitted at Manchester in 1835, it was 'the industrious portion of the
niddle classes to whose use Mechanics' Institutes are more especially
levoted'. Six years later, on 11 March 1841, W. D. Gillon, described as
of 'extremely liberal principles', actually proposed in the House of
Commons that grants should be given to them.

In this latter year J. T. Barber Beaumont founded his New Philo-
ophic Institute, which he endowed on his death with a trust fund.
Forty-three years later, this began to develop with the aid of the
Drapers' Company into the body which we now know as Queen
Mary College of the University of London.[19]

One Mechanics' Institute lecturer, who was also a Congregational
ninister, felt that the barrenness of the instruction did not compensate
or the rigid exclusiveness of the existing institutions of higher learning,
nd deplored the lack of cultural influences in the very conception of
Mechanics' Institutes. Since Oxford and Cambridge were the pre-
erves of the upper classes, and since social discontents stemmed from
ck of intelligent adaptability, could not the people of Sheffield found
heir own college by popular subscription, and attend early in the
norning and late at night? This minister, the Rev. R. S. Bayley,
was fighting a hard battle. Rivals for his hold on the intelligence of the
own were G. J. Harney, the first English Marxist, and G. J. Holyoake,
ne leading secularist. Yet so powerful was his appeal that within the
winter of 1842-3 he enrolled 300 students, and when he left the town
ve years later, the Sheffield People's College continued as a self-
overning and self-sustaining institution, inspiring F. D. Maurice to
stablish the Working Men's College in London in 1854 and others
o establish similar institutions in Nottingham and Leicester.[20]

Thomas Peacock's Dr. Folliot could scoff 'science for all, schools for
ll, rhetoric for all, law for all, words for all, and sense for none',
et in many northern Mechanics' Institutes, as in Leeds, Bradford,
York, Wakefield, Manchester, and Newcastle, laboratories were built
nd carried on with great success. Indeed, so vital did the movement

appear in Yorkshire, that in 1837 Edward Baines, the editor of the *Leeds Mercury*, proposed a Yorkshire Union of such institutes whereby permanent lecturers could be engaged to itinerate amongst the various towns 'to give a regular course of instruction on those sciences which have the most direct bearing on the manufacturing operations common to the district'. Thus an unbroken series of lectures could be afforded instead of a tantalising introduction. The Yorkshire Union was duly organised, and in 1849, 113 institutes were able to employ a paid secretary and lecturer. With 8,500 members and 83,000 books in its libraries, it was truly the most extensive confederation for adult education in the kingdom. Well might a Royal Commission, urging the claims of physical science to the University of Oxford in 1852 write:

> a large proportion of the middle, and even of the labouring classes are daily advancing in the cultivation of those branches of knowledge. Unless, therefore, the clergy and gentry who are educated at the university are compelled or encouraged to keep pace with the progress of society at large, it is to be feared that from their ignorance of a branch of knowledge so generally diffused they may find themselves placed below persons in many respects inferior and that an opposition may arise between Physical Science and other branches of knowledge, which would do serious injury both to the one and the other.[2]

7

'Durham,' wrote one supporter of the Established Church, 'affords a successful illustration of the benefits arising from Cathedral endowments when applied under episcopal sanction.' Similar application of church endowments for the establishment of colleges in diocesan areas was urged by Pusey as early as 1837, for the National Society was much preoccupied with the training of teachers for its schools.

The most coherent case for these colleges was put by G. F. Mathison in 1844. He had played a great part in the establishment of St. Mark's College in Chelsea and urged that similar colleges should be established in every diocese throughout the country:

> Healthy grafts on the old university tree, not pale exotics . . . founded upon the English Church, consonant with English feelings, suited to English habits and parallel with English, as contradistinguished from Scottish and foreign universities. At each of these, national boarding schools, parallel with our grammar schools . . . would provide children to form a practising school.

But Mathison was not concerned solely with the training of teachers. Where local industrial needs demanded it, science would be taught. Thus

In a Devon and Cornwall College no degree of science, theoretical or practical, which mining pursuits require in a mining country, need be excluded. . . . Collegiate foundations in a humbler sphere might easily open the door to future Davies.

Mathison was aware of other efforts made to establish regional universities, for not only did he mention the University of Durham with approval, but devoted an appendix to the earlier attempt at Ripon.[22]

The development of the professional training of teachers, however, was the work of the teachers themselves. True, John Minter Morgan had, in 1833, urged the University of London to establish a chair of education and the Rev. James Bryce, at University College, had run classes for schoolmasters with some success, but the efforts of Stein Turrell, a Brighton schoolmaster who established the College of Preceptors, did more. According to the charter, which it received in 1849, the College was to 'afford facilities for the teacher to acquire a sound knowledge of his profession . . . and to give certificates of the acquirements and fitness for their office of persons engaged in, or desirous to be engaged in, the education of youth'. Twenty candidates presented themselves. The idea was a good one: teachers themselves were to be responsible for maintaining the standards of their profession. The College Board, composed of teachers, judged each candidate 'as to the amount of knowledge and the art of conveying it to others'. It maintained a steady pressure on the authorities for a register of teachers to eliminate charlatans, and awarded its diplomas with scrupulous care. The Associateship (A.C.P.) corresponded to the matriculation, the Licentiate (L.C.P.) to the pass degree, and the Fellowship (F.C.P.) was intended to be the equivalent of the honours degree.[23]

8

Professional needs in other spheres stimulated further suggestions for local universities or specialist colleges. Thomas Arnold, in a letter to the *Sheffield Courant* in April 1832 remarked:

the classical schools throughout the country have universities to look to . . . but anything like local universities . . . held out to encourage exertion at a commercial school, it is in vain to look for.

'The interference of Government,' he commented, 'seems to me indispensable.'

But such commercial needs had to wait. Others, however, obtained some institutional response. Largely at Wellesley's request the East India

Company established two: one for soldiers at Addiscombe and one for civilians at Haileybury. Haileybury was opened in 1808, and from its classical porticos Colvin, Edmonstone, and Lawrence sallied out to rule the sub-continent. The professors at both institutions could challenge comparison with those in any university of Europe, Haileybury being singular compared to the Oxford and Cambridge of that day, in affording some systematic instruction in law. Indeed, Haileybury was linked with the first practice of the Benthamite principle of 'open competitive examination' for public employment. Mooted by Lord Grenville in 1813, it was not established for the Indian service till twenty years later. Macaulay secured its acceptance for all candidates for the Indian Civil Service in 1853, and, after great delays, the Home Civil Service followed suit in 1870. From there T. R. Malthus (product of a Dissenting Academy) published his famous essay on *The Nature and Progress of Rent* in 1815, and exercised a great influence on the developing science of economics from his chair of history and political economy, while his successor Richard Jones foreshadowed that philosophy of social evolution which the Marxists call the materialist conception of history. At Addiscombe, John Shakespear compiled his famous dictionary of Hindustani and William Sturgeon experimented with electro-magnets and worked on his dynamo: his *Annals of Electricity* was the first electrical journal in England. Sturgeon also tried to establish at Manchester in 1843 an 'Institution for Natural and Experimental Science' but met with little support and died in 1850. Addiscombe closed down completely after the Mutiny, but Haileybury, sold at a public auction in 1861, became yet another of the so-called 'public schools' then being founded on the pattern of Cheltenham, Marlborough, Wellington, and Clifton. It was from these that the next generation of pro-consuls was to be largely recruited.

Musicians owed much to Lord Burghersh whose efforts resulted in the foundation in 1822 of the Royal Academy of Music. The King gave a charter and a subsidy. William Crotch, Cipriani Potter, and Sterndale Bennett guided its destinies with great success, until in 1864 further financial help was needed. Gladstone gave them a grant of £500 a year, but Disraeli withdrew it in 1867 because 'the results of the institution were not of a satisfactory character'.

Another professional body was Putney College, one of the few places where some scientific and technical engineering training could be obtained. It was here that Edward Frankland, a former student at the Museum of Practical Geology and at Marburg, obtained the chair of chemistry in 1850. He became one of the most distinguished chemists of his generation. The students formed the Putney Club, from which grew the Society of Engineers in 1854. Nor was this the first of the Engineering Societies which advocated professional training; for the Institution of Civil Engineers dated from 1818, its Royal Charter from 1828, and its association with Great George Street, Westminster, from 1838. Its *Minutes of Proceedings* covered the whole field of engineering science and practice, and it went on to promote a number of special researches. In 1847 the Institution of Mechanical Engineers established itself for thirty years at Birmingham, where it too conducted a vigorous research and educational programme.

9

Even the lawyers were stirred from their gastronomic quietude in the Inns of Court, and began to awake to their professional responsibilities towards the education of new members. In 1833 the Law Society introduced lectures for solicitors and articled clerks and their example was followed by various local societies. In the same year, the Inner Temple tried to introduce compulsory lectures for their students, but the requirement was defeated by the students joining other inns where such lectures were not prescribed. In 1836, when the examination of solicitors was introduced, the legal profession may be said to have recognised the need for professional examination, though many of their members opined that the questions set were 'wholly beside the mark' and further that 'an examination even if successfully passed is no fair criterion of a young man's knowledge, and if he was plucked at that examination it would be no proof of his ignorance'. This examination was made obligatory in 1843, and in the following year the Inns of Court followed suit, but their requirements were not made uniform until 1852 when the embryo of the present Council on Legal Education was established. Even then, and up to the year 1872, a student could either attend lectures, or submit to an examination in order to be admitted to the profession. Perhaps the most interesting impact of this need for the professional education of lawyers upon the universities can be seen in the *Report of the Select Committee on Legal Education* of 1846. This committee, which took evidence from the Inns of Court, the Universities, the Law Society, and various other bodies, was of the opinion that

> the present state of legal education, both professional and unprofessional, is extremely unsatisfactory and incomplete and in striking contrast and inferiority to such education in all the more civilised states of Europe and America. . . . No legal education worthy of the name of a public nature is to be found.

So it recommended that there should be a great increase of the teaching of law at the universities, together with rigorous examination tests, and suggested that the Inns of Court should co-operate to form one great legal university providing full courses of lectures and discussions with a thorough examination system, opened to articled clerks as well as intending lawyers. But two centuries' lethargy in the matter of legal education could not be so easily shaken off.

How persuasive was this tendency to establish professional colleges may be seen among the Methodists—an increasingly important section of the community. Their membership had, in the forty-four years between 1790 and 1834, increased five-fold to 365,857.

As early as 1806, the great Dr. Adam Clarke (who spent thirty years of his life on his great commentary on the Bible) had written from City Road Chapel, 'We want, God knows! we want some kind of seminary for educating workmen for the vineyard of our God as need not be ashamed. We need without delay to get such a place established, either at Bristol or London. The time is coming, and now is, when illiterate piety can do no more for the interest and permanency of the word of God than unlettered irreligion did formerly.'

But there were many who argued that theological education would damp down the fires of evangelical zeal, and who, when a Methodist College was proposed, scented secularism around the ark. The advocates of a Methodist College—a 'Literary and Theological Institute' as they preferred to call it—put forward their proposals at the Methodist Conference of 1833 'to promote the improvement of the Junior Preachers in the Methodist Connection'. The project was submitted to the Conference of the following year, when a storm of protest was raised, chiefly by Dr. Samuel Warren, superintendent of the Manchester District. In spite of the fact that the promoters denied that the proposed institution was to be a 'college' and its tutors 'professors', Dr. Samuel Warren took such offence that he withdrew from the movement to found the Grand Central Association, which became the Wesleyan Methodist Association, and, in 1857, the United Methodist Free Church.

The promoters carried the Conference with them, and went ahead with their Literary and Theological Institution. The buildings of the old Dissenting Academy at Hoxton were rented, and by January 1835 were housing students, who attended some of the lectures at King's College, London. This experiment was so successful that further buildings were rented at Abney House, Stoke Newington, from a company which intended to use it as a cemetery. By 1839, Hoxton housed forty students and Abney twenty-nine.

But these arrangements were purely temporary. Helped by generous grants from the Wesley Centenary Fund, sites for permanent colleges were acquired at Didsbury near Manchester and Richmond near London. These were opened and occupied by students in 1842 and 1843 respectively, and Richmond later became a school of the University of London.[24]

10

During this period, the University of London was overshadowed by the Royal Institution. Michael Faraday, when offered the chair of chemistry in 1827, refused it, because he preferred the research facilities of the Royal Institution, where two years previously he had discovered benzene, the hydrocarbon found in oil gas (which was to serve as a basis for aniline dyes) and been elected to the directorship of the laboratory. In this capacity he had organised Friday evening meetings of members interested in science and these quickly developed into weekly lectures which became so noted a characteristic feature of the Institution's work. Well might Carlyle call it 'a kind of sublime *Mechanics' Institute* for the upper classes',[25] for it mirrored the wealth and ministered to the appetite for knowledge displayed by the fashionable society of the metropolis.

Hitherto, much of Faraday's research had been on behalf of others. By metallurgical research he had risen from being a laboratory assistant (with a short interlude as a valet) to his directorship, and he was increasingly convinced of the need for him 'to enjoy the pleasure of working his own thoughts'.

These 'own thoughts' revolved around electro-magnetic theory. Ampére and Arago were demonstrating the powers of electricity to produce magnetism, and Faraday suspected that a moving magnet was capable of generating electricity. His epoch-making experiments, a full account of which can be read in his diary for 29 August and 17 October, 1831, ushered in the neotechnic age. The dynamo and the transformer were born, and mankind was endowed with a new prime mover which was to revolutionise life.[26] The Royal Institution rode on his rising reputation. In 1833, Thomas Fuller endowed a chair of chemistry, to be held by him for life. A chair of physiology, also endowed by Fuller, was held by P. M. Roget who had projected the Northern Dispensary in 1810 and became secretary of the Royal Society in 1827, earning an incidental immortality for his famous *Thesaurus of Words and Phrases.*

Michael Faraday once wrote: 'There are three necessary steps in useful research—the first to begin it, the second to end it, the third to publish it.' The formation of a number of learned societies during this period shows not only that the importance of research was being recognised, but that its popularisation and dissemination were seriously considered. Round about 1810 Nash, the planner of Regency London, suggested that Metropolitan learned societies should be collectively housed in a square to be built round the Central Station at Charing Cross—later to be Trafalgar Square.[27]

The proliferation and strength of these societies enabled scholars and scientists of all kinds to sharpen their specialisms and discuss ideas; endowed them with grants in aid of research; and carried the results of such research in the columns of journals. Many of the professors at the newly founded University of London were active both in the formation and sustentation of these societies. Leonard Horner, for instance, the first warden of Gower Street was devoted to the work of the Geological Society (founded in 1807) and gave up much of his time to arranging its collections. Thomas Graham, professor of chemistry at University College, London, 1837-55 and founder of the science of colloid chemistry, was the first president of the Chemical Society; T. L. Donaldson, also of University College, was a founder of the Royal Institute of British Architects; A. McConochie was secretary of the Royal Geographical Society; William Pole of the Institution of Civil Engineers. The list could be extended.

By 1830, the number of these societies had grown so great, and their activities so multifarious, that Charles Babbage in his *Reflections on the Decline of Science in England* could acidly remark: 'Those who are ambitious of scientific distinction may, according to their fancy, render their name a kind of comet, carrying with it a tail upwards of forty letters at the average cost of £10. 9*s*. 9¼*d*. per letter.' Babbage, who was no novice at society-forming himself (he had been a moving spirit in the establishment of the Astronomical Society ten years earlier) was not the first to lament their number, though he correctly diagnosed the cause: the inability of the Royal Society to keep abreast of the scientific progress of the time. Sir Joseph Banks, who was president of the Royal Society from 1778 to 1820, feared the worst after the deliberate revolt of the Geological Society from his control, and lamented: 'I see plainly that all these new-fangled associations will finally dismantle the Royal Society, and not leave the Old Lady a rag to cover her.'[28] But the Old Lady, like the old universities, survived the societies, to gain added vigour from their activities. She lived to wear the new fashions of thought, and listen to the new trends of research, and the letters F.R.S. became an accolade in themselves. The only serious challenge to pre-eminence came from the British Association, which soon assumed a character of its own.

This had a Yorkshire origin. John Phillips, nephew of William Smith (the father of British Geology) and secretary of the Yorkshire Philosophical Society (founded in 1821 'to promote science in the district by establishing a scientific library, scientific lectures, and by providing scientific apparatus for original research'), was asked by David Brewster, then winning recognition for his discoveries in the polarisation of light, to convene an assembly on the model of the Deutscher Naturforscher Versammlung. The Corporation of York, when approached by Phillips, proved agreeable, and the first meeting of the British Association took place in that city on 26 September 1831. It is significant that the Baconian dream was quoted by the third co-founder and first general secretary, William Vernon Harcourt, a year later.[29]

Ridiculed by Charles Dickens as 'The Mudfog Association for the Advancement of Everything' with a full complement of crackpot doctors and by John Keble as a 'hodge-podge of philosophers', the British Association lived on to give powerful assistance to the movement for establishing civic universities.

It was originally proposed that applicants should be members of a 'philosophical society', and by holding its annual meetings in large towns up and down the country it undoubtedly opened the eyes of civic authorities to the need of encouraging such societies. Though Murchison told Whewell in 1845 that the Association should 'repudiate the idea that the chief aim of our existence is to stir up a few embers of scientific warmth in the provinces' and refused to 'play pantaloon or clown in the strolling company', he could not stem the tide. During this period the Association met twice at Birmingham ('39, '49); once at Liverpool ('37), Manchester ('42), Newcastle ('38), York ('31), and Southampton ('46). From 1833 it resolved on the motion of Harcourt to help research by compensating labour and paying the expenses of apparatus, and from 1848 onwards half the total receipts of membership tickets for annual meetings has been devoted to grants-in-aid of scientific research. Perhaps its most distinguished member was the Salford-born brewer J. P. Joule, who established the mechanical equivalent of heat. Joule, whose chemical education had been received from John Dalton in Manchester, was such an enthusiastic researcher that he carried a thermometer with him on his honeymoon.[30]

II

Manchester was, in fact, the hub of a new *élite* of merchants which was, as Thackeray said, emerging to 'manly opulence'.

Here in 1829 William R. Whatton addressed two letters to the Manchester Royal Institution, urging it to expand into a university for Literature, Science, and the Arts. Though an eminent Manchester historian recently described Whatton's scheme as 'having no bearing on the possibilities of the time'[31] it is interesting to see that such subjects as Geography, Botany, Architecture, Music, and Modern Languages were included. Whatton's idea persisted, and was repeated seven years later by H. L. Jones, an absentee curate of Ely, who proposed that a university college should be established to work in conjunction with the newly founded University of London.

Jones stressed the life and intelligence of what he called 'the Circle of Manchester'—a district extending from Liverpool to the West Riding and from Lancaster to Warrington. He urged them to follow the example of fourteenth-century Florence and refine the Circle.

> Not one Roscoe but many are wanted; not one Dalton standing like a Patriarch of Science at the head of the scientific part of the nation but a body of men who may appreciate and follow up his experiments or make similar advances in other branches of natural philosophy.[32]

His scheme provided for a university where the Fine Arts, Arts and Manufactures, and Medicine could be studied by a student body some 300 strong. The example Manchester set in this, might, he hoped, be followed by Liverpool.

This idea was taken up by James Heywood, a cultured Unitarian banker whose brother had taken a leading part in founding the Manchester Mechanics' Institute. Heywood had a great interest in university matters and seven years later, at his own expense, he commissioned and published an English translation of V. A. Huber's work on the English Universities, to which H. L. Jones contributed a paper on the University of London.[33] Heywood published Jones's original suggestion in 1836, and invited him to address the Manchester Athenaeum at their first general meeting. A circular was issued from the Pine Street School of Medicine for a university based on annual subscriptions. These were not forthcoming and the project fell through; for interest was diverted by other institutions. The Manchester Dissenting Academy returned from York in 1840 and in 1843 the Lancashire Independent College was established at Whalley Range, near where, a year later, Joule established his private laboratory. Mancunians were also preoccupied by the assault on the Corn Laws and the religious tests at Oxford and Cambridge, to say nothing of social discontent.

But the idea persisted. In 1845 John Owens, a shrewd bachelor who had made a fortune in the Chinese and American trade in Manchester cotton yarns, bequeathed £96,654 11*s.* 6*d.* for an anti-test college. In 1851 this opened its doors in Richard Cobden's old house at Manchester, purchased for the college by Owen's partner, George Faulkner. The first principal was A. J. Scott, formerly professor of English Literature at University College, London. This foundation was to serve as the rallying point for future efforts to establish a northern university.[34]

Owens was not the only merchant who desired to benefit his native town, for in 1850 Henry Robinson Hartley left an even greater sum—£102,000—to the Corporation of Southampton to be used for the 'study and advancement of the sciences of natural history, astronomy, antiquities, and classical and oriental learning'. Unfortunately his will was disputed. After twelve years of law suits the Corporation were left with only £42,425 which they could only use under certain conditions.[35]

12

James Heywood was also responsible for another landmark in university history—a Royal Commission on Oxford and Cambridge: the first victory of the liberalism in those ancient foundations. True, the groundswell had been felt since the beginning of the century: efficient examination systems had been established, and the exponents of the new and revolutionary science of geology were subjecting the chronology of Archbishop Ussher to a careful and critical scrutiny. William Buckland at Oxford and Adam Sedgwick at Cambridge were particularly active in promoting the study of a science which would enable an inquisition of the earth's riches to be made. In doing so they helped to establish the chronology of the world's creation, and undermined the hitherto accepted bases of belief.

Fed by the *Edinburgh Reviewers*, critical opinion outside these universities began to criticise the religious tests, and in 1834 mounted the first real assault. Covered by a barrage of over thirty pamphlets, G. W. Wood, a Unitarian, introduced a Bill in the House of Commons to abolish them, reinforcing his arguments by a petition signed by one-third of the residents of Cambridge, two college heads, and nine professors. Dr. Arnold had tried to secure the support of Oxford for this petition, but got little hearing. The Cambridge signatories included amongst others, Adam Sedgwick, Cornelius Hewitt (the Downing Professor of Medicine), and Connop Thirlwall, who lost a fellowship at Trinity for his tolerance towards Germanic scholarship. Among scenes of great 'clamour and disorder' (with Sir Robert Peel and W. E. Gladstone voting against it) the Bill passed the House of Commons by 185 votes to 44, but in the House of Lords, it was defeated by the victor of Waterloo, who said:

never has there been such an invasion of the established institutions of the country. . . . This Bill will inflict a mortal wound between Church and State.

For the *Edinburgh Reviewers*, this rebuff stimulated further criticisms. Sir William Hamilton vehemently italicised his conclusions that 'on the average, *there is to be found among those to whom Oxford confides the business of education, an infinitely smaller proportion of men of literary reputation, than among the actual instructors of any other university in the world*'. He coupled his remarks with some searching criticisms of collegiate usurpation of university duties.

As a result, no major assault was mounted against the Test barriers for the next ten years. Lord Radnor, it is true, skirmished with spirit, but it was not until Newman exposed the fallacy of the Thirty-Nine Articles guaranteeing orthodox Anglicanism in *Tract XC* (1845) that the struggle could be renewed. For if Newman could sincerely claim that subscription to the Thirty-Nine Articles was not inconsistent with adherence to the Roman Catholic Faith, then their efficacy as Anglican filters was open to serious question. Thus a liberal party took shape within the walls of Oxford itself, led by Benjamin Jowett, A. P. Stanley, and John Conington: the last two both old pupils of Thomas Arnold. Jowett saw the danger of allowing the anti-Test campaign in Parliament to be sustained by Dissenting ministers, and established communicative control over the efforts of W. D. Christie, M.P. for Weymouth, who moved for the appointment of a Royal Commission in 1845. Two years later, Jowett was urging Roundell Palmer to represent the views of the Oxford reformers in the House of Commons and in 1848 he published an anonymous pamphlet urging:

Our only defence against attacks from without is to build up from within, to enlarge our borders that we may increase the number of our friends. We have no one to fear but ourselves. At this moment . . . are we not living 'behind our dykes' in fear of the German Ocean? There may be enemies from whom it is right to fly, but the tide of opinion cannot be escaped in this way.

The 'German Ocean' referred to the Prince Consort, who had become Chancellor of Cambridge in the previous year. With Adam

Sedgwick as his secretary, he soon began to talk of professors and their duties: so much so that William Whewell, also an active reformer (he was responsible for the institution of the triposes in moral and natural sciences in 1848), remarked that there were 'tolerable plain indications that the old universities are not to expect a continuance they have been accustomed to receive at the hands of government'.[36]

Now James Heywood had studied at Trinity College, Cambridge, but in spite of considerable ability was prevented from taking his degree because he was a Unitarian. As a friend of Adam Sedgwick's, an enthusiastic geologist, and as a Fellow of the Royal Society he was in touch with liberal feeling inside the university; while as M.P. for North Lancashire he was sustained by liberal feeling in the country. In 1848, he and Bonamy Price, another of Arnold's pupils, initiated a memorial to the Prime Minister expressing the general gravamen of the complaints against the Oxford and Cambridge of that time. Among the 224 signatories of this memorial were Thomas Arnold's son Matthew, Charles and Erasmus Darwin, Sir Charles Lyell, and Thackeray. But the Prime Minister, Lord John Russell, who knew that reforms were contemplated at both universities, took no action.

Heywood waited for two years to give the reformers full scope. Then, on 23 April 1850, he moved an Address to the Crown. It ran:

> That all systems of academical education require from time to time some modification, from the change of external circumstances, the progress of opinion, and the intellectual improvement of the people. That in the ancient English and Irish Universities, and in the Colleges connected with them, the interests of religious and useful learning have not advanced to an extent commensurate with the great resources and high position of those bodies: that the Collegiate Statutes of the fifteenth century occasionally prohibit local authorities from introducing any alterations into voluminous codes, of which a large proportion are now obsolete; that better laws are needed to regulate the ceremony of matriculation and the granting of Degrees, to diminish the exclusiveness of the University Libraries, to provide for a fairer distribution of the rewards of scientific and literary merit, to extend the permission of marriage to Tutors of Colleges, and to facilitate the registration of electors for the Universities; that additional checks might be considered with reference to the continued extravagance of individual students; and that the mode of tenure of College property ought to be ameliorated, particularly in Ireland: That, as it is Her Majesty's right and prerogative to name Visitors and Commissioners to inquire into the ancient Universities and Colleges of England and Ireland, an humble address be presented to Her Majesty, praying that Her Majesty would be graciously pleased to issue her Royal Commission of Enquiry into that state of the Universities and Colleges of Oxford, Cambridge, and Dublin, with a view to assist in the adaptation of those important institutions to the requirements of modern times.

Lord John Russell, though he would not accept the motion, advised Her Majesty to issue the Royal Commission. He followed this by letters to the Prince Consort (Chancellor of Cambridge) and to the Duke of Wellington (Chancellor of Oxford) explaining that the Commission would receive evidence voluntarily given, and assuring them that 'the utmost care will be taken in selecting Commissioners, who may not only be well qualified for their important task, but who may inspire confidence and respect by their character and position'. On the last day of August 1850 the names were announced.

13

William Sewell, one of the Oxford tutors, who had dramatically burnt Froude's book, *The Nemesis of Faith*, in Exeter College hall the year before, now published four lampoons, *The University Commission, or Lord John Russell's Post Bag of 27th April 1850*. In these, he professed to discover through a series of imaginary letters addressed to the Prime Minister, the motives behind the establishment of the Commission. One of them suggested that in the Great Exhibition Building 'sufficient space should be set apart to exhibit to advantage a new specimen of a Model University, which it is the intention of his R.H. to manufacture in England. His R.H. trusts, that by the infusion of new principles from Germany, the nearly exhausted and effete efforts of our English art in this department may be brought to compete with those of the Continent'. To the influence of the Prince Consort was added that of Harriet Martineau, whom he fancifully depicted delivering a lecture on Eudaemonology:

> 'The world you know (I won't now glance
> At proofs that it was made by chance)
> But surely it was never intended
> To be what 'tis—and must be mended.'

He sketched the arrival of one of the proposed Commissioners at an Oxford College:

> 'I beg your pardon, Mr. Rector
> But I'm the Government Inspector.
> The Privy Council, in anxiety
> To aid this ancient, learned society,
> Begged me, as I was passing by,
> Just to drop in promiscuously
> And ascertain what steps your college
> Is taking in its useful knowledge.'

He catechises him in

'Law, grammar, music, diatetics,
Optics, with swimming, and aesthetics,
Gymnastics, surg'ry and conchology
And The — no — no I mean *Ge*ology
Colonization, economics,
Brewing, baking, and mnemonics
With rhetoric, and the art vehicular
And history general and particular,
Algebra, skating, and astronomy,
With metaphysics and gastronomy;
Give me an outline of pneumatics;
Explain how you would cure rheumatics;
Define rent, wages, and mahogany,
What's the last theory of cosmogony?'

The Inspector's significant slip of the tongue in almost mentioning theology was not lost upon Sewell's readers, and was to be given striking point two years later when Newman lectured at Dublin. But Lord John Russell was unmoved. To his way of thinking 'as the Reform Bill was to the Borough Proprietors, and the repeal of the Corn Laws to the Landlords, so is a Commission on the Universities to those who are in enjoyment of fellowships'.

14

Sewell's jeers at the Prince Consort and Jowett's remarks on the German Ocean were reflections of a profound influence on English academic life at this time. For German influence too can be traced in the foundation of another metropolitan institution in 1842, when Dr. John Gardner, Professor of Chemistry to the Society of Apothecaries, outlined a scheme for establishing a College of Chemistry based on that of Giessen, where he had studied. It was to be christened the 'Davy College of Practical Chemistry', and to establish it, a provisional committee consisting of well-known names was formed. The prospectus illustrated the direction of their thoughts. The college, it hoped

will be mainly devoted to *Pure Science*; at the same time, to meet the exigencies of this country, and to adopt the latest improvements in the continental schools, an appendage will be provided, devoted to the Economic Arts, where enquiries to Pharmacy, Agriculture, and other Arts may be pursued.

Unfortunately, however, the space at the Royal Institution was limited. At the first meeting of an enlarged council for the new college held on 14 January 1845 a number of arguments were advanced and published on the utility of the proposed college, not only to the mining industry, but also as a remedy to the existing agricultural depression. Six months later, a college council was formally elected, a constitution adopted, and the Prince Consort named as president. By October, temporary buildings were opened in Hanover Square, and twenty-six students enrolled under von Hofmann, among them such men as Abel, Bloxam, Galloway, Rowney, Nicholson, and de la Rue. Special buildings were erected in Oxford Street, and the number of students rose to forty.[37]

The example of, and his own experience at, Giessen stimulated J. S. Muspratt, son of the founder of the alkali industry in Lancashire, to found a private college of chemistry at Liverpool in 1848. He tried to secure its recognition by the University of London, the College of Surgeons and the Society of Apothecaries. But the latter proved awkward. As an institution it achieved some success, being well reported in the *New York Times* as late as 29 September 1860.

The Prince Consort's devotion to the cause of industrial education was reflected in his relations with the Society of Arts, whose President he became in 1843. From that time onwards the torpor and ineptitude which had characterised it under the previous president fell away, and the Society initiated a series of industrial and fine art exhibitions. These proved so successful that a great international exhibition was organised in London: the Prince Consort playing a leading rôle in securing official co-operation. The lessons of this exhibition, held in Hyde Park in 1851, were profound. They involved a new outlook on university problems, and began a new chapter in university history.[38]

REFERENCES

1. *Table Talk and Omniana of S. T. Coleridge* (Oxford, 1917), 175. C. Kelsall, *Phantasm of a University* (London, 1814), 118, 170; J. Yates, *Thoughts on the Advancement of Academical Education in England* (London, 1826), 172–3, 178. The Liverpool Royal Institution, officially opened on 25 November 1817, was modelled on its London counterpart. ORMEROD, H. A., *The Liverpool Royal Institution* (Liverpool, 1953).

2. BRANDE, W. T. (1788–1866), was elected Fellow of the Royal Society in 1809; Copley Medallist in 1813 and was joint secretary from 1816–26. In association with Michael Faraday he edited from 1816 to 1836 *The Quarterly Journal of Science and Art*, and was the author of manuals on Geology (1817), Chemistry (1819), and Pharmacy (1825) and also edited *A Dictionary of Science Literature and Art* (1842) which reached a third edition by 1853. For the Apothecaries see Olinthus Gregory, *Memoirs of . . . John Mason Good.*

3. The Apothecaries were forced to abandon their idea of a medical school because of the opposition of the College of Surgeons, B. Hamilton, 'The Medical Profession in the Eighteenth Century,' *Economic History Review*, IV (Cambridge, 1951), 168. For Charing Cross Hospital and Medical School see *Historical Account* . . . by William Hunter (London, 1914).

4. WHEELER, A. E., *A Short Account of the University of Leeds* (1924), 7. John Marshall 1765-1845, who became the father-in-law of William Whewell, was a pioneer of flax spinning by machinery, a supporter of the local mechanics institute and also sat on the Council of London University. R. V. Taylor, *Biographia Leodiensis* (London, 1865), 411-15.

5. WHITING, C. E., *The University of Durham*, 119-22; G. Grey-Turner and W. D. Arnison, *The Newcastle-on-Tyne School of Medicine* (Newcastle, 1934).

6. WILKINSON, K. D., *The History of the Birmingham Medical School* (Birmingham, 1925); Vincent and Hinton, *The University of Birmingham* (Birmingham, 1947), 39-46.

7. MUIR, Ramsay, *A Plea for a University of Liverpool* (1901), 7; *William Roscoe* (Liverpool, 1906), 25, ORMEROD, H. A., *op. cit.*, 31.

8. THOMPSON, J., *The University of Manchester* (1886), 29.

9. COTTLE, B., and SHERBORNE, J. W., *The Life of a University* (Bristol, 1951), 4.

10. BICKERTON, T. H., *A Medical History of Liverpool from the Earliest Days to 1920* (Liverpool, 1936).

11. *Report of a Select Committee on Medical Education*, Parliamentary Papers, xxii (1834). For an account of further struggles between the apothecaries and the colleges of Physicians and Surgeons see Arvel B. Erickson, *The Public Career of Sir James Graham* (Oxford, 1952), 244-55.

12. HALE BELLOT, H., *University College*, London (London, 1926).

13. PATTERSON, M. W., *Sir Francis Burdett and his Times* (London, 1931), ii, 554-5.

14. HALE BELLOT, *op. cit.*, 143. 'The reform of medical education was regarded by some at least among the promoters of the university as the most practicable part of the project, and their expectations were fulfilled. It is hardly too much to say that in its early years, the university owed its survival to the success of its medical school.'

15. HEARNSHAW, F. J. C., *A Centenary History of King's College, London 1828-1928* (London, 1928), 35ff. It is significant that in 1834 the young Thomas Lovell Beddoes should write to his uncle 'in England, the profession (i.e. medicine) must be almost intolerable, and the want of real universities renders the attainment of a chair to any but the most favoured sons of science almost impossible'. *Times Literary Supplement* (London, 1952), No. 2,645, 668.

16. STANLEY, A. P., *Life of Dr. Arnold* (London, 1890), 260-1. Arnold thought that 'Unbelief was making a catspaw of Dissent', and was so troubled about university affairs that he wrote to his wife (p. 334) 'when the faults of the London University revive all my tenderness for Oxford, then the faults of Oxford repel me again, and make it impossible for me to sympathise with a spirit so uncongenial. Wherefore I wish the wish of Achilles, when he looked out upon the battle of the ships, and desired that the Greeks and Trojans might destroy one another, and leave the field open for better men.'

17. WHITING, C. E., *op. cit.*, 33. E. A. Hughes, 'The Bishops and Reform 1831-3', *E.H.R.* (1941), lvi, 459-89.

18. DICEY, A. V., *Law and Opinion In England* (London, 1905), 320-1.

KELLY, T., 'The Origin of the Mechanics' Institutes', *British Journal of Educational Studies* (1952), 17-27.

19. Burns, C. D., *Birkbeck College* (London, 1924), J. L. and B. Hammond, *The Bleak Age* (Penguin, 1947) 169; George Godwin, *Queen Mary College* (London, 1939).

20. Moore-Smith, G. C., *The Sheffield People's College* (Sheffield, 1912).

21. *Report of the Royal Commission on the University of Oxford* (1852), 79–80.

22. Mathison, G. F., *How Can the Church Educate the People?* (London, 1844), 74 and 91.

23. *Fifty Years of Progress in Education. A Review of the work of the College of Preceptors from its Foundation in 1846 to its Jubilee in 1896* (London, 1897).

24. Bardsley Brash, W., *The Story of our Colleges* (London, 1935).

25. Carlyle, A., *New Letters of Thomas Carlyle* (London, 1904), i, 47.

26. Martin, T. (ed.) *The Diary of M. Faraday* (London, 1932), i, 367–430.

27. Summerson, J., *John Nash* (London, 1935), 128.

Howarth, O. J. R., *The Evolution of Scientific Societies* (Glasgow 1941).

28. Weld, C. R., *History of the Royal Society* (1848), ii, 103–205; H. C. Cameron, *Sir Joseph Banks* (London, 1952), 177. Banks' death in 1820 removed another munificent private patron of science whose house in Soho Square had been previously accessible to scientific men of every nation.

29. Howarth, O. J. R., *The British Association for the Advancement of Science—A Retrospect 1831–1931* (London, 1931), 43. As also did Owen, president in 1858, claiming that it 'realised the grand Philosophical Dream . . . of Francis Bacon'. Local lecturers were long familiar with the theme e.g. on 6 April 1824 Dr. Williamson of Leeds addressed the Sheffield Literary and Philosophical Society on 'the influence of Lord Bacon's philosophical speculation in promoting the advance of experimental science'.

30. Joule, J. P. (1818–89) was elected F.R.S. in 1850. From 1844 onwards he had a laboratory at Whalley Range and was librarian (1844), secretary (1846), Vice-President (1851), and President (1860) of the Manchester Literary and Philosophical Society.

31. Fiddes, E., *Chapters in the History of Owens College and of Manchester University* (Manchester, 1937), 206.

32. Jones, H. L., *A Plan of a University of Manchester* (1836).

33. Huber, V. A., *Die Englischen Universitäten* (1839), English translation by F. W. Newman (a younger brother of J. H. Newman, and professor of classical literature at Manchester New College), London, 1943, was described by Rashdall (iii, 2) as 'one of the most worthless university histories which it has been my lot to peruse' yet it contains as an appendix Thomas Wright's *Historical Doubts on the Biography of Alfred attributed to Asser* which exposed the myth that King Alfred founded The University of Oxford.

34. Thompson, J., *History of the Owens College* (1886).

35. V.C.H. *Hampshire* (1903), ii, 385–6.

36. For the full story of this see A. I. Tillyard, *A History of University Reform* (Cambridge, 1913), 101–61; Lewis Campbell, *On the Nationalisation of the Old English Universities* (London, 1901), 72–95; and W. H. G. Armytage, 'James Heywood's Resolution: Prelude and Finale', *Universities Review* (Bristol, 1950), xxii, 139–45.

37. Humberstone, T. L., in *London and The Advancement of Science* (1931), 171–3.

38. Steegman, John, *Consort of Taste* (London, 1950), 140–2.

CHAPTER NINE

The Conflict of Ideas, 1851-67

THE lessons of the Great Exhibition of 1851 were sketched in a series of lectures delivered before the Society of Arts in the following year. In one of these, Lyon Playfair, a professor in the School of Mines in Jermyn Street and a juror of the Exhibition, attacked the complacency of his fellow countrymen, and warned them not to 'nourish their vanity' on such industrial success as they had achieved. He continued:

a rapid transition is taking place in Industry; raw material, formerly our capital advantage over other nations, is gradually being equalised in price, and made available to all by improvements in locomotion, and Industry must in future be supported, not by a competition of local advantages, but by a competition of intellect.[1]

Lyon Playfair's remedy was a simple one: the establishment of Industrial Colleges for scientific research and teaching. His observations were underlined by Henry Cole who expressed a hope that his hearers would see 'the foundation of an Industrial University' on a site opposite that occupied by the Exhibition.[2]

I

Alarmed at the evidence of foreign industrial expertise, and animated by the lively sentiments of percipient minds like Playfair and Henry Cole, Parliament voted a grant of £150,000 which, with the £186,000 profits of the Exhibition, purchased three vast estates at South Kensington (the Gore House, Villiers, and Harington) where all the technical institutions of the metropolis could be centralised. Here, six years later, was established the Department of Science and Art (formed by the amalgamation of a Department of Practical Art founded in 1852 and a similar Department of Science in 1853) which was placed under the control of the Education Department of the Privy Council. The Science and Art Department, under a series of energetic administrators like Lyon Playfair, Henry Cole and John Donnelly, built up a vast system of grants-in-aid to organised science schools up and down the country, awarded on the results on annual examinations.[3] These examinations were regarded by T. H. Huxley as 'the most important engine for forcing science into ordinary education'. Huxley in fact was one of the reasons for their success, for not only was he an examiner, but he also lectured for the Science and Art Department.

The grants of the Science and Art Department, lasting as they did until the Department ceased to exist in 1899, incubated a number of provincial schools, at least three of which were later to emerge as university institutions. Exeter's school of art, founded in 1855, was enlarged ten years later when the Royal Albert Memorial Building was erected in Queen Street for the study of art, science, and literature. So too in Reading art classes were established in 1860 which later merged with science classes to become a school of some standing. At Southampton, a science and art department was opened in 1871 in connection with the Hartley Institute.

2

The proposed Industrial University would, it was hoped, grow around the Museum of Practical Geology, opened by the Prince Consort in 1851. This institution, designed to offer instruction in Mining and Applied Science, sprang from the Geological Survey's collection, accumulated in a house in Craig's Court, near Scotland Yard. Its promoter, Henry de la Beche, was appointed director, and when the Museum opened in Jermyn Street, he had gathered together a distinguished staff: Warington Smyth for Mining and Mineralogy, Andrew C. Ramsay for Geology, John Percy, 'the father of English Metallurgy', Robert Hunt for Mechanical Science, Edward Forbes for Natural History, and Lyon Playfair for Chemistry.

When Lyon Playfair was offered the secretaryship of the newly created Science and Art Department in 1853 his vacant chair was given to Hofmann, and the Royal College of Chemistry was incorporated into the Jermyn Street establishment, though still retaining its Oxford Street building, and its title. Its most famous student W. H. Perkin, the discoverer of the first aniline dye, joined it in that year. He like William Crookes (of the high-vacuum Crookes tube) and F. A. Abel (co-inventor of cordite)—also pupils of Hofmann—won a knighthood for his contributions to science. In the following year, when Edward Forbes was succeeded in his lectureship by T. H. Huxley, a further impetus was given to the broadening of the curriculum, for Huxley favoured the extension of its scope to cover the whole field of applied science, and not merely those allied to mining. The Prince Consort thought so too, he visualised it as 'a Government educational establishment for the diffusion of science generally as applied to productive industry'. Since the number of students taking the mining course was small, it looked as if the title adopted in 1853—The Metropolitan School of Science applied to Mining and the Arts—was going to be justified.

But the bright hopes were clouded. On the death of Sir Henry de la Beche in 1855, a new Director, Sir Roderick Murchison, was appointed and he was determined that the school should stand or fall by the success of its mining students. The title was changed in 1857 to the Government School of Mines, and again in 1863 to the Royal School of Mines. 'I view it simply as the school of British Geology and mines: the affiliated sciences are all subordinate to that fundamental point,' he wrote, and for the rest of this period, so it was, despite the vigorous efforts of Huxley to alter it.[4]

3

Meanwhile, the commissioners appointed by Parliament were wrestling with the shortcomings of the existing curriculum offered at Oxford. Wrestling is perhaps too robust a verb, for Stanley, the secretary of the commission, told Jowett that 'the raw material had to be dragged through a den of lions'.[5]

The lions who resisted them included the Bishop of Exeter who replied by return of post to the Commissioners' invitation to co-operate that he could not see

> without deepest concern and astonishment, the name of our precious Gracious Sovereign used by Her advisers to 'authorize and empower' your Lordship and your colleagues to institute an inquisition which no precedent could justify, and which, even if it can claim as precedents similar Commissions, issued within our living memory, for visiting other Corporations, has yet, as related to the venerable bodies which are now concerned, had absolutely no parallel since the fatal attempt of King James II to subject them to his unhallowed control.

Equally hostile was the Professor of Poetry, an anti-tractarian pluralist, who expressed the forebodings of his kind that

> no respect for the abilities, attainments and position of the members of your body can remove from thoughtful men the apprehension that formidable innovations, and, in our opinion, disastrous changes, are contemplated under the present Commission, to ascertain what, for all practical purposes, is already known. There is nothing to reassure us of the future.[6]

For five months, no sign of co-operation was forthcoming from the Hebdomadal Board which, having taken legal advice and found that the Commission was illegal and unconstitutional, sat back and waited for the Commissioners to make the next move.

Though such replies to their initial letters as they did receive were most unhelpful, the Commissioners employed fourteen meetings in compiling seven papers of questions. These were sent to the authorities of the University, the Professors, the Vice-Chancellor, the Assessor in the Vice-Chancellor's Court, the Public Examiner, the Colleges as corporate bodies, and the individual members of colleges. It was a wide net, cast with great skill. Many colleges evaded it: Christ Church returned no reply; the ninety-five-year-old president of Magdalen in a letter addressed to 'the Rev. A. P. Stanley, Fellow of University College', declined to answer, so did Brasenose and University Colleges. New, Oriel, Queen's, Trinity, Jesus, Worcester, and Wadham Colleges were very unhelpful. But others were more gracious, and though Balliol, as a College, refused to give evidence, the Dean and the Bursar supplied information, and so did many individual fellows. All Souls, St. John's, Pembroke, Magdalen Hall, St. Alban Hall, and St. Edmund Hall answered the questions. Corpus co-operated wholeheartedly. Merton reserved its documents, and Lincoln referred the Commissioners to the Bodleian for its statutes, but otherwise were of great use.

At their twentieth meeting, held on 18 March 1851, the Commissioners received the official reply of the Vice-Chancellor that the Commission was illegal and unconstitutional. They submitted it to the law officers of the Crown, who came to the rescue with a much more competently worded opinion, which was relayed to Oxford. But even this did not quell the opposition: for a petition to Her Majesty in Council was sanctioned in the House of Convocation by 249 votes to 105 on the 21 May 1851, and was followed by a similar petition by Brasenose College on the 12 July. Since the Privy Council advised the Queen to entertain neither of these two petitions, the question was tactfully dropped.

By this time, the Commission had held no less than fifty-one meetings, the last twenty of which had been occupied in drafting a report. This report occupied them for a further thirty-six meetings till the 23 April 1852. It was published in May. Its recommendations went further than the evidence suggested. Divided under the four heads—state and discipline, studies, revenues, and colleges—the compact and orderly nature of its presentation did much to wean Gladstone from uncritical support of his Alma Mater. It deepened his insight into the nature of the change required, and changed the nature of his relationship to his constituency. As a contemporary observed, 'he is liberalising them, instead of their torifying him. He is giving them a push forwards instead of their giving him a pull backwards'.[7]

The Report suggested that some initiating power should be vested in a remodelled Congregation, to consist of the heads, senior tutors, proctors, professors, and lecturers, conducting their debates in English instead of the traditional Latin: that all distinctions between noblemen, gentlemen-commoners, and commoners should be discontinued: and that liberty should be given for the extension of the University, both by the foundation of new halls, and by permitting members of the University to live in private lodgings without connection with a college or hall. In their recommendations on the course of studies to be followed, the Commissioners explicitly stated that they did 'not believe that any measures which the University has yet adopted are sufficient to remedy the evil' of the extensive decay of learning which was either professional, or preparatory to a profession. The Commissioners instanced the complete absence of a school of medicine—'those few persons who take medical degrees there with a view to the social consideration which these degrees give, or the preferments in the University for which they are necessary, study their profession elsewhere'. The clergy were as badly off as the doctors, for the Commissioners reported 'no efficient means at present exists in the University for training Candidates for Holy Orders in those studies which belong particularly to their profession', and instanced the rarity of learned theologians in the University. On legal studies, they opined that the majority of barristers were educated at Cambridge: 'the connection of Oxford with the Profession of the law is also unsatisfactory.'

Appreciative as they were of the statute of 1850 (due to come into operation in 1853) establishing, among other things, the four final honours schools of Literae Humaniores, Mathematics and Physical Science treated Mathematically, Natural Science, and Law and Modern History, the Commissioners wanted the Physical Sciences given greater recognition. They regarded it as 'encumbered with the necessity of continuing the study of Literae Humaniores to the end of the university course'.

Though they were not prepared to make Physical Science compulsory for all, they urged that it should be allotted a fair share of fellowships and prizes. The existing Museums were surveyed and found inadequate, the Commissioners quoting with approval Dr. Acland's plea for the erection of a great 'Museum of Science'.[8] They also appended a letter from Professor Liebig, written from Giessen on the 2 December 1851, in which he remarked that everywhere but in

England it was regarded as necessary to incorporate the Natural Sciences into University courses.

That the Commissioners should quote German authority is scarcely surprising: two of them (Tait and Stanley) had been to Bonn in 1839 especially to examine the German University system, and urged their colleagues to revive the professoriate, and the physical scientists supported them.

The witnesses before them also agreed—with the exception of Mark Pattison, and he was converted later—on this point. H. H. Vaughan—perhaps the most able of Arnold's pupils—who since 1848 had held the Regius Professorship of Modern History, argued that Professorships should be awarded not merely for teaching, but also for the support of learned men, saying:

> The great want of Oxford hitherto has not been merely nor chiefly that the Professors have not been sufficiently active in teaching, but that the system has disfavoured the existence, and missed the general effects, of Professorial learning. Some powerful men we have had; a considerable body, or a constant succession of such we have not had; men who could give authoritative opinions on matters connected with the sciences; whose words when spoken in public or private could kindle an enthusiasm on important branches of learning, or could chill the zeal for petty or factitious erudition; men whose names and presence in the University could command respect for the place, whether attracting students of all kinds and ages to it, or directing upon it the sight and interest and thought of the whole learned world; men whose investigations could be perpetually adding to knowledge, not as mere conduits to convey it, but as fountains to augment its scantiness and freshen its sleeping waters.

To Bonamy Price—another old Rugbeian—the professoriate was 'the very kernel of University reform'.

To assist the professoriate the Commissioners advocated the appointment of 'lecturers' instead of the private tutors then monopolising instruction at Oxford. These proposed 'lecturers' would also be able to undertake the instruction of non-collegiate students (though the Commissioners never used that term) as well as 'furnishing a body of competent candidates in each Faculty from which the successors to vacant Professorships might be selected with less risk of mistake'.

The decay of professorial teaching was, as the Commissioners revealed, due to collegiate monopoly of instruction. The Professorship of Greek was only worth forty pounds a year, and many others were barely worth a hundred pounds: these compared very unfavourably with the few examples of college stipends about which the Commissioners could get evidence. For investigation into the arcana of college life was strongly resisted and the Commissioners had to consult the Public Record Office, the British Museum, the Bodleian, and Lambeth Library for their evidence. Here too, James Heywood was most helpful, for, said the Commissioners in their opening paragraph, 'he liberally furnished the Commission, not only with copies of the translations of the various statutes published by him, but with several manuscripts which he had caused to be translated at his own cost'.

Laxities of study, residence, and employment of revenues prevailed with restricted elections and preferments to fellowships. Only four per cent. of the total fellowships in the whole university could be described as open in the sense 'that a young man, on first coming up, sees his way clear towards them with no other bar than may arise from his own want of talents or diligence'. This four per cent. comprised ten Balliol, and twelve Oriel fellowships; both of them colleges which had good reason to be proud of the results of such a policy. Frederick Temple himself from Balliol, told the Commissioners that restricted fellowships were 'that whose remedy is most needed and most important'. He continued:

the effect of these restrictions is most mischievous. Men who are naturally well fitted to be country clergymen are bribed, because they are born in some parish in Rutland, to remain in Oxford as Fellows, until they are not only unfit for that, but for everything else. The interests of learning are intrusted to those who have neither talents nor inclination for the subject. The Fellowships are looked upon and used as mere stepping stones to a living. A large number of Fellows live away from the place, and thus in reality convert the emoluments to a purpose quite alien from that for which they were intended. On the other hand, the undergraduates suffer a double loss: first in being deprived of the legitimate stimulus to study, and secondly, in having their instruction intrusted to an inferior body of men.[9]

4

Though a future Archbishop of Canterbury might think like this (and nine years later he was to provoke unmerited suspicions of his orthodoxy by his essay on *The Education of the World*), the rest of the Church party in Oxford did not. Many of them, led by Dr. Pusey, regarded the introduction of a lay professoriate as most prejudical to morals, religion, and the unity of the university. For those who could not follow Pusey's high dialectics on the priestly element in university teaching, there was Henry Mansel to poke among the ribs with his *Phrontisterion*:

'Professors we,
From over the sea,
From the land where Professors in plenty be;
And we thrive and flourish, as well we may,
In the land that produced one Kant with a K,
And many Cants with a C.'

The Hebdomadal Board appointed a committee to consider the proposals which, after six months' consideration, reported in December 1852 that to adopt them would be disastrous. An Association of tutors, led by James Mozley of Magdalen, and Charles Marriot, the sub-dean of Oriel, strongly opposed the system of professorial teaching, the removal of religious tests, the admission of lay fellows, and the remodelling of Congregation.[10] Yet even they admitted the need of some reforms: they would sanction affiliated halls, limit local restrictions on college emoluments, and tax college property for university teaching. Opinions, stated with emphasis before both the Royal Commission and the Hebdomadal Board's Committee, were further ventilated in pamphlets by Vaughan[11] and Pusey[12]. Even Roundell Palmer entered the arena with a pamphlet of *Suggestions*.

In the thick of the debate, the task of preparing a Parliamentary Bill was confided to W. E. Gladstone, M.P. for Oxford and now Chancellor of the Exchequer. He had opposed the Commission in 1850, now in the autumn of 1853 he changed his mind. 'In none of the enterprises of his life', recorded his biographer, 'was he more industrious or more energetic.'[13] Gladstone himself told a correspondent: 'as one of your burgesses, I stand upon the line that divides Oxford from the outer world, and as a sentinel, I cry out to tell you what I have seen from that position.' He certainly had much to cry about: three hundred and fifty letters written by him at this time on this subject survive in transcribed form among his papers.

The Cambridge Commission put into his hands a weapon which he pressed upon the Cabinet to the exclusion of Jowett's idea that the University should be left to manage its own affairs: the Executive Commission, endowed with statutory powers to manage the details of university reform. Apart from this suggestion, the Cambridge report, which appeared in November 1852, contained nothing so radical as the suggestions of their Oxford colleagues. Whether the astral preoccupations of two of the Cambridge Commissioners (George Peacock and Sir John Herschel), or the tenderheartedness of a third (Adam Sedgwick is said to have broken down while reading his own peroration), or the legal cautiousness of a fourth (Sir John

Romilly was the Attorney-General) prevailed in their deliberations is not known. What is more likely, they seem to have had less to deplore, since a year before they were appointed the University had appointed a reforming syndicate, whose report, published a month after the Oxford Royal Commission had made theirs, was highly endorsed by the Cambridge Commission. Nevertheless, the Cambridge Commission did, as the late D. A. Winstanley says, 'produce a fairly complete plan for the reorganisation and extension of the educational system of the University'.[14] They recommended that Boards of Studies should be established for Classics, Theology, Law, Moral Science, Natural Science, and Medicine; that a General Council of Studies should be set up, that Civil Engineering and Mathematics should be encouraged, that the ordinary degree should be made a reality, and that ten new chairs in Practical Engineering, Descriptive Geometry, Chemistry, Anatomy, Divinity (2), General Jurisprudence, International Law, Latin, and Zoology should be created; that a large staff of lecturers should be appointed, and that the individual colleges should contribute out of their revenues to maintain this university expansion. This latter proposal was greeted by Whewell, Master of Trinity, as 'a violation of the ordinary rules of property so strong, as to belong only to times of revolution and confiscation'.

As soon as Gladstone's Bill came before the House, Lord John Russell announced that the Government did not see its way clear to abolish the religious tests. James Heywood was ready. After a reasonably argued plea for the removal of restrictions, he gave notice that he would move an amendment. This he did on the 27 April: objecting to the clerical constitution of the proposed Hebdomadal Board; and pleading for more justice to private tutors, and the relaxation of the celibate rule for fellowships. He was strongly supported by other Dissenters in the House. But in spite of their efforts, and the rather factitious support of Disraeli, the amendment was rejected by 172 votes to 90.

With Heywood and his associates hammering at every clause, the Government realised that to get the Bill through the House, it would have to be cut down. So sixteen clauses of great detail (including one which gave the colleges power to contribute up to one-fifth of their income for the support of university Professorships and Lectureships) were jettisoned with the idea that the ensuing Statutory Commission would take them up. Yet even when this lightweight Bill appeared once more on the 15 June, Heywood was ready. He moved the insertion of a clause rendering it unnecessary for a person to make any oath except that of allegiance before matriculating; the object being to put Oxford on a level with Cambridge in this respect. This was carried by 252 votes to 161 in the face of a plea from the Prime Minister to drop the matter. Encouraged by his success, James Heywood then moved another clause which went a step further, i.e. that the religious test should be abolished for any of the degrees in Arts, Laws, or Medicine. But this was negatived by 205 to 196. So he moved it again on the 26 June, and this time carried it by 233 to 79. 'Great cheering' followed the announcement of the results of the division.

In the Lords, the Bill proved rather indigestible. Lord Winchilsea, whose hatred for the Catholic Emancipation had led him to fight a duel with the Duke of Wellington twenty-four years earlier, now burst out with most violent language against this equally liberal measure of relief. 'The present Bill,' he exploded to his fellow peers, 'proposes to effect the most dreadful confiscation of property that ever took place in an enlightened country, and is the grossest violation of justice that has ever characterised the Legislature of England. There never was a measure so fraught with evil, so unjust in principle, so iniquitous in its details, as this accursed Bill.' His fellow peers allowed both his language and the Bill to pass. On the 7 August, it received Royal assent.

5

Two years later, a similar bill to reform the University of Cambridge was entrusted to the son of the Earl of Radnor, Pleydell-Bouverie. In the general discussion which began on the 30 May 1856, James Heywood once more championed the cause of his co-religionists, moving that the tests be abolished for prospective holders of college emoluments, and for membership of the governing body of the university. Both clauses were added to the Bill. He tried to ensure that the statutes of the colleges should henceforth be framed in the English language, but this was negatived by 74 to 58. In a series of amendments on the 9 June, he proposed that the colleges should have power to frame statutes regulating the duration of 'headships'; that words should be inserted in the Bill 'providing for the encouragement of studies in Modern History, Science, and Languages'; and that students conscientiously objecting should be exempt from compulsory attendance at chapel. All three amendments were likewise negatived by large majorities.

The Lords refashioned Heywood's anti-test clause: eighty-nine-year-old Lord Lyndhurst, as High Steward of Cambridge, moving that 'it was a most important thing to take care that those who governed the University should be members of the Church of England'. Lyndhurst got his way, by a majority of 47.

The Cambridge Bill was drafted by Dr. Philpott from the provisions of its Oxford predecessor and they had much in common. The Hebdomadal Council at Oxford, and a Council of the Senate at Cambridge were in future to be elected from the Heads of Houses, the Professors, Doctors, and other Masters of Arts in certain proportions. Oaths, tests, and declarations were abolished for all Cambridge Degrees (except those in Divinity) and for Matriculation and all Bachelors' Degrees at Oxford (where they were retained for the Masters' and Doctors' Degrees).

6

To effect changes in both universities, Executive Commissions were established with powers previously denied to the Commissioners of 1850: they could compel the production of documents and the donation of information. By these means they were able to regroup endowments and to derestrict fellowships.

Oxford colleges (with the exception of St. John's, who declined to accept the Commissioners' ordinance and the matter had to go to the Privy Council) yielded up rich prizes. Chichele Professorships of Modern History and International Law at All Souls were refashioned out of ten previously existing fellowships; Waynflete Professorships of Moral and Metaphysical Philosophy, of Chemistry, of Mineralogy, and of Physical Geography were established at Magdalen; Corpus agreed to support one and possibly two Classical Professors; Merton, to endow a Linacre Professor of Physiology, Queen's, to pay part of the salary of the Sedleian Professor of Natural Philosophy; Christ Church, to appoint two Lee Readers in Anatomy and Chemistry; Wadham, a Reader in Experimental Philosophy. There were other changes. Paring of the powers of heads of houses, relaxation of obligations to ancient founders' wishes, uniformity of salary (as far as possible). simplification of procedure, recasting of statutes: these were some of the many changes that opened the pores of Oxford to the world.

At Cambridge there were similar changes. Obligations of residence were enforced; Trinity College ceded its presumptive rights to the Regius Professorships of Hebrew, Divinity, and Greek; new Mathematical Professorships were created out of Lady Sadler's bequest for Algebra Lectureships in all the colleges; boards of studies were established; and antiquated offices like those of the Taxors and Scrutators were abolished. Looking back upon it, Cambridge's latest historian admits that 'a new academic world was created by the revised code'.[15]

7

The revived élan of Oxford and Cambridge awakened a consciousness of their national duty and several attempts were made to 'colonise' the provinces. There was certainly an open field for such colonisation, for both the local philosophical societies and the mechanics' institutes were in bad shape. Thus J. W. Hudson, the secretary of the Manchester Athenaeum, lamented in 1851:

> The provincial philosophical societies have completed their career, they are the debris of an age that has passed away. Originally formed upon the contracted basis of improving rather than diffusing or popularising the truths of science . . . they fear that any fusion with the *people* would reduce them to the impure commercial amalgam of general usefulness. The managers of the Philosophical Societies of Birmingham, Leeds, and Sheffield have adhered to difficulties and inactivity, rather than sanction the development of one united and well directed institution. These societies, in addition to those at Liverpool, Bristol, and Manchester, find it difficult to secure the number of persons requisite to constitute a meeting.[16]

From Oxford, William Sewell (who had rushed into print in 1834 with a pamphlet violently refuting the claims of Dissenters to be admitted to the University of Oxford, exclaiming 'I deny the right of liberty of conscience wholly and utterly') actually suggested before the Royal Commission of 1850 that local professoriates at Birmingham and Manchester should give instruction as a preparation for degrees at Oxford and Cambridge, financed by payments from the students themselves, by private endowments, benefactions, and the generosity of the university presses. Though the Commission snubbed him (they could do nothing else in view of his recent action in burning a colleague's book in the quadrangle of the college and securing that colleague's dismissal), others returned to the suggestion as a means whereby the intellectual hegemony of the two universities might be maintained in the provinces.[17]

From Cambridge, Lord Arthur Hervey (later to be Bishop of Bath and Wells) saw quite clearly that it was 'already common for the elder boys of grammar and commercial schools to attend their lectures' (of the mechanics' institutes) and lamented their 'desultory and unconnected character'. He calculated that there must be over a thousand of such institutions in the United Kingdom, and asked why the railway could not be utilised to carry lecturers to them from the universities. Instancing his own University of Cambridge he calculated that four 'circuit professors' of Natural Philosophy, Geology, Astronomy, and Literature should each be able to cover twenty towns, and cited Manchester, Birmingham, and Brighton as examples. The necessary finance could be provided by each town subscribing £20 a year towards the salary of the professors.[18] Yet Hervey inadvertently observed that by so doing, the masses could also be led to appreciate 'the advantages which the noble Universities of this land confer upon the wealthier classes'.

The implications of this so-called 'extension policy' of Oxford and Cambridge were foreseen by an anonymous author who in 1851 published a pamphlet on the *Public Right to the Universities* in which he forecast:

> It would be a repetition, in a more Spartan form, of Mrs. Mother-country, of Downing Street, over her unfortunate progeny across the seas. The Universities of Oxford and Cambridge would have supreme control over her provincial offshoots; the colonist graduates would have no power even in the sense of that much used phrase of mystery—a 'virtual representation'.[19]

Yet both these suggestions, Sewell's from Oxford, and Hervey's from Cambridge, initiated a response in 1858 when Oxford and Cambridge agreed to administer the local examination of the Society of Arts and certify completion of work done at the mechanics' institutes.[20] This stemmed also from T. D. Acland's proposal that Oxford should award to pupils in middle-class schools the letters 'A.A.' or Associate in Arts, and developed into the 'school certificate' examination.[21]

A third, and by far the most original suggestion, emanated from James Hole, the secretary of the Yorkshire Union of Mechanics' Institutes. In 1853 he proposed that mechanics' institutes should be assisted by government grants, and become constituent colleges of the proposed industrial university which had been mooted. This was an ambitious scheme, even for 1853.[22]

A fourth scheme, less ambitious and more realistic, was that of Henry Chester, chairman of the council of the Royal Society of Arts. He advocated a national union of mechanics' institutes, which should be examined by the Society. Published in the spring of the following year, his scheme included mathematical and experimental sciences, sciences of observation, mechanical sciences, social sciences, fine arts, moral and metaphysical sciences, and literature. Such a formidable list so discouraged the institutes that only one candidate presented himself. But, in a modified form, these examinations drew 62 candidates to the

Society's premises two years later, and proved so successful that provincial centres were established under local committees. By 1867 about 2,000 candidates were forthcoming.[23]

8

What James Heywood and others were doing to open the pores of Oxford and Cambridge to the world, Sir Richard Bethell (later Lord Westbury) tried to do for the Inns of Court. As Solicitor-General, he supported a motion for a Commission of Inquiry into their working, saying in the House of Commons on 1 March 1854:

> I would like to see the Inns of Court erected into one great legal university, not only for the education and instruction of persons who intend to follow the law as a profession, but for the purpose of co-operating with the Universities of Oxford, Cambridge, and London in the education of the public at large.

His energy and convictions ensured him a place on the Royal Commission, and were largely responsible for the Commission's Report in January 1856 that a university should be constituted, with a senate having the power of conferring degrees in law: Constituent members of this university being the Chancellor, the Vice-Chancellor, and Masters of Law.

The Middle Temple and Inner Temple were quite willing to carry these proposals into effect, but the other two Societies refused. And though Sir Richard Bethell's convictions were later promoted with equal vigour by Sir Roundell Palmer (later the Earl of Selborne), there were too many lawyers in the House of Commons to allow an Executive Commission to be appointed on the Oxford and Cambridge model. And perhaps a further deterrent to action was that the Commission did not find proof that there had been any misuse of funds.[24]

The medical profession was more successful in promoting a scheme for professional regulation, and in 1858 secured the passage of the Medical Act which established a General Medical Council. This body, charged with the duty of maintaining a register of qualified practitioners, also recommended and inspected the curricula and examinations leading to qualification. Amendments to the original act have added subjects to the required course of study, but in essence the scheme remains as established by that act, with the university medical schools and the medical corporations working within an agreed framework. Their example has been followed by other, less eminent professions.

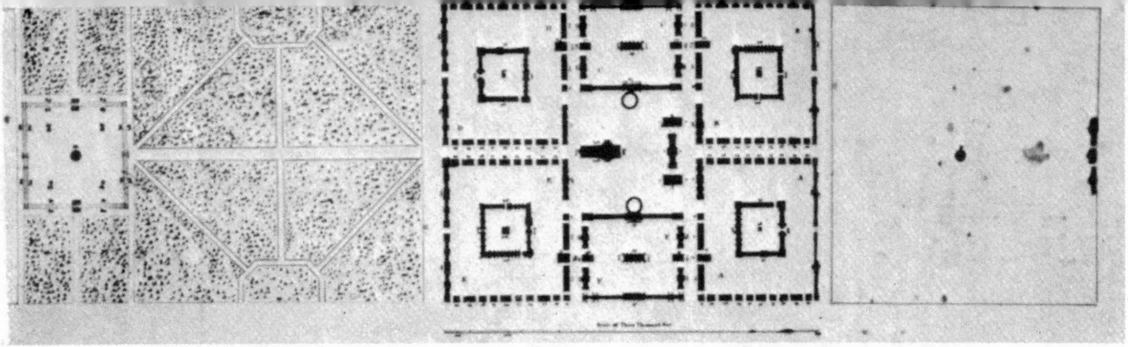

A. The College of Civil Polity and Languages B. The College of Fine Arts C. The College of Agriculture and Manufactures
D. The College of Natural Philosophy E. The College of Philosophy F. The College of Mathematics

The elevation is of the portion marked with circles in the ground plan

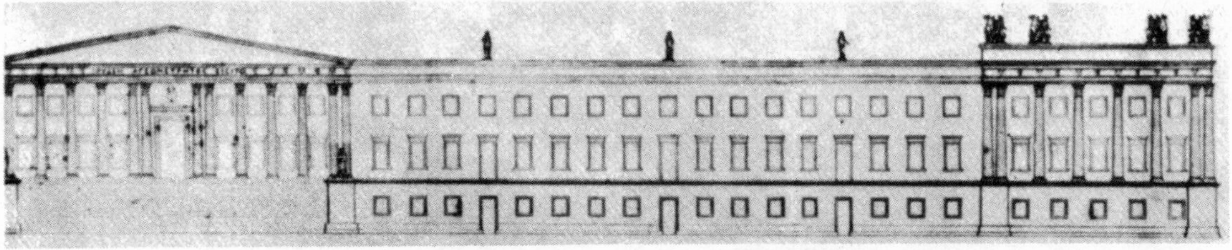

PLAN FOR A STAFFORDSHIRE UNIVERSITY, 1814

From Charles Kelsall, *Phantasm of a University*, 1814

See page 168]

PLATE 6

COCKNEY COLLEGE

Lord Brougham, here shown hammering at a hot iron bar (philosophy) c an anvil (public support), is helped by Lord Lansdowne, who pulls a lev to work the bellows. The title Cockney University was bestowed on Lond University by Theodore Hook in *John Bull* 18 December 1825, who hat it as a political measure [*By courtesy of the British Museu*

See pages 171–5]

THE BATTLE OF FAITHS

From a broadsheet caricature in the Huxley Papers in the Imperial Colleg of Science and Technology, London

See pages 187–9]

9

Fear of further changes in the structure of Oxford and Cambridge stimulated another interesting suggestion: that of Earl Fortescue for establishing 'a new middle-class university' which would co-ordinate the work of the county colleges that he had pioneered in Devonshire. 'In my proposal of a new middle-class university,' he wrote, 'I am not actuated by any dislike of the old. On the contrary, it is from my high appreciation of their value to the gentry of England that I seriously doubt the desireableness of such great alterations as would be implied if the wishes of many ardent reformers were carried out.' 'The progress of the present principles of university reform', he continued, 'is operating to the destruction of many close and local foundations, which had the effect of connecting counties and neighbourhoods with the influence of great centres of education.'

Fortescue's suggestion was laid before the meeting of the Bath and West of England Society's meeting as early as 1855, but his advocacy of it slackened while Acland and Chester's schemes for local examinations were being promoted. But after 1858, when he and Prebendary Brereton had established the Devon Farm and County School, he redoubled his energies to prepare his case, with care and ingenuity. For he wished the examinations of this, and similar county colleges, to be conducted by an institution of university standard, an institution which he described as

> analogous to London University . . . to supplement without superseding it, as it has itself supplemented without superseding the old universities.

It was to be empowered to award degrees, 'furnishing for the first time an authoritative standard of what . . . education ought to be for the middle classes'. It was to be a county university because of the 'value of county feeling and county ties'. Above all, it was to be a federal university:

> It need not have at the outset any central abode, for its examinations might be conducted in different centres, and its professors and teachers might be distributed among the County Colleges and Schools, which in affiliation to it would be formed in the several county towns.

In his federal university scheme, he pointed out the opportunities for specialisation in the particular regional needs:

> In one county college, the means of teaching chemistry, in another mechanics, in more than one agriculture would form the distinguishing feature; but in all the same general course would be pursued, and this would be determined by the standard adopted by the proposed university for its degree.[25]

O

But the middle classes for whom Fortescue advocated this schem would have none of it. Now that Oxford and Cambridge wer opened, they were determined to send their sons there, and, to enabl them to do so, public schools in ever increasing numbers sprang up t help them. *Tom Brown's Schooldays* (first published in 1857) drew th image for them, and its astounding success in the two decades tha followed still further enhanced the value of a public school an university education, especially as Thomas Hughes followed his nov of Rugby with another entitled *Tom Brown at Oxford*.[26]

10

Fortescue's main idea was to remove his 'county schools' fro possible control by the bureaucracy of the Education Department Whitehall—a bureaucracy which had already obtained control of th elementary schools, and of certain training colleges. Its paralysin effects at this time were well described in Charles Dickens's portrait Mr. M'Choakumchild in *Hard Times*.

> He and some one hundred-and-forty other schoolmasters had been late turned at the same time, in the same factory, on the same principles, like many pianoforte legs. He had been put through an immense variety of pac and had answered volumes of headbreaking questions. Orthography, etym logy, syntax and prosody, biography, astronomy, geography, and gener cosmography, the sciences of compound proportion, algebra, land-surveyi and levelling, vocal music and drawing from models, were all at the ends his ten chilled fingers. He had worked his stony way into Her Majesty's m Honourable Privy Council's Schedule B, and had taken the bloom off t higher branches of mathematics and physical science, French, German, Lat Greek. He knew about all the watersheds of the world (whatever they ar and all the histories of all the peoples, and all the names of all the rivers a mountains, and all the productions, manners, and customs of all the countri and all their boundaries and bearings on the two and thirty points of t compass. Ah! rather overdone Mr. M'Choakumchild. If only he had lear a little less, how infinitely better he might have taught much more.[27]

Those in the closest contact with the teachers trained for service the state-aided elementary schools of that time agreed with Dicke Thus Henry Chester, in an address to the United Association Schoolmasters in 1861, declared

> I conceive that the great want of popular education is a university wh may do for the middle and lower classes what Oxford and Cambridge, ap from their collegiate life which is in them, but not of them, do for the hig classes.[28]

He asked his hearers why there should not be created a university at South Kensington in which all training colleges would be incorporated, together with the Royal Academy of Art, the Royal Academy of Music, the School of Mines, and the College of Preceptors. Only by the establishment of such a liberal body could the teachers be liberalised.

Such a scheme won converts, among them Derwent Coleridge who in 1841 had been appointed first principal at St. Mark's College, Chelsea, a post he held till 1864. He wrote that it had 'long floated in his mind as a not undesirable issue of the training system'. He hoped that such a group of colleges would provide 'not a school, but something analogous to an university training for the sons of yeomen, tradesmen, artisans of the higher, and professional persons of the lower grade', adding

> Such a scheme would fill up the space downwards in the social scale, which the elder universities and public schools have long since left vacant, and which I do not think it is desirable that they should attempt to resume.[29]

But the reforms they advocated were rendered impracticable by the hierarchical nature of English society, a hierarchy which placed little value on the education as an instrument either of social mobility, or of national welfare. The teachers for the public schools (and such schools multiplied during the period)[30] were recruited from Oxford and Cambridge, where despite the almost revolutionary changes which had taken place, the classics still dominated the university course, and it was not until 1866 that a master in a public school could register a public protest against such domination.[31]

Yet in this sphere the training colleges, in spite of their drawbacks, did achieve one notable educational advance. For in them, as their most recent historian has pointed out, organised science teaching was essayed.[32]

II

When Henry Chester and Derwent Coleridge suggested that a convenient nucleus for another university existed in London, they were but bearing witness to a profound educational revolution which had been taking place in the existing one since 1851.

The traditional Arts Faculty had been widened by the inclusion of the study of English Language, and in 1859 special provision was made for including English philology and literature in examinations for degrees and honours. There was also founded, for the first time in

England, a Faculty of Science, which in 1860 began to award degrees of bachelor and doctor. In 1863 degrees in surgery were also instituted.

Even more important than the widening of the curriculum of the University of London was the widening of its constituency. A further charter in 1858 exempted postulants for external degrees from attendance at any of the 'approved institutions' named in previous charters, and threw all degrees other than those in medicine open to all who cared to sit for them. As a result, candidates for examinations increased from 450 in 1858 to 1,450 by 1870. This umbrella proved a very real shelter to other struggling institutions. The 1858 charter also recognised the right of graduates to participate in government of the university.

Yet another experiment was made in 1867, when by a further supplemental charter, diplomas and certificates were opened to women. This was an acknowledgement to the women's colleges founded in the metropolis and the standard of the education they afforded. Nineteen years after this experiment was made, the University admitted women to full degrees, the first university to do so.

Not without some cause, therefore, did London obtain what had long been the jealous prerogative of Oxford and Cambridge—representation in parliament. In 1867 they elected their first burgess: Robert Lowe.

12

By 1861 Parliamentary action with regard to the universities had progressed so far that without setting up a preliminary commission of inquiry, a Durham University Act was passed to provide for the better government and extension of that university. It had fallen on such evil times, that only nineteen degrees and licences were conferred in that year. As a result of this Act, a Royal Commission was appointed. This used its sweeping powers. New degrees in Science and Theology were to be established; baccalaureates were to be obtainable after two years; new professorships of Chemistry, Geology, and Mining were to be established; permission for the appointment of teachers of modern languages, book-keeping, surveying, and other cognate subjects was to be given by the Senate; and the warden was to be pensioned. After much dispute and reluctance to accept these and other changes, an Act of Chapter passed in 1865 brought many of them into effect.[33]

But the policy of giving direct State aid to the university colleges, though mooted, was never entertained. In November 1852, Owens College had applied for a grant, and a deputation was received at

Whitehall in July of the following year, but nothing was done. Opinion was, however, crystallising on the relationship of the universities to the State, as can be seen from the pamphlet *The Public Right to the Universities*, published in 1851 by a 'university man'. He wrote:

> The university being a public corporation created by the State, having duties entrusted to it for the general good, it is clearly responsible to the State, its creator. The power which created can annul; and if it may annul, it can alter or amend. No one can dispute this.

Yet at the same time he cautioned his readers:

> We must take care that reform of the university does not become the first step to a control of national education by the central government. In all our efforts to reform the universities, let us insist that, with complete responsibility, there shall also be complete self-government; otherwise the result is too sure to be the transfer of irresponsible rule from King Log to King Stork.

13

We have seen the ferment of ideas and suggestions directed towards the improvement of upper and middle-class education, and it now remains to consider the efforts made amongst the working classes. Class divisions in Victorian society were, as one penetrating observer wrote, so rigid that a state of war between them could be said to exist.[34] It was partly to soften the collisive impact of this class struggle that the Christian Socialists established in 1854 a Working Men's College in Red Lion Square, where Charles Kingsley, D. G. Rossetti, Ruskin, and Ford Madox Brown lectured to students. This college, itself founded on the model of one established at Sheffield eleven years earlier, stimulated other foundations of a similar kind at Wolverhampton (1857), Salford (1858), and Liverpool (1860).[35] But their purpose was largely recreational; 'recitations and songs given in a pleasant style' were the usual staple. Indeed, 'instruction blended with amusement' was often the rule in other, more pretentiously named institutions like The Society for the Illustration and Encouragement of Practical Science, which used to exhibit in the Adelaide Gallery.

The condition of the Welsh labouring classes had exercised the Government ever since the Rebecca Riots of 1843, and so adverse was the report of a commission upon the country's condition that a public outcry arose. The Association of Welsh Clergy in the West Riding of Yorkshire petitioned Parliament for a Welsh University in 1852, and in the following year B. T. Williams published a pamphlet on the same theme, citing Glasgow as a suitable model. Sir Hugh Owen, G. O. Morgan and E. J. Salisbury lent their powerful voices to the outcry, the Eisteddfods amplified them, and in 1863 a representative meeting was held in the Freemasons' Tavern in London to promote a Welsh University. By 1867, the provisional committee appointed as a result of this meeting managed to purchase, for £10,000, the Castle Hotel, Aberystwyth. This, bought from a bankrupt who had intended it for the tourist traffic expected from the opening up of the Cambrian Railway, was opened in October 1872 as the University College of Wales.[36]

Some of these organisations established for the popularisation of science in the provinces were really important in the light of subsequent developments. One of these was the Birmingham and Midland Institute, founded in 1853 for the education of miners and artisans and described forty years later as 'une sorte d'universitaire populaire'.[37] It consisted of a general department and a school of industrial science: the first included the management of libraries, museums and mining records; the second organised class instruction in chemistry, geology, mechanics, and minerology. Institutions like this, together with such of the mechanics' institutes as were thriving, undoubtedly benefited from the South Kensington grants, and swelled the total of 212 'Science Schools' which the Science and Art Department found were teaching some 10,230 students in 1867.[38]

14

One task of the historian is to examine the nature of revolutions, to display the logic and sequence of events that led up to them, and to discover any inherent novelties in the pattern. The period under review is exceptionally difficult to map, partly because the high tide of Victorian prosperity floods every inlet of national life, partly because the middle classes accepted the attitudes of their aristocratic contemporaries in cultural matters, but chiefly because of the deadlock that developed between the denominational interests in educational matters.

Yet, difficult as it is to map, certain contours stand out. The main feature of interest is the enhanced prestige with which both Oxford and Cambridge emerged from the purging and enrichment effected by the Royal Commissions set up, as we have seen, in 1850. And if a disproportionate part of this chapter seems to be taken up with the impact of those commissions on the two universities, it is because a new academic world was created by them for the civic universities of the next generation to imitate. Science was still not 'respectable' in Peacock's *Gryll Grange* (1861), however.

'Science is one thing, and wisdom is another,' remarks Dr. Opimian. 'Science is an edged tool, with which men play like children, and cut their own fingers. If you look at the results which science has brought in its train, you will find them to consist almost wholly in elements of mischief. See how much belongs to the word Explosion alone.'

Underlying everything was the tradition of suspicion inherited from previous generations: suspicion of the Dissenters by the Established Church, and suspicion of 'new' subjects by established academic interests. It is not surprising that the issues were confused: the classics held the field and the novelties had to win their spurs, and, in the mêlée that ensued, many hard, unjust, and sometimes flagrantly wrong accusations were made. Then too, there emerges the almost evangelical fervour of the new scientific agnostics, epitomised in T. H. Huxley, and often associated with liberal politics.

Defenders of the old order and supporters of the new struck off some inspiring redefinitions of the terms they used. Particularly notable was the re-minting of the term 'university'—hitherto generally accepted as describing a corporation or gild of teachers, empowered, like other gilds, to admit postulants to mastership after the performance of certain specified exercises. But the mastership, in common with a number of other medieval legacies, had lost its original corollary, the *jus ubique docendi*. Professions, alien to the medieval trinity of the law, the church, and medicine, had intruded upon the traditional domain of higher education, and had begun to secure recognition of their professional expertise by the universities. Moreover, the growing importance of research as an argument for reform provoked a natural reaction.

It was inevitable, too, that these issues should be coloured by the particular religious controversies of the time; that the advocates of scientific training and research should be stigmatised as godless and secularist by the defenders of the existing order which wished the universities to remain as nurseries of the church. The conflict between them, raging as it did at white heat, produced some of the gems of our university literature.

Consider, for example, the words of Newman who, misled by a mistake in Johnson's dictionary, helped to popularise the concept of a 'university' as a place for teaching 'universal knowledge'. Newman was so perturbed at the implications of 'universal knowledge' that he urged the teaching of theology as the keystone around which should be grouped the individual subjects. He also stressed the primary function of a university as that of 'freely communicating knowledge' not research:

research, for him, was the business of special institutions. His definition of a university was minted in 1852, when the controversies about the Universities Commissions were hot. Lecturing in Dublin in that year, as President of the newly founded Catholic University, he said:

> An assemblage of learned men, zealous for their own sciences and rivals of each other, are brought by familiar intercourse and for the sake of intellectual peace to adjust together the claims and relations of their respective subjects of investigation. They learn to respect, to consult, to aid each other. Thus is created a pure and clear atmosphere of thought, which the student also breathes, though in his own case he only pursues a few sciences out of a multitude. He profits by an intellectual tradition which is independent of particular teachers, which guides him in his course of subjects and duly interprets for him those which he choses. He apprehends the great outlines of knowledge, the principles on which it rests, the scale of its parts, its lights and its shades, its great points and its little, as he otherwise cannot apprehend them.[39]

The second change in meaning, that of the word 'culture', was not so generally accepted as the first, and, indeed, was to be vigorously challenged in the year 1868 by Matthew Arnold. But all the scientific progress of the period animated writers like William Whewell, Michael Faraday, John Tyndall, Thomas Huxley, and Herbert Spencer to reorient the concept. Of these, Huxley was perhaps the most liberal. 'For the purposes of attaining real culture,' he wrote, 'an exclusively scientific education is at least as effectual as an exclusively literary education.' Huxley was, in fact, against the monopoly of higher education by either, and declared he would be profoundly sorry 'even to observe a tendency to starve or cripple literary or aesthetic culture for the sake of science'. His use of the adjectives illustrates the fragmentation of a word which should have described understanding, manners, and taste.[40]

But a third change was needed before the civic universities could emerge to inherit the ideal defined by Newman: a change of attitude towards the so-called 'provinces'. With a civic university established in London, much provincial effort in the sphere of higher education was harnessed in the leading strings of the London examination system. This was a reflection of the average professional man's attitude. So it is interesting to see at the end of this period when George Eliot was writing *Middlemarch*, that she put into the mouth of Lydgate the advice:

> a born provincial man who has a grain of public spirit as well as a few ideas, should do what he can to resist the rush of everything that is a little better than common towards London. Any valid professional aims may often find a freer, if not a richer field, in the provinces.

The next generation was to discover that.

REFERENCES

1. PLAYFAIR, Lyon, 'The Chemical Principles involved in the Manufactures of the Exhibition as indicating the Necessity of Industrial Instruction', in *Lectures on the Results of the Great Exhibition of 1851* (London, 1852), i, 193. See also p. 197, 'Until our schools accept as a living faith that a study of God's works is more fitted to increase the resources of a nation than a study of the amours of Jupiter or Venus, our Industrial Colleges will make no material headway against those of the Continent.'

2. *op. cit.*, ii, 449.

LLOYD, J. A., *Proposals for Establishing Colleges of Art and Manufactures* (1851).

REID, T. W., *Lyon Playfair* (London, 1899).

COLE, H., *Fifty Years of Public Work* (London, 1884).

3. ARMYTAGE, W. H. G., 'Sir J. F. D. Donnelly 1834-1902', in *The Vocational Aspect of Secondary and Further Education* (Bolton, 1950), ii, 6-21.

4. REEKS, M., *The Royal School of Mines* (London, 1920); *Centenary of the Imperial College of Science and Technology* (London, 1945).

5. PROTHERO, R. E., and BRADLEY, G. C., *Life and Corr. of A. P. Stanley* (London, 1894), i, 224.

6. *Report of the Royal Commission on the University of Oxford* (1852), Appendix B.

7. MORLEY, *Life of Gladstone* (1908), i, 371.

8. H. W. Acland (1815-1900) had formed, since being elected Lee's Reader of Anatomy, an anatomical and physiological museum on the lines of the Hunterian Museum in London and in 1865 was the first to deliver the Hunterian Oration in English at the Royal College of Physicians. He found the faculty of medicine almost medieval in character and lived to see it equipped with the latest means of scientific investigation. He also fought for the introduction of biology and chemistry into the curriculum, see *Memoir* by J. B. Atlay (1903).

9. *Evidence*, p. 169.

10. See *Papers published by the Tutors' Association* (1853-4).

11. VAUGHAN, H. H., *Oxford Reform and Oxford Professors: A Reply to Certain Objections urged against the Reports of the Queen's Commissioners* (1854).

12. PUSEY, E. B., *Collegiate and Professorial Teaching and Discipline, in answer to Professor Vaughan's Strictures* (1854).

13. MORLEY, J., *Life of Gladstone* (1908), i, 369-79.

14. WINSTANLEY, D. A., *Early Victorian Cambridge* (Cambridge, 1940).

15. *ibid.*, 337.

16. HUDSON, J. W., *The History of Adult Education* (1851).

17. JAMES, Lionel, *A Forgotten Genius, Sewell of St. Columba's and Radley* (London, 1945), 253, 258. See also Sidney Herbert's suggestion to the Oxford Commission that theological schools affiliated to the Universities should be established at cathedral centres.

18. HERVEY, Lord Arthur, *A Suggestion for Supplying the Literary and Mechanics' Institutes of Great Britain and Ireland with Lecturers from the Universities* (London, 1855).

19. In the Library of the University of London.

20. WOOD, H. T., *The Royal Society of Arts* (London, 1913), 369-72, 377, 425.

21. ACLAND, A. H. D., *Memoir of T. D. Acland* (London, 1902).

22. HOLE, James, *History and Management of Literary, Scientific, and Mechanics' Institutes* (London, 1853). He put the case of Leeds to the Vice-President of the Council in 1867.

23. For the scheme, which by 1855 had developed to suggesting that, where practicable, mechanics' institutes should be converted to industrial colleges, see J. Booth, 'On the Examinations of the Society of Arts', in *Transactions of the National Association for Promotion of Social Science* (1858).

24. NASH, T. A., *Life of Lord Westbury* (London, 1888), i, 148–9. Paradoxically enough, Bethell was one of the council who in March 1851 condemned the Oxford Commission as 'not constitutional or legal'.

25. FORTESCUE, Earl, *Public Schools for the Middle Classes* (London, 1864), 23ff.

26. See E. C. Mack and W. H. G. Armytage, *Thomas Hughes, The Life of the author of Tom Brown's Schooldays* (London, 1953).

27. *Hard Times* (1854), Chaps. 1–3, 10, 14. For the perseverance of this view, see Sir James Duff, at the *Conference of Home Universities—Report of Proceedings* (1946), 59.

28. CHESTER, Harry, *The Proper Limits of the State's Interference in Education* (1861).

29. COLERIDGE, Derwent, *Teachers of the People* (1862), 60–2.

30. Notable examples are Bradfield (1850), St. John's, Leatherhead (1851), Victoria College, Jersey (1852), Wellington (1856), Ardingley (1858), Birkenhead (1860), Beaumont (1861), Clifton and Haileybury (1862), Cranleigh (1863), Malvern (1865), Trent College (1866). The increased emphasis on these schools may be seen from the activities of the Clarendon (1861–4) and Taunton (1864–8) Commissions.

31. James Heywood called the attention of the British Association in 1861, 1862, and 1864 to the disproportionate time spent by the schools and by Oxford and Cambridge upon Greek and Latin and their neglect of science. F. W. Farrar raised the question again in 1866 and was appointed with Huxley, Tyndall, J. M. Wilson of Rugby, and Joseph Payne on a Special Committee of the British Association to consider the question.

32. RICH, R. W., *The Training of Teachers* (Cambridge, 1933), 159.

33. WHITING, C. E., *The University of Durham* (1932), 97–117.

34. HODGIN, Margaret T., *Workers' Education in England and the United States* (London, 1925), stresses this 'class' aspect.

35. DAVIES, J. Ll., *The Working Men's College* (London, 1904).

36. ELLIS, T. I., *The Development of Higher Education in Wales* (Wrexham, 1935) 18–20. This was, strictly speaking, not the first university college in Wales. St. David's, Lampeter, founded in 1827, was empowered to confer the degree of B.D. in 1852, and that of B.A. in 1865. It provided a training for prospective clergymen of the Established Church.

37. LECLERC, Max, *L'Education des classes moyeunes et dirigeants en Angleterre* (Paris, 1894), 239.

38. See H. Solly, *Working Men's Clubs* (London, 1867) for other clubs, and *Report of the Science and Art Department for 1867*.

39. NEWMAN, J. H., *The Idea of a University* (London, 1912), 101. In 1845, the year in which Newman became a Catholic, the Government had established secular Queen's Colleges at Belfast, Cork and Galway, open to both Catholics and Protestants.

40. HUXLEY, T. H., *Science and Education* (London, 1905), written in 1869.

CHAPTER TEN

Portents and Polytechnics: The Efflorescence of Civic University Colleges in England, 1867-98

WHEN English industrialists heard that their exhibits at the Paris Exhibition of 1867 were characterised as 'slovenly intruded heaps of raw material mingled with pieces of rusty iron',[1] intimations of their industrial mortality began to dawn upon them. A Parliamentary Select Committee, presided over by Bernhard Samuelson, one of the greatest ironmasters of the day, was appointed to survey the field of technical instruction, and it reported that the field should be substantially cultivated—with state aid where necessary.

Others prescribed specific reforms. John Scott Russell, a former disciple of the Prince Consort and a promoter of the 1851 Exhibition, seized the occasion to urge the establishment of a great technical university with a hundred chairs, federated with fifteen local colleges, each with twenty-five chairs based on local industrial expertise. Even this, Scott Russell argued, would only provide for one-fifth of the youth requiring education of the sort that would enable England to keep abreast of her industrial competitors.[2] Another, more oblique advocacy of the local college was Sir Charles Dilke's enthusiastic description of the State University of Michigan as 'the most democratic school in the whole world' in his *Greater Britain* (1869). The implicit question he posed was, if a mid-western American state could maintain such a foundation, could not Britain do likewise?

The inadequacy of the reforms effected at Oxford and Cambridge during this period were revealed by that percipient observer, Matthew Arnold. Arnold had studied the Continental systems of education as a governmental commissioner both in 1859 and 1865, and was much moved by England's backwardness at all levels. Commenting on the class-nature of English education, he described the cast of ideas at the Oxford and Cambridge level as 'characterised by its indisposition and incapacity for science, for systematic knowledge'. He continued:

If there is one thing which my foreign experience has left me convinced of—as convinced of as I am of our actual want of superior instruction—it is this: that we must take this instruction to the students, and not hope to bring the students to the instruction. We must get out of our heads all notion of making the mass of students come and reside three years, two years, or one year, or even one month, at Oxford or Cambridge, which neither suit their circumstances nor offer them the instruction they want. We must plant faculties in the eight or ten principal seats of population, and let the students follow lectures there from their own homes with whatever arrangements for their living they and their parents choose. It would be everything for the great seats of population to be thus made intellectual centres as well as mere places of business; for the want of this at present, Liverpool and Leeds are mere overgrown provincial towns, while Strasbourg and Lyons are European cities.

He was well aware of the effects of the constant channelling of endowments and argued:

All future application of Oxford and Cambridge emoluments to national purposes might, with advantage to the country, and honour to Oxford and Cambridge themselves, be made in this direction for endowing chairs for professors and exhibitions for students in university faculties to be organised in the great towns of England.[3]

At Cambridge, the challenge was clearly discerned. 'The long, long, canker of peace is over and done,' wrote Henry Sedgwick to a friend, 'the only thing soon will be to avoid radicalism'.[4] And Henry Sidgwick showed the way to avoid it by taking the lead in the deliberations which resulted in the assignment by Trinity College, Cambridge, of a fellowship every third year to a natural scientist. At Oxford, Mark Pattison published his *Suggestions on Academical Reform* in 1868 in which he too urged the claims of new specialisms:

Civilisation in the West has now reached a point where no further triumphs await mere vigour undirected by knowledge. Energy will be beaten in the practical field by combined skill. . . . The necessary tendency of advancing civilisation is to divide and sub-divide the applications, as of labour, so of thought. The professions tend to split into branches; and skill in one becomes more and more incompatible with skill in the other. The more a subject has been explored, the more time does it take each succeeding student to follow the steps of his predecessors. To prevent the disabling effects of this speciality of pursuit, it becomes the more requisite to secure at starting a breadth of cultivation, a scientific formation of mind, a concert of the intellectual faculties.

The very muteness of the existing civic colleges at this time was an index of the trouble. London was declining in numbers. Durham had seriously considered closing. Queen's College, Birmingham, was in debt for £10,000 and its charter was repealed in 1867. Owens College, Manchester, was fighting against 'half-hearted sympathy and openly expressed contempt'.

I

The response to the challenge of the times came from the provinces. Thomas Nussey of Leeds had visited the Paris Exhibition, and in 1867 G. H. Nussey and A. Nussey published a pamphlet *A Technical Institute for Leeds and District*. Two years later, the authors established on South Parade, 'The Leeds Art and Science Institutions', where six teachers were engaged to teach the sciences relevant to the industries of the district, like mechanical engineering, and woollen dyeing and manufacture. The town was roused by a meeting in the Town Hall on 5 November 1869 when a resolution was adopted that it was desirable to establish a college of science in Yorkshire. An executive committee was appointed for the purpose. Behind this project were the Nusseys, Col. Ackroyd, M.P., Col. Walter Morrison, M.P., Isaac Holden, E. Baines, M.P., Titus Salt, and the Cavendish family. This committee duly sent a deputation to visit Owens College, Manchester, and King's College, London: it reported in 1872 to the Yorkshire Board of Education that £60,000 would be needed to found a college. By 30 April 1874 the project was sufficiently advanced for a constitution to be decided upon. Twenty governors were appointed and three professors for mathematics and experimental physics, geology and mining, and chemistry. Three hundred and twenty-six students attended a first year's course of lectures: 80 being day students, 101 afternoon students, and 145 evening students. The Bradford Philosophical Society, alive to the advantages of such teaching, employed the professors to lecture under their auspices as well. Certainly the promoters of the Leeds scheme were conscious of its high importance, and if any amongst them were not, Lyon Playfair's words at the inauguration of the second session should have converted them. For he warned them that even nations as far afield as China were to be reckoned with as industrial competitors: 'she may even now astonish us,' he prophesied, 'by burying antiquity and walking among the nations of the present.'[5]

The first student of the Yorkshire College of Science (which opened in a rented building in Cookridge Street, Leeds) was a coal miner. And mining had been very much in the mind of Nicholas Wood, the founder of the Northern Institute of Mining Engineers, who died in 1865. Wood had tried to establish a college at Hatton for the cultivation, teaching, and improvement of mining science—a project which had led directly to the founding of the Government School of Mines.

Wood's example, and the stimulus of the Paris Exhibition, led to a resurgence of a similar project in the north-east.

The authorities at Durham were at first anxious to revive and extend the science side at the university there, but the mining adviser to the Dean and Chapter, who had succeeded Nicholas Wood as President of the North of England Institute of Mining and Mechanical Engineers, preferred Newcastle. A new Warden of the University, Dean Lake, appointed in 1869, was of the same opinion, holding that 'of Durham itself, there is little to be made, except as a college for educating clergymen'. So, on 2 August 1870, a conference took place. The same industrialist class who had worked to such purpose at Leeds, rallied at Newcastle: I. Lowthian Bell and Joseph Cowen of the *Newcastle Chronicle* being most prominent. Their efforts in raising £20,000 by public subscription enabled a college to open at Newcastle in October 1871.

The Newcastle College of Physical Science, affording advanced scientific education to the North Riding and the four northern counties, actually antedated the Yorkshire College of Leeds by three years. Like the Yorkshire College, it bore the impress of the times: not only was the senate of the University of Durham represented, but the mining and engineering industries of Tyneside, the Literary and Philosophical Society, and men of wealth in the locality. It was also a makeshift affair, housed in some vacant rooms in the Coal Trade Buildings in Neville Chambers, and in the Wood Memorial Hall, and using the library of the Literary and Philosophical Society. The College of Medicine offered a laboratory on its ground floor to the professor of chemistry, who, in return, taught the medical students. Its staff too, afforded added indications of its ancestry. Theophilus Bunning, secretary to the college, was also secretary to the Mining Institute; Professor Aldis (Mathematics) was a Senior Wrangler and Smith's prizeman but had been debarred from a chance of a Cambridge fellowship because of his nonconformist opinions; Professor Herschel (Physics) was the grandson of Sir William Herschel, the astronomer; and Professor Friere-Marreco (Chemistry) was a product of the College of Medicine. When a chair of Mining was established by several leading coal owners in 1880—the first of its kind to be established in England—its occupant was J. H. Merivale, son of the famous historian, and the first student to register at the new college.[6]

As with textiles and mining, so with hardware. At Birmingham, centre of the hardware trade (which had been steadily losing ground to the more ingenious American products), Josiah Mason executed a foundation deed for a third college on 12 December 1870. Mason had been a shoemaker, a baker, a manufacturer of split rings and pens, and a partner in a large and successful electro-plating works. Since his success was founded on the scientific discoveries of previous generations, he was anxious to 'provide enlarged means of scientific instruction on the scale required by the necessities of the town and district ... upon terms which render it easily available by persons of all classes'. His friends, J. T. Bunce, editor of the *Birmingham Daily Post*, and George Shaw, professor of law at Queen's College, helped him acquire a site in Edmund Street. There on 23 February 1875 the foundation stone of his college was laid. It was by far the most ambitious essay in college founding by any industrialist of the decade, for Mason's total expenditure was over £200,000. And when it was formally opened in 1880, with an inaugural address by T. H. Huxley, its Victorian Gothic, red-brick front, rising over a hundred feet above street-level, was considered the finest in Birmingham. Like Owens, he repudiated all religious tests.[7]

A fourth new foundation was a College of Science for the West of England established at Bristol. Here the precedents of Newcastle and Birmingham were openly cited by the promoters, W. L. Carpenter (a mechanical engineer who specialised in the manufacture of soap, candles, lubricants, and glycerine), W. Procter Baker, and Lewis Fry. In their circular convening a public meeting in the Victoria Rooms to discuss the foundations of the college, they wrote:

> It is generally admitted that the prosperity of British industry must in future greatly depend upon the proper scientific and technical training of those by whom the commerce and manufactures of the country will be carried out.

But their aims were consciously broader than those of their fellow college founders in the darker northern towns, since they acknowledged:

> At the same time there is a growing conviction that culture in all the subjects which form the staple of university teaching should be made more widely accessible.

Balliol and New College, Oxford, offered their help, and the Bristol Medical School and the Museum showed themselves willing to cooperate. The capital fund to be raised was £25,000; the sustentation fund £3,000 a year. Civic support was promised by the mayor, and the Merchant Venturers of Bristol matched the Medical School's gift of £1,000. Joshua Dixon of Winslade led the van of private munificence, and on 9 August 1876 the Board of Trade licensed the incorporation of University College, Bristol, as a limited liability company. Two professors and four lecturers began their work in a Georgian house on Park Row, holding classes in Mathematics, Mechanics, Physics, Geology, and Economics, with Classics, Law, Textiles, Logic, and Hebrew soon to follow. For its second session, the college was fortunate in securing the services as principal, of the great economist, Alfred Marshall. Over 300 students were enrolled, a number which remained relatively constant for the rest of the century.[8]

Civic pride was responsible for a fifth foundation at Liverpool. As a result of a town meeting convened in 1879 the Corporation granted a site and £50,000 was raised by subscription. In January 1882 University College, Liverpool, opened in a disused lunatic asylum in the midst of a slum district. Between its conception and its creation, Liverpool itself had become a city, and, with commendable civic pride, the city authorities supported the new college most generously.

2

A more sophisticated response to the contemporary challenge was elicited from H. E. Roscoe, the energetic and imaginative professor of chemistry at Owens College, Manchester. He and his principal investigated the Universities and Technical Hochschulen of Germany and Switzerland for their own extension committee. Their report was handed to the Royal Commission on Scientific Instruction appointed by the Government in 1870. In it, Roscoe declared:

> Very great evils must result from this tendency to multiply institutions—a tendency springing, probably, from the difficulty of modifying old institutions to meet new wants.[9]

and called attention to 'the serious harm' which would come from the separation of polytechnics from universities proper: harm to both the polytechnics and to the universities. He set himself to remedy this state of affairs in Manchester, especially since German influence was strong there. With the active co-operation of Thomas Ashton and other princes of the cotton trade, two new Acts of Parliament were secured in 1870 and 1871 to enable the civic authorities to participate in the building of a real university for the city. But before full university status could be obtained, Roscoe set himself and his colleagues the task of showing that they were worth it. By the prosecution of basic research, the importation of professors of distinction, by uniting the Medical College, the Extension College and Owens College in new

BIRMINGHAM UNIVERSITY

From a painting by Henry Rushbury

See pages 243–4]

THE RADIO TELESCOPE

An artist's drawing of the great steerable radio telescope being constructed at Jodrell Bank. This project began in 1945, greatly assisted by the Nuffield Foundation and the Department of Scientific and Industrial Research, which between them have promised the £335,000 necessary to build the telescope

See page 309]

buildings on the Oxford Road, Roscoe and like-minded colleagues worked steadily towards a charter.

These like-minded colleagues, A. W. Ward, Morgan, and the principal, A. W. Greenwood, based their case for a charter on the complete inability of the existing universities to tap hidden strata of ability in the population. Their arguments were supported from outside by powerful public men like Lyon Playfair (who had, in his early days, been professor of chemistry at the old Manchester Institute) and Mark Pattison (who came out strongly in their favour at the Social Science Congress of 1876). After a decade of pressure, the Privy Council gave way. In 1880 the Victoria University was chartered, with Owens College becoming its first, and for a time its only, constituent college.[10]

The Victoria University had a tremendous attraction. Certain responsible educational reformers like Sir George Young actually wanted University College, London, to become one of its constituent colleges in order to enjoy emancipation from the London examining machine.[11] Though University College, London, did not join, two other northern colleges did. The first was University College at Liverpool which became a constituent college of the Victoria University on 5 November 1884. The second was the Yorkshire College at Leeds, almost exactly three years later. Both these foundations brought with them their local medical schools.

3

A further stimulus to provincial college founding occurred in the year 1867, when James Stuart, a young fellow of Trinity College, Cambridge, delivered a series of lectures on the law of gravitation to audiences at Liverpool, Manchester, Sheffield, and Leeds composed mainly of schoolmistresses. These schoolmistresses, the rank and file of the North of England Council for the Higher Education of Women, were in their own modest way an effective pressure group, working with methodical purpose to secure academic qualifications for their sex. Their demand was itself an answer to a growing social problem: that of the surplus women in society who desired a professional career.[12]

James Stuart was a young man (he had graduated in 1866), a good lecturer, and had an imaginative conception of his work: 'a sort of peripatetic university of professors which should circulate in the big towns.' So he responded eagerly to other invitations: lecturing at

Crewe (on the invitation of the local Mechanics' Institute), at Rochdale (where the Co-operative Society devoted two and a half per cent. of their profits to education), and at Nottingham.

Now at Nottingham the Mechanics' Institute was destroyed by fire in 1867. When the members assembled together to discuss its rebuilding, it was obvious that they should hear suggestions that university extension teaching should begin in the town. Two of the leading spirits were John Brown Paton (who in 1866 had become the first principal of the local Congregational Institute) and Richard Enfield (a supporter of the Mechanics' Institute). They suggested that working men should be admitted to such classes. They also supported the North of England Council for Promoting the Higher Education of Women, the Crewe Mechanics' Institute, and the Rochdale Co-operative Society in memorialising the University of Cambridge to systematise such university teaching as James Stuart had been undertaking on his own account. James Stuart himself, in a letter addressed to resident members of Cambridge University, hoped that permanent university establishments in the provinces might be secured by this means.

He was right. When Nottingham rebuilt its Mechanics' Institute, the first university extension course, so called, was held there under Henry Sidgwick, who acknowledged that university extension 'would have remained an idea, but for the action taken by Nottingham'. Endowments for this new venture were soon forthcoming: one anonymous donor giving £10,000 on condition that the Corporation erected a suitable university extension building within a reasonable time. Stimulated both by this, and by the holding of the annual general meeting of the University Extension Movement in the town that year, the civic authorities advertised for tenders. 'Plans for the new Culture Buildings' as they were officially called, were approved; the mayor laid the foundation stone on 27 September 1877, and another university college was born.

Yet the real significance of the Nottingham University College was not so much that it was the child of the University Extension Movement, as that it was sustained by a town rate. This was a new departure; for the other science colleges were more specifically the creation of manufacturers. The Nottingham University College was, if anything, more cultural than scientific; its main supporters were the trade unionists of the town. That the civic authorities should spend over £100,000 in the erection of the building, and in addition, levy a three half-penny rate for its maintenance, makes the building on what was

Horse-Fair Close a landmark in university history. It was, literally, a civic university college.[13]

Other colleges owed much to the University Extension Movement. In near-by Sheffield a local steelmaster, Mark Firth, whose family had already built a college for ministers in training for the Methodist New Connection circuits, endowed a college to house the University Extension Movement. His generosity was so liberal that it retained his name till it merged in 1897 with the local medical school and a technical college to form University College, Sheffield. It was articulated with the local School Board: a higher-grade school being built at the entrance to the building. A similar, if later, university extension college was formed at Reading by the amalgamation of the Reading University Extension Association with the government Science and Art School in 1892, and was sustained by the dynamic personality of H. J. Mackinder. The first buildings of the Reading College were a symbolic trinity: the School of Art, the School of Science, and a vicarage. The School of Science, by an even apter chance, was housed in what had once been part of the great Abbey of Reading. The new clerisy were occupying old cells with a vengeance.[14]

4

John Scott Russell's idea of a national University for Industrial and Technical Training was promoted with vehemence and enthusiasm. In 1871 a committee was formed, which, working from 4 Storey's Gate, St. James' Park, attempted to secure the interest of the government. Two M.P.s, E. T. Gourley and J. M. Carter, pressed the matter, and Gourley wrote a private letter to W. E. Gladstone, but to no effect.[15]

For Gladstone had already appointed a Royal Commission to consider Scientific Instruction and the Advancement of Science under the Duke of Devonshire (who in 1870 had been responsible for the inauguration of the Cavendish laboratory at Cambridge). It sat for five years. From voluminous evidence certain specific recommendations were distilled. One was the necessity of a school-leaving examination in which both scientific and literary subjects would be equally represented. Another was that universities should recognise the 'primary duty' of research, and give professional instruction where needed. They further proposed research laboratories with adequate staffs, a scientific professoriate, and the creation at Oxford and Cambridge of a doctorate of science on the London model.[16]

While the Devonshire Commission was laboriously gestating these recommendations, metropolitan energies wrestled with the urgent necessity of establishing a satisfactory system of technological instruction. The Royal Society of Arts resolved on 20 July 1872:

It has long been acknowledged that if this country is efficiently to maintain its manufacturing supremacy in the markets of the world, the technical education of our artisans must be improved, and we . . . are of the opinion that technological examinations (which do not form part of the systems either of the universities or of the Government) would be of great use in furtherance of this end.[17]

Architect of the examinations, which were set in the technology of cotton, paper, silk, steel, and carriage-making, was J. F. D. Donnelly of the Science and Art Department. The system so established lasted for six years, during which time the number offering themselves for examination rose from six to sixty-eight.[18]

The wealthy City Companies had a twofold interest in the matter. Not only were their individual members vitally concerned with the products of British industrial expertise, but as corporate bodies they viewed with alarm the motions made by radical M.P.s to confiscate their funds and re-apply them for their original purpose of technical instruction. In 1876, the very year in which one of these radical motions was proposed in the House of Commons, they met in the Mansion House and resolved to act.[19] A provisional committee was formed in the following year, which drew the blueprint for the City and Guilds of London Institute for the Advancement of Technical Education. This, incorporated in 1880, took over the system of technological examinations pioneered by the Royal Society of Arts. This committee also resolved to assist technical classes already existing elsewhere, and amongst other things, founded the Central Technical College, and resolved to subsidise the proposed chairs of Chemical Technology and Mechanical Technology at University College, London. Their deliberations were doubtless accelerated by some remarks of T. H. Huxley's, delivered at the Royal Society of Arts on 3 December 1879:

As far as London is concerned, I think it would be an utter scandal and robbery if one shilling were asked for out of the general revenue to pay for technical education. There are in the City of London, at the present moment the possessors of enormous wealth, inheritors of the property and traditions of the old Guilds of London meant for this very purpose, and if the people of this country do not insist on this wealth being applied to its purpose, they deserve to be taxed down to their shoes. . . . It will be well if those who have charge of the matter will understand that they are morally bound, and if they don't see this, they will one of these days be legally bound to do this work for the country.[20]

The City Companies hastened to respond to the challenge. The Drapers' Company gave £10,000 to build the Finsbury Technical College, opened on 19 February 1883 to provide instruction in Mechanical and Electrical Engineering and Industrial and Technical Chemistry. Till 1888 the Drapers continued to be very generous to this college, but in that year they diverted their munificence to another, more promising foundation.

Nor were these grants confined to the metropolis. The Clothworkers' Company, in its desire to help the textile industry, created the Textile and Dyeing Department of the University College at Leeds, to which, up to the year 1924, it had given nearly a quarter of a million pounds. The same college owed its Leather Department to the Skinners' Company, while subsequent subsidies by the Drapers not only enabled scholarships and exhibitions in cotton, linen, silk, jute, and wool to be awarded at various institutions, but also made possible the creation of a Department of Applied Science at Sheffield.

Other provincial institutions helped by the London Livery Companies were the Manchester Technical School, the Leicester Technical School, colleges at Huddersfield, Bradford, and Halifax, and similar foundations at Batley, Keighley, Stroud, and Trowbridge. Over a period of forty years, the sums so expended exceeded two million pounds.

Other new foundations which owed much to the charity of the City Companies were the London Polytechnics. The original Polytechnic in Regent Street had been erected by Thompson in 1838, and enlarged ten years later. It contained a hall of manufactures with machines worked by steam power, lecture theatres, a diving bell, and a machine for generating electricity. But, though intended as an educational institution for the neotechnic age, it did not prosper, and its decline was accelerated by the fall of a staircase on 3 January 1859, when one person was killed and many others injured. On 12 November 1860 it had been re-formed under a new company, and the classes were reorganised into a college inaugurated by the Earl of Shaftesbury on 7 October 1872. But even this venture failed, and the affairs of the college were wound up in 1882 and the plant sold for £2,000. At this stage, the visionary philanthropy of Quintin Hogg saw the possibilities of the place, and to it he transferred the evening classes which had previously been held in the Long Acre Evening Institute since 1878.

The Polytechnic idea caught on. The publication of Besant's *All Sorts and Conditions of Men* in 1882 stimulated the establishment of the People's Palace and East London Technical College, to which the

Drapers' Company were most generous, giving in all £400,000 to enable the latter to become the real university of the East End. A second polytechnic which flowered into a constituent college of the University of London was founded by the Goldsmiths' Company at New Cross. There, at a cost of some £110,000, the former Royal Naval School was altered for use as the Goldsmiths' Institute, and opened in 1891. When, thirteen years later, the buildings and land were presented to the University of London, the Goldsmiths gave a further capital sum of £10,000, and continued their annual grant of £5,000 for eight years. In all, this particular college cost the company a quarter of a million pounds.

Strength and permanence was given to the polytechnic movement by the City Parochial Charities Act of 1883, which redeployed the endowments of 109 minute city parishes by offering a million pounds to London for establishing polytechnics if the sum was matched by private subscription. The Clothmakers came forward to endow the Islington Polytechnic, and various other bodies helped to build nine other Polytechnics.[21] When Sidney Webb assumed the leadership of the Technical Education Committee of the London County Council these were integrated into the general educational pattern of the metropolis. Well might Webb's fellow Fabian, Bernard Shaw, make his unconventional hero, Jack Tanner, say in *Man and Superman*:

> His university, Octavius, not Oxford, Cambridge, Durham, Dublin, or Glasgow. Not even those Nonconformist holes in Wales. No Tavy, Regent Street! Chelsea! the Borough!—I don't know half their confounded names: these are his universities, not mere shops for selling class-limitations like ours.

5

Those 'Nonconformist holes in Wales' were being extended and linked. Aberystwyth, opening in 1872 with a deficit of £2,500, had unsuccessfully supplicated for State aid. Stirred by Hugh Owen, whose national fervour was responsible for the reform of the Eisteddfod and the revival of the Cymmrodorion Society, a hundred thousand artisans and labourers rallied with their pittances to raise £50,000 for the college. The hard struggle seemed to have been worth while when the Aberdare Committee reported in 1881 that a proper educational network of secondary and university education should be established in Wales. Aberystwyth, as one of the links in this network, was recommended for a grant of £4,000 from the central funds, which it duly obtained. Similar grants were also given to two new university colleges founded at Cardiff in 1883 and at Bangor in 1884. These two colleges received charters in 1884 and 1885 respectively followed by Aberystwyth in 1889. To federate them, a movement began in 1888. This was successful, and on 30 November 1893, the University of Wales received its charter as a federal university, entitled to give its own degrees, and emancipated from the leading strings of the London examination system.

Two further developments worked to provide these Welsh Colleges with students. The first was the Intermediate Education Act of 1889, which established secondary schools as feeders on the plan sketched by the Aberdare Committee; the second was the recognition by the Education Department at Whitehall, of Day Training Colleges attached to universities and colleges of university rank. One provided the students, the other gave them an occupation. The local education authorities, themselves new bodies, lent their aid and advice, and the Prince of Wales, as chancellor, agreed with Viriamu Jones, the first vice-chancellor, that the university was 'Wales itself organised for the guidance of learning, the pursuit of science, the promotion of research.'[22]

6

In England, great events were also going forward, notably in Oxford and Cambridge which were certainly responding to the needs of the times, and indeed, contributing much to the development of the new civic colleges. Perhaps the most significant symbol of the resurgent university of Cambridge was the newly founded Cavendish Laboratory, to which Clerk Maxwell lent his brilliant talents after his appointment in 1871 to the first chair of experimental physics. Under his successors Lord Rayleigh (from 1880) and J. J. Thomson (from 1894), himself a product of a civic university, the Cavendish Laboratory became a nursery for physicists who themselves contributed much to these colleges.[23]

For from the Cavendish Laboratory emerged a number of scientists who helped to mould the civic university colleges then taking shape in the industrial towns. Perhaps the most active of these was William Garnett, Clerk Maxwell's first assistant from 1873 until 1879. Garnett, a friend and fellow undergraduate of W. M. Hicks (later principal of University College, Sheffield), had lectured to working men under the auspices of Professor James Stuart's extension scheme. When Lord Rayleigh succeeded to Clerk Maxwell's chair of Experimental Physics at Cambridge, Garnett was elected to a chair at University College,

Nottingham, where his extension work continued. After two years of successful work at Nottingham, he became principal of the Durham College of Science at Newcastle in 1884. There, with such congenial friends as Dr. R. Spence Watson, a leading Liberal, Dr. J. T. Merz, an industrialist, and Dr. Thomas Hodgkin, a well-known banker, he literally forced the governing body to buy the site for a new building. The foundation stone of this was laid in 1887 and in the same year, Garnett played no inconsiderable part in helping Charles Parsons improve his early turbo-electric generators. In 1893 he left Newcastle for the secretaryship of the London Technical Education Board, where he worked under Sidney Webb to organise the metropolitan educational system into the largest capacity-catching machine in the world.[24]

In a similar way, Arthur Schuster, who worked at the Cavendish Laboratory from 1876 to 1881, carried the mathematic-physical skills he had learned there to Manchester, where, as professor of applied mathematics from 1881 to 1888, and from 1888 to 1907 as professor of physics, he discovered the constitution of cathode rays, and did much to develop the mathematics of the so-called Heaviside Layer. And just as Garnett was an administrative figure of the first importance in the history of Newcastle, so Schuster was a leader in the movement which was to displace the federal Victoria University by autonomous civic universities.

Other changes at Oxford and Cambridge were accelerated by parliamentary action. In 1872, a Royal Commission under the Duke of Cleveland was charged with the investigation of collegiate expenditure. Its report implied that more money might be allocated to university as opposed to college teaching. The Marquess of Salisbury, who happily enough was both a member of the Government and Chancellor of Oxford, introduced a bill along the lines of the Cleveland Report, but it was dropped in favour of an executive commission empowered to frame statutes under the Oxford and Cambridge Act of 1878. In four years, much of the formal pattern of university life in both universities was changed. The Latin statutes were repealed. In reframing them in the vernacular, easier methods of amendment were introduced. Life fellowships were further limited, and the celibacy rule was abolished, together with a number of clerical restrictions upon elections to headships of colleges. College revenues were drawn upon for the establishment of university chairs and readerships.[25] Tests had already been formally abolished in 1871, and the seal was set upon the liberalising of Oxford when Samuel Alexander was elected to a fellowship at Lincoln College. This marked the first admission of a professing

Jew to the teaching body of either of the two universities. Alexander himself was a force for change, insisting that the course in Greats needed quickening from moral science and psychology.[26]

Freed from the heavy incubus of collegiate teaching, teachers could now develop their own tutorial work along individual lines, taking up the duty of hearing work in their own rooms and so developing the system of tutorials which did much to re-animate their academic prestige. Moreover, the work of Mark Pattison in stressing the importance of research (his convocation of a gathering at the Freemasons Tavern in London on 16 November 1872, and subsequent memorialisation of the government showed that reform was desired as much within the university as without),[27] and of Henry Sidgwick in promoting the admission of women to university teaching and examinations, played no small part in creating the atmosphere in which new ideas could flourish. The changing nature of the humanities was reflected in the growth of the history schools at both universities—schools which in the intensity of their research, the inspirational teaching, and the philosophic depth of approach were to supplant the classical schools as nodes of the Arts course.

7

James Bryce, who lectured at Manchester from 1868 until 1874, returned to Oxford as Professor of Law. In 1885 he pointed out that Germany, with a population of 45 millions, had 24,187 university students, whereas England, with a population of 26 millions, only had 5,500. 'Nothing,' he asserted, 'could more clearly illustrate the failure of the English system to reach and serve all classes.' Bryce saw three causes operating to retard English university development: suspicion of the influence of Dissenters, the cost of existing university institutions, and their non-professional character.[28]

Even as he wrote, events were shaping which were to alter the complexion of affairs. In that very year a Royal Commission was appointed to investigate the nature of the economic depression through which Britain was passing. Among the numerous opinions offered by witnesses before this commission, there was a strong measure of agreement that foreign competitors, especially in Germany and America, enjoyed greater educational facilities through the active help of their respective governments. Since the passage of the Morrill Land Grant Act in 1862, American states were able to equip themselves with 'at least one college, where the leading object shall be, without excluding other scientific studies . . . to teach such branches of learning as are related to agriculture and the mechanic arts, in such a manner as the legislatures of the states shall respectively provide, in order to promote the liberal education of the industrial classes in the several pursuits and professions of life'. In Germany similar foundations established at Karlsruhe (1825), Darmstadt (1826), Munich (1827), Dresden (1828), Stuttgart (1829), Hanover (1831), Aachen (1865) were crowned by the magnificent Physikalische-Technische Reichsanstalt at Charlottenburg, built in 1884 at a cost of nearly half a million pounds.

The menace of German and American competition, based as it was upon such superior institutions for industrial education, was further stressed by T. H. Huxley who wrote to *The Times* on 21 March 1887:

> We are entering, indeed we have already entered, upon the most serious struggle for existence to which this country was ever committed. The latter years of the century promise to see us in an industrial war of far more serious import than the military wars of its opening years. . . . We must be careful to organise victory. To those who remember the cotton famine and reflect how much worse a customer famine would be, the situation appears grave.[29]

To organise victory in this industrial race, the National Association for the Promotion of Technical Education was formed, aptly enough in the rooms of the Royal Society of Arts. Its moving spirits, Huxley and Sir Bernhard Samuelson, together with a number of enlightened Liberal M.P.s, invited the co-operation of the chief towns and industrial centres. The Liberal M.P.s numbered Henry Roscoe and A. J. Mundella amongst their leaders, both anxious to promote state aid to provincial colleges. Mundella indeed, on 7 March that year, had asked G. J. Goschen, Chancellor of the Exchequer, whether the Government would authorise local authorities to contribute towards the maintenance of technical colleges.[30] Goschen's negative was followed by intensive campaigning on the part of the Technical Education Association, and by outspoken letters from Benjamin Jowett of Balliol, who, realising that the Leeds, Newcastle, Sheffield, Nottingham, and Bristol colleges were not in a satisfactory condition, declared that to wait for private munificence would delay the work for half a century. 'They have proved their value,' he wrote, 'and, like every other educational institution they have proved that they cannot live without external help. The only help that is likely to be permanent and that will enable them to feel secure is help from the State; and, in a moderate degree, it will be worth the State's while to give it.' Henry Roscoe agreed:

> The localities have in almost all cases now practically exhausted the power of raising funds from private sources. . . . We cannot afford to wait until

public opinion has reached the point at which ratepayers generally are convinced that it is to their advantage to support such colleges. The only alternative, therefore, is that the State as a whole shall, through the Government acknowledge its obligation.[31]

Yet in the localities, initiative was not lacking. At Southampton, for instance, the council of the Hartley Institution were convinced that after its twenty-five years' existence as a superior library and museum, the foundation they controlled should be expanded into a local university college. In a pamphlet entitled *The Hartley Institution and its Proposed Extension as a Local University College* (1887) they pointed to the action of the Government in assisting the foundation of three university colleges in Wales, and announced their determination to urge 'on the Government the claims of various local centres in England to assistance of a similar kind to that now accorded to colleges in Wales'. After communicating with other provincial colleges, a public meeting was held at Southampton on 9 May 1887 in which various speakers drew attention to the flood of educated Germans which was beginning to penetrate as far as China. To check this, they asked for State aid for the English university colleges of £50,000 a year.

The prime minister at this time was the same Lord Salisbury who had taken such an active interest in the reform of Oxford in the previous decade. His ministry passed the Technical Instruction Act, arming the newly created county and borough councils with powers to levy a rate specifically for technical education. Such funds helped to revive the local colleges. Bristol, to take but one case in point, voted the sum of £2,000 on condition that three civic representatives were added to the governors of the local university college.

But perhaps the most important step which Salisbury's ministry made to foster civic university colleges was taken when in the Treasury Estimates of 1889 the sum of £15,000 was put down for distribution to university colleges. A memorandum stated that since all these foundations (with the exception of Oxford, Cambridge, and Manchester) were in financial straits, the Treasury recognised their need. A committee was appointed to advise on the disbursement of the grant. Its members were Sir John Lubbock, Sir Henry Roscoe, J. Percival, G. F. Browne, R. C. C. Mowbray, and Henry Oakeley. Though not specifically so-called, a University Grants Committee was thus launched.

A year later, in 1890, a further windfall dropped from the State into the coffers of the local colleges. The secretary of the Technical Education

Association persuaded the chancellor of the exchequer to divert three quarters of a million pounds, intended for publicans who had lost their licenses, to the further assistance of technical education. Some of this 'whisky money' went to the university colleges, and proved a stimulant at the very time when they needed it most.

8

Concomitantly, the country was experiencing an agricultural depression. This led to further attempts to foster scientific expertise. The Board of Agriculture established in 1889, was, from its foundation, authorised to inspect and aid any higher schools offering practical or scientific agricultural instruction. For the purpose, £5,000 a year was placed at its disposal.

At this time, the only facilities for higher agricultural education were those provided at Cirencester, Downton, and Aspatria; all private-enterprise foundations. The only State encouragement of agricultural teaching was confined to Science and Art Department grants. As a result of the 'whisky money' given to the local county councils, the Board was able to pursue a policy of establishing national centres of agricultural education, associated where possible with a university. The first college to receive a grant was Bangor, but in 1890 Yorkshire College, Leeds, also established an agricultural department, helped by a grant. The College of Science at Newcastle followed in 1892, and University College, Nottingham, and the University Extension College at Reading in 1894. In 1896 the Agricultural College at Wye was founded and associated with the University of London. All these centres were assisted by the Board of Agriculture to the extent of some £800 a year each.

In 1896 the Northumberland County Council established the first experimental farm at Cockle Park, placing it under the control of the agricultural department at Armstrong College, and the Board gave an additional £200 a year to assist its maintenance.[32]

9

All this was accompanied by jarring discords in the great examination machine misnamed the University of London. Matthew Arnold, Walter Bagehot, and Lyon Playfair, each so different in outlook, all agreed on the utter inadequacy of the London system to solve the problem of wide education in a mixed society. The prime causes of discord were the strident professional demands of the lawyers and the doctors. In 1868 the Law Society revived the project for a legal university, once sponsored by Lord Westbury. A pressure group, calling themselves the Legal Education Association, formed under the presidency of Roundell Palmer (later Lord Selborne) and supported his bills for a legal university which he introduced into the Commons in 1871 and 1872, and into the Lords in 1873, 1874, 1875, and 1876. Selborne failed to arouse professional enthusiasm for his project because he coupled it with a wider scheme for a general reform of the Inns of Court.

The University of London also opposed Selborne's bills, mainly because his scheme would prejudice the existence of their own law schools. Their intransigence in this, as in other matters, was not congenial to members of the individual colleges, and, as we have already noticed, there was a suggestion made in 1878 that University College should affiliate with Owens College in the projected Federal University Scheme. When Leeds joined the Victoria University the London colleges decided to act, and in 1884 there was founded an Association for Promoting a Teaching University for London. The protagonists of this scheme for a second university, to be called the Albert University, were the Inns of Court, the Law Society, the Royal Colleges of Physicians and Surgeons, and the disaffected colleges. When in 1887 University College and King's College petitioned the Privy Council for power to award their own degrees, the government appointed a commission, singularly enough under Lord Selborne, 'to inquire whether any and what kind of new university or power is or are required for the advancement of higher education in London'.

The Selborne Commission reported in 1889: agreeing that the case for a teaching university was not proven. They recommended that time should be given for the existing university to apply for a charter extending their teaching functions along lines proposed for the so-called Albert University. But, owing to friction between Senate and Convocation, the university did not apply for such a charter.

So in 1892 the Government set up yet another Royal Commission, under the chairmanship of Lord Cowper. Professor Burdon-Sanderson, the first Waynflete Professor of Physiology at Oxford, who had been head of the oldest research institution in the University of London (the Brown Animal Sanitary Institution), was one of the members of this commission. Two years later it reported that there should be one university in London, not two, and that the new university should be established by legislation.

Burdon-Sanderson's nephew, Richard Burdon Haldane, a lawyer of ability and foresight, joined forces with Sidney Webb (a founder of the London School of Economics, and indirectly of the numerous polytechnics that had sprung up in London) to draft a Bill which would prove acceptable to both parties.

The difficulties were great. The professors of the colleges wanted a teaching university. The holders of external degrees feared that their own position would be jeopardised. All through the summer of 1896 Haldane worked on the bill, only to find that the opposition of the bishops killed it. But he persevered, and presented it in the session of 1897. It suffered a similar fate. Realising that a privately sponsored Bill would have no chance, Haldane enlisted the help of A. J. Balfour, who promised to get Sir John Gorst to take it up.[33]

Not till 1898 did the Bill come up for the second reading in the House of Commons, when it was tentatively launched by Gorst, and sternly opposed by Sir John Lubbock, the member for the University. In a vigorous speech, all the more effective for being unprepared, Haldane showed the real reason behind the Bill. Asking members to consult the map of London published by the Technical Education Board of the London County Council, then spending £170,000 a year in technical education, he pointed to the polytechnics as offering teaching 'of a very high type'. He argued that if the university took these polytechnics under its wing, 'cheap and efficient university education' would be given to workmen 'which it is absolutely necessary we should give to them if we are to keep pace with the artisans of Germany and France'.

This, described by both Asquith and Chamberlain as almost the only case in their recollection in which a single speech had turned opinion in the House, carried the day. The Bill was passed, and under the Act, Haldane's friend, Lord Davey, was appointed to chair a commission charged with drafting statutes and regulations for the reconstituted university. Nor was this Haldane's last service, for in response to the consequent need for administrative buildings, he conducted the negotiations which resulted in the acquisition by the university of part of the Imperial Institute Buildings at South Kensington.[34]

London's reorganisation was a prelude to further changes in the provincial colleges hitherto oriented towards it. Since London was now committed to cultivating and organising its own regional resources, it was but natural that provincial colleges should soon begin to claim that right as well.

10

'Have the Universities created a Frankenstein that will threaten his makers?' asked Lewis Campbell at the close of the century. 'Will the newer growths ultimately supersede the old?'[35] His admiration for the evolution of these polytechnic schools to university college status in a single generation prompted him to raise the questions with his readers. To him, not only the established colleges of Manchester, Leeds, Newcastle, Sheffield, Birmingham, and Liverpool had a future, but the university extension colleges of Reading, Exeter, and Colchester as well.

They were certainly phenomena so characteristic of the age that they formed the subject of a novel, *Born in Exile* (1892) written by George Gissing, a former student of Owens College. This was the story of a 'son of the people' and in the lineaments of Sir Job Whitelaw's College one can recognise the quintessential spirit of similar foundations, whose red-brick walls were rising above the smoke-canopied streets of the industrial towns. And it was Gissing, the provincial, who tried to diagnose the evils of his own society. 'Science' was for him 'the remorseless enemy of mankind'. Living as he did in an age when many of the Western values were crumbling under the pressure of alien and misunderstood forces, it is not without significance that he should confess himself 'specially interested' in the age of Cassiodorus.[36]

Gissing's delineation of a civic college should be compared with Thomas Hardy's picture of the oldest university, which appears as Christminster in *Jude the Obscure* (1895). To Jude, an ambitious stonemason, the gothic splendours of Biblioll, Sarcophagus, and Rubric Colleges were centres of 'high and fearless thought'; but to his second wife they were 'nests of commonplace schoolmasters whose characteristic is timid obsequiousness to tradition'. The author, in a revealing aside, commented on the frustrated clericism of his hero:

> He did not at that time see that medievalism was as dead as a fern-leaf in a lump of coal; that other developments were shaping in the world around him in which Gothic architecture and its associations had no place. The deadly animosity of contemporary logic and vision towards so much of what he held in reverence was not yet revealed.[37]

The full force of that contemporary logic and vision was to be demonstrated in the century to follow.

The drabness of Gissing's urban reportage, and the pessimism of Hardy's outlook must, however, be offset by the regenerative optimism of Andrew Carnegie and Cecil Rhodes, both archetypes of the period. Carnegie saw human nature in terms of the steel that had made him wealthy, and laid out his vast fortune to ensure that humanity should be 'dephosphorised'—purged of gross ignorance—by science. To enable the Anglo-Saxons to participate in the fuller development and enrichment of the world he established public libraries,—over eight hundred and fifty in the English-speaking countries alone—; helped the universities of his native Scotland—over fifteen million dollars were expended by the Trust which he established—; and founded the institute which bears his name at Washington. But to appeals from the older, upper-class English universities, he remained relatively indifferent; a letter in Mr. Gladstone's trembling nonagenarian hand on behalf of the Bodleian met with no response. Oxford, however, had little cause to lament, for at this very time it was enhanced as an imperial studium by the will of Cecil Rhodes, bestowing sixty scholarships for students of the British Empire, and a hundred for students from the United States. Rhodes also established a university college in the country where his fortune had been made.[38]

The undertones of the whole generation were caught up and harmonised by the aristocratic A. J. Balfour, whose own interest in these things was sustained and profound. In a letter to Carnegie, Balfour declared that 'it is to science that we have to turn for the future progress of the race' adding:

> we ought to regard our universities not merely as places where the best kind of knowledge already attained is imparted, but as places where the stock of the world's knowledge may be augmented. One discovery which adds to our command over the forces of nature may do more for mankind than the most excellent teaching of what is already known, absolutely necessary to our national welfare though this latter is.[39]

Carnegie's sympathetic agreement was to be of material value in the years to come.

REFERENCES

1. Quoted D. L. Burn, *Economic History of Steelmaking* (Cambridge, 1940), 4–5. See also his article 'The Genesis of American Engineering Competition 1850–1870', in *Economic History*, ii (1931), 292–311.

2. *Systematic Technical Education for the English People* (London, 1869). He continued (p. 327), 'The object of these "Suggestions" has been to insist that the university shall be no longer a class school. . . . It is a national institute for the preservation and tradition of useful knowledge.'

3. ARNOLD, M., *Schools and Universities on the Continent* (London, 1868), 276, 290.

4. WINSTANLEY, D. A., *Later Victorian Cambridge* (1947), 241.

5. WHEELER, A. E., *A Short Account of the University of Leeds* (Leeds, 1924). BROWN, E. J., *The Private Donor in the History of the University* (Leeds 1953).

6. WHITING, C. E., *op. cit.*, 186-99.

7. VINCENT, E. W., and HINTON, P., *The University of Birmingham* (Birmingham, 1947).

8. *Report of a Public Meeting held on 11th June, 1874 in the Victoria Hall* (Bristol, 1874).

9. *Report of the Royal Commission on Scientific Instruction* (Devonshire Commission) (H.M.S.O., 1872), i, 506. He also approved (Q 7436) of an executive council to advise the state on matters of scientific instruction.

10. CHARLTON, H. B., *Portrait of a University* (Manchester, 1951), 53–77.

11. HUMBERSTONE, T. L., *University Reform in London* (1926).

12. DRAPER, W. H., *University Extension 1873-1923* (Cambridge, 1923).

13. BECKETT, Edith M., *University College of Nottingham* (Nottingham, 1928), 9-43, WOOD, A. C., *The History of University College, Nottingham* (Oxford, 1953).

14. CHILDS, W. M., *Making a University* (London, 1933), 13.

15. MILLS, John, in *What is Industrial and Technical Education* (London, 1871), wrote: 'We are beaten in many of the open markets of the world. Other nations are beating us simply because they have been taught how to do it.'

16. *Royal Commission on Scientific Instruction Third Report* (1873).

17. MILLIS, C. T., *Technical Education, its Development and Aims* (London, 1925), 58.

18. ARMYTAGE, W. H. G., 'J. F. D. Donnelly: Pioneer in Vocational Education', in *Vocational Aspect of Secondary and Further Education*, ii (1950), 6-21.

19. TAYLOR, J. R., *Reform your City Guilds* (1872), set the note, W. James, M.P. for Gateshead, and Arthur Pease, M.P. for South Durham, took it up in Parliament in 1876 and 1877. Indignant ratepayers supported them.

20. MILLIS, C. T., *Technical Education* (London, 1925), 54.
MAGNUS, Sir Philip, *Educational Aims and Efforts* (London, 1910), 84-108.

21. *Special Reports on Educational Subjects* (H.M.S.O., London, 1898), ii, 58–75.
SADLER, M. E., *Continuation Schools in England and Elsewhere* (Manchester, 1907).
WEBB, S., *London Education* (London, 1904), 133–74.
Our Partnership by Beatrice Webb, ed. Barbara Drake and M. I. Cole (London, 1947), 57–107.

22. DAVIES, W. C., and JONES, W. L., *The University of Wales* (London, 1905).

23. *History of the Cavendish Laboratory* (Cambridge, 1910).

24. ALLEN, B. M., *William Garnett* (Cambridge, 1933), 31–53.

25. WINSTANLEY, D. A., *op. cit.*, 253–9.

26. LAIRD, J., 'Samuel Alexander 1859-1938', in *Proceedings of the British Academy*, XXIV, 1938.

27. WINSTANLEY, D. A., *op. cit.*, 267–8.

28. CONRAD, J., *The German Universities for the last fifty years*. With a preface by James Bryce (Glasgow, 1885), xiv-xxx.

29. *Life and Letters* (ed. L. Huxley), London, 1900, iii, 9.

30. Armytage, W. H. G., *A. J. Mundella 1825–1897* (London, 1951), 269–73.

31. *The Times*, 3 and 7 January, 16 March, 3 and 5 May, 16 and 20 December 1887.

32. Comber, N. M., *Agricultural Education in Great Britain* (London, 1948), 14–20.

33. Allchin, W. H., *An Account of the Reconstruction of the University of London* (H.M.S.O., 1905–12).

34. Maurice, Maj.-Gen. F., *Haldane 1856–1915* (London, 1937), i, 77–93.

35. Campbell, Lewis, *On the Nationalisation of the old English Universities* (London, 1901), 236.

36. *Letters to Edward Clodd* (London, 1914), 35. For two contemporary French evaluations of these developments see Max Leclerc, *L'Education des Classes Moyennes et dirigeantes en Angleterre* (Paris, 1894), and *L'Education Populaire des Adultes en Angleterre* (Paris, 1896), avec un préface de M. F. Buisson.

37. *Jude the Obscure*, Chapter V, sect. vii; Chapter 11, sect. ii.

38. Aydelotte, Frank, *The Vision of Cecil Rhodes* (Oxford, 1936).

39. Hendrick, B. J., *Life of Carnegie* (London, 1933), 572ff.

CHAPTER ELEVEN

Community Service Stations: The Transformation of the Civic Universities, 1898-1930

I

It is not your wonderful machinery, not even your unequalled supplies of minerals, which we have most cause to envy. It is something worth both of these combined, the class of scientific young experts you have to manage every department of your works. *We have no corresponding class in England.*

SO an English steel magnate lamented to Andrew Carnegie who, amongst his many other generosities to this country, offered to give £50,000 to help the City of Birmingham to establish a university on the American model where such young experts could be trained. That he did so was largely due to the dynamic parliamentary representative of Birmingham, Joseph Chamberlain, who became the first president of the newly incorporated Mason University College in 1898. Chamberlain had first made his name as an advocate of efficient primary education: now he worked to crown the many civic schools with a civic university. At a luncheon before the first meeting of the Court of Governors of Mason University College on 13 January 1898 he said:

To place a university in the middle of a great industrial and manufacturing population is to do something to leaven the whole mass with higher aims and higher intellectual ambitions than would otherwise be possible to people engaged entirely in trading and commercial pursuits.

He appealed for an endowment of a quarter of a million pounds, additional to the existing endowment of £235,000, so that application could be made for a charter. Birmingham responded by convening a meeting on 1 July 1898 to appoint the requisite executive, canvassing, finance, and management committees. By February of the following year the target figure was passed by £76,500. So Birmingham applied for a charter, which was sealed on 24 March 1900. It was only right and proper that Joseph Chamberlain should be the first chancellor.

One of his first acts in that office was to appeal for yet another quarter of a million pounds with which to erect new buildings.

American influence was strong in the new foundation. Professors J. F. Poynting and F. W. Burstall with G. H. Kenrick, a city father, had made a special trip to the United States to investigate the teaching of applied science. Carnegie confirmed their observations that the existing buildings and apparatus of Mason College were quite inadequate as a nucleus for the new university. So Chamberlain secured from Lord Calthorpe an initial tract of twenty-five acres on the Bournbrook side of the Edgbaston Estate where the new scientific departments were to be planned. Chamberlain selected as Vice-chancellor Oliver Lodge, then Professor of Physics at Liverpool. He also chose the architect of the new buildings.

Aptly enough, the first building ready for use was the power station, where an engine was in motion by 1904. Burstall and the architect, in conjunction with the professors of mining and metallurgy, planned the lay-out, and captured the sympathy of Sir James Chance, a local industrialist, who endowed a chair of engineering. R. A. S. Redmayne, the Professor of Mining, conceived the idea of establishing a model coal mine within the vicinity of the main university buildings.

The marriage of university and region, so happily consummated, bred a number of new university studies, which in turn led to new faculties. Thus a degree in commerce was inaugurated under the guidance of W. J. Ashley, who was much influenced by German and American examples, and pioneer studies in economic history, public finance, accounting, and commercial law flourished under his wing. New subjects, like the biochemistry of fermentation, stemmed from the needs of the brewing industry, and these, under the capable direction of Professors Adrian J. Brown and A. R. Ling, subsequently expanded to include malting, brewing, and other fermentation processes.

Not all the studies fell into such banausic categories however. Music was stimulated by the establishment of a chair in 1904—held successively by Sir Edward Elgar and Sir Granville Bantock; philosophy by the presence of J. H. Muirhead and Walter Moberly; History by J. H. B. Masterman and C. R. Beazley; English Literature by Macneile Dixon, Churton Collins and E. de Sélincourt. Thus the Faculty of Arts grew. Thus Birmingham University set the pattern of a scientific and cultural service station, as it catered for the two million inhabitants of its area.[1]

2

The tricuspid Victoria University of Manchester fell apart under similar strains. Sympathetic detonations in Liverpool were set off by the shock of Birmingham's success. Such explosions might have been foretold as early as 1890, when Leeds and Liverpool quarrelled violently over the proposal that a chair of theology should be established, and Manchester, as the senior partner, was much offended. There were other combustible elements which accumulated over the years. Continual travelling to Manchester for meetings of examiners and of the Court of Governors was a perennial exacerbation, especially since the lay members of court felt that they were assisting the growth of Manchester rather than their own local colleges.

Liverpool was the first to move. Ramsay Muir published *A Plea for a Liverpool University* in 1901, stressing the menace of foreign competition and reiterating

> the university is the only possible vitalising force in general education, which aims at producing intelligence; it is the only possible vitalising force also for technical education, which aims at developing capacity for a particular profession.

England, he continued, had fewer universities in proportion to her population than any other civilised country except Turkey. He urged the conscious imitation of America, Germany, and Scotland and proudly advanced the claims of Liverpool to enjoy a university of the same status as Munich or Leipzig. He pointed to its existing achievements:

> the first to treat architecture as on a level with other professions by devising a university curriculum for it; one of the first to bring primary teachers under university influence; the first to attempt high commercial education; the first to bring modern science systematically to bear upon the plagues which hinder trade in tropical regions.

But Leeds, which had greatly benefited from the federal connection, did not feel strong enough to stand alone, and was therefore as anxious to continue the relationship as Liverpool was to end it. Manchester's attitude would turn the scale, and Manchester declared for abolition. So in October 1903 Manchester and Liverpool received charters, leaving Leeds as the sole member of the Victoria University. Leeds, anxious to secure the title of Yorkshire University, met opposition once more, this time from University College, Sheffield, formerly an unsuccessful applicant for inclusion in the federal scheme. Sheffield's rejection by the Victoria University, and Leeds' determination to secure a Yorkshire title, fired the leading citizens of Sheffield to emulate Birmingham, Liverpool, and Manchester, and obtain a civic university of their own. So, a year after Leeds received its charter in 1904, Sheffield too became a university.[2]

A fifth new university also won its charter in this decade. A committee of Bristol citizens was formed to obtain a charter for their university college, and the Colston Society was formed in 1899 to collect funds for it. At a governors' meeting in 1901 Percival spoke on the subject. R. B. Haldane, addressing the University College Colston Society in 1902 pointed to the rich western area which such a university could serve, and sketched the possible constitution of a West of England university on the Victoria pattern, with a court at Bristol and units at Southampton, Exeter, and Reading. The Professor of Chemistry, M. W. Travers, added his voice, pointing out that Bristol was the largest city in England without a university.

The agitation was not without effect, and in 1908 the Colston Society were informed that Henry Overton Wills, member of the tobacco family, offered £100,000 if a charter could be obtained in two years. A royal visit provided the opportunity to supplicate, and on 24 May 1909, with Henry Overton Wills as Chancellor, the University of Bristol was chartered. A link with the north was provided by the appointment of Isambard Owen, formerly principal at Newcastle, as Vice-Chancellor. But the university had been launched in troubled waters. In the years before the first world war it suffered greatly, and was saved by timely assistance from the Wills family.

Bristol, in addition to encouraging civic and industrial technologies, cultivated rural sciences. It became responsible for the administration of the Agricultural and Horticultural Research Station at Long Ashton (founded in 1903 by the National Fruit and Cider Institute) where research was carried out on problems of fruit culture, and problems of pest control were investigated. Another research station at Chipping Campden was associated with the University after 1921 and became the research centre of the fruit and vegetable canning industry in England.[3]

So discredited was the federal principle, that two emerging civic colleges at Southampton and Exeter preferred to remain autonomous.[3] Exeter Extension College was founded in 1901, and in the following year, thanks to the efforts of the Rev. Edmund Kell, the Hartley University College at Southampton was incorporated and recognised by the Treasury as worthy to receive a grant.

3

The promoters of these civic universities also played a great part in securing treasury assistance for them. In 1901 Sidney Webb, an architect of London's integrated educational system, urged

> Nothing would be more widely popular at the present time, certainly nothing is more calculated to promote National Efficiency, than a large policy of Government aid to the highest technical colleges and universities. The statesman who first summons up courage enough to cut himself loose from official pedantries on this point, and demand a grant of half a million a year with which to establish in the United Kingdom, a dozen perfectly equipped faculties of science, engineering, economics, and modern languages would score a permanent success.[4]

Sidney Webb's advice can be best appreciated when one considers the actual amount then given by the State to the universities, £25,000, as compared to his suggested £500,000.

The volume of support for his suggestions grew steadily. Joseph Chamberlain remarked, in a trenchant letter to *The Times* on 6 November 1902, that 'university competition between states is as potent as competition in building battleships, and it is on that ground that our university conditions become of the highest possible national concern'. And when at the same time Germany was giving to one university more than the British were giving to all their universities, Chamberlain's arguments were pointed enough to hurt. Politicians like A. J. Balfour, scientists like Sir Norman Lockyer, and the university colleges themselves all combined their forces to present the case for increased subventions. University grants, they argued, were investments, since universities were agents of economic progress. The examples of America and Japan were conjured up to reinforce their case, and stimulate action.[5]

The response came in 1904, when, by a Treasury minute dated 30 March, the university grant was doubled from £27,000 to £54,000, and its allocation referred to a committee of four. This committee was to consider the necessity of 'stimulating private benevolence in the locality' and to confine its assistance to those bodies which afforded 'education of a University standard in the large centres of population'.

The most prominent member of this committee was R. B. Haldane. Not only did he coin the adjective 'civic' for the newly chartered universities, but he was constantly on guard against the proliferation of technical high schools unconnected with them. 'You cannot, without danger of partial starvation,' he told an audience, 'separate science from literature and philosophy. Each grows best in the presence of the other.'[6] And the civic universities which he so carefully nourished responded by inviting him to open their buildings and preside over some of their most important functions.

4

Three other factors worked to entangle universities with the state.[7] The first of these was the pressure of the population upon existing food supplies. By special acts of parliament in 1909 and 1910, £2,900,000 was set aside to develop agriculture, rural industries and fisheries, and a Development Commission of eight members was established to allocate these funds after consultation with the appropriate ministries.

University College, Reading (whose new buildings Haldane opened in 1906), showed the way by sending a deputation to visit three leading agricultural colleges in Canada and two in America. Expenses were defrayed by L. Sutton, a seed merchant, and Alfred Palmer, a biscuit manufacturer. The report of this deputation, published in 1910, was a challenging testament of the lead which a college could and should give in the improvement of agriculture. Though only eighteen years old at the time, this department of agriculture at Reading was the largest in any civic university, and the largest in England and Wales with the exception of Cambridge. The members of the deputation urged from their trans-atlantic experience that it should become 'the aggressive distributor of the best ideas and methods of agriculture', serving the 14,925 farmers in the Reading area. They continued:

> The true aim and ambition should be to build up a Department which should in effect become an Agricultural University, providing first and foremost for the needs of the great agricultural community around it.

They called for more effective co-operation with county councils, and the institution of an extension section to deal with the external work of the agricultural department. With shrewd insight, they pointed to the difficulty with which a new university in an old social order was faced. For Society, inured to neglect, was suspicious of theory and clung to the traditional ways. Looming with ever-increasing significance on the horizon were the energetic examples of the United States and Canada where a university was regarded

> as a lever to be used in numerous ways to advance the interests of civilisation. Because the University in Canada and the United States is so conspicuous a

unit in the intellectual organisation of society, and because its work ministers so directly to public needs, there is far less hesitation in Canada and in the United States about the propriety of liberal State aid.[8]

The Development Commissioners caught on. A survey of the existing facilities for agricultural education and research in the United Kingdom was made and in 1911 a plan was adopted with two main objects: to create well-equipped and well-staffed institutions for prosecuting specialised research, to link these research institutes with agricultural schools on one side and farmers on the other. Both objects involved the universities. Five original research institutes for plant breeding (Cambridge), plant nutrition (Rothamsted), animal breeding (Edinburgh), animal nutrition (Cambridge and Aberdeen), and economics (Oxford) expanded to twenty-five, mostly connected with universities and under their own governing bodies. By 1931 they were receiving £185,000 a year from the Development Fund. The second object of linking these research institutes with agricultural schools involved the training of chemists, mycologists, entomologists, economists, and veterinary surgeons both for schools and for advisory centres. By 1931 the advisory centres alone were costing £85,000 a year—also from the Development Fund. And these advisory centres were divided into seventeen 'provinces'; regional needs were at last recognised. In addition to this a training scheme was adopted whereby twelve students a year were selected for special post-graduate training. So great became this organisation for the scientific study of agriculture that in 1931 an Agricultural Research Council was created by Royal Charter under the Lord President of the Council, and held its first meeting on 9 July of that year.[9]

Having planned the improvement of agriculture, the Development Commissioners turned to fisheries. Here the problem was vastly different for there was no tradition of recorded observations to be handed on. True, the *Beagle* and the *Challenger* had sailed, but they were voyagers in uncharted waters. So the Development Commission encouraged free research to build up a 'complete knowledge of the sea and the life in it'. While the Marine Biological Associations Laboratory at Plymouth, the Ministry Laboratory at Lowestoft, and two Scottish Laboratories were the main centres of such research, three civic university laboratories were also assisted: Port Erin (Liverpool), Cullercoats (Armstrong College), and Hull. The stimulating effect of these opportunities upon the biologists, and the impetus they gave towards the study of marine biology, was considerable.[10]

5

A sense of imperial responsibility undoubtedly stimulated the convening in 1912 of a Congress of the Universities of the British Empire. This congress established the Universities Bureau of the British Empire, a body intended to provide a centre of university information, and to serve as a link between the imperial universities. This developed into the Association of Universities of the British Commonwealth, and began to publish the *Universities Yearbook*. One of the results of its work has been the institution of quinquennial congresses, at which various problems are discussed. As far as Great Britain is concerned, the staff of the association act as the secretariat to the Committee of Vice-Chancellors and Principals of the Universities of Great Britain and Ireland.

At the first of these congresses, held in 1912, a suggestion was made that British universities should institute the post-graduate degree of doctor of philosophy in order to attract research students who were flocking to America and Germany. The Foreign Office strongly urged the adoption of this degree, and in 1917 the five civic universities of Manchester, Liverpool, Leeds, Sheffield, and Birmingham held a conference on the subject and agreed on a common course of action. They agreed that it would be preferable to adopt the Ph.D. as the degree desired, rather than to lower the standard of the D.Litt. or the D.Sc. A year later, their resolution was adopted by all universities except Cambridge.

The institution of the Ph.D. has enabled the civic universities to build up strong reputations in particular fields, not all of them concerned with science and technology. Perhaps the most notable example was Manchester, where under the able and energetic direction of Professor Tout, a powerful school of medieval history was created.

The Ph.D. degree did not succeed in fulfilling the hopes of its promoters. As the University Grants Committee reported in 1930:

> It is true that the institution of the Ph.D. degree has had less effect than was originally expected in the way of attracting to our Universities students from other countries, but it is perhaps not wholly to be regretted that our Universities have not had among their other serious preoccupations to improvise arrangements for dealing with a large and sudden influx of foreign students in search of some particular academic label.[11]

In the sciences, this was not surprising, in view of the intensive programme of State aid to research which other countries had been adopting since the first world war. But in the arts it was. And perhaps a reason for that might have been found in the melancholy fact that in 1925–6 all the grant-aided Universities and Colleges of Great Britain put together did not spend as much on books as the four American Universities of Illinois, Michigan, Minnesota, and North Carolina, and only a little more than Harvard and Yale.

6

We have seen how national concern for the utilitarian aspects of higher education prompted an increase in State grants to universities, how the pressure of population compelled State action to stimulate agricultural education and fisheries research, and how the growing sense of responsibility for the welfare of backward races generated a pooling of imperial university experience. But these three aspects of State assistance were completely overshadowed in 1914 by a fourth: the dominant needs of national defence.

With Germany as the national enemy, the nation found itself immediately deprived of the very materials needed to fight the war: optical glass, khaki dye, magnetos, drugs, tungsten, and zinc, so a committee was appointed under Lord Haldane to consider ways and means of supplying them.

The universities branch of the Board of Education prepared a memorandum pointing out the failure of the universities to train a sufficient number of research workers and suggesting means by which the weakness of native industries could be remedied. This memorandum was referred to a small committee presided over by Sir William M'Cormick, then chairman of the Advisory Committee on grants to universities. In 1915, when the Royal Society and other bodies waited on the Presidents of the Boards of Trade and Education, asking for 'government assistance for scientific research for industrial purposes, the establishment of closer relations between the manufacturers and scientific workers, and teachers, and the establishment of a National Chemical Advisory Committee for these purposes', the government acted boldly. A month later they established the Department of Scientific and Industrial Research, and constituted it as a Committee of the Privy Council.

The Department of Scientific and Industrial Research, designed to 'operate over the Kingdom as a whole with as little regard as possible to the Tweed or the Irish Channel', proved a very real help to the civic universities. For the Department's small advisory committee was placed under the chairmanship of Sir William M'Cormick, who had already been acting as chairman of the committee which had been advising the Board of Education since 1909, on the distribution of university grants. As chairman of both the Advisory Council of D.S.I.R. and the Committee on University Grants, he was in a position to exercise a powerful influence on university development.

For, as the White Paper (Cmd. 8005), dated 23 July 1915, declared when it established D.S.I.R.:

it is obvious that the organisation and development of research is a matter which greatly affects the public educational systems of the Kingdom. A great part of all research will necessarily be done in Universities and Colleges which are already aided by the State, and the supply and training of a sufficient number of young persons competent to undertake research can only be secured through the public system of education.

This the Advisory Council did in three ways: by proposals for specific researches; by proposals for developing special institutions and by establishing research studentships and fellowships. Working in intimate collaboration with the Royal Society and the principal scientific and professional institutions as well as with the universities, the D.S.I.R. established a system whereby suggestions could be initiated for consideration. Some measure of public surveillance was secured by the obligation to present an annual report.[12]

At the same time, in 1916, the Consultative Committee of the Board of Education reported on the need for enlarging the output of the universities. The Committee under Sir William M'Cormick, which had been distributing grants under the aegis of the Board of Education, was now retransferred to the Treasury, and in 1919 was charged

to enquire into the financial needs of university education in the United Kingdom and to advise the Government as to the application of any grants that may be made by Parliament towards meeting them.

And, symbolising both the insufficiency of private endowments to meet the tasks ahead and the need for a national stimulus of scientific research in all available universities, Oxford and Cambridge accepted grants from the University Grants Committee.

The choice of Sir William M'Cormick to chair both the University Grants Committee and the Advisory Council of D.S.I.R. until his death in 1930 was significant, for the work of the latter bore enormously upon the universities.

Fundamental research under the creative guidance of professors was encouraged, especially by Sir George Beilby. This policy was implemented in three main directions: first by the distribution of maintenance grants to young researchers; secondly by the award of more senior grants, which in 1928–9 were consolidated into Senior Research Awards, equivalent to university fellowships in status and tenure; lastly, by direct grants to heads of departments and senior lecturers for research with an immediate application, but needing assistance from outside.

The Advisory Council of D.S.I.R. were also responsible for the consideration of the need of special institutions. Since both the National Physical Laboratory and the Geological Survey came under its control after 1920, it was in a special position to co-ordinate scientific research. It advised the creation of a Fuel Research Board, established in 1917 with Sir George Beilby as Director, and a Fuel Research Station, established at Greenwich a year later. In 1918 too the Food Investigation Board was established under W. B. Hardy, and in 1919 a Low Temperature Research Station was established at the University of Cambridge to study problems of refrigeration. In 1920 a Building Research Board was established, in 1921 a Forest Products Research Board, in 1922 a Chemistry Research Board, and in 1927 a Water Pollution Research Board. These boards, though they possessed their own laboratories, stimulated collateral research in a number of universities. Forestry at Oxford, the Imperial College, and St. Andrews; and the colloids of sewage by University College, London, were notable cases in point.

Like a beneficent deity, D.S.I.R. moved in a mysterious way its wonders to perform. Sometimes it co-operated with a specialist body, like the Institute of Metals (founded in 1908) in order to finance research into a particular problem such as the corrosion of aluminium and other non-ferrous metals. Sometimes it relinquished control of a specific technology to a university. This was notably the case in Glass Technology, which it encouraged Sheffield to develop as a speciality.

Following the channels it created was the fount of charity controlled by the Livery Companies of London, who were anxious to stimulate industrial expertise. To the new Department of Glass Technology at Sheffield, the Worshipful Company of Glaziers contributed; while the Clothworkers having already built and equipped the Department of Textiles and Colour Dyeing at the University of Leeds, continued to give an annual endowment of £10,000. The latter also gave a further £7,000 a year to the City and Guilds Engineering College and other sums to technical colleges all over the country. The Drapers, by numerous gifts to universities throughout the country, were responsible amongst other things, for the buildings of the Applied Science Laboratories at Sheffield University and those of Queen Mary College in the University of London. Both University and King's College in the same university received substantial aid from them. The Fishmongers helped, amongst other bodies, the University College of Hull. The Goldsmiths endowed both the Library and the college which bear their name at the University of London. The Ironmongers founded fellowships and scholarships at Sheffield University. The Skinners helped to endow the Leather Department of the University of Leeds. The Armourers and Brasiers offered prizes and certificates for technical students at Sheffield University. The Founders endowed research and study, chiefly at King's College, London. The Paviours founded in 1928 a part-time professorship of Highway Engineering at the Imperial College in 1928. The Cutlers, amongst their numerous benefactions, have maintained scholarships and exhibitions at Oxford and Cambridge.[13]

The flow of students and research workers to the universities was also materially sustained by the cumulative charity of a number of public bodies. The Board of Education, by its award of grants for further education and training to ex-service men, made 26,000 awards in the immediate post-war years to enable students to resume their university courses. In addition, a system of State scholarships was established in 1921 enabling the more promising pupils of grammar schools to proceed to universities with their fees paid and a generous maintenance allowance. The Local Education Authorities also co-operated by instituting a similar system of awards.

7

There was yet another service for which the universities were paid by the State—Medical Research. As a result of the Insurance Act of 1911 the Medical Research Committee was established in 1913 from funds derived from the contributions of insured persons. This source of revenue sustained it for six years until 1919 when it was reorganised as the Medical Research Council and placed, like D.S.I.R., under the Privy Council with funds voted directly by Parliament. These funds have been supplemented from time to time by grants from public bodies and private benefactors, and a third of its income is devoted to the National Institute for Medical Research at Hampstead.

The other two-thirds of its funds sustain various researches conducted in hospitals and universities throughout the country. Pathology,

Bacteriology, Optics, Microphotography, Biochemistry, Pharmacology, Applied Physiology, and Hygiene have all benefited from the grants so received from the Medical Research Council. It also awards travelling fellowships.

Sub-committees, composed of medical and scientific workers from all over the country, have been set up to examine specific problems of nutrition, mental disorders, tuberculosis, radiology, anaesthetics, epidemics, and many others, while special attention is devoted, through an Industrial Health Research Board, to the problems of working conditions in modern factories. As the Prince of Wales truly said in his presidential address to the British Association in 1926:

> There can surely be no plainer duty, for a State charged with the health of an industrial civilisation, than to promote with all its resources the search for such knowledge as this, as well as to provide for its application when obtained.

8

'I have sometimes thought,' wrote Sidney Webb in 1904, 'that the dwindling Arts faculty would be saved, even without its reform, by the inrush of teachers.'[14] He was right. The 1902 Act, of which he was so efficient, if invisible, an architect, created both a demand for qualified teachers for the new secondary schools which the universities alone could satisfy, and a reservoir of talent upon which the universities were to draw so much that the very curricula of those schools were oriented towards their matriculation requirements. In 1902 36 per cent. of existing teachers had never passed the examination for the teachers' certificate and 55 per cent. had never been to a training college of any kind.

All the civic university colleges had possessed 'day training colleges' since 1890. These were designed to help primary school teachers acquire degrees, and survived until 1911. They were superseded because they combined professional training and the degree course to the detriment of the degree course. After 1911 a four-year course was instituted in which the intending teacher took three years for a degree and one for professional training. This professional year was tested by the award of a Board of Education certificate. A third change gave more responsibility to the universities when in 1926 the Board allowed diplomates of the education departments to obtain their certificate without a further examination. In that year too, the universities were endowed with representation on the newly created Regional Boards, set up to examine non-university trained teachers from the training colleges, and thus to influence their curriculum as well. Some results of this latter relationship meant yet more university students, for where the training colleges were near enough to be affiliated to their regional universities, students were allowed to become undergraduates. Durham was notable in this respect, recruiting students from Bede College, St. Hild's, and Neville's Cross. London University also incorporated Goldsmiths' College for a similar purpose.

The low financial status of teachers, who always struggled against inadequate salaries, proved a deterrent to many aspirants for university courses. As late as 1914 a male certificated teacher received only £129 per annum and his woman counterpart £96. In 1917, however, H. A. L. Fisher, called from the Vice-Chancellorship of the University of Sheffield to be President of the Board of Education, obtained an increased exchequer contribution towards the cost of teachers' salaries. Two years later in 1919, he established a committee under Lord Burnham which established national scales of remuneration for primary teachers. Other committees did similarly for secondary and technical teachers till by 1921 a series of scales was in operation. These scales, together with the increasing amenities offered by the schools, did much to attract university students to accept what was informally known as the 'pledge', i.e. they undertook a university degree course, financed by the Board of Education, under the obligation of accepting appointments at the end of their course.

The economic troubles of 1926 and the further crisis of 1931 tended to divert even more of the secondary school pupils towards universities, since other avenues were closed. The attraction of an established superannuation system, established in 1918 and 1925, and based on a pension proportionate to length of service and status, did much to create a feeling that in an insecure economic world, the teacher was at least insured.

Indeed it is not too much to say that the civic universities in their struggling years, and the university colleges all along, owed the very existence of their arts faculties and in many cases their pure science faculties to the presence of a large body of intending teachers whose attendance at degree courses was almost guaranteed by the state.

9

With such stimuli, the growth of the civic universities was remarkable. London became almost the embodiment of Haldane's dream: a great imperial university covering every aspect of human knowledge.

Though the Davey Commissioners had not included the four schools of music, nor the four Inns of Court, they had reconstituted twenty-four other colleges as schools of the University of London. These were University College, King's College, six colleges in the Faculty of Theology, two women's colleges (Holloway and Bedford), the Royal College of Science, the South East Agricultural College, the ten medical schools of the great London Hospitals, the Central Technical College, and the London School of Economics.

To these twenty-four were added another eleven during the period 1902-25: Westfield (1902), the London School of Tropical Medicine (1905), the East London College (1909), University College Hospital Medical School (1909), the London Day Training College (1910), the Royal Dental Hospital School (1911), Birkbeck College (1920), and the School of Pharmacy (1925). The Royal Army Medical College and the Royal Naval Medical School were admitted to the Faculty of Medicine in 1908 and 1913 respectively.

Haldane's vision of a great metropolitan university, offering advanced instruction to students in every field of human endeavour seemed to materialise at last. Research Institutions like the Lister (1905), the School of Oriental Studies (1918), the Institute of Historical Research (1921), the Maudsley Hospital and Bethlem Royal Hospital (1924), the Cancer Hospital (1927), grew up under its wing. New degrees were established in Engineering and Economics (1903), Agriculture (1905), Commerce (1919), Horticulture (1918), Household and Social Science (1920), and Estate Management (1921). Diplomas in a yet wider range of subjects were offered in Education, Geography, Theology, Anthropology, Archaeology, Bacteriology, Biology, Fine Art, Journalism, Librarianship, Psychology, Public Administration, Slavonic Studies, Sociology, Town Planning and Civic Architecture, and the network of extension classes covered every field of human endeavour.

To administer this vast congeries of colleges, research institutions, and classes, a central administrative building was needed, and in 1920 the government offered the university 11½ acres of land in Bloomsbury, on condition that King's College moved there and sold their site to the Government. King's refused, so the Government sold the land back to the vendor. Seven years later, thanks to a grant from the Rockefeller trustees, the university were able to buy the land on their own terms, and throw up the functional crag that now towers over the British Museum and Russell Square. That it should face Boyle's house in Southampton Row, and Cavendish's on the corner of

Montague Street and Gower Street, was apt acknowledgement of its intellectual patrimony.

Yet the most difficult institution for the University of London to digest was the Imperial College of Science. This, an amalgamation of the former Royal College of Science, the Royal School of Mines, and the Central Technical College, was intended for advanced teaching and research in technology. Architect of the scheme was Sidney Webb's spiritual agent in politics: R. B. Haldane. He not only induced the L.C.C. to promise an annual grant of £20,000, but chaired a Departmental Committee of the Board of Education appointed in 1904 whose report suggested the amalgamation. Its establishment was accelerated by the will of Alfred Beit, which provided some £60,000 for the purpose. Chartered in 1907, the Imperial College of Science and Technology developed a strong antagonism to the University of London, and many of the teachers and students campaigned for a separate university. So a Royal Commission was appointed under Haldane, which sat from 1909 until 1913. In the latter year a Departmental Committee was established to execute its recommendations. But the War put an end to its activity, and it was not until 1924 that another Departmental Committee was appointed, after a controversy that raged through the correspondence columns of *The Times*. This in turn reported in 1926, recommending the now familiar engine of a statutory commission. This, established by the University of London Act of that year, drafted new statutes which came into operation on 21 March 1929.

These statutes welded the University of London into an administrative whole under a Court, to whom the grant-giving bodies like the University Grants Committee and the London County Council made block grants for subsequent distribution to individual institutions. And one of the first and most important tasks of this newly established Court was to concentrate the University around Bloomsbury, where a self-contained estate had been secured by the financial assistance of the Rockefeller Foundation (which gave £400,000 for the purpose in 1927) and the administrative assistance of the London County Council (which allowed certain roadways to be enclosed).

10

As London University tended to nucleate around Bloomsbury, so the provincial universities and university colleges tended to develop communities, usually, however, on the periphery of the towns which nourished them. This removal, as it were, from the traffic of busy cities was accompanied by a corresponding widening of intellectual perspectives. Birmingham seemed to have set the example in 1900 by its Edgbaston estate which more than doubled in size throughout the period by adding in the decade after the war, new buildings to accommodate departments of Botany, Brewing, Zoology, and Oil Engineering. Thanks to a generous gift by the Anstruther-Gough-Calthorpe family, another 41 acres was added to this estate, and plans were drawn for the transfer of the two main Birmingham Hospitals to an adjacent site. Leeds also embarked in 1924 on the rehousing of their entire university, and, in response to a public appeal, obtained a magnificent endowment for a new library from Sir Edward Brotherton. Reading, which received its charter in 1926, acquired a further 20 acres of land.

And when, in 1926, the University of Reading received its charter, it became the ninth degree-giving university. Since its inspection by the Treasury Commissioners in 1901, Reading had held the status of a university college. Four years later after moving into a new and extensive site, it developed two characteristic features under its persevering and energetic principal W. M. Childs. The first was its department of Agriculture which was expanded to embrace Horticulture in 1907, and elevated to the status of a faculty in 1913. The second was its early and steady development of halls of residence—a new thing in the civic universities.

University Colleges followed suit. Exeter acquired a hundred acres of land on the outskirts of the city to which they planned to transfer their existing urban departments. Southampton built itself into the framework of Wessex, establishing a chair of music amongst other things, and acquiring a fine old house, once the property of the Sloane family, as a men's hostel. For Nottingham, Jesse Boot did what the Wills family had done for Bristol: building a magnificent group of new departments at Highfields, three miles from the city. These three became, in a very real sense, regional service stations, even though their degrees were awarded by the University of London.

In 1922 a fourth university college was founded for Leicestershire and Rutland, and rechristened University College, Leicester, in 1927. A fifth college was promoted in 1926 at Hull, and formally incorporated under the Companies Act of 1929 as 'an institution for the promotion, in all their branches, of higher learning, science, the arts and knowledge in general'. Its governing body consisted of representatives of the Royal Society, the British Association, the Law Society, the

Dental Association, the Royal Institute of British Architects, the Pharmaceutical Society, the Trades Council, the Co-operative Movement, the Free Churches, the Urban Districts and County Councils. So comprehensive were the professional and political needs which new universities were supposed to satisfy! In their articles of association, the promoters frankly acknowledged that their purpose was

> To establish, organise and maintain classes and lectures . . . for the purpose of promoting education and research, and to provide instruction in such branches of education as shall be required for the training of entrants to the learned, teaching and technical professions, industry and commerce, and in such other branches of education as shall from time to time be directed by the managing Body or Bodies.
>
> To grant diplomas of merit and efficiency.
>
> To act in conjunction with, and to receive grants from, and co-operate with any University, Institute, College, School, Society or Association whose objects are altogether or in part similar to those of the Association.
>
> To co-operate with and receive grants from and make arrangements with County Councils, City and Borough Councils, Educational Societies and Committees, Railway Companies, and other public bodies, with a view to promoting and forwarding all or any of the objects of the Association.

No better definition of a community service station could have been conceived at that time.

This University College, endowed with a quarter of a million pounds by T. R. Ferens (who had also presented an Institute of Otology to the University of London) also received £150,000 from the Corporation of Kingston-upon-Hull and a site of 18½ acres. Foundations were formally laid on 28 April 1928, and plans were envisaged for a university of nearly two thousand students. But the immediate advances were, in their way, solid. For by collaboration with the local technical college, a diploma in aeronautics for aircraft designers was developed, and, with government help, a special scheme of fisheries research was inaugurated.

II

Though the nine universities and five university colleges developed during this period into vital cores of their respective regions, there was a strong current of feeling that they should and could develop even more. Patrick Geddes called for a great renewal along Baconian lines, in which 'the university militant, affirmative, selective, predictive' was to play a leading rôle:

> the reawakening movement of the universities has been slow, timid, blindfold, because lacking in civic vision. Now, therefore is urgent an arousal of the

universities to their spiritual responsibilities for the fullness of life in all its phases, individual and social. In every region is needed a comprehensive working together of city and university on each plane of the ascending spiral from home to humanity.[15]

Geddes saw clearly that the domination of English universities by the Germanic idea of complete objectivity should be overthrown. To him, regional capitals each had responsibilities to their respective regions: Newcastle to North England, Manchester and Liverpool to Lancashire, Leeds to Yorkshire, Sheffield to Peakdon, Birmingham to the Severn area, Nottingham to Trent, Southampton to Wessex, Norwich to East Anglia, Oxford to Central England, Plymouth to Devon, and London and Bristol to their own environs. Response to the specialised needs of each of these areas would, he argued, revitalise the curricula of the universities in these capitals. And to enable the regions to be adequately served in this respect, he proposed further universities at Plymouth, Norwich, and Northampton.

Geddes and his disciples wrote before the foundation of Hull or Leicester University Colleges, and their views, tinged by admiration of mid-western universities in Wisconsin and Michigan, provoked derision in more orthodox academic circles. Yet there were some, even among the orthodox, who agreed that the march of American mind had far outpaced anything accomplished in England. Ramsay Muir, for instance, cited the example of Iowa, which, with a population of two millions, sustained as many universities as all England: the State University being larger than both Oxford and Cambridge combined. Ramsay Muir commented on the respect for scientific methods of enquiry which pervaded all branches of American life, the 'immense facilities for research in every subject bearing upon industry', and the sustained output of great numbers of employable university graduates.[16]

All this, Ramsay Muir regretfully concluded, had a most important social consequence: 'the absence of that acute class feeling which is today one of the chief obstacles to progress in England.' But he lamented in vain. The liberalism of his own youth had lost the power to animate, much less to endow, similar institutions in England; while his own warnings were derided by the disillusioned generation of the late twenties. This generation's viewpoint was well expressed by Aldous Huxley in *Point Counterpoint*, where the 'easiness' of a life devoted to erudition, scientific research, philosophy, or criticism was mocked:

It's the substitution of simple intellectual schemata for the complexities of reality: of still and formal death for the bewildering movements of life. . . .

The intellectual's life is child's play; which is why intellectuals tend to become children—and then imbeciles and finally, as the political and industrial history of the last few centuries clearly demonstrates, homicidal lunatics and wild beasts.

Mark Rampion, one of the vocal ideologues of the novel, was a graduate of Sheffield University, who by marrying above his class, emancipates himself from what he regards as the fate of most of his fellow students. 'Teaching, teaching,' he exclaims to his wife-to-be, 'does it surprise you that I should feel depressed?' His talents lead him into art and journalism, and one of Huxley's most expressive satires on the contemporary world emerges in a description of Rampion's drawing 'Fossils of the Past and Fossils of the future'. In this, J. J. Thomson and other intellectual leaders of the time, are depicted as marching towards extinction. 'And a damned good thing too,' Rampion comments, 'only the trouble is they're marching the rest of the world along with them.'[17]

12

It was during this very period that the University of Manchester was fostering the most significant scientific research of modern times: the concept of the nucleus of the atom. The pioneer in this field was Ernest Rutherford, a brilliant New Zealander and the first post-graduate student to work at the Cavendish Laboratory in 1895. After experiments there with another old Manchester student, J. J. Thomson, on the ionisation of gases he was elected to the chair of physics at McGill University, Montreal, where he put forward the theory of spontaneous atomic disintegration leading to the discovery of isotopes.

Rutherford's election to the Langworthy chair of physics at Manchester, which he held from 1907 to 1919, marked another step forward in atomic research: that of the nucleus of the atom, which stemmed from his experiments on the scattering of α particles (doubly ionised helium ions). By utilising these particles to bombard nitrogen and thereby change it into an isotope of oxygen, he made the wildest dream of the alchemists come true.

By so doing, Rutherford opened vast and illimitable vistas. Not only did he help to endow mankind with a new prime mover, destined to react as powerfully on society as electricity had done in the previous century, but he helped to fashion another powerful inquisitor of nature. He stood at the gates of a new era, just as Faraday did a century before him. And it was but fitting that when, in 1930, the chairmanship of the Advisory Council of the Department of Scientific and Industrial Research fell vacant, he should be appointed to the post.[18]

REFERENCES

1. AMERY, Julian, *Life of Joseph Chamberlain* (London, 1951), iv, 209–21.

VINCENT and HINTON, *op. cit.*, 29. For the influence of America in Educational circles see R. H. Heindel, *The American Impact on Great Britain* (Philadelphia, 1940), 273–98; and *Special Reports on Educational Subjects* (H.M.S.O., 1902), ii, 419–32.

2. See *Case for the Liverpool University Committee* and *Case and Appendix of the Yorkshire College, Leeds*. R. B. Haldane, on p. 78 of the former petition, argued that Leeds and Sheffield should constitute a Yorkshire University. It is interesting that soon afterwards, in 1906, W. H. Owen should present detailed proposals to the city council for the establishment of a university at Hull. For insights into the ideals of civic university teachers at this time see A. Smithells, *From a Modern University* (Oxford, 1921), and Ramsay Muir, *An Autobiography and Some Essays* (London, 1943).

3. COTTLE, B., and SHERBORNE, J. W., *The Life of a University* (Bristol, 1951), 1–36.

4. Fabian Tract No. 108, also published in the *Nineteenth Century* for September, 1901.

5. For Lockyer's efforts, and those of the British Science Guild, see T. M. Lockyer, *Life and Work of Sir Norman Lockyer* (London, 1928), 184–93.

6. *Education and Empire* (1902), 32–3, 85. See also *An Autobiography* (London, 1929), in which Haldane wrote (p. 90): 'By this time [1902] I had come to see that what we needed badly in our own country was more universities and universities of the civic type, in different parts of these islands. Turning to these matters, one of the first of the new university movements on which I set to work was that in Liverpool. . . . I addressed the men of business of the city in a speech . . . warning them of their peril from German rivalry if they continued to neglect science and education. Liverpool made a splendid response. I also worked hard at London and at Bristol, where the university was ultimately founded of which I am now Chancellor.'

Haldane was elected Chancellor of the University of Bristol in 1912, and his inaugural address emphasises this theme.

7. The precedent was set by the establishment of the National Physical Laboratory in 1902, which grew out of the work of the British Association's Committee on Standards, formed to provide industries with accurate methods of measurement and grading. This played an important part in the evolution of mass-production. The then Prince of Wales said at its opening: 'I believe that in the National Physical Laboratory we have almost the first instance of the State taking part in scientific research . . . to bring scientific knowledge to bear practically upon our everyday industrial and commercial life, to break down the barrier between theory and practice, to effect a union between science and commerce.'

8. *The Problem of Agricultural Education in America and England with Special Reference to a Policy of Developing the work . . . at University College, Reading* (Reading, 1910).

9. COMBES, N. M., *Agricultural Education in Great Britain* (London, 1948).

10. See the Reports of the Development Commission.

11. *Report of the University Grants Committee* (1930).

12. HEATH, H. F., and HETHERINGTON, A. L., *Industrial Research and Development in the United Kingdom* (London, 1946), 251-6. In fairness to the champions of the humanities, it must be said that they were most active at this time. On 4 May 1916 a letter appeared in *The Times*, replying to that of the scientist's on 2 February, under the title 'Educational Aims and Methods', and urging a proper balance in the curriculum. The Classical, English, Geographical, Historical, and Modern Language Associations took up the matter, and with the co-operation of the British Academy, formed the Council for Humanistic Studies which met the representatives of the scientific bodies to draft seven resolutions in January 1917. For a detailed account of these discussions see I. L. Kandel, *Education in Great Britain and Ireland*, U.S. Bureau of Education, Bulletin (1919), 47ff.

13. HEATH and HETHERINGTON, *op. cit.*, 307-10.

14. WEBB, Sidney, *London Education* (London, 1904), 81.

15. GEDDES, P., and BRANFORD, V., *The Coming Polity* (London, 1917, 2nd ed., 1919), 214-15, 343, and C. B. Fawcett, *The Provinces of England* (London, 1919).

16. MUIR, Ramsay, *America the Golden: An Englishman's Notes and Comparisons* (London, 1927), 27-31. This should be contrasted with the judicious endorsement of the 'structural efficiency' of English universities to be found in William S. Learned, *The Quality of the Educational Process in the United States and in Europe* (New York, 1927).

17. Aldous Huxley was thinking of D. H. Lawrence, a former student of Nottingham who died in 1930. He published an edition of Lawrence's letters in 1932.

18. EVE, A. S., *Rutherford* (1939), 163-266.

CHAPTER TWELVE

Flexner to Truscot: The Readjustment of Perspectives, 1930-44

> The creation of the University Grants Committee, the Medical Research Council, the Department of Industrial and Scientific Research, indicates recognition of the fact that England lacks modern universities. The organisations just named give temporary relief—a block grant, support for a promising investigator or an important investigation. Such agencies are not superfluous; under all circumstances they have their uses; but they are no substitute for universities, amply endowed, amply equipped, and amply attended by a sufficient group of men and women dedicated to the search for truth. They seem to say: 'We lack developed universities. While we are waiting for them or in preparation for them, let us train this or that promising man, let us get this or that thing done.' It is all very well but it does not answer.[1]

SO Abraham Flexner described English university policy in 1930. The makeshift *ad hoc* character of the civic colleges to that date, their mushroom growth, and their lowly position in public estimation also provoked another foreigner, the German, William Dibelius, to make the sardonic remark

> From the purely academic point of view, the new universities may beat the old on this or that point. It makes no difference. The average Englishman rates them far below Oxford and Cambridge. If a post is to be filled, the academic qualifications of the M.A. of Liverpool or Leeds will not prevail against the social status of the Oxford B.A., which bears no mark of coal dust and the fumes of the brewing vats.[2]

Such was the external assessment of progress up to the year 1930.

I

Others saw nothing to challenge in these verdicts, and much to applaud. For pruning and controlling rather than fostering and encouraging was the order of the day. This was partly due to the general discrediting of scientific progress which characterised the times, a kind of neo-Thomist tightening of attitude. It was reflected in T. S. Eliot's indication of the worm-eaten fabrics of liberal thought and in W. H. Auden's attack on a decaying social order in his First *Poems* (1930):

> 'The horns of the dark squadron
> Converging to attack;
> The sound behind our back
> Of glaciers calving.'

and epitomised by the Bishop of Ripon's suggestion to the British Association in 1931 that science should 'take a ten years holiday'.[3] The almost fundamentalist faith in technological progress cherished by previous generations was ridiculed by Aldous Huxley in *Brave New World* (1932).

Faced with the distempers of contemporary society, a number of academic teachers turned with nostalgia to the middle ages, and projected a romantic picture of the medieval clerk for the modern university teacher to imitate. Julian Benda (whose work became current in this country through the translations of Richard Aldington in 1928 and Herbert Read in 1930) indicted the treason of university teachers in abandoning the pursuit of abstract truth in order to pander to utilitarian needs. Benda called upon the universities to eschew the power, security and comfort which bound them to their regions as scientific and cultural service-stations, and to return to the spartan life of the medieval clerisy.[4]

Benda's indictment was documented with characteristic energy by Abraham Flexner, who also deprecated the tendency of the universities to serve their regions. Flexner denounced institutions like the King's College of Household and Social Science—founded in 1929 and since 1953 called Queen Elizabeth College—as 'out of place in a university'. 'What does such a school gain by being a School of the University?' he asked, 'and what does "University" mean when such a school is included?' Interlaced with his patronising commendation of the civic universities appears a similar indictment of their technological activities as 'too highly developed': examples he cited being certificates of Higher Commercial Studies, in Photographic Technology and in Industrial Administration at Manchester, the diploma in Brewing and in Social Study at Birmingham, the degree in Domestic Science of Bristol, the diplomas in Dyeing, in Gas Engineering, and in Colour Chemistry at Leeds, and the diploma in Glass Technology at Sheffield. 'Equally shortsighted and absurd,' he continued, 'are such excrescences as the School of Librarianship and the course in Journalism at University College, London, the Department of Civic Design at

Liverpool, and the work in Automobile Engineering at Bristol. This technical development,' he concluded, was 'deplorable.'[5] In a more urbane and philosophic fashion, Ernest Barker lamented the 'danger of technical zeal' and said 'it is a great mistake to blur the distinction between university and technical colleges'.[6]

As principal of King's College, London, Ernest Barker issued a warning against the planless expansion of higher education:

'There is a certain danger in modern times,' he wrote, 'of what might be called the clericalisation of society. The general spread of education, if it works by the book and directs itself only to the intelligence, readily produces a great supply of would-be clerical workers, which pours in a flood towards every grade of clerical service. The channels are not adequate for its flow; the discontented product of a clerkly system of education may become a revolutionary force.'[7]

That England had only 1 student for every 1,150 per head of population (as compared to 1 for 690 in Germany or 1 for 125 in the United States) was, to Ernest Barker, an adequate proportion: this was 'as much as we can safely attempt at the present time'. He continued:

those who know our universities best are haunted by the fear that a democratic enthusiasm, as genuine as it is ill-informed, may result in an attempt to increase the quantity of university education at the expense of its quality.[8]

Contraction was also advocated by H. G. G. Herklots, in his book *The New Universities, An External Examination* (1928). 'This should be a period of retrenchment and reform: it should not be a period of further expansion,' he argued:

One cannot but deprecate the attempts that are being made to found universities up and down the country . . . if matters continue as they are at present we are promised a spate of new universities. These will either lower the standard of education in the universities that are already in being, and widen further the breach that exists between the old and the new, or else they will form a new and surely unnecessary type, perhaps most like the American small town college.[9]

2

That standards were being lowered seems obvious from the complaints of various responsible authorities within the civic universities themselves. The Vice-Chancellor of the university most closely associated with brewing vats, Charles Grant-Robertson, in his survey *The British Universities* (1930), remarked:

As education advances, the general level of trained intelligence rises, but not, unfortunately, with the result of producing more and more of the really first class. . . . A highly competent mediocrity is a real danger to a nation, and above all, to a university. For the more competent and widely distributed that mediocrity becomes, the more it fears and resents those who rise above it; a latent but ineradicable antagonism between mediocrity and quality is inevitable.[10]

Grant-Robertson feared that the graduate of mediocre attainments would have anything but mediocre ideas of the remuneration and responsibility owed to him by society. He also expressed grave doubts that the percentage of real honours students at the universities could be raised: 'it is,' he wrote, 'much smaller than the indulgent universities care to assume', and urged his readers not to confuse that percentage with the obviously greater percentage of those who were fitted for a full secondary education to the age of eighteen. 'Narrow the gates of entry,' he urged.

The pages of the *Universities Review*—an organ established in 1922 by the Association of University Teachers—were filled with speculations of a similar kind. Thus E. R. Dodds, in an article entitled 'What is wrong with the Modern Universities?' in October 1931, commented on the failure of such civic universities as Birmingham, Leeds, and Liverpool to achieve a position comparable to that held by newer universities like Frankfurt, Cologne, and Hamburg in Germany. 'Why is it,' he asked, 'that in both the educational and the business world the majority of those responsible for making appointments (not excluding the modern universities themselves) still show a marked tendency to prefer not merely a man of first rate ability from Oxford and Cambridge, but also a second rate one, to a first rate graduate of a modern university?' Dodds deplored the fact that most civic universities were serving only as vestibules for the teaching profession, with the result that courses in subjects commonly offered as principal subjects for the Higher School Certificate became crowded to an extent which both jeopardised their efficiency and produced a glut in the educational market. P. Mansell Jones, writing from Cardiff, in the *Universities Review* for October 1932 on 'Where Modern Universities are wrong', saw that the civic universities only worked as machines, 'devised to produce graduates furnished with qualifications which will help them to earn a livelihood'. Another civic university teacher, R. C. McLean, stressed the necessity of research to counteract such a mechanistic tendency:

'Go on as we are going', he prophesied, 'and we shall sink down to a middle place under sheer weight of the mediocrities who have diluted and deteriorated the universities they have so copiously invaded. If that ever happens, an educational disaster of the first magnitude will have occurred.'[11]

That 'copious invasion' (an increase of 11 per cent. in the years 1929–34 as opposed to 3 per cent. in the years 1923–9) led, as was to be expected, to an excess of graduates. The sluices to the teaching profession overflowed, and others were blocked. It was a world-wide phenomenon, so serious that in 1932 the International Student Service (a body originally stemming from a student refugee organisation formed in 1919 and called European Student Service) undertook an enquiry into the extent and nature of graduate unemployment. Its general secretary at Geneva, Dr. Walter Kotschnig, directed the study, and the results were embodied in *Unemployment in the Learned Professions* (1937). He came to the conclusion that 'compared with most countries on the European continent, professional men and women in England can still be counted amongst the *beati possidentes*'.[12]

3

Lord Eustace Percy was alive to the overcrowding of the universities, and rightly attributed it to an outlook inherited from an older, more aristocratic civilisation, whereby the universities were regarded as the 'sole avenue to the coveted status of educated man'. Such a view in a democratic age he described as superstitious and costly: superstitious since it paid lip service to the opportunities offered by the liberal professions; costly because it diverted ability from natural channels in industry and commerce to flood the universities with undergraduates basically unfitted for university study.

In *Education at the Cross Roads* (1930) he warned his readers: 'Ours is no longer a country to be enjoyed and exploited for its advantages, it is a country to be saved.' To save it, Lord Eustace Percy proposed that technical colleges, whose neglect he described as 'surely one of the worst examples of waste in all educational history', should be rehabilitated. He advocated the linking-up of schools of technology, commerce, and arts in each locality into 'one federated centre of learning'.[13] These colleges, controlled by the civic authorities, were designed to serve the industrial needs of their regions, and grew, partly by the efforts of local administrators and partly as a result of the deficiencies of the civic universities. These deficiencies were described as far back as 1911 by the secretaries of the Barnsley, Ealing, West Bromwich, and St. Helens authorities who in the course of a tour of inspection of the technical and commercial colleges of the North American continent had commented on 'the serious shortcomings' of English universities compared to those they visited.[14] But it was only after 1918, when the Local Education Authorities were allowed to levy more than a 2*d*. rate to finance such colleges, that they could really grow. At Hull, for example, the council resolved in January 1919 to 'proceed without delay with the plans for an adequate technical college in preparation for a university'. And with promise of further aid from the State, they did, encouraged still further by the Board of Education circular 1358 of 1925 which stimulated the construction of new buildings, a stimulus greater than was officially expected. As a result of this, technical colleges of advanced design began to rise all over the country.[15]

These new technical colleges were advanced in curriculum too. For as secondary education improved, they were not only able to shed their own make-shift courses, but to recruit from Junior Technical Schools, Day Continuation Schools, and evening classes. They even obtained a small proportion of the university population, owing to their cheapness and to their orientation towards the London as opposed to the provincial degree. Paradoxically, the right to confer degrees only after a period of full-time study within the walls seems to have prejudiced some of the smaller civic universities from recruiting the better type of poor student, and the local technical college with its part-time facilities, often drew off the very industrial postulants for whom they had originally catered.

The Association of Teachers in Technical Institutions fought to obtain recognition of their colleges as legitimate partners with the universities at the head of the educational system, and it was not without significance that in 1923 the University Grants Committee had appointed a sub-committee 'to enquire into existing facilities for education in coal mining at the Universities and Technical Schools in Great Britain'. The National Certificate Scheme (first established in 1921) enabled the various professional bodies to utilise technical colleges for the teaching necessary for their various qualifications. Thus the Institute of Mechanical Engineers established a scheme in conjunction with the Board of Education in 1922, the Chemists in 1922, the Electrical Engineers in 1923, the Naval Architects in 192[illegible] and the Builders in 1930.

Lord Eustace Percy, as President of the Board of Education, had appointed two committees, the Clerk Committee on Education for Industry, and the Goodenough Committee on Education for Salesmanship. These had reported in 1929 and 1931 and their conclusions added yet further to the prestige of technical colleges.

The Association of Technical Teachers, with their ancillary

professional associations, now began a vigorous propaganda campaign to convince the country of the need for technical and higher technological education. They studied technical education in Canada, France, and the Continent, and in 1936 published a stirring pamphlet on *Technology and the Commonwealth*. County and Borough Councils, animated by similar enthusiasm, sent delegations to the Continent, and Birmingham and Middlesex published reports on what they found there.

In 1937, four of the professional bodies concerned with technical education issued a *Report on Policy*, in which they called attention to the problem of technological unemployment, and urged that technical education should not only transmit skills, but cultivate adaptability. This, they continued, would mean more full-time instruction at technical colleges, and more co-ordination within the various regional authorities responsible for technical education. Hitherto, the Board of Education had been exerting all its resources towards putting an end to the pupil-teacher system in the schools, and building up a national system of secondary schools, and the technical colleges had suffered accordingly. But by the thirties, the factors retarding their growth (apathy of employers, suspicion of employees, false status of white-collar workers, and north-country traditions of early wage-earning) had begun to lose their force. Certainly the hopeful note sounded by the Board of Education circular 1444 dated 1 January 1936 impressed G. A. N. Lowndes so much that he wrote, 'perhaps our future historian will see in this the starting point of a new era of expansion comparable to that which in the case of secondary education began in 1902'.[16]

And certainly, with some kind of established channels to catch capacity at the secondary stage, the technical college at last began to develop specialities in response to local industrial and social needs. Mining Departments at Wigan, Sunderland, Chesterfield, and Cannock; Metallurgy at Rotherham and Sheffield; Engineering at Coventry, Birmingham, and Wolverhampton; Ceramics at Stoke-on-Trent; Navigation at Hull, Cardiff, and Liverpool: all these grew with great rapidity under the stimulus of official encouragement and local aid. By 1939, it could be asserted with truth that 'The University and the Technical College are, in fact, parallel institutions, providing alternative means of further education'.[17]

4

Yet the applied sciences were also making great progress within the universities, often in face of overt hostility and suspicion. It was an applied scientist, J. D. Cockcroft, originally a graduate in electrical engineering at Manchester, who in 1931 with E. T. S. Walton succeeded in disintegrating lithium by means of proton bombardment, and thus making a further stride in the utilisation of atomic power. But so strong was the prejudice against the vast expenditure involved in the application of 'applied' techniques to 'pure' physics that it was only in America that the real significance of the discovery was appreciated. And by 1937 America had over thirty cyclotrons for atomic bombardment, while Great Britain had none.

In Britain, the decade was, administratively speaking, more marked by the establishment of the Agricultural Research Council which held its first meeting on 9 July 1931. Endowed with funds of its own, and responsible for advising the Development Commissioners, its purpose was to plan and co-ordinate research over the entire field of agricultural research, in which task it was helped by three standing committees. It sustained thirteen Agricultural Research Institutes in England and fostered special units within the universities themselves. Other university departments whose members were engaged in research which might come under the generic title of agriculture also obtained grants, while a steady sustention of research studentships, training grants, and fellowships was pursued to ensure an adequate supply of trained agricultural scientists.

As with agriculture, so with other advancing technologies of the period. Aeronautics were developed and recognised at Cambridge, London, and Southampton, Building Construction (as opposed to the existing schools of architecture) at London and Manchester, Fuel Technology at Leeds, London, Sheffield, and Nottingham, Industrial Relations at Cambridge and Leeds, Naval Architecture at Durham and Liverpool, Oil Technology at Birmingham and London, and Technical Optics at London were some outstanding developments. Such applied sciences, often fostered by the various professional associations, sometimes led to the association of technical colleges with universities in a vague and empirical manner. Such exiguous connections as were sustained can be conveniently summarised as prevailing at London, Durham, and Manchester: the three types of such association. The first was typified by the London Polytechnics, several of which were recognised as internal schools of the University of London, and allowed to prepare students for degrees in Science, Engineering, and Music. The second, a more limited type, can be seen in Sunderland Technical College, which was recognised by the University of Durham in that the principal and heads of departments were given a certain measure of representation on the Senate and the Faculty of Applied Science, and the students were allowed to take pass degrees in Mechanical, Civil, Electrical, and Marine Engineering. The third, and closest relation existed at Manchester, where the Municipal College of Technology became the Faculty of Technology for the university, but retained its own governing body.

Yet, broadly speaking, the relations between universities and technical colleges left much to be desired. In 1944, the four technical colleges of Birmingham, Wolverhampton, Coventry, and Rugby had little connection with the technological department at Birmingham University; Bradford and Halifax had no relations with Leeds; Salford, Bolton, Wigan, and Stockport none with Manchester; nor Rutherford College at Newcastle with Durham.[18] Some degree of co-ordination and planning of these and other facilities was, however, in the air.

5

Co-ordination of the universities themselves was however the major prerequisite, and this was felt to be so necessary that in 1934 the University Grants Committee obtained its first full-time chairman in Sir Walter Moberly, formerly Vice-Chancellor of the University of Manchester. Moberly was most anxious to soften the impact of the U.G.C. upon the universities, and wrote:

> The bogy of State-interference has been much overworked. There are other forms of interference more sinister, and, in Great Britain and America at least, more common; and these are often tolerated by academic tories. Indeed, the State may approach the university as a rescuer rather than a dragon. . . . Indeed the dogma of freedom from external interference may be, and in the past often has been, used to deny internal freedom. . . . State action is truly a 'hindrance of hindrances'. It does not stifle, but augments or even creates, freedom. To raise the standard of 'autonomy' against such intervention would be hypocrisy.[19]

Two classic examples of the enfranchising effect exercised by the State concerned Newcastle and Nottingham. The first occurred in the very year of Sir Walter Moberly's appointment. A Royal Commission reported on the affairs of the University of Durham and, by the now time-honoured device of an executive commission, a University of Durham Act of 1935 made arrangements for Commissioners to frame a new constitution. This came into force in 1937, and created King's College, Newcastle, from the Newcastle School of Medicine and Armstrong College. This was recognised as a constituent college of the

University of Durham, which itself obtained a University Court. The other occurred in 1938 when Nottingham University College, which still suffered from its 'civic' character in not having sufficient representatives of the academic staff upon the governing body, was brought into closer conformity with other university institutions.

The grant disbursed by the University Grants Committee for the first quinquennium 1931-6 was £1,830,000, and for the second, £2,100,000. This was to be regarded, in the words of the report for the first quinquennium as 'a stimulus to other benefactors, whether corporate bodies or private individuals, and as such, it has hitherto been most effective'. And since those other benefactors provided £5,250,000 in the period 1929-35, the remark was not unjustified.

The University Grants Committee found that nearly four-fifths of the student population of Great Britain were attending civic universities, and that half of these began their education in public elementary schools. They offered numerous suggestions for the development of halls of residence and the establishment of tutorial systems and efficient appointments boards. They too entered caveats against the over-professionalisation of university studies, and pointed out that 'the objective of the best training for a vocation in life is not easily reconciled with the objective of the best training for life itself, and universities in the course of their history have always been faced with this dilemma'.

6

The resolution of that dilemma was an especial preoccupation of the years under review. For many of them had developed, in the compartmentalised Faculty system, a curriculum which was either rigidly professional, as in the applied sciences or medicine, or directly oriented towards the requirements of the teaching profession, as in Arts and Pure Science. In Arts the problem was most acute, for nearly 50 per cent. of the student population of the country were so enrolled.

Now another problem of many of the Faculties of Arts and Pure Science in the civic universities was their divorce from each other, a divorce which was made absolute by the fiercely competitive nature of the examination system, which put a premium on early and intensive specialisation in the schools. Indeed, the lock-step which developed in the universities operated to the detriment of new studies, like Russian and Spanish.

This compartmentalisation of the university curriculum was lamented by many. A. N. Whitehead wrote in 1929

A man who knows only his own science, as a routine peculiar to that science, does not even know that. He has no fertility of thought, no power of quickly seizing the bearing of alien ideas. He will discover nothing, and be stupid in practical application.[20]

This stimulated a number of suggestions for the regrouping of traditional subjects and a redeployment of the university resources. The *speculum mentis*, it was felt, needed remapping, along the co-ordinates of the newer mental, moral, and natural sciences.

A bold and impressionist sketch map was that drawn by M. Alderton Pink in *If the Blind Lead* (1932). He proposed that the first degree should consist in the study of a group of what he called 'Modern Humanities', based on the social and natural sciences and philosophy. The Master's degree was to be taken after further study had been undertaken in one of these subjects, while the Doctorate involving original research would only be taken by those who had already attained a Mastership. To supervise and co-ordinate the work of all the universities, Pink proposed that there should be a general academic council of the nation, consisting of university teachers, with a certain proportion of laymen represented on it.[21] His suggestions were given considerable publicity and in October 1933 the *Universities Review* printed his 'Suggestions for a Reformed University Curriculum'.

Students were as critical too, even more than usual. Terence Greenidge, in *A critical study of a Modern University* (1930), said that at Oxford

many thoughtful undergraduates are growing very weary of pursuing half-heartedly a course of study which they know to be none too good, and vaguely attempting to supplement it with occasional gems picked up from the side-shows.[22]

In 1932, Bertrand Russell attributed the vapidity and cynicism characteristic of many clever young university students of the period to 'the consciousness that their work has no real importance'.[23]

The National Union of Students was particularly vocal in the last decade before the war. They instituted inquiries into teaching methods and curricula at Manchester, Birmingham, Nottingham, and Bedford College. They made a study of graduate employment. They organised conferences. In a conference held in 1937, one speaker expressed the feelings of many of his generation that a more widely diffused system of education had not brought a golden age; while another lamented the tendency of civic universities to be 'regional minded'. In 1938 they issued *A Challenge to the University: A Report on University Life and Teaching in Relation to the Needs of Modern Society*. This report urged the reduction of technical limitations on combinations of degree subjects so as to make it possible for students to read in both the Faculties of Arts and Science; the institution of general lectures; the relation of subjects to their historical background and other branches of learning; the establishment of general honours courses equal in academic estimation to the single honours degree; and the holding of a university entrance examination separate from the higher school certificate examination.

Other student groups, like the Student Christian Movement, were also active along these lines. David Paton's pamphlet *Blind Guides, A Student looks at the University* published in 1939 was emphatic enough:

> The university is not, in fact, meeting the needs of our time. It is not meeting them because it does not understand the times in which we are living very much more profoundly than the leaders of society outside the university.

Paton indicated the pernicious effects of the 'pledge', or teacher's grant, and spoke of students deliberately failing in their diplomas in education in order to evade the unpleasant necessity of teaching in a school.[24]

7

So it is not surprising that these fourteen years witnessed a number of attempts to reorganise civic university studies. Scientists complained of the frustration of their energies.[25] Teachers of the humanities, faced with the rapid changes effected by the social as well as the natural sciences, sought by analysis and reinterpretation to adjust the university curriculum to satisfy the needs of their students. These needs were emphasised by observers like Walter Kotschnig in 1932, who lamented the 'lost unity of truth and learning' and pointed out that 'one reason there was unemployment amongst university graduates was because they were unemployable'.[26]

The Arts Faculties registered the greatest disturbances. With the classics deposed as the norm of the curriculum, the teachers of history, English, and modern languages each made claims to supplant them, but all found that the scope of their subjects was wider than they imagined. History, alienated from law, tended to become an introduction to the social sciences, while English Studies became a vestibule to Philosophy and Philology. Not a little of the teaching of English was affected by the decline of organised religion. Yet little wisdom could accrue while university teachers were harassed with the plethora of committees, examination boards, and administrative matters which filled the diary and often the life of the average university teacher.

Reflection, meditation, leisure: all prerequisites of a university atmosphere, were rendered virtually impossible.

As specialisms proliferated, it is not surprising that shrill demands for integrated curricula began to be heard.

The second world war accelerated a number of changes. Its approach sharpened the need for co-ordination. In November 1938, the Committee of Vice-Chancellors and Principals submitted a memorandum on the organisation of their universities for wartime service. Two months later they were met by the Lord Privy Seal who asked them to work out schemes for inter-university co-operation if war materialised. Meanwhile members of the academic staff were registered with the Ministry of Labour and National Service.

The war itself, involving enforced migrations of staff and students, undoubtedly freshened and stimulated a flow of communication between institutions and specialities; liberating much free discussion on the curriculum.

It was argued by one school, represented by Dr. Löwe in *The Universities in Transformation* (1941), that since the root of the trouble was specialisation, a new humanist synthesis should be effected around the social sciences so that universities could produce enlightened experts to hold key posts and direct the planning of society. This humanist synthesis, he declared, should fulfil the same purpose as that of the nineteenth-century curriculum at Oxford which effected a reconciliation not only between cultural and technical education but also between the spiritual and material elements in civilisation.[27] It was argued by others that the new humanist synthesis was to be found elsewhere. Thus Dr. Leavis stressed the idea that

> it was more than ever the raison d'être of a university to be, amid the material pressures and dehumanising complications of the modern world, a focus of humane consciousness, a centre where, faced with the specialisations and distractions in which human ends lose themselves, intelligence, bringing to bear a mature sense of values, should apply itself to the problems of civilisation.[28]

The relation of specialisms in a non-specialist centre of consciousness was, as Dr. Leavis argued in his *Education and the University* (1943), to be found in the English school, for which he suggested a curriculum.

Both Lowe and Leavis showed distinct stigmata of American influence, Leavis especially, since he acknowledged that he was stimulated to work out his suggested curriculum of English studies by the publication of Alexander Meiklejohn's *Experimental College* in 1932. This was an account of a successful experiment carried out under the auspices of the University of Wisconsin. Leavis also cited Brooks

Otis, another American who had been stimulated to constructive suggestion and had published an essay, *Thoughts after Flexner*.

And American influence began to bear more powerfully on England with the arrival of large numbers of American troops, and even of an American University Extension department in these islands. Americans were facing, as Dr. Leavis indicated, much the same cultural impasse only on a more exaggerated scale. Frank Aydelotte's *Breaking the Academic Lockstep* and Howard Lee Nostrand's *Ortega y Gasset on the Mission of a University*—both in their different ways containing suggestions for overcoming the specialist impasse in America—were both given English currency.

Yet of all the books and pamphlets published on university affairs during the war, none had such an immediate and widespread appeal as Bruce Truscot's *Red Brick University*, which went through two impressions in 1943. In this, the late professor of Spanish at Liverpool pleaded for a metanoia both in the public served by, and in the teachers of, the civic universities. Taking advantage of the rising tide of wartime idealism and of the fact that the whole educational system was currently under ministerial review for the purposes of reconstruction, he pleaded for full parity of esteem for all English universities. As he wrote:

> What is the ideal towards which we need to work—for no revolution which involves the building up of a new tradition can be accomplished quickly?
>
> An England, surely, in which there are no longer two large residential universities for those who are either well-to-do or brilliant, and nine smaller universities, mainly non-residential, for those who are neither. Let there be eleven, of approximately equal size, all in the main residential and each having certain Schools in which it excels the rest. Let the standards of admission at all universities, as well as the minimum standard for graduation, be raised, as nearly as possible, to the same level. . . . Let every boy or girl entering a university go where his or her particular subject is best taught. And finally, let a levelling of standards pave the way for the interchange of pupils where this is in the interests of the pupils themselves.[29]

To accomplish this revolution, Bruce Truscot suggested three reforms, all to be based on a substantial increase in the Treasury Grant: the development of residential facilities, more open entrance scholarships, and the concentration of special schools within each university. He further argued that an inter-change of teaching staff, if only for short courses of lectures on special topics, would help to bring about the necessary levelling process.

Dramatic changes were at hand.

REFERENCES

1. FLEXNER, A., *Universities, American, English, German* (Oxford, 1930), 255-6. One vice-chancellor complained of the way in which Flexner used his information: 'I well remember Abraham Flexner, the American educationalist, coming to Cambridge in between the wars when he was writing his book, *Universities; American, English, German.* I entertained him royally at Clare College and expended two whole evenings explaining the difference between the two universities. He went away and wrote a chapter upon Oxford and then said, in effect, that Cambridge was just the same. I have seldom been more annoyed.' Sir Raymond Priestley, *The English Civic Universities* (a paper read to Teaching Officers of Overseas Universities at Cambridge in August 1949). C. E. Thomas, in his *European Universities* (Boston, 1936) omits them in favour of a chapter on English public schools.

2. DIBELIUS, William, *England* (translated by M. A. Hamilton, 1930), 440.

3. The Bishop of Ripon, preaching before the British Association, suggested this, since mankind was, in his opinion, gaining new scientific knowledge and acquiring control of 'stupendous new forces faster than it was exhibiting capacity to be entrusted with their use'. For the atmosphere, see Julian Symonds, 'Of Crisis and Dismay: A Study of Writing in the 'Thirties', in *Focus One* (London, 1945), 90–111.

4. BENDA, Julian, *The Great Betrayal* (translated by R. Aldington, London, 1928): Herbert Read, *Julian Benda and the New Humanism* (London, 1930).

5. FLEXNER, *op. cit.*, 255-6.

6. BARKER, E., 'Universities in Great Britain', in *Universities in a Changing World*, ed. W. M. Kotschnig and E. Prys (Oxford, 1932), 119.

7. BARKER, E., *National Character and the Factors in its Formation* (London, 1927), 244.

8. BARKER, E., 'Universities in Great Britain', in *Universities in a Changing World*, ed. W. M. Kotschnig and E. Prys (Oxford, 1932), 118.

9. HERKLOTS, H. G. G., *The New University, An External Examination* (1928), 87-8.

10. GRANT-ROBERTSON, Sir Charles, *The British Universities* (London, 1930), 75.

11. *Universities Review* (Bristol, 1931·3). In 1933 -4 the status of an Oxford or Cambridge degree was reinforced by the fact that 88 and 87 per cent. respectively of their students had never been to an elementary school; that 78 and 74 per cent. respectively of their scholarships were held by boys from public and private schools; and that the percentage of ex-elementary school students which they obtained, represented the cream of the secondary schools. D. V. Glass and J. L. Gray 'Opportunity and the Older Universities' in *Political Arithmetic*, ed. L. Hogben (London, 1938), 418-70.

12. KOTSCHNIG, W., *Unemployment in the Learned Professions* (Oxford, 1937), 121, 158-73.

13. *Education at the Cross Roads* (London, 1930), 57.

14. Education in relation to Industry (Leeds, 1912), *A Report on Technical Trade, Applied Art, Manual Training, Domestic, Commercial and Public Schools in Canada and the United States*, by W. P. Donald, J. B. Johnson, J. E. Pickles, and Percival Sharp.

15. Swansea Technical College actually secured admission as a constituent member of the University of Wales in 1919. Evans, *op. cit.*, 104. One reason why technical education was neglected was that technology did not offer a path to the directorate, T. H. Burnham and G. O. Hoskins, *Iron and Steel in Britain 1870–1930* (1943), 248. For municipal encouragement, see J. Sykes, a *Study in English Local Authority Finance* (1939), 217.

16. LOWNDES, G. A. N., *The Silent Social Revolution* (Oxford, 1937), 193–4.

17. RICHARDSON, W. A., *The Technical College* (Oxford, 1939), 69. The overlap between students in the university faculties of Agriculture, Engineering, Applied Science, Art and Music and those in technical colleges who were in full time attendance was serious even then—see Olive Wheeler, 'The Importance of the Non-University College' in *Educating for Democracy* (London, 1939), 82–3.

18. *Times Educational Supplement*, 8 April 1944. S. J. Curtis, *History of Education in Great Britain* (London, 1950), 491.

19. MOBERLY, Sir Walter, *The Crisis in the Universities* (London, 1949), 234. See also p. 241: 'When all deductions are made, it remains true that the prevailing type of relation between our universities and the State is a fruitful one. Indeed, our tradition in this respect is the envy of many other countries; it is something to hold on to and develop.'

20. WHITEHEAD, A. N., *The Aims of Education* (London, 1929).

21. PINK, M. Alderton, *If the Blind Lead?* (1932).

22. GREENIDGE, Terence, *Degenerate Oxford, A Critical Study of Modern University Life* (1930), 38.

23. RUSSELL, B., *Education and the Social Order* (1932), 157.

24. PATON, D., *Blind Guides, A Student looks at the University* (London, 1939), 51, 53.

25. e.g. J. D. Bernal's indictment of university science in *The Social Function of Science* (London, 1939), 105–7, and compare with that amusing satire by R. A. Knox, *Let Dons Delight* (London, 1939), 254–80.

Lancelot Hogben in *Science for the Citizen* (London, 1938), self-styled as 'the first British Handbook to *Scientific Humanism*', condemns the universities: 'In Britain a realistic study of how social institutions assist or impede the satisfaction of human needs united to an inventory of scientific instruments now available for satisfying them will not come from our universities, where the teaching on current social problems is dominated by the dreary futilities of deductive economics'. p. 1090.

26. Kotschnig in the *University in a Changing World* (Oxford, 1932), 13, wrote: 'It is time that European intellectual circles ceased to look down upon American Universities and Colleges, and sought instead their co-operation in the common quest for a New University.' See also his *Unemployment in the Learned Professions* (Oxford, 1937).

27. LÖWE, Adolph, *The Universities in Transformation* (London, 1941).

28. LEAVIS, F. R., *Education and the University* (London, 1943), 30.

29. TRUSCOT, Bruce, *Redbrick University* (London, 1943), 37; title altered to *Red Brick University* in the second edition.

CHAPTER THIRTEEN

The Universities and Social Reconstruction, 1944-54

I

BRUCE TRUSCOT'S obbligato was quickly followed by numerous arpeggios designed to loosen the strings of the public purse. Virtuosos like Sir Ernest Simon (as he then was) touched chords calculated to reverberate when he described university provision in England as 'parsimonious' compared with that of the United States of America. His pamphlet, *The Development of British Universities*, was published in January 1944 with the help and advice of the vice-chancellors of the two great civic universities of Manchester and Birmingham. It called for 'considerable expansion of university teaching and research and more positive planning in the field of university work'.

Planned expansion was the theme of other, more orchestrated, works. Two months later, in March 1944, the Association of Scientific Workers submitted a report to the University Grants Committee entitled *Science in the Universities*, which called for immediate expansion of the modern universities, to an average of 3,000 students each, the raising of university colleges to university status, and for Government assistance to colleges like Hull and Leicester. It estimated that at least £10,000,000 in grants would be required in the first five post-war years. More comprehensive was the *Report on University Developments* adopted by the Association of University Teachers on 16 December 1943, and discussed with University M.P.s on 25 October 1944, which not only called for a 50 per cent. increase in the student population but added:

> These universities and university colleges, which we shall call regional universities, stand most urgently in need of review and reform as far as their structure is concerned. . . . Many of our regional universities are only slowly releasing themselves from the ties and controls operated by the Local Authorities, individual benefactors, and other institutions, which were inevitable in the early history of colleges when the teaching body was small and immature in experience. But a stage in their history has now been reached when decisive steps should be taken to give these universities a status comparable to that enjoyed by Oxford and Cambridge.[1]

This status animated many of the Association's recommendations: higher salaries, a more adequate representation of academic opinion on governing bodies, and a wider curriculum of studies both in the natural and social sciences. Other segments of the thinking community elaborated these themes. The British Association's special committee on the Universities (originally appointed in August 1941) published its report in August 1944. So also did the National Union of Students. And in an attempt to see the question in its entirety a special number of the *Political Quarterly* was devoted to the universities, in the last quarter of 1944. In it, John MacMurray set the tone of the contributions:

> there can be no serious doubt that there is a great need to rethink and replan our university system, if indeed it can be called a system.

adding the equally important rider

> Yet any attempt to force a systematic reorganisation upon our university institutions from outside would prove impossible.[2]

2

The abrasion of outside realities sharpened the arguments for expanding the universities. The Service Departments put forward plans for post-war establishments involving the employment of scientists on a scale scarcely less than that prevailing during the war. Then again, scientific and industrial expertise was needed to promote the export trade: a trade upon which the feeding of an overcrowded island, shorn of its overseas investments, increasingly depended. A third reality was the acceptance, by the President of the United States, of the report of Vannevar Bush (embodied in *Science, The Endless Frontier*) in the Spring of 1945: a report which so impressed the Royal Society that they discussed the problem and made representations to the Treasury that a similar investigation was needed in this country. The Lord President of the Council on 9 December 1945 appointed a committee under Sir Alan Barlow, composed of five independent members and some civil servants. This reported that the existing 55,000 scientists in the country should be increased to 90,000 by 1955, and came to the conclusion that there was a sufficient reserve of talent if it could be brought up to the requisite standard for entry into the university.

The Barlow Report, presented by the Lord President of the Council to Parliament, testified to the willingness of the English civic universities to expand their numbers by 86 per cent., and added 'we consider that in some instances even this is an appreciable underestimate of what could be done'.[3]

3

The extensive redeployment of national talents involved in post-war organisation inevitably affected the universities, both at the regional and at the national level. As one distinguished university teacher wrote in 1943: 'The two world wars mark the close of an epoch which began with the Reformation. They bring us, whatever we may wish, to the certainty of a planned society.'[4] The blueprints of the plans were drawn by the Barlow Report on the Distribution of the Industrial Population (1940), and the Scott Report on Land Utilisation (1942); which both agreed that it was essential to have the planning machinery at regional level. Subsequent essays in social welfare followed the regional idea, and all demanded participation of the universities.

The McNair Report of 1944 set the precedent, by proposing that universities should assume the main responsibility for the training of teachers by establishing University Institutes of Education in conjunction with the Training Colleges of their areas. After internal struggles, many of the universities adopted this scheme.

That precedent was quickly followed. In 1945 the Percy Committee, advocating greater numbers of highly qualified technologists, recommended the establishment of regional advisory councils on which the universities and technological colleges would be represented with the industrial and local authorities. This recommendation was endorsed by the Minister of Education in a letter (Circular 87, dated 20 February 1946) addressed to the local authorities. Ten of these councils, covering England and Wales, came into existence, each with representation on a National Advisory Council. This latter body advises the Minister on general policy.

A third regional responsibility was placed upon the universities by the National Health System. Under this, Professors of Medicine were called upon to discharge a variety of services on committees, services which, as Sir Lionel Whitby said, 'must be endured since, otherwise, the control of medical education would revert to Whitehall and be open to the danger of political influence'.[5]

Such categorical regional responsibilities imposed by the State were but additions to a considerable regional burden which the civic universities had been accumulating throughout the century. Bruce Truscot might assert that 'the chief business of a university is not, and never can be, the service of a region—still less the creation of numerous contacts, whether social or educational, with a region',[6] but the withering away of the various and vigorous scientific and literary societies imposed a greater burden on the extra-mural work of the universities—a burden which was only alleviated by the appointment of numerous full-time teachers and organisers. And even here the significant diocesan arrangements adopted by extra-mural departments tended still further to emphasise the regional setting of universities.

At the national level, professional societies began to look upon the universities as natural agents for undertaking the education and certification of their postulants. Thus the Vice-Chancellor of the University of London could say in 1946:

> The truth is that all the professions are pressing us, as universities, to take on a greater part, if not the whole, of the requisite professional or technical training for their own professional subjects. I think I could mention at least five professions which have recently been in contact with the University of London with a view to our undertaking, or, at least, extending our present facilities for what is really technical or professional training. I refer to the accountancy profession, veterinary medicine, estate management, youth leadership, and journalism.[7]

4

Other professional needs were articulated by the University Grants Committee, which, like Agag, walked delicately to avoid giving offence. In addition to the McNair and Barlow committees, four other committees appointed by the Government all presented their reports during the three years after 1944, and each of them advocated a greater participation of the universities in training various specialist professions. The recommendations of these committees, when adopted, involved close co-operation between the University Grants Committee (as the body recommended to distribute the government grant to implement these recommendations) and the Committee of Vice-Chancellors and Principals (as the representatives of the universities to receive them). They also involved the establishment of a number of specialist sub-committees by the University Grants Committee, as well as a redefinition of their own sphere of responsibility.

The report of the Barlow committee on Scientific Manpower in May 1946 was used as an argument for doubling the existing grant to universities. As from July of that year, the terms of reference within which the University Grants Committee had operated since 1919 (i.e. 'to enquire into the financial needs of university education in the United Kingdom, and to advise the Government as to the application of any grants that might be made by Parliament towards meeting them') were expanded by the Lords of the Treasury. It is obvious that 'planned expansion' was in their minds, for the new terms read:

> To enquire into the financial needs of university education in Great Britain; to advise the Government as to the application of any grants made by Parliament towards meeting them; to collect, examine and make available information on matters relating to university education at home and abroad; and to assist, in consultation with the universities and other bodies concerned, the preparation and execution of such plans for the development of the universities as may from time to time be required in order to ensure that they are fully adequate to national needs.[8]

A full-time deputy chairman was appointed three months later. Three years earlier, the Lords of the Treasury had found it necessary to abandon the practice whereby members of the committee were not in the active employment of a university, and the new blood thus acquired stimulated their deliberations.

In 1947 the quinquennial grant system was reintroduced, with the innovation that the U.G.C. added in their report to the Treasury that the capital needs of the universities during the same period would amount to £50,000,000. The increases which the Barlow Report had asked for in ten years were satisfied in two.

The close liaison with the Committee of Vice-Chancellors and Principals was followed by the formation of a number of specialist committees to assist the U.G.C. Thus Sub-Committees on Medical and Dental Education, Science, Technology, the Social Sciences, Oriental and African Studies, Slavonic and East European Studies, Agricultural Education, and Veterinary Education played, with co-opted experts, an important part in introducing or consolidating these subjects as university studies.

Medical education, designed to inculcate fundamental principles and methods rather than the distillation of factual knowledge, was replanned by the *Goodenough* Report, May 1944, and accepted by the Government.[9] This involved the creation of a medical sub-committee of the U.G.C. to distribute the extra State subvention required, which also distributed the special grants for dental education, designed to treble the annual entry into dental schools, that had been recommended by the *Teviot* Report of October 1945.[10] The Royal Society's *Report on the Needs of Research in Fundamental Science after the War* stimulated the establishment of a second committee of the U.G.C. which took evidence from professional and public bodies, and then asked universities to co-operate in filling such gaps as existed in subjects like cytology, virus diseases, taxonomy, microbiology, metrology, and acoustics. This sub-committee also suggested the purchase of field stations, laboratories, and marine stations.

A third sub-committee on agriculture was set up as a result of the *Loveday* Report on Higher Agricultural Education, 1945,[11] which had recommended that agricultural grants should be transferred to the U.G.C. To encourage the universities to eliminate agricultural teaching below degree standard, earmarked grants were given. As a result of these earmarked grants a number of notable developments took place. Nottingham formally incorporated the Midland Agricultural College at Sutton Bonnington; London the Wye Agricultural College—a combination of the S.E. Agricultural College at Wye and the Horticultural College for Women at Swanley (the buildings of which had been destroyed by enemy action); while Newcastle established the first chair of Agricultural Engineering in the country. A fourth sub-committee on veterinary education,[12] appointed in 1948, co-operated with the Ministry of Agriculture to bring existing veterinary schools within the province of universities, and established further schools at Cambridge and Bristol.

As a result of the *Scarbrough* Committee's recommendation in 1946 that the U.G.C. might be the channel for grants to encourage the study of Oriental, Slavonic, East European, and African Studies, two more specialist sub-committees were appointed: one for Oriental and African languages, the other for Slavonic and East European Studies.[13] In addition to 195 studentships, the University Grants Committee went ahead with a number of plans for encouraging these studies in various universities. A seventh sub-committee to plan distribution of another quarter of a million pounds grant for social studies was appointed in 1947 as a result of the *Clapham* Committee.[14]

Well might the University Grants Committee describe the changes effected by their grants as 'dramatic'. Capital, earmarked, and annually increasing recurrent grants flowed like water into the academic Sahara. Students multiplied, new buildings arose, halls of residence appeared. The annual grant rose from a pre-war total of two million pounds to nine in the first post-war year, to sixteen in 1947, till by 1953 it reached twenty-five millions. And it was symptomatic that Sir Walter Moberly, the chairman of the University Grants Committee which had been so intimately connected with all these developments, should, on retiring from his post in 1948, publish a book on the philosophy of university education entitled *The Crisis in the University* (1948). By virtue of his position, he was one of the few capable of so doing.

5

An even more dramatic change was the direct participation of the State in the field of fundamental research. Hitherto, as we have seen, it participated indirectly through bodies like the Development Commission (1909), the D.S.I.R. (1916), the Medical Research Council (1920), and the Agricultural Research Council (1931). But the widening of State responsibility for the economic life of the nation led to a complete reorganisation of the Scientific Civil Service in September 1945, and scientists in Government service were given pay and conditions of employment comparable to those prevailing in universities, with similar facilities for prosecuting their own fundamental research.

The Government also established at Harwell in October 1945 a vast research centre of its own, based round the two atomic reactors 'Gleep' and 'Bepo', organising it into twelve divisions, each with its own head, comparable to university departments. These departments were in turn responsible for the prosecution of basic research in Chemistry, Chemical Engineering, Engineering, Metallurgy, and Physics. The isotope division at Harwell and the radiochemical centre at Amersham were also responsible for the running of short courses.

These developments involved yet further integration of the universities with national needs, and so in January 1947 an Advisory Council was appointed to assist the Lord President of the Council in the formulation of scientific policy. Twelve of the fifteen members of this Council were chosen from scientists in the universities and included the permanent Deputy-Chairman of the U.G.C. At the same time a Defence Research Policy Committee was established to assist the Minister of Defence. Both these bodies were presided over by Sir Henry Tizard (a former member of the U.G.C.) and replaced the Scientific Advisory Committee to the War Cabinet.[15]

The first of these bodies, the Advisory Council on Scientific Policy, established a number of committees: the Committee on Scientific Manpower, the Atomic Energy Committee, the Scientific and Technical Committee, and a Committee on Overseas Scientific Relations. And just how much the Advisory Council on Scientific Policy was concerned with university development may be seen from their reports, to which we shall refer later.

6

'Much-needed professional training' was also one of the main reasons why the Asquith Commission (appointed in August 1943) recommended in May 1945 the establishment and development of at least six new universities in the British Colonies overseas. These professional needs arose from a welfare policy towards the dependent seventy millions inhabiting the Colonial Empire, which had only three universities, Malta (founded 1769), Hong Kong (founded 1911), and Ceylon (founded 1942) with a total student population of less than 2,000. And since the number of students from the Colonial Empire attending universities in the British Isles was less than half that number, it meant that the existing ratio of university students to total population was 1 to 20,000.

But as the home universities needed to double their own output of scientists, it was obvious that they could do little to meet the needs of the colonies. Moreover, the existing colonial universities—Malta, Hong Kong, and Ceylon—were dispersed and small: Malta, for instance, had less than 300 students. There was no university at all which could serve the African territories where over two-thirds of the Colonial population were contained.

The problem of creating an informed political leadership in these colonies, capable of co-operating with the Home Government, attacking mass-illiteracy, and guiding the energies of demobilised troops was an acute one. It was sharpened by the fact that the movement for self-government had been accelerated by the war years. As the Asquith Commission observed:

> It is the university which should offer the best means of counteracting the influence of racial differences and sectional rivalries which impede the formation of political institutions on a national basis. Moreover, universities serve the double purpose of refining and maintaining all that is best in local traditions and cultures and at the same time of providing a means whereby those brought up under the influence of these traditions and cultures may enter on a footing of equality into the world-wide community of intellect.[16]

The African territories (which for these purposes included the condominium of the Anglo-Egyptian Sudan) obtained, as a result of the Asquith Commission, a new university college at Ibadan to serve Nigeria, upgraded institutions at Makerere (to serve East Africa), and Khartoum (to serve the Sudan). Provision was also made for a fourth university college at Achimota to serve the Gold Coast. These four African university colleges entered, also as a result of the Asquith Commission's report, into a special relationship with the University of London; a relationship which was wider and deeper than that which existed between such colonial university institutions as Codrington College, Barbados (which had sixteen students in 1944), and Fourah

Bay College in Sierra Leone (which also had 16 students in 1944) enjoyed with the University of Durham since 1875 and 1876 respectively.

Africa, however, was a comparatively simple problem when compared to the British Caribbean Colonies. There, three million islanders were stretched in little packets of population over an area comparable to that encompassed by lines joining London, Danzig, Moscow, Odessa, and Ankara. The largest of these packets at Jamaica contained almost half the total, and Trinidad one-sixth. So the Asquith Commission appointed a special committee under Sir James Irvine to go out and survey the area, which they did, early in 1944. The result of their visit, embodied in their report (Cmd. 6654) was published in August of that year, and presented to Parliament in June 1945. This report recommended the establishment of a University College of the West Indies at Jamaica, established by grants from the Colonial Development and Welfare Funds and sustained by the colonies. This University College was also to enjoy the special relationship with the University of London proposed for its African counterparts.

The sixth foundation, stemming from the Asquith Commission's report, was the University of Malaya, embodying the King Edward VII College of Medicine and Raffles College, both at Singapore. This university immediately took its place as a worthy partner of existing colonial universities like Malta and Hong Kong, and, as regards buildings, was better off than either of the others.

To assist the development of these six university institutions, an Inter-University Council for Higher Education in the Colonies was established, composed of one representative of each of the home universities and one of the four existing colonial universities. This body elected Sir James Irvine as its chairman, and set about transmitting the experience gained in English universities and modifying it to suit colonial needs. Four and a half million pounds were allocated from Imperial funds to assist the work, and a Colonial University Grants Advisory Committee was established to administer them.[17]

In essence, the idea was to project to the colonies the prevailing pattern set by the modern universities. And, as the secretary of the Inter-University Council wrote as these proposals were being implemented in 1947:

> the Colonial colleges will be more squarely confronted than we at home by the problems of the relationship between vocational training and general education. In thinking through this question and experimenting in methods of solving the problems raised, the Colonial colleges will certainly have valuable experience to offer to the home universities.[18]

7

Since the available university buildings at home were 'inadequate even to accommodate properly the existing population', the Barlow Committee argued that the five university colleges of Nottingham, Southampton, Exeter, Hull, and Leicester 'ought to be able to make a substantial contribution towards filling' the gap.

'there is nothing sacrosanct about the present number of Universities in the Kingdom', the committee went on, 'and we are attracted by the conception of bringing into existence at least one University which would give to the present generation the opportunity of leaving to posterity a monument of its culture. Moreover there is some reason to believe that a number of able teachers from the existing Universities would welcome the opportunity of re-enacting in the twentieth century the exodus which is said to have led to the foundation of Peterhouse in the thirteenth.'[19]

Nottingham, Southampton and Hull duly received their charters in 1948, 1952 and 1953, and the University College of Leicester was recognised as a grant-earning college. But these institutions were modelled on the existing pattern of a civic university. The hope of the Barlow Committee for a university which 'would give to the present generation the opportunity of leaving to posterity a monument of its culture' was to materialise elsewhere.

A new university, more than any other institution, must embody a particular idea, and the idea which had been voiced by most of the contemporary critics of university curricula was their lack of span. Ortega y Gasset (an English translation of whose *Mission of the University* was given to the English-speaking public in 1944 by Howard Lee Nostrand) would have students brought 'up to the height of the times' by being made aware of the vital ideas embedded in the physical, biological, philosophical, historical, and sociological sciences.[20] Jacques Maritain argued cogently in *Education at the Cross Roads* (1943) that the traditional medieval liberality of the arts curriculum should be restored in a new context: for the medieval master's degree involved a study of mathematical sciences (arithmetic and geometry) and the physical sciences (astronomy and music).[21] It was expressed equally forcibly by Professor MacMurray in the *Political Quarterly* in 1944 when he wrote, 'So far no satisfactory method has been found for bringing scientific studies within the cultural synthesis which the older curriculum provided.' MacMurray urged that a university should not be 'a common house for disjointed specialisms' but 'a place where knowledge is unified'; and that this unification should be 'in constant and vital relation to the cultural life in the community around it'. The crux of the cultural problem lay, in short, in the unification of arts and science.[22] His words were echoed by Professor Bonamy Dobrée, who in the same number wrote, 'The old structure of the Arts Faculties, proper to a state of society which has vanished, must go; new structures must be devised, aiming at providing the new heterogeneous class of cultured men.'[23] In more sober language, the proportions of the problem were sketched in a study published by Nuffield College entitled *The Problem Facing British Universities*. The pressures of the professions, the proliferation of sub-specialisms, and the general obliteration of the speculum mentis by various sectional accretions to the curriculum stimulated the authors of this survey to pose the question whether universities could properly discharge their duties.

Circumstances after the war, however, made it possible to embark on an experiment aimed at correcting the prevailing departmentalism of university teaching. For the 1944 Education Act stimulated a demand for teachers in the new type of secondary modern school; and the managerial revolution created a number of posts in public and social administration, which, it was felt, could only be satisfied by graduates trained, not only in the natural sciences, but with wider reserves of humane knowledge upon which to draw.

Alderman Horwood of the city of Stoke-on-Trent pointed out that there was in North Staffordshire a strong tradition of adult education, and it was decided to campaign for a new university college for the area. On 27 March 1946 an informal discussion took place with the University Grants Committee, and three weeks later the Stoke-on-Trent City Council set up an exploratory committee, composed of representatives of the four neighbouring local authorities which promised contributions. As chairman of this committee, Lord Lindsay of Birker, then Master of Balliol College, Oxford, was elected.

The University Grants Committee communicated with this committee on 6 December 1946 that they would 'consider sympathetically an application for financial assistance in respect of a new University College in North Staffordshire provided that the basis of studies in Science and Arts be adequately broadened'. The necessary sponsors were obtained and on 14 May 1947, the Lord Chancellor could say in the House of Lords: 'might it not be an experiment which is well worth making. Here is a new experiment—that the North Staffordshire people should have the right of setting their own examinations.'

Now Lord Lindsay had for many years been one of the most persistent critics of university departmentalism, and, as an Oxford tutor, he had taken a leading part in the establishment of Modern

Greats, a school which aimed at infusing the traditional history course with a mixture of philosophy and economics. Lindsay was concerned with the problem of general education in a free society, and in the course of a number of addresses before the war, he dilated on the necessity for spanning the ever-widening rift between the arts and the sciences. The success of contemporary American experiments in this and kindred fields led him to tap the now traditional source of strength for a new university college—the University Extension Movement—to found a new college based on a year's preliminary survey of the frontiers of both the arts and the sciences before the degree course.

A Victorian mansion, set in an estate of 154 acres at Keele, three miles from Stoke-on-Trent, was secured. Around the main hall an army camp had been constructed. The huts of this camp were renovated and redeployed to form a university campus, where staff and students lived. With Lindsay as first principal, the course for the bachelor's degree was integrated with the professional training required for posts in educational and social work. The L.E.A.'s generously recognised these four years in their system of awards, and the new college opened its doors in 1950.

Studies were regrouped under a tripartite division of Arts, Social Studies, and Experimental Science. After their common first-year course, students were to carry a subject chosen from each division to their degrees: two at an advanced level. The aim was a bold one: to solve the basic problem of the time by enabling all students to assimilate the significance of contemporary scientific advances without losing sight of the basic values, and so to enable a twentieth-century viewpoint to crystallise. In a letter to me, dictated three days before his death, Lord Lindsay wrote:

> I remember Stopford at Manchester at a meeting where I explained what we wanted to do saying, 'Yes of course we all want to do that, but you will find your Professors won't let you.' And I replied, 'Yes, but if you can start with a staff who believe in the experiment you won't have all those vested interests to grapple with.'

The precedents set by this new college both in its curriculum and in its initial emancipation from the University of London (though under the sponsorship of Oxford, Manchester and Birmingham) illustrate the enfranchising effect of State aid. Well might the University Grants Committee call attention to the fact that 'never before have the founders of a university institution in this country been in a position to dispense with an endowment and put their plans into effect with the backing of the State.'[24]

8

The balance of the university curriculum stimulated further suggestions that universities of yet another new type should be founded, since the students of technology numbered less than 10 per cent. of the total student enrolment, whereas arts students numbered 43·6 per cent. of the whole.[25]

The dimensions and implications of expansion had been foreseen by the Barlow and Percy Reports. Commenting on the latter, the Barlow Report observed that it supported the development of full-time technological courses of university degree standard at a selected and limited number of technical colleges, and also Lord Percy's own suggestion that the Government should treat Colleges of Technology as a group and develop amongst them some major university institutions. These major university institutions were envisaged as being situated in University cities, and others 'geographically remote from existing universities, might qualify for independent university powers'.[26]

The imperative national need for more technologists was stressed by the Advisory Council on Scientific Policy, which advocated the establishment of colleges of applied science closely integrated with universities, for the post-graduate training of applied scientists. The Council lamented that

> in this country there has been a long-standing prejudice in favour of a career in the pure sciences as against the applied sciences; it is important that this prejudice, which does not exist in other countries, should be removed.[27]

The Advisory Council also indicated the higher levels of productivity enjoyed by the United States of America, and the 'considerable industrial prosperity' of other European countries which did not enjoy 'our natural advantages', and concluded that it was

> largely due to the employment in industry of men who have received an education of university standard in technology. And in the long run, our own precarious economic position cannot be expected to improve unless industries employ a sufficient number of men adequately trained to apply and develop the discoveries of pure research.

The various professional associations recruited from the universities did not seem to welcome the notion of separate colleges of technology, but urged that the existing universities should be expanded to meet the national need for such men. Thus the Association of University Teachers issued a report which claimed that 'it should not be beyond the capacity of our existing machinery, with due expansion of resources and equipment, to provide the true technologists we require'. They admitted that technological studies had an important contribution to make to university education, and were obviously anxious not to allow the universities to develop too far towards being 'pure' arts or 'pure' science colleges.[28] The Association of Scientific Workers also called for an expansion of the smaller universities to cope with the demand.

The University Grants Committee issued a cautious *Note on Technology in the University* (1950), declaring that university courses should be based on more extended courses in fundamental science than hitherto, but they considered the respective rôles of technical colleges and universities in technological education were not identical, and called for an increase of research in Engineering.[29]

But the need for increased productivity kept the demand for colleges of technology alive. A team led by Dr. Percy Dunsheath toured the universities of America for the Anglo-American Council on Productivity in the Spring of 1951 and returned with some startling facts. The United States was spending seven times as much per head on scientific research and engineering education as Great Britain; and that, comparing the American bachelor's degree in technology with the British Higher National Certificate, 52,000 of the former were awarded to only 5,000 of the latter. The team called for 'immediate attention' to be given to the provision 'as rapidly as possible' of extended facilities for preparing a large number of young men for industry, giving them a broad general education on a full-time basis with a technical standard at least as high as that of the Higher National Certificate courses. Though many of the exhortations of this team were directed towards the recruitment by industry of such scientists and technologists, their last recommendation read

> In general, we recommend the encouragement of a closer association between the universities, technical colleges, and industry.[30]

In a White Paper issued in 1951, the Labour Government postponed the establishment of a technological university because of the strain it would impose on the national resources. But the Conservatives proclaimed in June 1952 their intention to build up at least one institution to university rank, and in addition, to develop higher technology in the technical colleges.[31]

9

The challenge was obvious. As an American scientist wrote in 1950 (and his remarks were given wide currency)

> Great Britain doesn't have the numbers of scientists at its disposal that other major industrial centres have, and it would take decades to achieve such levels.

> Switzerland for instance has almost three times as many fully-qualified scientists and engineers in proportion to its population. The proportions of qualified men in Germany and the United States are similarly overwhelming. In these countries a pattern of research and development has arisen which uses seven or eight graduates in the more specifically applied aspects for every scientist pursuing fundamental investigation. In Britain the present ratio is about three to one.[32]

In the world where Britain was, like Switzerland, living on the products of national ingenuity and not, like Russia or the United States, on a massive imperial economy, his observations were most pertinent. Especially so since fundamental discoveries, like rubber substitutes, though pioneered in Britain, were being exploited in hard-currency areas like the United States and Switzerland.

By 1952, the shortage of technologists had become so acute that the Advisory Committee on Scientific Policy appointed a committee under Professor Solly Zuckerman 'to study the future needs of scientific and technological manpower for employment both at home and abroad'. The conclusions of this committee constituted the whole of the Fifth Annual Report of the Advisory Council on Scientific Policy, which supported the view that technical colleges could be re-geared to increase the output of science graduates, and suggested that a few of them could be selected for special development with the object of training graduates. The Zuckerman Committee accused the public schools of failing to encourage boys with a scientific bent, concluding

> Essentially there is an insufficient appreciation of the contribution that science makes to a liberal education, and a lack of awareness of the great opportunities for scientific, and especially engineering, training that are available in Universities other than Oxford and Cambridge. Without some change in these influences and attitudes, we do not think it likely that the public schools will play their proper part in sending a reasonable proportion of their best boys forward for a scientific and, in particular, a technological education.[33]

So it was not surprising that on 11 June 1952, the Lord President of the Council (as the minister responsible for civilian scientific matters) should officially turn down the proposal, originally made in 1950 by the Advisory Council for Education in Industry and Commerce, to create a non-teaching, non-award-making Royal College of Technology, and announce that the Government was going forward with the idea of a technological university. This was followed by the announcement on 29 January 1953 of the Government's policy to increase the size of the Imperial College of Science and Technology from 1,500 to 3,000, to recognise it as a technological university, and to improve the status of certain other colleges of technology.

Five months later, the Chancellor of the Exchequer invited the U.G.C., in consultation with the universities and colleges concerned, to work out plans for the development of higher technological education outside London. The universities and colleges responded, and after the technology sub-committee of the U.G.C. had examined the proposals and reported to the Chancellor, he was able to announce in July 1954 that Glasgow, Manchester, Leeds and Birmingham were to be the main centres in which the Government's plans for 'concentrated development' of higher technological education were to be applied. And in these plans, it was explicitly stated that the 'dispersal of effort' involved in increasing the number of university institutions concerned with such education was to be avoided. Finally, on 7 December 1954, the Government announced that it would try and avoid either excessive centralisation or undue dispersal of resources by concentrating its efforts on institutions already receiving Government grants. In short, it expressed the view that higher technological education must be closely linked with other university studies.[34]

REFERENCES

1. *Universities Review* (Bristol, 1944), XVI, 59.

2. MacMurray, John, 'The Functions of a University', *Political Quarterly* (1944), XV, 277. See also 'In Aid of Universities', *The Economist*, cxlvii (1944), 270–2.

3. *Scientific Manpower. Report of the Committee appointed by the Lord President of the Council.* (Chairman, Sir Alan Barlow, Bt.) H.M.S.O., London, 1946, Cmd. 6824.

4. Laski, H. J., *Reflections on the Revolution of Our Time* (London, 1943), 163.

5. *Conference of Home Universities, Report of Proceedings* (1950), 28.

6. *Redbrick University* (1943). Yet cf. his article 'The University and its Region', in *Political Quarterly* (1944), XV, 298–309.

7. *Conference of Home Universities, Report of Proceedings* (1946), 54.

8. *University Development from 1935 to 1947, being the Report of the University Grants Committee* (H.M.S.O., London, 1948), 6–7. This was slightly amended in 1952, when the Committee were relieved of the duty of collecting and making available information relating to universities overseas: the words 'throughout the United Kingdom' replacing 'at home and abroad' in line 4. University Development: Report on the years 1947 to 1952 (H.M.S.O., London, 1953), 6.

9. *Medical Schools. Report of the Inter-Departmental Committee.* (Chairman, Sir William Goodenough, Bt.) H.M.S.O., London, 1944.

10. *Dentistry. Final Report of the Inter-Departmental Committee.* (Chairman, Lord Teviot.) H.M.S.O., London, 1945 (Cmd. 6727).

11. *Higher Agricultural Education in England and Wales. Report of the Committee.* (Chairman, Dr. T. Loveday.) H.M.S.O., London, 1945 (Cmd. 6728).

12. In response to the *Second Report of the Committee on Veterinary Education*

in Great Britain. (Chairman, Dr. Thomas Loveday.) H.M.S.O., London, 1944 (Cmd. 6517).

13. *Oriental, Slavonic, East European and African Studies. Report of the Inter-Departmental Committee of Inquiry.* (Chairman, The Earl of Scarbrough.) H.M.S.O., London, 1946.

14. *Social and Economic Research. Report of the Committee.* (Chairman, Sir John Clapham.) H.M.S.O., London, 1946 (Cmd. 6868).

15. *Government Scientific Organisation in the Civilian Field.* A Review prepared for the Lord President of the Council by the Advisory Council on Scientific Policy, H.M.S.O., London, 1951.

16. *Report of the Committee on Higher Education in the Colonies.* (Chairman, Mr. Justice Asquith.) H.M.S.O., London, 1947 (Cmd. 6647).

17. For accounts of these various university colleges see articles by Margery Perham, 'The Relation of Home Universities to Colonial Universities', T. W. J. Taylor, 'The University College of the West Indies', K. Mellanby 'University College, Ibadan', and Bernard de Bunsen, 'Makerere University College', in *Universities Review* XVIII (1946), 32–9; XXIII (1950), 6–17 (1951), 100–5; XXIV (1952), 70–81.

18. Adams, W., 'Higher Education in the British Colonies', *Universities Quarterly*, 1 (1947), 152.

19. *Op. cit.*, 17.

20. His influence can be seen by the number of people who quoted him in contemporary discussions.

21. *Education at the Cross Roads* (Oxford, 1943), 71.

22. *Op. cit.*, 279–80.

23. *Ibid.*, 341–52.

24. Horwood, Alderman T., 'A New University College', *Universities Quarterly*, 2 (1947), 77–81.

25. 'The situation calls for a drastic revision of University curricula', E. G. Cullwick—'Engineering Education and the Universities', *Research* (1950), v, 302. See also 'Impressions of a Discussion on Technical Universities', *Brit. Journal of Applied Physics*, 2 (1951), 245–8.

F.B.I. Industrial Research and Education Committee. *The Education and Training of Technologists* (1949); 'Japanese Science and Technology', *Research*, III (1950), 341–4. *The Case for a Technical University* reprinted from the *Times Educational Supplement*, 1950, argued by Lord Cherwell, M. W. Perrin, Patrick Johnson, H. Lowery and James R. Killian.

26. *Op. cit.*, 10–11.

27. *Second Annual Report of the Advisory Council on Scientific Policy.*

28. Printed in *Universities Review* (Bristol, 1950), xxiii, 86–92; *Science and the Universities* (1951), 31.

29. *A Note on Technology in the University* (H.M.S.O., London, 1950).

30. *Universities and Industry* (London, 1951), 23–4.

31. Board of Education Circular. C. 255. 14 July 1952.

32. Meier, R. L., 'The Role of Science in the British Economy', *Manchester School of Economic and Social Studies*, xviii (1950), 120.

33. *Fifth Annual Report of the Advisory Council on Scientific Policy* (H.M.S.O., London, 1952).

34. *Nature*, clxxv (1955), 22.

CHAPTER FOURTEEN

Prospects and Perspectives

'UNIVERSITY education has grown up in the casual English way,' remarked Sir Richard Livingstone in 1948. 'It has never been viewed, much less planned as a whole. A cynic might give a book on the subject the title of *Drift*.'[1] A book with such a title would, as the preceding pages have tried to show, be somewhat misleading, for the civic universities owe their existence to certain national needs, and if present tendencies warrant prognoses, they are likely to respond even more to these needs. Will this increasing response affect their essential character as universities and result in a diminution of their independence? Some observers, like Michael Oakeshott, fear so: 'The doctrine that the university should move step for step with the world, at the same speed and partaking of every eccentricity of the world's fashion, refusing nothing that is offered, responsive to every suggestion, is a piece of progressive superstition and not to be tolerated by any sane man . . . the contemporary world offers no desirable model for a university.'[2]

I

There are four material factors to be taken into consideration when the independence of the universities is considered. The first of these is the acknowledgement of the Committee of Vice-Chancellors and Principals made in July 1946 that:

> the universities entirely accept the view that the government has not only the right, but the duty to satisfy itself that every field of study which in the national interest ought to be cultivated in Great Britain is in fact being cultivated in the university system, and that the resources which are placed at the disposal of the universities are being used with full regard both to efficiency and economy.[3]

As the agent of national pressure, the University Grants Committee observed:

> In an age both of crisis and planning, some increase of planning in the university world is inevitable. A somewhat quicker adjustment of universities to major social needs is imperative[4].

To effect this adjustment involved 'a certain measure of central planning' in which the U.G.C. would have to devise 'appropriate means of reconciling the operation of planning with the maintenance of the essential academic freedoms'. Though the U.G.C. recognised the right of universities to refuse to undertake developments against their own considered wishes, yet the policy of 'ear-marked grants', whilst it existed, proved a great persuasive force. By the end of the second post-war quinquennium, the U.G.C. was meeting, on an average, seven times a year, and its sub-committees seventy. It had also visited every institution on its grant list, the second visitation taking 107 days.

A second, less coherent, pressure is that exercised by the region. Over half of the total enrolment of students have been hitherto drawn from the immediate localities of the civic universities, though this decreased as numbers doubled between 1930 and 1948. The engulfing wave of suburban students eroded still further the traditional non-vocational defences of their universities. For their needs were immediate and obvious and, to cater for them, standards were modified. 'The "Redbrick" universities at least cater predominantly for a clientèle which is "suburban" without roots and without standards: and they have too much taken their colour from their environment,' lamented Sir Walter Moberly.[5] But, as the University Grants Committee agreed in 1953, there has been both a decline in the proportion of students who live at home as well as of those who live within a thirty-mile radius of home. These declines are much more marked in England and Wales than in Scotland, as the following figures illustrate:—

Percentages of full-time students whose homes are within a thirty-mile radius or who live at home during term.

	Homes within 30 miles			*Living at home during term*		
	1938–9	1947–8	1951–2	1938–9	1948–9	1951–2
English Civic Universities and Colleges	55·7	52·2	44·5	51·0	46·0	37·8
University of Wales	65·8	52·3	48·3	45·9	31·5	32·6
Scottish Universities	64·4	63·0	60·2	60·5	59·4	57·0

Yet so strong was the pressure of this suburban clientèle (aided by Local Authority grants) that the Vice-Chancellor of Liverpool University expressed fears that Local Education Authorities might 'try to exert on the Universities a pressure as regards selection of students and courses which the University Grants Committee and the Treasury would never attempt to exert'. And since the L.E.A. grants were of sufficient magnitude to make the difference between solvency and bankruptcy, there was need, he urged, for safeguards against such abuse of powers.

Nor did he end here, for, taking as his text the newly enlarged terms of reference of the University Grants Committee, he asked who were the 'other bodies' referred to in their obligation 'to assist, in consultation with the Universities and other bodies concerned, the preparation and execution of such plans as may from time to time be required in order to ensure that they are fully adequate to national needs'. He categorically asserted that there were 'serious doubts in some University circles with regard to the wisdom of some of the recommendations of the Goodenough, the Clapham, and the Scarbrough Committees'.[6]

One of the other bodies might well be considered as a third factor. This, the Federation of British Industries, convened a national conference, the first of its kind, to promote and develop the interest of the universities in industrial research. This conference, held in London in March 1946, was attended by 1,400 delegates, and was opened by Sir Robert Robinson, President of the Royal Society, who invited more industrialists to make contact with university departments where topics in which they were interested were being studied. Such contact, concluded Sir Robert, enabled the university professor 'to keep a better sense of proportion . . . and acts as a corrective against many of the intellectual maladies to which professors are apt to succumb'.[7]

No one can accuse the F.B.I. of exerting undue pressure on the universities to promote technological studies as such. For at a conference held at Nottingham University on 24 September 1952, Lord Hives (the chairman of Rolls-Royce) insisted on the need for universities to produce trained and flexible minds. He did not believe that universities could deal with specialised technological education because they were too remote from the changing requirements of society. Yet, as a body, the F.B.I. realise that industry must necessarily rely to a much greater extent than before on university graduates to supply its future leaders, since the chances of recruiting from those leaving school has greatly diminished. And the Vice-Chancellor of Queen's University, Belfast, produced figures to support this trend. Since 1912, he pointed out, the reservoir of persons 18 years old has decreased by 74,000, and the number of students who have entered the universities has increased by 12,537.[8]

In one sense, however, the F.B.I. is committed to encouraging technological studies in view of its membership of the British Productivity Council, a non-party organisation established on 30 June 1952 to implement the suggestions made by the Anglo-American Council on Productivity. This last body, which lasted from 1948 until 1952, was much concerned with the longer period of formal education prevailing in America and also with the greater relative number of research workers in, and students of, technology. With D.S.I.R., the British Productivity Council has been endowed by the United States with funds amounting to nearly one and a quarter million pounds, for amongst other things, the promotion of technological studies in universities.[9]

The fourth factor stems from one of the basic growing points of the constitution: Parliamentary control of State expenditure. All government grants are for one year only, and can only be prolonged by a specific statute defining the nature of the service to be rendered by the agency receiving the grant. Now the Chancellor commits the Exchequer to help the universities for five years at a time and, though Parliament confirms his yearly allotment, they do not know how much of the surplus reverts to the Exchequer: in fact, they do not, nor does the Comptroller and Auditor General, receive accounts of the universities' expenditure.

Such an anomaly has elicited unfavourable comment from the Committee on Public Accounts appointed by Parliament. From 1946-7 onwards this Committee expressed great dissatisfaction with the tendency of university accounts to escape Parliamentary control, and in the following year, Sir Edward Bridges of the Treasury defended the practice on the grounds that once statutory guidance on these matters was sought, all sorts of other encroachments on university independence would occur. This satisfied the Committee until 1950 when it again returned to the attack, asking whether it was possible to secure 'adequate Parliamentary control over this large expenditure of public money'. The Treasury agreed to examine in 'considerable detail' the question of possible extravagances.

But the Committee on Public Accounts were not satisfied. Following a suggestion of the Select Committee on Estimates in their fifth report for the Session 1951-2 that the non-recurrent grants made to universities should be subject to public audit; and in spite of a Treasury demurrer embodied in a memorandum dated 28 May 1952; it argued that the independence of universities would be no way minimised by such an audit. Indeed, seizing on instances where the University Grants Committee had disallowed certain costs incurred by universities, it argued that this itself was an argument for an audit. Well might a leading scientific journal comment:

'there is some lack of public understanding of the position of universities in Great Britain, of the way they function, and their true relations to the Government . . . certainly . . . on the part of those who are elected to Parliament'.[10]

2

Against these strings the universities can pull with some strength, confident of reserves of strength and of known sympathy on the part of those who hold them. Their first asset is the undoubted fact that British universities serve the *élite*. Their small student population—some 85,000 as opposed to the 2,000,000 of the United States—does, as the President of Princeton sagely observed in 1952, 'greatly restrict the area of popular interest in the universities and possible political pressures rising therefrom'.[11]

A second asset consists of the severely professional nature of their task. The traditional 'dual entry' to a profession, and traditional English empiricism have prevented the universities from becoming the sole exit from the educational escalator. The very fact that they do not afford the broad general education of American liberal arts colleges, and do not educate 'the whole man', prevents them from exciting such popular enthusiasm. That forty-four per cent. of the total number of English university students were reading 'arts' in 1949-50 in no way invalidates this general contention that British universities provide professional training, for most of these arts students are postulants for professional posts in teaching, the civil service, and the social services. Indeed, so strong are professional objectives in the minds of university students, that when a group from Nuffield College, Oxford, examined the position of the universities, the criterion of optimum expansion which they employed was that of 'intake to the professions'.[12]

The third defence, and in England perhaps the most powerful guarantee of their autonomy, lies in the high character of the University Grants Committee, and the peculiarly sympathetic relationship between its personnel and those of the Treasury Departments. The President of Princeton, observing this, wrote:

> the facetious observation that the Committee succeeds only because its members, the chief Treasury Officials, and the vice-chancellors are all members of the Athenaeum Club really expresses a deep truth.[13]

Much the same observation was made by Sir Walter Moberly when he said that, after all, the country was really a large parish.

3

In another place, Sir Walter Moberly observed that the 'rationalising and standardising of education which is now in vogue may prove to have been carried too far', adding

There is a place for idiosyncrasies redolent of particular classes, callings, and localities for a diversity of cultures enriching one another, and so perhaps for the special concern of a particular university or college with a particular region.[14]

This 'special concern of a university or college with a particular region' is all the more significant in view of the demands being made for regional government. The Fabian Society's 'New Heptarchy' plan of 1905 has been modified in the light of subsequent developments in economic life.[15] Water and electricity supplies, for instance, demonstrated its necessity, and so did the Post Office. One of the first to realise the universities' rôle in such regional devolution was C. B. Fawcett[16] and he was followed by G. D. H. Cole, who, in his *Future of Local Government* (1921) jettisoned Fawcett's idea of provincial parliaments and substituted elected councils. Political necessities popularised the regional idea, and when, in 1925, the Government feared the disruptive effects of a general strike, the country was divided into eleven regions under Civil Commissioners. The situation which they had to face was repeated *mutatis mutandis* fourteen years later when war broke out in 1939. The eleven wartime Civil Defence Commissioners were 'to exercise the powers vested in the Government' if communications should break down. These commissioners, in turn, developed the idea of regional government and, before their demise, four important schemes were published to utilise the experience thus gained.[17] The first, outlined in a Fabian pamphlet in 1942, argued that, at the end of the war, these regional commissioners should be succeeded by regional councils.[18] The second, sponsored by the County Councils Association, proposed to reduce the counties from 61 to 47, and the major local authorities from 144 to 88.[19] The third scheme, sponsored by the Labour Party, envisaged a regrouping into 60 regions.[20] The fourth proposal, outlined by Professor Cole in the *Political Quarterly* of October-December 1941, and modified and expanded in *Local and Regional Government* (1947), made provision for 18 provinces quite different from the local defence regions, and specifically so.

As one of the public services which most clearly called for unified administration in the provinces, G. D. H. Cole selected education.

In doing so, he stressed that the universities should be both independent of, and above, their regions as centres of teaching and research. Yet, at the same time, he saw that regional groups looked to the universities for services which they could not obtain elsewhere. To make these services more effective, Cole examined the existing distribution of universities and found that all but two of his proposed eighteen regions were served by universities or university colleges. So, to make the service more adequate, he proposed that the two excepted regions (East Anglia and the Cumberland-Westmorland-Furness Region) should obtain university colleges at Norwich (or Bury St. Edmunds) and Carlisle. Furthermore, to strengthen the other regions, he suggested that Nottingham, Southampton, and Exeter should be raised to university status, followed in due course by Hull and Leicester; and that further university colleges should be founded at Lincoln and Stoke-on-Trent. Some of his proposals have, as we have seen, been implemented. Yet, though he advocated the strengthening of the regional links of universities, he opposed any limitation of their independence, or any rigid assimilation of their areas with those of the proposed regional governments, concluding, 'No one, I hope, will suggest that the Universities ought to be made subject to control by the Regional Authorities.'[21]

4

The regional responsibilities of the universities have been growing rapidly. As early as 1894 the Bryce Commission discussed the establishment of provincial administrative districts for education coextensive with existing university areas[22] and today their examining boards do influence the curriculum of the secondary schools. In 1905 (the year of the Fabian Society's 'New Heptarchy plan') the Workers' Educational Association was founded and by the time Cole's *Local and Regional Government* was published in 1947, this was serving, in concert with the universities, some 103,000 students in 21 regions. These regions were divided, as one veteran observed, by boundaries 'like iron curtains'.[23]

The growth of the social services also offered rich opportunities for regional study and teaching: opportunities which the universities like Liverpool eagerly grasped.[24] This work led to the further expansion of the university curriculum: courses in clinical psychology, psychiatric social work, industrial administration, and town planning evolved as a result of the co-operation between region and university, to the mutual advantage of both.

Perhaps the most startling extension of the diocesan responsibility of the universities was inaugurated in 1948 by the National Health Act. As a result of this Act fourteen Regional Hospital Boards were created on which the universities were not only represented but were exhorted to play their part in encouraging post-graduate study. That the universities should have an intimate knowledge of the hospitals within their regions was still further ensured by the Medical Act of 1950 which demanded that all medical students should hold a house appointment at a hospital approved by the university of a particular region before they could be registered.[25]

5

As a direct result of the extension of regional responsibilities for the training of teachers being placed upon the universities, new bodies have emerged—the University Institutes.

Academic training colleges were condemned as obsolete as far back as 1922, when the Trades Union Congress and the Labour Party published a joint pamphlet describing them as a survival of the times when there were only three universities, and calling for recognition of the necessity that every teacher should be a graduate. They argued that the existing system of some 92 small, scattered colleges was wasteful, that it was as expensive to keep a student at a civic university as at one of these, and that a university training would raise the standard of the teaching profession generally. These proposals were strongly supported by the National Union of Teachers, who added that they looked to the time when the universities would ultimately absorb the training colleges. It was admitted by the Departmental Committee, established at that time to examine the whole question of the training of teachers for public elementary schools, that university training of teachers would raise the standard of the profession and thereby attract better recruits, but it doubted whether it would increase the recruitment of such teachers for elementary schools.

The universities, however, did not warm to these proposals, nor did the training colleges. In fact Miss Winifred Mercier, the principal of Whitelands Training College, called a conference at Whitelands Training College where representatives of the Labour Party were invited to present their case, and at this conference, and later before the Departmental Committee, she ably defended the existence of the two-year colleges. Indeed, her biographer, contemplating her activity in these years, remarked, 'It has often been said that Winifred Mercier saved the life of the two-year training colleges. If her last arguments be granted, it would also appear that she saved the life of the universities.'[26]

As we have seen, the McNair Report of 1944 resulted in the establishment of Area Training Organisations, comprising the universities, local authorities, training colleges, and serving teachers of a university region. But not even these satisfied the critics of training colleges, one of whom declared, 'I want, as soon as possible, to put an end to their existence, *in their present form*.'[27] This present form is most unsatisfactory: it tends to recruit the mediocre, and (except in certain colleges which we have noticed) affords no incentive to a late developing student to study in depth for a degree, and to obtain span by mixing with students preparing for other professions. In addition, many of them are too small to be run as economic units and are finding it increasingly difficult to recruit students. Graham Wallas once observed that 'regular teaching produces a kind of disgust which is more profound than that produced by any other kind of work'.[28] Training college products, who are destined for the teaching profession and no other from the age of eighteen, have become the Janissaries of the schools: a sturdy helot army, jealous of the degree, and exalters of 'method' as opposed to the content of knowledge.

If the educational system is designed with escape hatches for ability from the age of 11 onwards, it is surely inconsistent to insist on the perpetuation of a system which fossilises methodological techniques, and starves the postulant teacher of any real contact with creative knowledge. It is to be hoped that the next decades will see the Area Training Organisations making a realistic attack on this problem, disregarding the arguments which will most certainly be advanced by the entrenched vested interests both in the training colleges and the universities. In this connection it is perhaps worth noting the reflection of 'Bruce Truscot':

> I have sometimes wondered if a three-year course should not lead to a special type of degree—a degree of Pass, or General, type, with the mark of distinction allowed, covering the entire field of subjects studied, together with the theory and practice of teaching—to be called 'Bachelor of Education'. The prize does not seem excessive; so long and full a course, if it is planned and followed in close connection with the university surely merits the recognised university hall-mark.[29]

6

The institute idea might also inspire those who wish to help technical colleges, whose desperate needs were acknowledged by the Select

Committee on Estimates in 1953 in a special report. This report stated that the desire of students for degrees often diverts them to universities from less costly courses of study more suited to them and subscribed to the view that 'some kind of national label and national status' should be accorded them. This was no new state of affairs for the McNair Report actually recommended that technical colleges should enjoy a greater measure of contact with universities, and also suggested that the professional institutions should be invited to co-operate by enabling industry and the technical colleges to exchange staff. The Percy Report, which did not claim to be a final solution of the problem, proposed, as we have seen, the establishment of Regional Advisory Councils to co-ordinate technological studies in universities, colleges of technology and technical colleges in each region. And to prevent the preponderance of administrators on these councils, it had further suggested that Regional Academic Boards of Technology should be created, composed of the academic heads of universities and technical colleges, together with members of their teaching staffs. These Academic Boards were to give advice on the co-ordination of higher technological education in each region as a whole. And above these was to be a National Council of Technology, responsible to the Minister and the University Grants Committee for the national implications of regional policies. The Ministry did take steps to carry out the main recommendations of this Report, and Circular No. 87, dated 20 February 1946, urged the immediate creation of the regional boards suggested, while Circular No. 98, dated 10 April 1946, suggested the establishment of colleges of technology.

Over two hundred technical colleges in London and the rest of England are attempting to give academic depth to part-time students for Higher National Certificates in engineering, science, and technology. Nearly half of these provide senior full-time courses in these subjects as well as in architecture, commerce, pharmacy and medicine. Teaching and research is, in many cases, of a high order. Thus students from one university college attend a polytechnic because it is only there that they can have access to a certain type of equipment. The number of students reading for degrees under the auspices of technical colleges is formidable. In 1949, 8,772 of these students were attending full time and 11,295 on a part-time day basis. These did not include the large number of students taking university degree courses by means of part-time evening study. Such external degrees were described by one principal as 'entirely undesirable'.[30]

The technical colleges are being overloaded with specialist courses;

witness the Urwick Committee's recommendation that they should offer courses in management. A Royal Institute of Technology (mooted, as we have seen, in 1950 but jettisoned in 1952) might have co-ordinated their efforts and enabled them to handle their load of teaching effectively. For technical colleges are interested in research: an inquiry in 1949 showed that 190 papers had been published by the staff of 21 technical colleges over the previous three years. Some universities, it is true, have entered into close relations with some of the technical colleges of their area, but others remain apart in pharisaical indifference, fearing lest the local authority which controls the colleges might, by implication, seek to control them. Yet some assistance to these struggling foundations is obviously necessary, and, as two shrewd observers of the situation wrote in 1952: 'If the professional institutions and the universities dislike the R.I.T. idea, it is for them to give a helping hand to the technical college, to negotiate with government for more money for it, and to aid it to some academic independence and breadth.'[31] The problem is becoming more acute as the technical colleges recruit from the new secondary technical schools and have succeeded in establishing a new ninth examining board to certificate the products of these schools.

There is also a group which might affect the curriculum or outlook of the universities. This comprises the national specialist colleges: the outstanding example being the College of Aeronautics, over whose birth the Aeronautical Research Committee presided. The Fedden Report (1944) envisaged that 'the college should start as a separate institution' but added

> Independence, however, should not mean isolation or competition. With the universities, with any similar higher institutions of Science and Technology that may be established, and with the research establishments, the College's relations should be intimate and continuous.

Similar colleges for Horology, for Heating and Ventilation, Rubber, Foundry Work, Food Technology and Leather Manufacture took the same plan and were in existence by 1950.

Perhaps the answer to the problem of the technical colleges is to associate them in regional institutes under university supervision. By so doing, the standard of teaching could be raised, and the problem of integrating research (an increasingly important one in both the natural and the social sciences) would be simplified. The University of London has built its polytechnics and Institutes into the framework of the university proper: and though the London Institutes are post-graduate, there is, in the existing schemes of other universities which affect training colleges, a pattern which might well be considered in framing civic institutes of technology.

7

The development of newly nationalised industries has sharpened this problem of the technical college and its status.

For over a quarter of a century, two distinct levels of scientific research have existed in industry: that carried out by individual firms in their own laboratories and that carried out by universities. Between these two levels, two further intermediate levels have developed. One, consisting of about forty special research associations, has grown up under the shadow of the second—the government-controlled D.S.I.R. Now these latter two, both dating from the first world war, have grown so much that D.S.I.R. (with, in some cases, the Medical Research Council and the Agricultural Research Council) is financing much fundamental research at university level and assisting much of the practical work at the level prosecuted by individual firms. Indeed, a scrutiny of its Annual Report for the year 1951-2 shows that the five largest grants of D.S.I.R. are to Universities: £487,500 to Liverpool for a 400 Me V. synchro-cyclotron, £317,700 to Glasgow for a 300 Me V. proton synchrotron, £191,000 to Oxford for a 140 Me V. proton synchrotron and £168,000 to Manchester for radio astronomy.

The sychrotron at Birmingham, the second largest in the world, was also financed largely by D.S.I.R. But, as the U.G.C. pointed out, the proportion of government expenditure on scientific research which goes to the universities is relatively small, which is as it should be.[32]

The very use of the term 'level' to describe the kinds of research carried out is symptomatic of the hierarchy of institutions undertaking research, a hierarchy which has led to a certain isolation of research projects from one another. In 1945, the Barlow Committee on the Scientific Civil Service regarded this isolation as peculiarly characteristic of a Government scientific branch. But it existed at other levels also, as Edmund Dews observed in 1952:

> Probably just as isolated from academic research is the technological research which goes on in industrial establishments. This can be attributed partly to the universities' reluctance to undertake research projects for industrial firms, partly also to the barriers of academic and social status which inhibit the free movement of graduate students between technical colleges, universities, and industry.

This observer concluded

It is attractive to consider whether nationalisation should not provide an opportunity for integrating research at three industrial levels.[33]

So far, however, little attempt has been made to utilise the academic scientist on the boards of electricity, steel, or transport. Yet, at the teaching level, they are being increasingly called upon to provide courses which lead to the award of certificates of efficiency: town planning and management studies are two cases among many. Being outside the framework of nationalisation, the objectivity of the university's assessment is all the more valuable.

8

There is *prima facie* evidence that the emancipation of the urban proletariat in the industrial towns has contributed to, and been assisted by, the development of the civic universities, and the process is by no means finished. This emancipated class, with its clamant need for relevant knowledge, has strained the traditional concept of the university: one which owed much to Plato and Newman in stressing that practical competence was a by-product of a liberal and intelligent attitude to things of the mind. The almost iconoclastic outlook of this emergent class has been censured by Michael Oakeshott:

In the past a rising class was aware of something valuable enjoyed by others which it wished to share; but this is not so today. The leaders of the rising class are consumed with a contempt for everything which does not spring from their own desires, they are convinced in advance that they have nothing to learn and everything to teach, and consequently their aim is loot—to appropriate to themselves the organisation, the shell of the institution, and convert it to their own purposes. The problem of the universities today is how to avoid destruction at the hands of men who have no use for their characteristic virtues, men who are convinced only that 'knowledge is power'.[34]

Yet, strained as it might be, the traditional concept of a university should be stated with all the emphasis that the times demand:

A university training aims at raising the intellectual tone of society, at cultivating the public mind, at purifying the national taste, at supplying true principles to popular enthusiasms and fixed aims to popular aspirations, at giving enlargement and sobriety to the ideas of the age, at facilitating the exercise of political power and refining the intercourse of private life.[35]

This links the ergasterial foundations of the ninth century with the cathedral schools of the eleventh, the universities of the high middle ages with the virtuosi of the seventeenth century, the scientific and literary societies of the last century with the civic universities of this.

For the civic universities are parceners of a great heritage. Oases of withdrawal in a complex urban structure, centres of creative endeavour in the arts and sciences, repositories of informed knowledge and opinion, powerhouses of ideas, nurseries of new disciplines: they embody some feature of all the forbears described in the foregoing chapters. And the future, as Sir Raymond Priestley told a conference of university teachers drawn from the British Empire, lies largely with them.[36] Yet, as they enter on their heritage, they should at the same time, beware of the nostalgia of looking back and lamenting their lack of cloistered walks and hallowed associations. For, as D. W. Brogan observed:

the civic university, near the civic reference library, the theatres, the concert halls, the pubs and the cinemas, the art gallery and the great civic churches, is well rewarded for its acceptance of the material drawbacks. Let the rulers of the civic universities of England (and Scotland) reflect that they, not Oxford and Cambridge (or Yale and Princeton) are the normal universities of the modern world.[37]

REFERENCES

1. Livingstone, Sir R., *Some Thoughts on University Education* (London, 1948), 13.

2. Oakeshott, M., 'The Universities', *Cambridge Journal*, II (1949), 523.

3. *University Development from 1935 to 1947* (H.M.S.O., 1948), 77-8.

4. *Op. cit.*, 81.

5. Moberly, *Crisis in the University*, 241. He continues: 'The chief danger to our universities today does not come from probable public interference nor are their gravest defects due to this. They are due to the pervasive influence of the mass mind, and it is this which is the most formidable menace. Against this the State may even be an ally, since the level of enlightenment in government circles and government offices is commonly much in advance of the man in the street.' *University Development 1947-52* (H.M.S.O., 1953), 24.

6. *Commonwealth Universities Congress* (1951), 19-20. See also Professor Robert Peers at the *Conference of Home Universities* (1950)—'There is some danger that regional interests may put pressure upon the civic Universities in the direction of certain applied studies or specialisms of the narrowest kind at the cost, possibly, of reducing relatively the contribution which the civic Universities can make in the field of the Humanities.' As a matter of fact, income from local authorities increased by 50·9 per cent., from £629,947 to £948,972 between 1946-7 and 1951-2.

7. Dunsheath, Dr. Percy, 'The Universities and Industrial Research', *Universities Quarterly* (1947), 185-8. *Industry and Research: Report of a Conference arranged by the Federation of British Industries and held at the Kingsway Hall, London, W.C.2* (London, 1946).

Report of a Conference on Industry and the Universities (London, F.B.I., 1953).

8. *Report of Universities and Industry Conference organised by the F.B.I. and the Committee of Vice-Chancellors and Principals of the Universities of the United Kingdom held at Ashorne Hall, Leamington Spa 24–26 October 1952* (London, F.B.I., 1953).

9. *U.S. Economic Aid under Mutual Security Act* Cmd. 8776 (Feb. 1953); Graham Hutton, *We too can prosper* (London, 1953) 168, 191.

10. HANSON, A. H., 'The Select Committee on Estimates', *Yorkshire Bulletin of Economic and Social Research* (1951), III, 103-30; Basil Chubb, *The Control of Public Expenditure* (Oxford, 1952), 161-8. *Nature*, CLXXII (1953), 556.

11. DODDS, Harold W., in Dodds, Hacker and Rogers, *Government Assistance to Universities in Great Britain* (New York, 1952), 103.

12. '*The Problem Facing British Universities*' (Oxford, 1948), 11-28.

13. Dodds, *op. cit.*, 112.

14. MOBERLY, Sir Walter, *The Universities and Cultural Leadership* (Oxford, 1951), 17. In his *Universities Ancient and Modern* (Manchester, 1950), 26, he wrote 'As interpreters of contemporary culture, the "Red brick" universities have possibly a rôle even more important than that of Oxbridge.'

15. See, for instance, their pamphlet of 1905 on 'Municipalisation by Provinces' which, using the examples of transport, electricity, and water supply, argued that 'narrow municipal boundaries are cramping the growth of the collective control of industry' (p. 8).

16. FAWCETT, C. B., *The Provinces of England* (1919).

17. For a detailed sketch of this trend, see V. D. Lipman, *Local Government Areas 1834–1945* (Oxford, 1949), 251-304. And for a description of a University's Regional work see 'The University and its Region', in Bruce Truscot, *Redbrick and These Vital Days* (1944), 106–23.

18. Regionaliter, *Regional Government* (1942) (Fabian Research Series No. 63), 13.

19. *Local Government Reform* (1943).

20. *The Future of Local Government*. See also P. Self, *Regionalism, A Report to the Fabian Society* (London, 1949).

21. COLE, G. D. H., *Local and Regional Government* (1947), 238-40. Bruce Truscot, *Redbrick and these Vital Days* (1944), 109–10 also suggests colleges at Carlisle, Norwich, Ipswich, and possibly Plymouth or Truro. So, too, the Nuffield College Report (*The Problem Facing British Universities* (1948), 101) says: 'The existing geographical distribution of universities needs supplementing. All the great industrial areas are provided for, but this leaves large areas with substantial, though less concentrated, populations, without universities of their own. . . . Today when certain studies, such as Medicine or Economics, are usually integrated with local activities, a wider geographical distribution is called for.'

22. *Royal Commission on Secondary Education* (1895), ii, QQ 106–9.

23. WALLER, Professor R. D., on 'The University as a Regional Focus', in *Conference of the Home Universities Report of Proceedings* (1950), 33.

S. G. Raybould, *The English Universities and Adult Education* (London, 1951), 81-86 also indicates the extent to which 14 English universities have accepted responsibilities for civilian aid to Forces education in their areas.

24. See, for instance, the work of the Universities of Liverpool and Manchester in the Development Councils during the depression of the thirties, on

which the Universities were represented, M. P. Fogarty, *Prospects of the Industrial Areas of Great Britain* (1945), 203-32.

25. WHITBY, Sir Lionel, *op. cit.*, 27-32.

26. GRIER, Lynda, *Winifred Mercier*, 181.

27. COLE, G. D. H., *op. cit.*, 237-8. About two thirds of these colleges offer two-year courses, the remainder—some 30 or more—offer three-year courses. In 1938-9 they produced 4,377 teachers a year, as opposed to 1,744 from the universities.

28. WALLAS, Graham, *Our Social Heritage* (1921), 147.

29. TRUSCOT, Bruce, *Redbrick and these Vital Days* (1945), 145.

30. *Education 1900-1950 The Report of the Ministry of Education* (Cmd. 8244) (H.M.S.O., 1950), 52. J. C. Jones, Director of the Regent Street Polytechnic, speaking on behalf of the Association of Principals of Technical Institutions at the Home Universities Conference (*Report of Proceedings*, 97-100). He added: 'Speaking as the Principal of the largest technical college in this country I should like . . . to draw attention to the fact that the Ministry has sent out circulars to the local education authorities suggesting that in instances where the college is of high standing, its governing body shall be given autonomy within a block grant estimate.' See also *The Problem Facing British Universities* (1948), 73. 'There is a good deal of overlapping, for technical colleges prepare for university degrees, and all university colleges, including some universities, undertake part-time and especially evening teaching in miscellaneous trade subjects that seem particularly the work of a technical college.' For their recognition by one professional body see Royal Institute of British Architects, *Report of Special Committee on Architectural Education* (1946) and for a general survey of the whole problem see *Twelfth Report from the Select Committee on Estimates Session 1952–53* (H.M.S.O., 1953), sub-titled *Technical Education.*

31. MAUDE, Angus, and LEWIS, Roy, *Professional People* (London, 1952), 227. R. A. Butler, 'The Study of Technology', *Universities Quarterly* (1946), I, 273-80. *New Fabian Essays*, ed. R. H. S. Crossman (London, 1952), 116-118, where an 'educational precinct' is outlined.

32. Cmd. 8773 (H.M.S.O., 1953). *University Development . . . 1947 to 1952*, 43.

33. DEWS, Edmund, in *Problems of Nationalised Industries* (ed. W. A. Robson) (London, 1952), 222.

The International Association of University Professors and Lecturers sent out a questionnaire to 551 heads of departments in the British Universities. The 270 replies received were made the basis of a paper by Dr. V. E. Coslett to the 7th Universities Conference at Amsterdam in April 1953, entitled *The Relation between Scientific Research in the Universities and Industrial Research.*

34. Michael Oakeshott, *op. cit.*, 538, referring to Ernest Green, *Education for a New Society*. For the social origins of the students in six university institutions in England and Wales see *University Students—A Pilot Survey* (P.E.P., London, 1950).

35. NEWMAN, *Idea of a University*, ed. May Yardley (Cambridge, 1931), 100-1.

36. PRIESTLEY, Sir Raymond, *The Civic Universities* (1949).

37. BROGAN, D. W., 'Redbrick Revisited', *Cambridge Journal* (1951), V, 210.

Index

Places associated in the text with university institutions are printed in capitals

Printed in Great Britain by The Camelot Press Limited, Southampton

The Academic Profession

An Arno Press Collection

Annan, Noel Gilroy. **Leslie Stephen:** His Thought and Character in Relation to His Time. 1952

Armytage, W. H. G. **Civic Universities:** Aspects of a British Tradition. 1955

Berdahl, Robert O. **British Universities and the State.** 1959

Bleuel, Hans Peter. **Deutschlands Bekenner** (German Men of Knowledge). 1968

Bowman, Claude Charleton. **The College Professor in America.** 1938

Busch, Alexander. **Die Geschichte des Privatdozenten** (History of Privat-Docentens). 1959

Caplow, Theodore and Reece J. McGee. **The Academic Marketplace.** 1958

Carnegie Foundation for the Advancement of Teaching. **The Financial Status of the Professor in America and in Germany.** 1908

Cattell, J. McKeen. **University Control.** 1913

Cheyney, Edward Potts. **History of the University of Pennsylvania:** 1740-1940. 1940

Elliott, Orrin Leslie. **Stanford University:** The First Twenty-Five Years. 1937

Ely, Richard T. **Ground Under Our Feet:** An Autobiography. 1938

Flach, Johannes. **Der Deutsche Professor der Gegenwart** (The German Professor Today). 1886

Hall, G. Stanley. **Life and Confessions of a Psychologist.** 1924

Hardy, G[odfrey] H[arold]. **Bertrand Russell & Trinity:** A College Controversy of the Last War. 1942

Kluge, Alexander. **Die Universitäts-Selbstverwaltung** (University Self-Government). 1958

Kotschnig, Walter M. **Unemployment in the Learned Professions.** 1937

Lazarsfeld, Paul F. and Wagner Thielens, Jr. **The Academic Mind:** Social Scientists in a Time of Crisis. 1958

McLaughlin, Mary Martin. **Intellectual Freedom and Its Limitations in the University of Paris in the Thirteenth and Fourteenth Centuries.** 1977

Metzger, Walter P., editor. **The American Concept of Academic Freedom in Formation:** A Collection of Essays and Reports. 1977

Metzger, Walter P., editor. **The Constitutional Status of Academic Freedom.** 1977

Metzger, Walter P., editor. **The Constitutional Status of Academic Tenure.** 1977

Metzger, Walter P., editor. **Professors on Guard:** The First AAUP Investigations. 1977

Metzger, Walter P., editor. **Reader on the Sociology of the Academic Profession.** 1977

Mims, Edwin. **History of Vanderbilt University.** 1946

Neumann, Franz L., et al. **The Cultural Migration:** The European Scholar in America. 1953

Nitsch, Wolfgang, et al. **Hochschule in der Demokratie** (The University in a Democracy). 1965

Pattison, Mark. **Suggestions on Academical Organization with Especial Reference to Oxford.** 1868

Pollard, Lucille Addison. **Women on College and University Faculties:** A Historical Survey and a Study of Their Present Academic Status. 1977

Proctor, Mortimer R. **The English University Novel.** 1957

Quincy, Josiah. **The History of Harvard University.** Two vols. 1840

Ross, Edward Alsworth. **Seventy Years of It:** An Autobiography. 1936

Rudy, S. Willis. **The College of the City of New York:** A History, 1847-1947. 1949

Slosson, Edwin E. **Great American Universities.** 1910

Smith, Goldwin. **A Plea for the Abolition of Tests in the University of Oxford.** 1864

Willey, Malcolm W. **Depression, Recovery and Higher Education:** A Report by Committee Y of the American Association of University Professors. 1937

Winstanley, D. A. **Early Victorian Cambridge.** 1940

Winstanley, D. A. **Later Victorian Cambridge.** 1947

Winstanley, D. A. **Unreformed Cambridge.** 1935

Yeomans, Henry Aaron. **Abbott Lawrence Lowell: 1856-1943.** 1948

[redacted]